**ABAP Objects: Application Development
from Scratch**

 PRESS

SAP PRESS is a joint initiative of SAP and Galileo Press. The know-how offered by SAP specialists combined with the expertise of the publishing house Galileo Press offers the reader expert books in the field. SAP PRESS features first-hand information and expert advice, and provides useful skills for professional decision-making.

SAP PRESS offers a variety of books on technical and business related topics for the SAP user. For further information, please visit our website: *www.sap-press.com*.

Horst Keller, Sascha Krüger
ABAP Objects
2007, 1,059 pp.
978-1-59229-079-6

Martin Huvar, Timm Falter, Thomas Fiedler, Alexander Zubev
Developing Applications with Enterprise SOA
2008, 336 pp.
978-1-59229-178-6

Rich Heilman, Thomas Jung
Next Generation ABAP Development
2007, 485 pp.
978-1-59229-139-7

Ulli Hoffman
Web Dynpro for ABAP
2006, 359 pp.
978-1-59229-078-9

Thorsten Franz, Tobias Trapp

ABAP Objects: Application Development from Scratch

Galileo Press

Bonn • Boston

ISBN 978-1-59229-211-0

© 2009 by Galileo Press Inc., Boston (MA)
1st Edition 2009

German Edition first published 2008 by Galileo Press, Bonn, Germany.

Galileo Press is named after the Italian physicist, mathematician and philosopher Galileo Galilei (1564–1642). He is known as one of the founders of modern science and an advocate of our contemporary, heliocentric worldview. His words *Eppur si muove* (And yet it moves) have become legendary. The Galileo Press logo depicts Jupiter orbited by the four Galilean moons, which were discovered by Galileo in 1610.

Editor Mirja Werner
English Edition Editor Jutta VanStean
Technical Review Horst Keller
Translation Lemoine International, Inc., Salt Lake City UT
Copy Editor Jutta VanStean
Cover Design Silke Braun
Cover Image Getty Images/Gail Shumway
Layout Design Vera Brauner
Production Kelly O'Callaghan
Typesetting Publishers' Design and Production Services, Inc.
Printed and bound in Canada

Contents at a Glance

Contents

7   GUI Programming 229

Preface

Many books have already been written about ABAP, which is a good thing, I have to say. However, many of these books highlight the same topic: After providing a short introduction to the software architecture of an ABAP-based SAP system (previously R/3, now SAP NetWeaver AS ABAP), they present the basic elements of the ABAP programming language and its development environment, the ABAP Workbench. The basic language elements in the majority of these books are long-established, and the focus is on modularization using subroutines and function modules. Material on ABAP Objects—the actual basic programming model for ABAP for the past ten years now—is, however, (except for the usual exceptions) unfortunately considerably less frequently found. There are books purely about the language, of course, and in addition, there are also a range of specialist books that cover specific topics of ABAP development, such as Web Dynpro ABAP, or interface programming. However, there is an almost complete lack of books about *actual application development using ABAP* or realistic books about *ABAP development for SAP customers.*

Therefore, I feel very honored to be allowed to write the preface for a book that closes this specific gap. The authors of this book bring with them experience from customer-specific ABAP application developments—something that authors who specialize solely in the ABAP language can only dream of. This book is therefore less of a textbook about the ABAP programming language and more of an introduction to application development using ABAP. I am particularly pleased that not only are traditional reporting and classic dialog programming (using transactions) used here for application development, but also that great emphasis is placed on using modern concepts that are based on ABAP Objects. The book covers everything from the design phase through the organization and modularization of software in packages and software components to the actual programming. It also includes topics such as Customizing, or modifying and enhancing delivered programs that you will not otherwise find very often in related books. In addition to examining the pure SAP NetWeaver layer (the SAP_BASIS software component delivered by SAP for the operation and customer developments on the AS ABAP), this book also takes a look at the SAP application basis in particular (the SAP_ABA software component also delivered with an AS ABAP), with ABAP and its development environment presented throughout as an extremely suitable tool for modern business application development.

All that remains for me to say is: enjoy reading the book. While this may not always be the easiest task, it will definitely be worth it.

Horst Keller
Knowledge Architect
NetWeaver Foundation ABAP
SAP AG

1 Introduction

Is SAP technology still current? Will it withstand future requirements? Today, we can answer these questions that were already posed by analysts some years ago with a resounding "Yes." After the SAP NetWeaver Application Server's ABAP stack was enhanced by the Java stack, SAP NetWeaver Process Integration (PI), SAP NetWeaver Master Data Management (MDM), and many other components, a powerful technology platform was born.

But is this statement also true for the oldest part of the platform – the ABAP stack? This question can also be answered with "Yes" without any reservation. With ABAP Objects, the SAP NetWeaver Application Server's ABAP stack (SAP NetWeaver AS ABAP, hereafter referred to as *AS ABAP*) has an object-oriented programming language, including a persistence framework and APIs for web-based applications, as well as complete solutions for workflows, organizational management, a comprehensive business partner application, parallel processing, several frameworks for business rules, and much more.

Even without complete ERP software or industrial solutions, developers can create powerful business software on AS ABAP alone. The techniques used in this book are based solely on the SAP_ABA and SAP_BASIS software components that are delivered with every AS ABAP. You can apply them anywhere in ABAP development, whether developing add-ons for SAP ERP, SAP Customer Relationship Management (SAP CRM), or to implement your own application systems.

Basis: SAP_ABA and SAP_BASIS

The strength of the SAP NetWeaver platform lies in its large portfolio of software products. Unlike your own application to be developed, these products have already proven their capabilities in live operations. It therefore makes sense to evaluate whether the SAP NetWeaver platform doesn't contain a solution that you can use completely or partially, because you can save costs and development time by increasing the number of standard solution components you use.

Challenges inherent in developing applications

Product designers and software architects face the following challenges:

- What parts of the standard SAP system are available and how do you integrate these parts into your own application as efficiently as possible?

- How do you create an architecture that you can enhance for customer processes and that is sufficiently flexible for further development?

- Which experiences from individual software development should you keep in mind? In what areas must you do some rethinking?

In this book, you will learn how to meet these challenges using ABAP Objects. The object-oriented concepts of ABAP enable developers to develop high-quality flexible software, and increase their own productivity. These techniques are therefore used throughout the entire book. You will also learn in detail how to apply object-oriented techniques in business programming, use the standard SAP system's object-oriented programming interfaces, and encapsulate them in an object-oriented way.

Important: modularization and software structuring

In ABAP development projects, you should place importance on modularization and software structuring. Unlike developing small add-ons for the standard SAP system, which has a software structure and therefore considerably influences your design decisions, developing applications gives you greater freedom and also greater responsibility for the design.

1.1 About this Book

Prerequisites

This book is not an introduction to the ABAP Objects language; however, you do need knowledge of this language which you can obtain from the book *ABAP Objects* (SAP PRESS 2007) by Horst Keller and Sascha Krüger. It is also helpful if you are familiar with standard SAP software, be it from the SAP ERP environment, SAP NetWeaver BI, or SAP CRM.

Structure of the book

You can read most parts of this book separately; however, some parts do build on one another as will be evident from the following chapter descriptions:

Chapter 2, Designing Application Systems, focuses on considering non-functional requirements and architectural aspects.

Chapter 3, Application Object, discusses a core theme of the book: identifying the central application objects of the application to be created. The term *application object* has been adopted from SAP development, because it is more readily known than the actually correct name *central business class of an application*.

Application Object

What does *application object* mean? An application has central entities: the central entity for the SAP Business Partner application is the *business partner*, to which other entities, such as the *business partner role* or *relationship* between business partners, are added. This shows that object orientation ensures that through the use of classes the entities from the concept correspond directly to the software. If you can identify and model these central classes and implement them as objects, you have already performed an important part of application development. Chapter 3 describes in detail the modeling of application objects at the database level as well as object persistence: a detailed description of Object Services and the classic and object-oriented concept of transactions is provided.

Chapter 4, Classes, Interfaces and Exceptions, highlights specialized object-oriented programming and object-oriented exception handling topics. You will also learn about ABAP Unit and classic modularization units and discover when you should use them.

Specialized topics

Chapter 5, Application Architecture, deals with the application system from a broad perspective: classes, reports and function groups as modularization units are too small for large application systems. This chapter therefore explains how to split an application into packages, define dependencies, and develop interfaces between them. In addition to splitting, the composition of the different subpackages as well as special interface techniques such as Business Add-Ins (BAdIs)—and also the very flexible Publish & Subscribe interfaces—are described in a modern, object-oriented context, with particular attention paid to handling system errors.

Implementing the application layer is the greatest challenge for software developers. **Chapter 6**, Application Layer, covers the implementation

Implementing the application layer

of application objects, as well as the subjects of Customizing and SAP Workflow. The latter is presented in object-oriented programming with which it is considerably easier and more efficient to develop than with the classic Business Object Repository. Because workflow is founded on event-based concepts, to understand this chapter it will help to know about the Publish & Subscribe interfaces from Chapter 5, Application Architecture.

Chapter 7, GUI Programming, introduces classic techniques such as maintenance dialogs and view clusters and shows how they can be enhanced with modern techniques. An example of object-oriented Dynpro programming is also presented using the BUS Screen framework. The chapter concludes with a look at modification-free Web Dynpro applications.

SAP Business Partner
The SAP Business Partner is one example of a modification-free extensible application. Because this central module is used by almost all business applications, in **Chapter 8**, SAP Business Partner, you will learn about its basic principles and enhancement options. This chapter also introduces you to Business Data Toolset (BDT) programming and to the SAP Locator Framework.

Chapter 9, Application Programming Techniques, focuses on special application programming techniques: logging data in the business application log and parallel application processing.

Information acquisition
Although the SAP Library is a good resource for AS ABAP documentation, developers often also have to do research during programming. **Chapter 10**, Information Acquisition, provides you with information sources and tricks and tips.

Appendix A covers the subject of Managing Development Projects and includes information about quality assurance and application system documentation. A description of how to add your own checks to the Code Inspector will provide plenty of ideas, in particular to those who will be performing these tasks.

To make it easier for you to work with this book, we use icons to highlight certain information in the book, as follows:

▶ **Caution**   **[!]**
This icon indicates boxes that contain information to warn you about risks and stumbling blocks.

▶ **Tip**   **[+]**
This icon indicates boxes that contain useful practical tips.

▶ **Note**   **[»]**
This icon indicates boxes that provide background knowledge or further information.

1.2 Sample Application and Technical Prerequisites

A sample application called "Vehicle Management" is used in this book. It supports, among others, the following processes of a transportation company:

Sample application

▶ Creating vehicle inventories

▶ Managing orders and contracts for transport services

The application consists of two modules: *Vehicle Management* and *Contract Management*. Contract Management consists of a list of orders, including references to business partners and *assignment options*: which vehicles are assigned to an order.

A functional requirement of vehicle administration is that it must be independently executable without assignment management. The reason for this is that assignment management only manages possible uses in the form of sales orders. The actual assignment falls into the area of vehicle planning, which is supported by non-SAP software, and in turn makes available other functions, such as creating and optimizing work schedules, schedules and round trip plans.

This sample application is used in the ABAP programming examples in this book, which shows ABAP developers instantly usable techniques and also provides application architects and project leaders with tips and tricks. In addition to presenting important parts of AS ABAP, such as SAP Business Partner and SAP Business Workflow, and proposing solutions for commonly recurring problems in business application development, the book also deals with theoretical aspects. Experience shows that the biggest and most painful errors are made during the architectural phase because, for example, many ABAP developers are not familiar with the options available with the new concept of packages.

Technical requirements The programming examples in this book are based on AS ABAP release 7.0. However, most of the APIs discussed are available in releases 6.40 and 6.20 and are contained solely in the SAP_ABA and SAP_BASIS software components. You can therefore use the techniques presented in this book in any AS ABAP, regardless of whether you want to develop add-ons for existing SAP applications or your own application systems.

Because of the wealth of material to be discussed in this book, we were unable to address a number of important topics. This includes frameworks for business rules (such as the Business Rule Framework or Formula Builder), advanced aspects of object-oriented BDT programming, the Switch Framework, as well as the Enhancement Framework, primarily the areas that are based on aspect-oriented programming. We also could only briefly touch on the topic of authorizations.

We are convinced that in this book we have bridged the gap between theory and practice and believe we can provide even ABAP experts with enough suggestions for programming projects.

We would like to thank Stefan Proksch, Mirja Werner, and Jutta Van-Stean of Galileo Press, as well as Marita Jockenhöfer, Dr. Horst Keller, and Dr. Thomas Müller. Very special thanks go to Florian Rothländer, who enriched this book with a section on the Code Inspector. Above all, we thank our families and friends for their understanding and support while we were writing this book.

Thorsten Franz

Tobias Trapp

"The house has to please everyone, contrary to the work of art, which does not. The work of art is a private matter for the artist. The house is not." (Adolf Loos from the essay "Architecture")

2 Designing Application Systems

Before you can begin developing a product, you must develop the product idea. Who are the customers? Which business processes must the product support? What is its unique selling point? How can it contribute to the economic success of the company?

Product idea

Each software product has a clearly defined scope. This means that you can identify what it can and cannot do. We can also often derive information about the design from the *product philosophy*. For example, which subcomponents does the product consist of? Which functions and interfaces have these subcomponents? The product philosophy can therefore contribute to a communication process where different groups include their interests:

▶ The *product vision* is often a significant factor for the sold-to party. How will the product maintain its position? Can it be developed further, and in which direction? This may also affect management, whose support is required for demanding projects.

▶ Is the completed application system part of a product portfolio, or must it be integrated into a company's IT architecture? In such a case, there must be a body of authority that ensures that the application is included into existing IT landscapes.

▶ The requesters (for example, user departments of the company) also need this information to communicate with contractors.

Successful products are characterized by the fact that product designers and developers know the defined philosophy that is required for developing the product.

Successful products

When you begin to design an application system, you must create the requirements for the software system to be developed. In this chapter, we will look at requirements analysis as a process. We will then describe *non-functional requirements* and their implementation in detail. We will conclude the chapter with general observations about the software architecture and using standard SAP functions.

2.1 Requirements

To make a product idea more specific, you must determine the product requirements. We will discuss aspects of requirements analysis in the following sections. To remain within the confines of this book's length, however, we can only provide an introduction to this topic. We will therefore focus primarily on non-functional requirements. Experience shows that these are the most difficult requirements to conceive, and while their subsequent implementation is often essential, it involves the greatest challenges and project risks.

2.1.1 Requirements Analysis as a Process

The design phase of an application system begins with the requirements analysis. Put yourself in the customer's shoes. What does the customer want? What is a product to be used for? Requirements analysis, however, accomplishes even more. It enables communication through the application system and is the basis for specifications and complete project management, because you can make decisions about deadlines and budgets at the end of the requirements analysis.

Risk During requirements analysis, you already face the greatest risk of production development – you want the system to be able to do everything. First, this is often either technically or financially unfeasible and, second, may not be possible from a purely logical perspective, due to conflicting requirements.

The core of requirements analysis involves answering the following questions:

▶ Which business processes do you want a system to support?

▶ Which requirements must be met to ensure that a business process is supported?

We must differentiate between an analyzed requirement and a specification. By *requirement*, we mean observable user behavior, whereas *specification* describes the system behavior at the system boundaries (for the user or other systems). A specification is more detailed and formalizes requirements, but it also contains additional aspects.

Requirement and specification

Proceed as follows to analyze requirements: Determine the requirements in interviews and workshops, and by analyzing systems to be replaced. Laws and regulations are another good source.

Determining requirements

You must manage requirements, as follows: Prioritize them and make a note of their complexity, and include the requester and current status: Is the requirement to be implemented or not? The requirements analysis usually ends with a review. Typically, you begin the system specification during the requirements analysis, as soon as you can foresee that a certain requirement must be implemented.

2.1.2 Functional Requirements

A large number of methods and templates exist for the functional requirements for an application to be developed. These include business blueprints, function lists, process lists, object lists, dialog networks, technical data models, different Unified Modeling Language (UML) models, and so on. When selecting the correct method, it is important to find a template the requester can handle, because requirements are the basis of all future project work.

A different approach is used for agile methods in requirements analysis. User stories, rather than use cases, are recorded on cards that describe the customer requirement in approximately three sentences. Development time is one to three weeks.

Agile methods

However, all participants must be included in the process for agile and "heavyweight" standard methods. It is also important that you understand the implicit prerequisites and assumptions on which the requirements are based, to be able to better analyze any inconsistencies.

2.1.3 Non-Functional Requirements

Implementing all functional requirements correctly does not guarantee a successful product. Previous requirements do not provide any information about performance, the volumes of data to be processed, or the required flexibility of the application system.

In general, requesters often initially forget about non-functional requirements. These then have to be implemented subsequently, with considerable effort, in a late phase of the project. Unfortunately, the greatest challenges are often the non-functional requirements the requester assumes will be included in the project, but that the developer does not think need to be included. This means the discrepancy only comes to light later.

Extensibility and Flexibility

Why must application systems be flexible? One reason is that business rules change. To support a business process, you must adapt and implement the software; the customer wants to activate the changed behavior at a certain point in time after transports are imported, or by selecting the relevant switch.

Customizing

Flexibility also makes it easier for you to maintain the application, and is another business factor and quality characteristic of the software. One reason for the success stories of SAP's ERP software was the ability to adapt it to your own business processes. *Customizing* enables you to modify the standard software to suit your own needs. Therefore, you will develop software components that you can parameterize extensively, saving application parameters in database tables—the Customizing tables.

Every ABAP developer is proficient in the basic techniques of designing an application system in such a way that it can be flexibly adapted for customers. You define the value range of data elements in value tables or using foreign keys here. You also store entire rule sets in transparent tables; therefore, they can be modified.

Strictly adhering to modularization

Customizing not only increases an application system's flexibility, but also its complexity. An important principle when designing Customizing is to adhere strictly to modularization. A Customizing table has exactly one responsibility for an aspect of the application system, for example, a calculation base or value range.

> **Check Functions for Customizing** [!]
>
> When you create your own Customizing tables, provide check and plausibility functions because experience shows that incorrect Customizing can lead to errors that are difficult to reproduce.

However, an application system that discloses sufficient parameters does not have to be implicitly extensible. Nevertheless, based on experience, flexibility is mainly a question of the application system's architecture. You will learn about a promising architecture in Section 2.2.1, Product Families: Separating Frames and Content.

Multitenancy

Multitenancy, in this context, means that an SAP system is divided into logical subsystems, where applications run independently of each other. This reduces administration costs for SAP systems and enables you to set up—in addition to production clients—test and training clients that work with application and Customizing data that is isolated from each other.

Multitenancy is easy to implement, because it is "bestowed" by AS ABAP. If application data together with Customizing data is client-specific, this also applies for the application. You must ensure that database tables cannot be accessed across clients; this will guarantee data *isolation*. Note that using a large number of clients will increase the time and effort required to maintain the application Customizing. For more information, refer to the section *Client Concept* in the SAP Library.

Data isolation

> **SAP Library** [»]
>
> Throughout this book, we often refer you to the SAP Library to obtain further information. Section 10.1.1, SAP Help Portal, describes how you can access the SAP Library. (Chapter 10 deals exclusively with the aspect of information acquisition.)

Mass Data Capability

One of the greatest strengths of AS ABAP is its scalability: you can easily set up additional application servers. Experience shows that, especially for mass processes, parallel processing options and strategies are the key

Scalability

for high-performance application systems. These aspects are detailed in Section 9.2, Parallel Processing of Applications.

Based on experience, performance is not a matter of individual ABAP commands. There are only a few exceptions where it makes sense to wonder about whether using field symbols for commands (such as READ or LOOP, for example) is more efficient than using field symbols from working areas. Programming guidelines that provide specific instructions with regard to this create a completely distorted view of performance. The instruction to transfer all values by reference and to always use field symbols is actually the first step towards an application system where an unintentional data modification may cause critical changes across several call levels. It may also result in unintended modifications in internal tables, which will seriously affect the robustness of the application system.

[!] **Do Not Begin Performance Optimizations Too Early**

You should not optimize the performance of the application system too early; instead, use the search functions presented in Section 10.4.3, Runtime Analysis, to identify areas of the program where optimization would be most worthwhile. Because database access is usually critical to performance, this is discussed in detail in Chapter 3, Application Object.

Administrability in a Live System

It is often useful to plan for a specialized *administrator* role for business applications.

Specialized administrator role

While system administrators in a data center maintain a wide range of different systems in terms of content and technology, they are not thoroughly familiar with their setup and details. A specialized administrator, on the other hand, specifically knows "his" application. He is typically an employee of the user department who has mostly system-based expertise, but who also has an affinity for technology and automatically positions himself as the link between users and development.

In daily system operations, the specialized administrator monitors the status of the application and, if necessary, intervenes to troubleshoot problems. If a job terminates, this administrator is the first contact partner for the data center. This is because he will know which processes are running, and when, and what to do if errors occur during these processes. For example, if a failed process can be restarted, should the processing chain continue? Where are the current processing logs located? The specialized administrator decides which errors are reported to development, and formulates the error message.

To support the specialized administrator in the best possible way, you can add an administration environment to the application. A simple option to implement such an environment is to create an area menu the administrator can easily access for the functions he needs:

> Administration environment

- ▶ Current processing logs
- ▶ Processing programs for manually restarting a system
- ▶ Reorganization and deletion reports for incorrect data
- ▶ Customizing transactions
- ▶ Check programs for Customizing and application data
- ▶ Generation programs for correcting incorrect generations (if parts of the application are generated from Customizing)

To accommodate the administrator even more, you can provide an *administrator cockpit*, which is a user-friendly overview transaction that provides the application status at a glance. The most important statuses can be displayed using traffic light symbols, and all relevant functions can be accessed from one central location.

> Administrator Cockpit

Administrability of Customizing Contents

The specialized administrator is also responsible for customer-specific Customizing. Entries often have to be adapted in the Customizing tables, in particular for release upgrades and modifications in specialized requirements. The specialized administrator will be sought after for this, because he will know how new business rules or processes can be implemented by parameterizing the application.

The *Implementation Guide* (IMG) provides user-friendly, straightforward and consistent access to the "adjustment screws" of the system, and can be accessed from Transaction SPRO, as shown in Figure 2.1.

> Implementation Guide

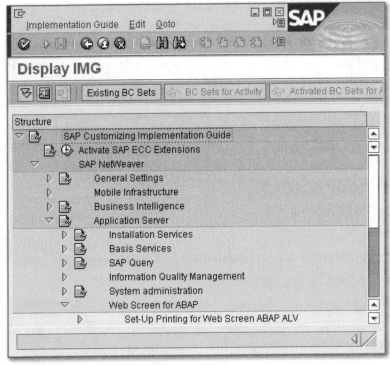

Figure 2.1 Transaction SPRO

It is usually sufficient to create the Customizing tables' maintenance views of your application as IMG activities. For a description on how to proceed, refer to the *IMG Structure Maintenance (BC-CUS)* section in the SAP Library. In terms of complicated applications, in particular those that allow comprehensive rule sets to be developed, view clusters and maintenance views are sometimes not sufficient to manage the content stored in Customizing.

Maintenance transaction

Comprehensive rule trees can consist of hundreds of entries in many different Customizing tables. This makes it difficult to obtain an overview, or display, process and manage a rule set as a whole. A custom-developed maintenance transaction for business rules or other Customizing content provides the opportunity to offer suitable display options and other functions for complicated Customizing content. For example, a test or simulation function may be helpful. In addition, version management, modification tracking, finely detailed authorization checks for maintenance purposes, and functions for creating, copying, deleting and transporting rule sets can make application administration easier.

Deliverability

The question of optimized maintenance for complex Customizing content leads immediately to the question of transport and delivery. In recent years, software development in the SAP environment has seen the growth of increasingly multilevel development models, where layers of software are successively superimposed over each other by different vendors.

As a hypothetical example, let's assume that SAP further develops the scope of SAP NetWeaver BI, based on the SAP NetWeaver Application Server. As an option, you can import and activate parts of the Business Content, such as extractors and evaluations for Finance, for example. A partner company provides an industry-specific add-on for the insurance industry, and a second partner provides content for private health insurance that is based on the add-on. **Example**

The customer, IDES-KV AG in Walldorf, Germany, is a company with several locations and independent reporting; therefore, a reporting template is created centrally in the group and delivered to the locations, where specific enhancements can be developed.

The result is a multilevel software pyramid, whose levels build upon each other. Enhancements or specializations represent the underlying levels: **Software pyramid**

1. Customer (location): Reporting enhancement at Walldorf location

2. Customer (head office): Central reporting template of IDES-KV AG

3. Development partner 2: "Private Health Insurance" division content

4. Development partner 1: "Insurance" industry content

5. SAP: Standard business content for "financial service providers"

6. SAP: SAP NetWeaver BI framework

7. SAP: SAP NetWeaver Application Server – ABAP stack

Figure 2.2 shows a possible software structure of an application system developed by you.

Figure 2.2 Possible Software Structure of Your Own Application

Significant effects   Modifications at one level can have significant effects on the overlying levels. In a worst-case scenario, modifications to the data model or extraction logic at one level may result in development objects in the levels based on that level to no longer be executable. Even worse, they may produce useless results, without this being noticed.

How can you prevent this without foregoing the advantages of multilevel software development? One possible answer is a well-considered inclusion of dependencies of lower-level objects and careful differentiation between released, stable interface objects on the one hand and internal objects not to be used on the other (as described in Chapter 5, Application Architecture).

Indeed, what do you do if this is not enough? This could be the case if, because of the specific properties of the application, many visible objects—whose stability in many cases cannot be guaranteed—appear on a few internal (but externally invisible) objects? In this situation, a merge process for received and enhanced content is inevitable for the customer. A multilevel development may also require this merge process at the intermediary levels where content is received and enhanced.

You can provide a merge tool for this task that includes functions such as explicitly activating new content, comparing data between existing and new content, and providing support when you merge received content and your own enhancements. The standard SAP system contains highly developed examples of these types of merge tools in Transactions SPAU and SPDD for ABAP Repository or ABAP Dictionary objects. Another example you may also use is a sophisticated, multilevel delivery and activation concept that was created for delivering Business Content to SAP NetWeaver BI.

Merge tool

For more information, refer to the SAP help options under CHANGING THE SAP STANDARD (BC) and under SAP BUSINESS INFORMATION WAREHOUSE • DATA WAREHOUSING • DATA WAREHOUSE MANAGEMENT • BUSINESS CONTENT (VERSIONS).

Merging Application Data

In the context of company mergers, data from two different installations of application systems may have to be merged. If you foresee this requirement, you can try to optimize the data model of the application to ensure that you can transfer tools at the database level using *Extract Transform Load (ETL)*. Strategies for generating unique primary keys across systems are presented in Chapter 3, Application Object.

However, you cannot assume that the standard SAP system data that your application uses, such as *Business Application Log* (BAL) logs or work items from workflows, can interact. In this case, you must restart the corresponding workflows, and also read BAL logs and create new ones. This example shows that merge projects can be difficult. It is unlikely that you will be able to foresee all conditions for a merge project and be able to react to them adequately during the development period.

Difficulties

However, if later merges of application data are likely, you should save the source in the form of a logical system name as an attribute at the database level in your central application objects. The logical system is saved in the table of the underlying V_TBDLS view; you determine it using the OWN_LOGICAL_SYSTEM_GET function module of the BDLS function group. You can use this approach after a data migration to start post-processing tasks and follow-up processes, such as reactivating workflows.

2.1.4   Limits of Functional and Non-Functional Requirements

Many subroutines and submodules do not arise from functional or non-functional requirements, but instead emerge during development and developer testing. These are of interest to experienced users, application consultants, and software testers and can be part of the application system.

Automatic System Test

Automatic workflow Customizing

If you have to implement comprehensive Customizing activities for an application system, the check functions suggested in Section 2.1.3, Non-Functional Requirements, are not sufficient. One example from the standard SAP system is automatic workflow Customizing (Transaction SWU3), which is displayed in Figure 2.3. There, you can easily test the effects of Customizing modifications on the workflow runtime environment by clicking on the start Verification Workflow button F5 .

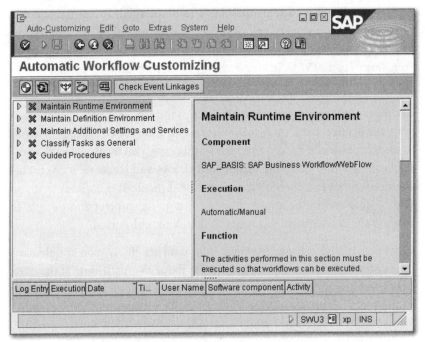

Figure 2.3 Customizing Maintenance and Test

Object Search Services

For most application objects, you need search functions you can use to search for specific criteria and navigate to the relevant editing area. The selection parameters in functional requirements are often motivated purely by specialization considerations, and are primarily intended to support the user. However, during development, quality assurance, and roll-out, emphasis may also be placed on additional search criteria and search strategies. A search based on the following criteria can support a developer or application consultant:

- ▶ Display all application objects that were created and modified at a certain time.   Criteria

- ▶ Determine all application objects where workflow terminations occurred when you were editing the objects, or where a correct person responsible could not be determined for their workflow and a special organizational unit was selected to be used to handle the error.

We recommend that you create flexible search services that will make it easier for you to implement different search strategies.

Verification Code and Sample Code

In some cases, application systems contain comprehensive frameworks, where users of specialized processes integrate their source code. A good way to test the functional options of frameworks and their user-friendliness, and to demonstrate how to use these options, is to provide verification code.

Here, when using the term *verification*, we do not mean that you check   Verification
important properties of an application system using formal tools. Instead, we mean that you can provide test code, perform a sample application scenario, and be satisfied with the correct behavior of a software module.

Verification and sample code can be delivered together with the application system. Here too, the standard SAP system contains examples, such as test workflows in Transaction SWUI_VERIFY (see Figure 2.4).

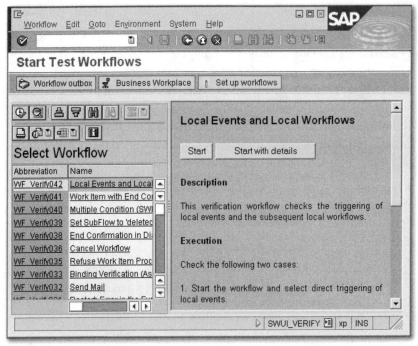

Figure 2.4 Verification

Effect on live data

Some development guidelines do not allow verification code to be delivered. An important reason for this precautionary measure is concern over the effect it may have on live data – if verification code changes the contents of transparent tables, this may affect the live dataset. Even if already existing application objects cannot be changed, simply creating new application objects can affect follow-up processes, such as reporting, replication, and also archiving. Effects are even more complex if loosely-linked follow-up processes are triggered by the Publish & Subscribe interfaces described in Section 5.5.3, Event-Based Interfaces. In such a case, you can prevent verification code from being executed in live systems by enabling the application to use the TR_SYS_PARAMS function module. This will check whether the system is live and, if so, terminates. You can also use special authorizations to protect the application.

However, if effects on live data cannot be avoided or implicitly occur during the automatic system test, you must implement special measures and explicitly provide the generated application objects with an attribute that separates them from the live dataset.

2.1.5 System Specification

The classic approach after requirements analysis is to create a specification or business blueprint that is the main and binding basis of the subsequent implementation. The system specification phase normally begins shortly after you start the requirements analysis. If the requirements are stable, you can describe them in a specification.

The specific goal of the specification is to maintain the interfaces of the system or of relevant subsystems for neighboring systems. The overall interface concept is summarized here:

Interfaces

▸ **GUI interfaces**
User interfaces are described in detail in the system specification.

▸ **Workflows**
Business processes that consist of several work steps and may involve several persons responsible are mapped by workflows. These must be displayed in the specification at a suitable abstraction level.

▸ **Data exchange process**
Systems often have external interfaces to other applications; master and transaction data from other systems is partly used. These data flows of underlying data exchange and replication scenarios must also be part of the specification.

However, not only do you require business processes to describe these items, you also need application cases and detailed data models.

In the development of individual software, the accepted point of view is that a system specification describes *what* a system does, not *how* it does it, whereby the latter occurs in a separate DP concept. In ABAP developing, adhering too rigidly to this dogma usually results in disaster. The strength of AS ABAP is that it provides a wide range of frameworks and has dialog standards. You can, of course, completely re-program the standard SAP system because, for example, users who are inexperienced at using SAP may not find certain dialog standards very user-friendly. However, this has the following consequences:

▶ **Budget risks**
If the proportion of standard software decreases and, in contrast, the proportion of software modules you created in-house increases, this raises the costs required for development and testing.

▶ **Quality problems**
Most AS ABAP software solutions are sophisticated and tested and have therefore been "refined" through hands-on use. Unlike independently programmed solutions, they are understood in the ABAP developer community, and documented and supported by SAP. Software modules you develop yourself must first reach this level of maturity. The fact that you may be aware of any weaknesses in existing solutions in the standard SAP system does not mean that your own development will not have any weaknesses – they will simply come to light at a later stage and may become acute in the pilot phase of the product.

▶ **Lack of conceptual consistency**
The strength of AS ABAP is its consistent implementation of different concepts. This relates to dialog standards and data replication scenarios. If you decide for no reason not to use the technologies contained in the standard system, this will increase the complexity of the resulting application system. You also give away synergy effects. By not sticking to dialog standards, you make it more difficult for experienced SAP users to learn and use the functions of the new application system.

[!] **Technical Expert Knowledge in Early Project Phases**

Although the focus of system specifications must be on presenting business processes, a technician should nevertheless assist in advising specialized staff on questions about how dialogs are designed, on replication scenarios, or on how add-ons are developed for the standard SAP system. This approach means that you will prevent specialized staff with superficial technical knowledge from including this said knowledge in the requirements, and avoid specifications based on a complete lack of knowledge from being created (the implementation of which would far exceed the scope of the budget and technical basis).

The question about how technical a system specification should be is therefore more of an academic question. The business processes and system or user interfaces are the central topic. Before you can specify user dialogs, which you can only implement with great effort using standard SAP system tools, the basic principle of the full technical neutrality of the system specification should be abandoned. This is also true for many master data processes. A live SAP application often already has comprehensive business partner data and equally comprehensive add-ons for this data. If this fact is ignored in a business blueprint, the likelihood that existing solutions will be ignored during the specification process is great. One indication of these types of specifications are abstract concepts, for which authors try to avoid entities that are already understood and used in the SAP system, only essentially to abstract them from the standard SAP system despite the fact that their use has long been established.

2.2   General Architectural Considerations

The description of implementing non-functional requirements shows that you often need to modularize the application system appropriately to be able to implement it. We will therefore discuss aspects of modularizing application systems in the next sections.

Separating technology and specialization is a basic principle in software development. It is already widely implemented in AS ABAP, because the database layer is encapsulated. We will discuss the implementation of database access layers in detail in Chapter 3.

Layer models

When you have complex applications that are particularly specialized or technical, it is useful to separate specialization (specialist logic, and dependencies) and technology (database access strategies) in the source code. We recommend proven models with layer architectures. We will discuss the implementation details of these architectures in Chapter 5, Application Architecture, as part of software structuring, and in Chapter 6, Application Layer, for implementing the application layer.

2.2.1   Product Families: Separating Frames and Content

In the SAP development environment, only one active version of a development element exists at any one time. Although there are versionings of objects, there are none for sets of objects. This means that you cannot restore a specific software status quickly, as you can in other software development environments, or store different versions of the same development object in parallel for possible use in the application system.

Product families Many SAP developers solve this problem by separating *frames* and *content*. Instead of developing one or two products, they plan and develop product families. In practice, this is structured as follows:

▶ **EDI procedure example**
Assume that you want to develop an EDI procedure for different processes, in which external data deliveries are transferred to the system, checked, and transformed into internal structures. In addition, the procedure allows for monitoring of processes and access options for the user. You can easily modularize this application by creating a common interface for the operations to be performed (transfer, check, and transformation) and integrating these into an application framework that will control these operations and communicate the outcome of an implemented operation ("check performed"), and possibly a result ("data delivery technically incorrect" or "intervention required by person responsible"), to the application framework. This means that you can jump to the process-specific data — the specific content that is unknown to the application framework.

▶ **Dispute case example**
Imagine an application that manages dispute cases for certain application objects such as invoices or contracts. Intervention from the persons responsible will be required. This application defines separate workflows, how to easily find persons responsible, escalation control, and jumps to the objects to be disputed. All mentioned functions — including jumping to the objects to be disputed, which is controlled by Customizing — can be implemented in such a way that the product works for dispute cases of any application objects. This represents real added value.

Frameworks The examples show that, by separating frames and content, the framework can be separated from the specialized processes. A *framework* is a system of classes that implements a reusable design of a certain application area.

A successful product is often characterized by the fact that, in addition to defining the frame, it also defines content (which in itself already adds value). An example of this type of separation in the SAP environment is the architecture of SAP NetWeaver Business Intelligence (SAP NetWeaver BI). The standard content with all of its capabilities is already a unique selling point of the product, but customers can also flexibly enhance it and define their own characteristics and key figures in InfoCubes.

SAP NetWeaver BI

This example also shows that the product offers real added value to customers, because they can add their own business processes to the product. It also opens up a new business area for product manufacturers because they can support customers in the integration of their own processes.

Requirements Management

Separating frames and content represents challenges for software architects and developers. The principle that "there is absolutely no place for specialization in the application framework" must enjoy top priority; otherwise, the architecture will immediately degenerate because an important basic principle of software technology has been violated: The separation of responsibilities, which generally increases the complexity of the software considerably.

Separating frames and content

> **Separating Responsibilities**
>
> The principle of separating responsibilities specifies that software modules must only be responsible for one purpose. At the level of an application system, it means that modules responsible for a similar task must be grouped and differentiated from other modules. This approach enables individual tasks to be modified independently of each other.

This section describes how specialized requirements creep into the application framework and how you safeguard yourself against this:

▶ **"My specialized process needs a special workflow."**
We have nothing against this type of requirement, except to say that you must not make the mistake of including it in the application framework. Retain the workflow template in Customizing tables and call it dynamically.

▶ **"I want to be able to search according to process-specific criteria in the general search dialog of the framework."**
With this, you will face a technical challenge. How do you search with a framework function for data that is — and must be — completely unknown to the framework? One solution are special search services the framework user implements. Chapter 5, Application Architecture, and Chapter 6, Application Layer, deal in detail with the techniques required to address this.

▶ **"I want to display special fields in the general display dialog that are relevant for my specialized process."**
This requirement is a logical consequence of the previous requirement. A user wants to display, on one initial screen, all of the information required to complete his tasks. In this situation, you might be tempted to simply transfer the process-specific data into the application framework, but this would have disastrous consequences. What happens in situations where a specific specialized process cannot deliver this data? Should the application framework be enhanced with new data elements when new processes are added? The only proper way to deal with these requirements is to implement them using the specialized process. To do this, you integrate a screen into a subscreen and determine the data to be displayed on the basis of specific processes.

▶ **"I must call process-specific functions in certain locations in the logic of the application framework."**
An inexperienced developer will simply program the functions into the application framework in very large CASE constructs. This means that you will not be able to extend the application framework flexibly; that is, you will no longer be able to modify the content independently of the application framework. However, you can easily do this by calling BadIs, which, as filter criteria, carry the name of the specialized process.

You can add to this list as you wish – the answer is always the same:

1. An application framework is always the lowest common denominator and not the highest common multiple.

2. Specialization is only applied in specific specialized processes. The application framework delegates to these processes.

If the framework developer does not implement requirements of specialized processes but instead creates interfaces to enable the developers of specialized applications to integrate their processes into the framework, requirements management results. Developers of specialized processes discover the pragmatism and difference between necessary requirements and highly desirable requirements when they have to implement these requirements themselves.

Different type of requirements management

The question of how to implement flexible architectures runs through this entire book. Chapter 4, Classes, Interfaces, and Exceptions, examines the smallest modularization units (classes and interfaces), while Chapter 5, Application Architecture, deals with aspects of structuring the application system and different interface technologies. Chapter 6 includes details on special aspects of application programming, such as implementing search services.

Development Coordination

If you, as the development lead, decide to create a framework, you must set the requirements for its design engineers:

Developer requirements

▶ **Technical competence**
  The development of frameworks is one of the most demanding activities and is therefore reserved for the best developers on the team. This is because experience shows that design errors, such as incorrectly defined interfaces for specialist processes, for example, will come back to haunt you bitterly. Software developers require a lot of discipline not to let the architecture degenerate, as well as good communication skills to explain the framework to users.

▶ **Specialized competence**
  A framework is not an end in itself, but rather performs a defined task in the application system. Because the focus of a framework is on reusability, there is always the risk that it will either be too specialized to be reused in the application system by other specialized processes, or too general to be used efficiently in the application to be implemented. Specialized competence helps developers find a happy medium and also enables them to estimate future requirements.

▶ **Practical rather than theoretical**

Framework developers need feedback from the people who will be using the framework; otherwise, the resulting frameworks will be purely theoretical in design and will require a great deal of effort to use. However, framework developers can alleviate this problem by also designing and integrating a specialized process. This approach means that framework developers are also framework users, which encourages pragmatism and a realistic approach.

2.2.2 Metadata

If you have highly configurable applications, it often makes sense to provide a metadata repository and a descriptive service that uses this repository. This helps the application to remain robust, flexible and, above all, transparent.

Number range management

Number range management provides a simple example of a metadata service. You can use number ranges for using primary keys in transparent tables or general document numbers, which we will discuss in detail in Chapter 3. So where is the problem with using number range objects? The answer is that using number range objects in data models is not transparent. Although you can assign a domain to a number range in the ABAP Dictionary, there is no where-used list for the number range object. If you specifically want to document which number range is used for generating a key for a database table, you can do this in your own Customizing table. This has the name of the number range object as the primary key, and the name of the table field and data element where it is used as the attribute. In this type of table, you can also define which number range interval is currently active.

Application data checks

Each application system performs checks on the application data. Special checks are possible, depending on the result:

▶ An error is reported in dialog processing, and the user is asked to correct the incorrect data.

▶ Although data can be saved in automated mass processes, the person responsible starts a workflow for correcting the error.

A typical example of these types of checks are definitions that specify which fields are mandatory, that is, which fields are required entry fields and which fields are optional entry fields. When you hard code properties in the screen properties of fields, this is often not acceptable for larger application systems:

▶ You must perform comprehensive source code checks to find out which dialog fields are mandatory and which are not.

▶ When data is modified these properties are not checked by BAPI interfaces or Web services.

▶ You cannot change these properties without making modifications.

You can avoid these restrictions by storing these properties in Customizing. Here, we will present a solution that is frequently used in the standard SAP system but is associated with specific GUI technology. We will also illustrate its advantages and disadvantages.

In applications controlled by the *Business Data Toolset* (BDT) (see Chapter 8, SAP Business Partner), you can determine these definitions in the form of field groupings (see Figure 2.5).

Field groupings

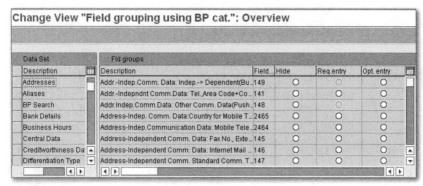

Figure 2.5 Field Groupings (Transaction BUSO)

This is a very clever definition because it directly influences the screen fields of an ABAP dialog application. However, questions remain about the software technology:

▶ **Data origin**
The requirements for data quality might depend on the origin of the

data: If data is generated from external systems, or through migration, it may sometimes not satisfy the quality requirements that might be required to enter data into the SAP system online. In this case, the strength of the same field groupings being used for processing the BDT application in the background (*BDT-Direct Input*) is also a weakness. In some applications, transparently defining a data quality requirement based on the origin of data is important.

▶ **No dependency on GUI technology**
Because field groupings are part of a specific GUI technology, transferring these criteria for another technology such as Web Dynpro ABAP, for example, is problematic. Can you guarantee that a BDT view corresponds to a Web Dynpro view? Certainly, when you look at BDT technology by itself, there are restrictions for using EnjoySAP Controls. When using editable ALV grids in BDT applications, you must first obtain the required information from BDT Customizing as to which fields can be edited or definitely have to be filled.

If you define the data quality requirements of an application object using process-specific metadata, you can differentiate these based on the origin of the data, or on the application case. This gives you greater flexibility.

2.2.3   Generative Programming

If the application system contains metadata, the obvious thing to do is generate parts of the application system. You will find sufficient examples of this procedure in the SAP system, from table maintenance dialogs (see Section 7.2, Table Maintenance Dialogs and View Clusters) to Web Dynpro technology in AS ABAP, and for the object services that are one of the topics of Chapter 3.

Domain-specific languages — Proceed as follows when generating programs: In an editor (which could be graphical), create a description of the functions to be generated in a domain-specific language (DSL). You must be able to create a description in a DSL at least as quickly as the programming of the corresponding functions in ABAP. This procedure is very beneficial if the descriptions can be created in the DSL by the relevant user department. This ensures that the user department's work is kept separate from development. The consultants will no longer have to draft their requirements and communicate these to the developers, but will instead be able to describe parts of the application logic directly — and also generate them directly, if necessary.

What are the advantages of generating programs? In addition to the potential savings when creating programs, there are also technical advantages. For example, generated source code is faster than a DSL executed at runtime by a separate interpreter written in ABAP.

Generative programmingis considered the ultimate in application development — and rightly so. Experience shows that the first success is quickly followed by disillusionment as detail level problems materialize: **Problems**

▶ Should you generate the programs transiently, in other words, should they only exist in the main memory to ensure that they disappear after generation and application?

▶ Should you generate the programs without modifications, that is, should you also be able to do this in live systems?

▶ If you generate the source code in the development system, how do you connect to the transport system?

Solutions are available for these problems. You can use the BUS_SEARCH_   **Solutions**
GENERATOR_MAIN function module to find an example of an existence check, of deleting and (over)generating function groups and function modules, and activation. You can generate programs using the GENERATE REPORT command and actually save them without modifications using INSERT REPORT. Note that these techniques are only intended for internal SAP use. There are even tools like the SAPlink open source tool (see *http://www.saplink.org*) that can generate ABAP development objects from an XML representation.

Aside from the previously described technical problems, there are other disadvantages. Based on experience, generated source code is hard to read, and transient programs are difficult to check and debug.

We know that generative techniques are only worthwhile for automating relatively simple tasks that are to be completed schematically, such as specialized checks. For additional requirements, we recommend a detailed cost-benefit analysis.

XSL
Transformations
One of the most powerful generating techniques are XSL Transformations, which you integrate into ABAP using the `CALL TRANSFORMATION` command. The advantage of this technique is that it also allows you to maintain DSL statements in external tools such as spreadsheets. Almost every office application lets you save its data in XML and can therefore be used as a data source for DSL statements.

2.2.4 Model-Driven Architectures

The classic software development process, whether performed in a standard or agile manner, consists of design, coding, and documentation. When you make a change, you must repeat the corresponding operations. Another step towards industrial software production is the paradigm of *model-driven architectures* (MDA).

MDA approach
The MDA approach involves developing models of the application system to be created. You convert a number of models (for example, platform-independent models become platform-dependent models), and these are converted into source code. You automate the software development process and solve the problem of keeping the software documentation up-to-date following modifications.

Web Dynpro ABAP
There are some frameworks in SAP development where a step in this direction has already been taken. The most well-known is the Web Dynpro ABAP framework. Developing models and generating source code is a normal procedure when you create graphical user interfaces. This also gives you enough flexibility to meet the new challenges of quickly developing standards and technologies for Internet technologies and web-enabled user interfaces.

Nonetheless, we still have a long way to go before we achieve completely model-driven applications. In particular, a great deal of time and effort is required to develop new frameworks. The cost-effectiveness of developing these frameworks is also questionable if their reusability cannot be considered a certainty.

Even more difficult are the organizational challenges you face when you develop or use an MDA framework that is not yet fully advanced. The development team then splits into two groups: The developers or experts for the MDA framework, and the application developers. This poses a risk of losses as a result of frictions within the team. Can you guarantee that the MDA framework can be used for implementing the functional and non-functional requirements? Is it flexible enough that the generated result can also be enhanced by its own source code? Or do the application developers have requirements that the framework cannot meet and that therefore, the framework experts must "protect" it?

Beyond a certain level of complexity, only large software companies or open source projects can accomplish good quality development of their own MDA frameworks.

2.3   Using the Standard SAP System

Every AS ABAP is delivered with two software components, SAP_BASIS and SAP_ABA, that comprise a large number of APIs and frameworks you can apply to use your business applications. Some of these APIs are described in this book, and include the SAP Business Partner, SAP Business Workflow, and a parallel processing framework.

Two software components

The components mentioned are released externally, which means that you can use them for your development (for more information, see SAP Note 109533). However, many components, such as the Business Application Log, for example, are not released externally even though they are extremely useful and frequently used in the standard SAP system. If you use these functions, SAP AG will not provide support. If you do want to use them nonetheless, you must be very familiar with these functions. You should also have analyzed the functions in the standard SAP system to enable you to assess the risk in terms of whether they will be available in future releases. If there are many SAP Notes for a function, you can assume that other developers also use this function and solutions to problems are provided.

External release

When using released and non-released functions, we recommend that you have an expert for these functions on your development team who will be able to advise other developers about its use, train them, and conduct reviews. If using a component means that there will be far-reaching consequences for the overall application, the relevant expert should also

Experts

49

be involved in the early phases of the project because only he can assess to what extent functional and non-functional requirements can be implemented using the component.

The expert should also regularly check the SAP Marketplace for notes about the component and study the corresponding SAP release notes. For details of where to find sources of information, refer to Section 10.1.2, SAP Support Portal.

If functional and non-functional requirements have been established for an application system to be developed and you have given basic consideration to the software structure and use of standard SAP components, you can begin designing the central application objects. These result from the domain models of the specialized design or from the data models developed in the system specification. Chapter 3 describes how application objects are modeled at the database level and how object persistence, together with transaction control, is implemented.

"Objects serve two purposes: They promote understanding of the real world and provide a practical basis for computer implementation." (James Rumbaugh)

3 Application Object

The paradigm of object orientation means that software is seen as a quantity of discrete objects that have a data structure and data behavior. This perspective is completely natural at the application design level, because this approach can be used to map the business entities of the conceptual design. Object-oriented programming involves creating an equivalent to the business entities in each case, such as invoices or documents. The following are characteristic features of an object designed and programmed in this way:

Paradigm of object orientation

▶ An *object identity* can be defined: An object exists but once and must be uniquely identified.

▶ An object has properties that are encoded in *attributes*. These are defined in ABAP by ABAP Dictionary data elements.

▶ Objects also have behaviors that are encoded as *methods*.

▶ Objects of the same type (in terms of the same attributes and behavior) are categorized. They are *instances* (or also copies) of a class. In the sample application presented here, the central objects are instances of a vehicle class.

▶ Classes have a hierarchical structure through *derivation*. Derived classes are more specific than their predecessors. The basis classes are therefore true generalizations.

Object orientation helps you implement business processes flexibly, because you can keep several instances of business entities in an internal session at the same time. This lets you implement methods that can compare, copy, or possibly consolidate these instances.

Implementing business processes flexibly

In this chapter, you will learn about the techniques required to do this. For the Vehicle Management sample application, you will design an application object at the semantic level and create a data and object model.

In Section 3.2, Modeling the Application Object at the Database Level, we will discuss the mapping of the data model at the database level in detail. Section 3.3, Implementing Object Persistence, deals with implementing object persistence, as the name suggests. For example, how are ABAP objects saved to the database? We will introduce different types of database access layers, where the focus will be on *Object Services*. The SAP transaction concept is illustrated in Section 3.4, Transaction Concept, because you must thoroughly understand databases and SAP transactions for developing and using database access layers. The chapter concludes with Section 3.5, where we present best practices for all topics already discussed. This section will also describe specific topics, such as using change documents for persistent objects, for which you will need a number of the techniques developed in this chapter.

3.1   What Is an Application Object?

At the core of typical applications for SAP systems is a relatively complex application object whose data is saved to one or more tables and which contains specialized methods that can be used to manipulate the application object. Typical examples include business entities such as customer, invoice, document, or delivery.

Object-oriented analysis | How do you identify application objects? In almost all cases, the application object results from the product idea, whereby the application will need to manage a central business entity. If a system specification is object-oriented, you will find application objects for object-oriented analysis.

In addition, more than one application object may exist in an application system, in which case it is useful to modularize the application into sub-applications. This is the topic of Chapter 5, Application Architecture.

You find application objects by breaking down an overall object model into logical parts. This procedure is the key to every successful modeling process. Instead of being analyzed in the overall model, each more complex system is initially identified in submodels of greater cohesion.

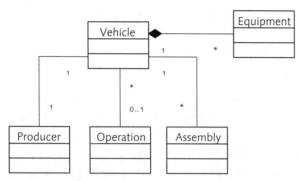

Figure 3.1 Application Object

There are two central application objects in this sample application, *vehicle* and *request*. Figure 3.1 illustrates the strategic structure of the *Vehicle* application object in Unified Modeling Language (UML). The semantics are as follows:

Example of an application object

A vehicle is normally assigned to exactly one operation where it is allowed. When a vehicle changes the operation to which it is assigned in an organization group, it temporarily might not be assigned to any operation. In fact, there is a *time frame* the user should also be able to recognize.

A vehicle has exactly one producer. To map the producer data, you can access the SAP Business Partner available on every SAP system. To map this producer, you can easily access the standard SAP system and create a field on the vehicle that you can use to refer to a business partner number.

A vehicle has a number of equipment parts, such as the type of passenger information (for example the recorded announcement of stops). However, this also includes fittings like seating, paintwork, and advertising (for example side panel, or full wrap advertising). You should model the equipment parts as independent objects. There is no provision made to enable you to assign a fitting to another vehicle.

Vehicles have assemblies. Unlike the equipment, they have a serial number, year of production, and so on. You should be able to assign assemblies to another vehicle.

Object-oriented design

The object-oriented analysis is followed by the design phase, where the object model that is used as the basis for the implementation is also developed. While the object-oriented analysis returns a domain model of the application, the result of the object-oriented design is a class model and sequence diagrams. Here, you should consider the class model and the requirements for database persistence, which must satisfy each business application object.

Different procedures exist in software technology for designing objects. Some software designers design an object model first and then develop a data model from this object model. However, the reverse is also possible, that is, you can design a data model and develop an object model based on it. Advocates of agile methods often favor incremental procedures. That is, for example, if you make modifications to the object model you will also need to make modifications to the data model, and vice versa. Agile methods in ABAP development are certainly a major challenge. If you choose this option, you will need detailed knowledge of the refactoring options of the ABAP Workbench, but should also be aware of the implications of a structural change to transparent tables.

Procedure

The procedure is as follows:

1. Starting with the class model from the analysis phase, you design the application object.
2. You then develop the data model at the database level, starting with the attributes and object model relationships.
3. Finally, you implement the object persistence, meaning you map the object at the database level.

Advantages

There are two advantages to this procedure: First, the focus early in the design phase is on the database model. You will be able to ensure in good time that it is optimized in terms of access paths, satisfies revisory factors, and can be found easily in the archive. Second, you can implement the object persistence using the *Object Services* of the ABAP Workbench.

In the following text, we will discuss the aspects you must take into account when designing application objects, such as the granularity of the object model.

In most cases, the application object is not an instance of an individual class, but instead consists of compositions and associations to other classes. Examples include header and item data that you frequently find in SAP ERP applications. It may prove useful to implement these types of compositions at the level of structured data types, rather than using a wide variety of classes, and therefore use the options of internal tables and, if necessary, also deeper data structures. This lets you reduce the number of runtime objects as well as easily access quantities of object attributes as internal tables. This approach is particularly beneficial in performance-intensive applications. This procedure is often used in EDI processes, where, for example, the *Data delivery (external)* application object has a quantity of raw data in an external data format that cannot be implemented as an independent object. In fact, after typing this raw data and instancing a new *Data delivery (internal)* application object, you must not model temporary data, such as address components (which may involve you having to update the master data at a later stage) as separate objects.

Granularity of the object model

In the next step, you should try to use business objects from the standard SAP system. You must define a producer for a vehicle in the sample application. It would be useful here to map the possible business partners as SAP Business Partners and include the business partner number as a reference in an attribute in the Z_CL_VEHICLE class. An example of the class model obtained using this approach is shown in Figure 3.2.

Using business objects from the standard SAP system

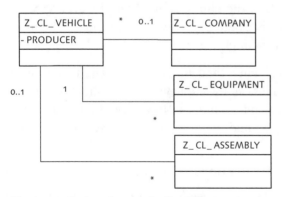

Figure 3.2 Design of an Application Object

The Z_CL_VEHICLE class has an attribute that specifies a business partner number in the producer role.

Virtual attributes

Not all attributes of an object must have a one-to-one correspondence to a field in a database table. In addition to database attributes that represent the fields of assigned database tables, do you also want virtual attributes that will be calculated, or read from other tables? In this case, you do not need to take the corresponding attributes into account in the data model. After you have finished designing the application object, you can begin modeling it at the database level.

3.2   Modeling the Application Object at the Database Level

The database design is a key component of every business application. You can develop it based on a model for object-oriented design. Alternatively, you can develop a semantic data model, implement it based on the ABAP Dictionary, and derive an object model from this. You will learn about this procedure in conjunction with the Structured Entity Relationship diagram in Section 3.2.1.

You must be particularly thorough when creating data models. It is difficult to modify the data model of an application that is already live because you have to write comprehensive conversion programs. If you have just archived live data, the effort required will be even greater, because you will have to check the effect on archiving objects (Transaction AOBJ) when a modification is made.

Two aspects

You focus on two aspects when modeling data: the data model must enable you to access data efficiently and have a simple structure so that it can be evaluated by DataSources for SAP NetWeaver BI, or enable you to display archives using methods of the standard SAP system.

3.2.1   Structured Entity Relationship Model

You can use the *SAP Data Modeler* integrated into the ABAP Workbench to create data models. Figure 3.3 shows a small portion of the SAP_10130 SAP Business Partner data model . This example also illustrates that you can use data models to document existing applications.

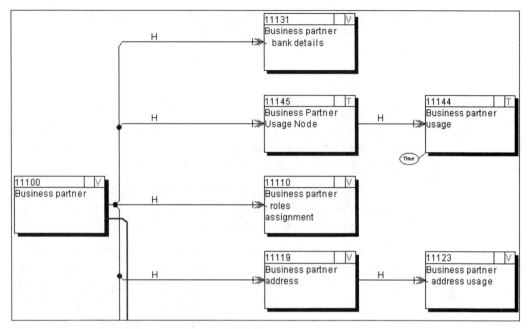

Figure 3.3 Partial SAP Business Partner Data Model

Unlike the Entity Relationship diagram, the *Structured Entity Relationship diagram* (SERM) consists of directional arrows. An arrow means that the target entity depends on the source entity in terms of the relationship of a header record to item records. An item record can therefore only exist if a header record exists (this is called *existence dependency*). In this case, the letter "H" above the arrow stands for "hierarchical". The double or single arrowheads indicate that several entities, or only one single entity, participate(s) in the relationship. A single line signifies that the relationship is optional, meaning that an element may also be missing on the target side.

Data Modeler

You call the Data Modeler from Transaction SD11, but it is also integrated into the ABAP Workbench. You can display data models or their entity types in Transaction SE80 under BUSINESS ENGINEERING • DATA MODELS OR BUSINESS ENGINEERING • ENTITY TYPES.

You will use the Data Modeler to develop an SERM diagram from the design model shown in Figure 3.2. You will create a data model called ZVEHICLE first.

You will set up a ZVEHICLE business object in Chapter 6, Application Layer; therefore, it will be useful to assign the data model using this approach.

To do this, you will create entity types for all classes:

Creating entity
types

▶ The ZVEHICLE entity type corresponds to the vehicle data.

▶ ZOWNER defines the assignment of a vehicle to a company. A vehicle is only assigned to one company at a time; you can use the time frame to map different transfers of vehicle ownership.

▶ ZEQUIPMENT represents the equipment data. Like ZOWNER, this has a hierarchical (that is, existence-based) dependency on the vehicle entity type, although no time dependency is involved here.

▶ ZASSEMBLY represents assemblies. These have a referential relationship to the vehicle entity (letter "R" above the arrow). Letter "C" (for "conditional") specifies a conditional relationship. This modeling demonstrates that an assembly can also exist without a vehicle if it is removed from one vehicle and built into another vehicle later.

Figure 3.4 shows the data model, visualized by the SAP Data Modeler.

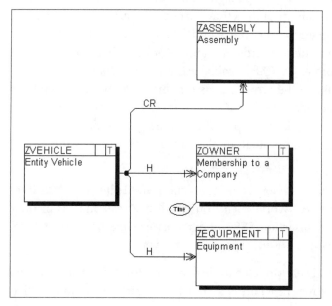

Figure 3.4 Vehicle Data Model

You can create this data model using the ABAP Workbench by first creating the entity types displayed in the figure. Other documentation options are also available here, for example, you can create SAPscript texts for all entities and for the data model. For each entity type, define detailed relationships (using the button of the same name or F6) to other entities that correspond to the arrows shown in Figure 3.4. You still have to assign the entity types to the data model using the Hierarchy button, as you can see in Figure 3.5. You can still subsequently move the entities if you think that the positioning selected by the Data Modeler is unclear.

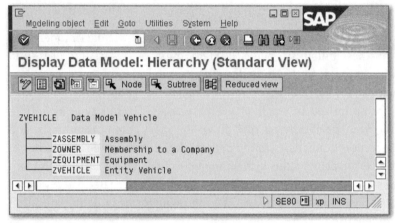

Figure 3.5 Data Model Entities

You will find the Data Modeler in the SAP Library under the keyword *Data Modeler (BC-DWB-TOO)*. The SAP SERM model also provides other relationship types (aggregating and external) and specializations for modeling inheritances. You can also create submodels, hierarchically nest them, use external relationships to refer to them and link data models to business objects to ensure that you achieve an integrated description of the application object, consisting of object behavior and object data, in the SAP system. SERM models are generally quite suitable for data modeling composite objects, because they are in the third normal form in terms of database theory.

Normalization can be seen as optimizing the data model, which results in redundancies and anomalies being avoided when you access databases.

We will not be able to discuss the theory of normal forms as it is beyond the scope of the book.

The SAP Data Modeler enables you to assign entity types to ABAP Dictionary elements such as transparent tables or views. This means that you can link SERM models to the database model. Mapping the SERM model in the ABAP Dictionary is the topic of Section 3.2.2, Data Modeling at the ABAP Dictionary Level.

Normalization   Knowledge about database normalization is an important basis for each data modeling, as well as an essential requirement here. Information about this topic can also be found in every book about databases.

Normalized data models correspond to the semantic data model from the business blueprint, and SAP SERM models are usually already in the third normal form. Normalized data models do not have any redundancies and no anomalies occur for database operations. However, they are not optimized in terms of database access. In this type of optimization, you specifically narrow down the most common requests, and also accept redundancies in the data model, to minimize the number of requests. You achieve this by keeping fields in database tables redundant and saving the results of calculations (such as aggregated values at the database level) in the database. The following forms of denormalization are widely used in SAP development:

Forms of
denormalization

▸ The most common form of denormalization is keeping attributes redundant. You usually save the last and first names of business partners or classification criteria from other tables.

▸ For temporary data, you can duplicate tables for which you expect large data volumes. If these tables are distributed to different partitions at the database system level, parallel access can be accelerated. You can use Customizing to control which tables to select for which transaction data.

▸ If you are sure that a number of attributes will not be populated in most cases, you can create a separate table for them and create the corresponding records only as required.

> **Denormalization** [+]
>
> The following rules apply for optimization of the database model:
>
> ▶ You must not use denormalization lightly; Denormalization is only useful for optimizing frequently-performed access to databases.
>
> ▶ Denormalization is often avoided for write-only applications to prevent change anomalies.
>
> ▶ Read-only applications are often considerably denormalized to prevent joins, aggregations, and calculations at the database level.

3.2.2 Data Modeling at the ABAP Dictionary Level

The ERM and SERM data models are characteristically semantic. You must develop a data model out of them that consists of transparent tables. The relevant aspects required for this are described in the following text, and include defining primary and foreign keys, indexes, database locks, saving unstructured data, and so on.

Primary Key

Each transparent table contains one primary key with a unique constraint. Two table rows must have different primary keys. Master and transaction data should also contain the client in the primary key to ensure that the application system has multitenancy capabilities.

Unique constraint

To create primary keys, you can define either specialized or technical keys. A specialized key is created by the attributes that define the identity of an object as a whole. You must use specialized keys with caution because if the specialization changes, or if you discover that the key has been modified, extensive recoding will be necessary.

Number ranges enable you to generate keys for application objects. This also allows you to store specialized information in the keys by defining subobjects and including fiscal years. You define number ranges in Transaction SNRO. Note the following when using number ranges:

Number range objects

▶ **Specialized components**
Specialized components in a number range help persons responsible when they are processing business objects, because they can memorize these components, if necessary. Specialized components also sup-

port developers and support. Under no circumstances should a program evaluate these specialized components because this would cause the disadvantages of specialized keys to be inherited. There can be exceptions if you want to merge data from different SAP systems as part of a merge project. However, this requires assigning the numbers disjointly in the different systems, which involves additional coordination effort.

▶ **Assigning external numbers**
You should assign the numbers outside of the SAP system using an *external number assignment*. These types of cases are common for migration projects or external data transfers from other systems.

▶ **Deactivating buffering**
If you want assigned numbers to have the character of a document, you must deactivate main memory buffering to ensure that the numbering is consistent, even if the Logical Unit of Work (SAP LUW) were to terminate. A *logical unit of work* (or SAP transaction) is a sequence of related database operations, which are discussed in detail in Section 3.4, Transaction Concept. For more information about number range buffering, refer to the *SAP Number Range Buffering (BC-CST-NU)* section in the SAP Library.

▶ **Assigning a number**
The NUMBER_GET_NEXT function module accesses the database and requires a certain amount of access time for activated main memory buffering.

▶ **Maintaining interval statuses**
Each customer must maintain the statuses of number range intervals. The statuses cannot usually also be delivered with the software, because the current values are also transferred in this way. This often makes no sense in the target system, or is even risky if you want to install the software again.[1]

---

1 You can, of course, use a report to set the initial statuses of the number ranges by manipulating the transparent NRIV table. However, this approach is extremely risky, because multiple uses mean that the uniqueness of the numbers may no longer be possible. Consequently, you may no longer be able to determine primary keys. We therefore advise you to always write these programs as securely as possible to eliminate the risk of statuses being reset that have already been maintained.

You create number range objects in Transaction SNRO, as shown in Figure 3.6. In this case, you define a domain for the number length, buffer the numbers in main memory, and specify to issue a warning if only ten percent of the numbers are still available. Transaction SNRO

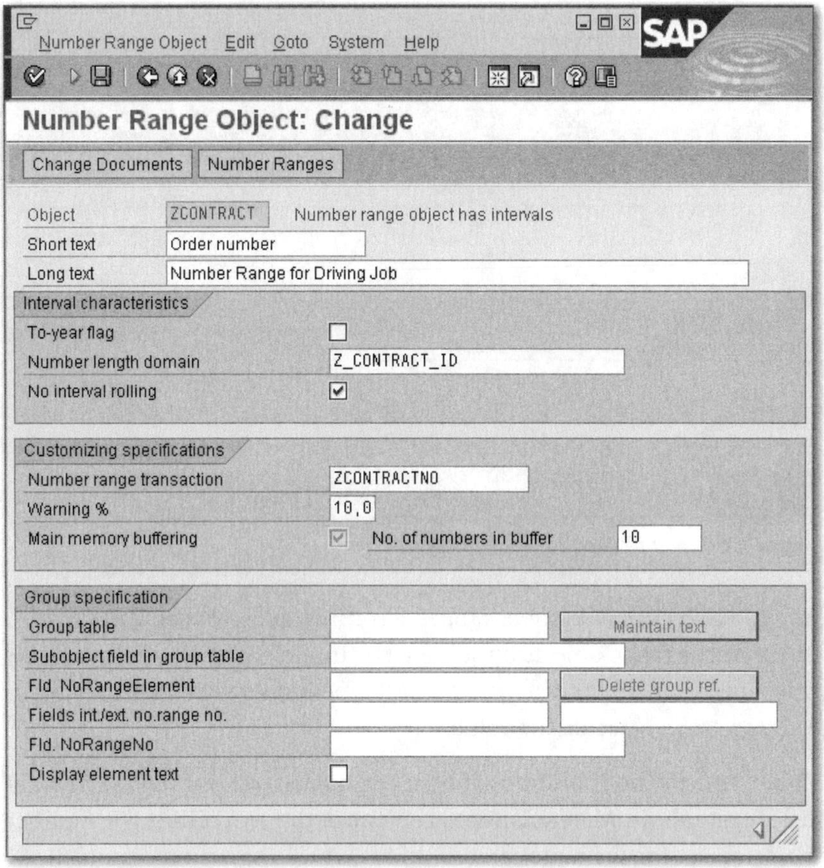

Figure 3.6   Creating Number Range Objects

After creating the number range object, you create the intervals. Intervals must not overlap; exceptions are only allowed if there is a reference to the fiscal year. If you assign a number, you must specify an interval where the generated numbers should be located. Alternatively, you can specify that the numbers roll back. This means that when you start an interval the numbers are assigned again from the beginning as soon as the upper limit is reached (Transaction SNUM, see Figure 3.7). You can Intervals also identify intervals as "external". In that case, the number is assigned by the user or an external system. This type of number range interval can also contain alphanumeric characters if this is allowed by the domain used. You can use the NUMBER_CHECK function module to check whether a number belongs to a certain number range interval.

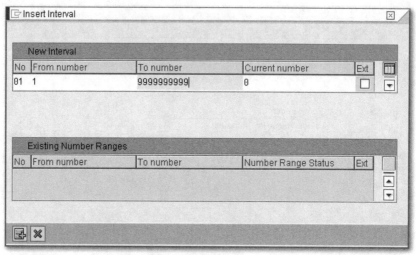

Figure 3.7 Creating Number Range Intervals

Fiscal years   You can also classify number ranges according to fiscal year. You can classify number range objects by subobjects. In the example, you can create a separate domain for different request types and assign your own intervals for each characteristic value.

Number range   Other structuring is also possible, using *number range groups*. The standard example in Materials Management is the MATERIALNR number range object for the material master, for which the material type (MTART data element) determines the number range interval using Table T134 (which is specified in the number range object).

You will find plenty of examples of this procedure in the SAP ERP environment. However, we advise against overdoing this by assigning numbers with too many specialized aspects. We will use a negative example to confirm this: Assume that you assign numbers for different materials depending on the vendor. As a result, you receive a key (either structured or concatenated as a fixed-length string) that contains a year, the domain value depending on the vendor, the interval number, and the actual number. You must first make sure that none of the parts of the key for specialized processes are evaluated in the application. If this is actually the case, there may be a risk of nasty surprises if the specialization changes, for example, if two vendors merge. Experience shows that the risks of complex number range objects together with subobjects and groups outweigh the advantages in most cases, unless sophisticated data modeling was maintained.

For more information about number ranges, refer to the SAP Library under BC EXTENDED APPLICATIONS FUNCTION LIBRARY • NUMBER RANGES.

Global Unique Identifiers (GUIDs) enable you to generate technical keys. Using GUIDs makes using number ranges effortless, and you get a purely technical key that enables you to merge data from different live instances of the application system again. You create GUIDs using the `GUID_CREATE` function module of the `SYGU` function group. As of Release 7.0, GUIDs have the benefit of distribution properties, which means that you can easily receive packaging options as part of parallel processing. We also recommend this key assignment for application objects that are used in cross-system processes and for which uniqueness is therefore essential. We examine this aspect in Section 9.2.2, Prerequisites, as part of parallelization strategies.

Global Unique
Identifier (GUID)

Based on experience, GUIDs are not suitable for display in screens. They are also not user-friendly for the person responsible; numbers are easier to use.

Defining External Keys

You can define external keys in the ABAP Dictionary but they are not represented by external keys in the database. Consequently, you cannot guarantee the referential integrity of the dataset using database tools.

However, this does not mean that you should forego defining external keys. You use them to document the data model of the application system. You can also use external key relationships to implement

F4 help and input checks on dialog boxes. You can generate complete maintenance dialogs specifically for maintaining Customizing tables and simple master and transaction data, as you will see in Chapter 7, GUI Programming.

Mapping Inheritance

Options Different options are available for expressing the inheritance of classes at the database level. You can use separate tables for each class and map the entire hierarchy in a single table:

▶ **Mapping an entire class hierarchy in one table**
The advantage of mapping an entire class hierarchy in a table is that one class can be converted easily into another class. This is the case in the example here when a vehicle changes its type. Database queries are also usually easy to organize. However, the disadvantage is that often, a lot of memory space is wasted in the database because not all attributes are required in every class. Perhaps more annoying than the waste of memory space is the lack of transparency: You cannot easily identify to which class attributes belong.

▶ **Mapping a class to a table**
Mapping a class to a table comes closest to object-oriented modeling. In addition, you can change each class irrespective of other classes, and delete and add attributes as you wish. The disadvantage of this approach is that the number of database tables is very high, and access can be complicated. The effort required also increases if you want to add attributes to or delete them from all tables when you modify the data model. Queries can be very complex when you have a wide range of tables.

Inheritance relationships In many business applications, inheritance relationships are expressed by different composition relationships to other objects. For example, the parent class is usually abstract and represents the header data of an entity. The different derived classes all have the same header data but may have different item data. The problem of mapping inheritance does not arise in these situations.

Locks

You use database locks to ensure that several internal sessions (users or jobs) do not access the same object at the same time, which could create inconsistent statuses, or situations where only data written by the last person would be saved. What effects could not having locks have? The first is lost modifications. When two programs read a value from the database in a local variable in parallel and change and write this value back, the last transaction that made modifications overwrites the modifications made by the previous transaction. Even if only one transaction writes data, while another transaction accesses read-only data, you will not be able to rule out inconsistencies in the second transaction. You must also protect reading processes against writing processes.

Dirty reads are another problem. If a transaction is working on an entry and later executes a ROLLBACK WORK, written entries will be reset again in the meantime. If another process is using this data before it is "released" by COMMIT WORK, there is a risk that invalid data will be used.

Dirty reads

Locks can have different granularities. For example, you can lock single records, but you can also lock entire tables or use different lock concepts, namely *optimistic* and *pessimistic* locks. The pessimistic lock concept involves locking a database before each access, whereas the optimistic lock concept means that you generally forego database locks and use a time stamp to check whether a record has changed in the meantime. This saves time and effort required to manage database locks. *Isolation levels* of the database management system are closely associated with this.

ABAP development also has a lock concept that is not based on database locks and is described in the SAP Library under *The SAP Lock Concept (BC-CST-EQ)*. Here, you manage locks in main memory on an *enqueue server* that exists on the central instance of the SAP system or on a separate server. If a work process is not running on the instance of the enqueue server, a lock request is sent through the dispatcher and the message server. Nevertheless, managing these locks does not require as much effort as managing database locks, because you manage them in main memory.

ABAP lock concept

INSERT, UPDATE, MODIFY or SELECT ... FOR UPDATE set database locks for database modifications only. This type of database lock is held until

Deadlocks

the next database commit, but not necessarily until the end of the LUW. These locks can be the cause of *deadlocks* if other processes access the same data and each process is waiting for the other process to release the lock again.

SAP locks and database locks

However, there are other differences between SAP locks and database locks. You can also create SAP locks for records that do not yet exist in the database. You must use SAP locks when you work with updates, because the database modifications are only implemented in the update and no database locks can exist beforehand.

Creating lock objects in the ABAP Workbench

You create lock objects in Transaction SE80, as shown in Figure 3.8. For example, create a somewhat more complex lock object for which you can lock several tables of an application object, that is, the equipment parts for a vehicle (ZEQUIPMENT table) and the owner (ZOWNER table). As a result, additional lock parameters are created for the components of the primary key of all tables involved.

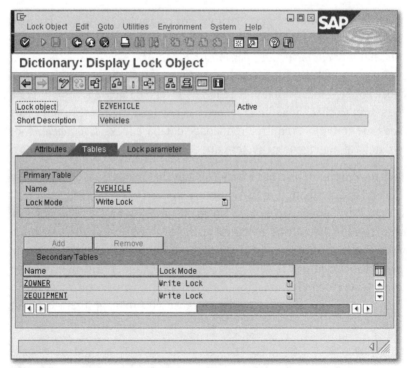

Figure 3.8 Creating a Lock Object

Secondary Tables with Lock Objects   **[!]**

If you create the primary keys of the dependent tables in such a way that they contain the primary key fields of the original table, and if you also define foreign key relationships, you can include the dependent tables as secondary tables in the lock object and also lock these tables. If this is not the case, you may have to define additional lock objects for dependent tables.

You generate an enqueue module for a lock object. This enqueue module has several standard parameters. The `mode` parameter specifies the lock mode. Some lock parameters you use to specify the area to be locked include the `_scope` parameter, which describes the interaction of locks and updates. You can use the `wait` parameter to configure the number of repeat attempts and the `_collect` parameter to buffer the lock requirements locally in a lock container before the `FLUSH_ENQUEUE` function module collects and transfers them into the lock table.

Enqueue modules

The following lock modes exist:

▶ The *exclusive lock* ("E" lock mode) can be requested several times per session by the lock owner but there must be no shared or exclusive locks from other lock owners. Exclusive locks cumulate and must be released again several times.

Exclusive lock and exclusive but not cumulative lock

▶ The *exclusive but not cumulative lock* ("X" lock mode) can be requested only once in the internal session, provided there are no exclusive or shared locks from the same lock owner or other lock owners.

▶ You can have several *shared locks* ("S" lock mode) in parallel but there must be no additional exclusive locks. You can use shared locks to protect displayed data records from being modified.

Shared locks

▶ *Optimistic locks* are shared locks you can convert to exclusive locks by calling a lock with the "R" lock mode. In that case, other existing locks will be invalidated.

> **Optimistic Lock Concept**
>
> Because the optimistic lock concept is relatively new, we will explain it in more detail at this point. SAP's optimistic lock concept sets shared locks, and therefore protects against modifications (provided other optimistic locks were not converted into exclusive locks). The SAP optimistic lock concept is suitable if different processes set shared locks, of which only a small number actually want to modify data later. This is the exact analogy for the lock concept from classic database development. There, you forego database locks and use time stamps to query whether a modification occurred in the meantime.

You call the lock module as shown in Listing 3.1.

```
DATA:
  ls_msg      TYPE          scx_t100key,

CALL FUNCTION 'ENQUEUE_EZVEHICLE'
  EXPORTING
    mode_zvehicle    = iv_enqmode
    mode_zequipment  = iv_enqmode
    mode_zowner      = iv_enqmode
    id               = lv_id
    _scope           = iv_scope
    _wait            = iv_wait
  EXCEPTIONS
    OTHERS           = 3.
IF sy-subrc <> 0.
  ls_msg-msgid = sy-msgid.
  ls_msg-msgno = sy-msgno.
  ls_msg-attr1 = sy-msgv1.
  ls_msg-attr2 = sy-msgv2.
  ls_msg-attr3 = sy-msgv3.
  ls_msg-attr4 = sy-msgv4.
  RAISE EXCEPTION TYPE zcx_locking_error
    EXPORTING        textid = ls_msg.
ENDIF.
```

Listing 3.1 Calling a Lock Module

The central component of this listing is the call for the generated ENQUEUE_ EZVEHICLE lock module, to which you transfer four parameters: the lock mode in the IV_ENQMODE parameter with the "E" default value, the IV_

SCOPE parameter with the "2" default value and the IV_WAIT parameter with the SPACE default value because generally, you will want to repeat unsuccessful lock attempts.

You can also use this lock object to delete the dependent tables, because no values are transferred for the NR and TIME parameters, which, together with the ID, create the primary key of the tables involved.

The "2" value of the SCOPE parameter is the default value for updates and causes the lock to be forwarded to the update process.

If locks are not transferred to the update and deleted there, you must remove them. You do this similarly to the way you set locks using generated function modules. The following sample source code shows the sequence of the call:

Removing locks

```
CALL FUNCTION 'DEQUEUE_EZVEHICLE'
    EXPORTING
        mode_zvehicle    = iv_mode
        mode_zequipment  = iv_mode
        mode_zowner      = iv_mode
        id               = lv_id
        _scope           = iv_scope
        _synchron        = iv_synchron.
```

The iv_synchron parameter used here means that the lock module might wait until the entry is actually deleted from the lock table. However, this is only useful in a few cases; therefore, you use a method to make this parameter optional when the removal of a lock is being encapsulated, and set SPACE as the default parameter.

Indexes and Buffering

Two techniques for accelerating read database access include buffering and using database indexes. Buffering and using indexes are two mutually exclusive concepts. In one case, you want to keep table contents in main memory; in the other, your objective is to be able to access the database efficiently. Buffering is a difficult topic for which you should refer to SAP-specific literature such as *SAP Performance Optimization Guide* by Thomas Schneider (SAP PRESS, 2008). However, we have compiled

Accelerating read database access

the most important features you need to be aware of with regard to buffering:

- ABAP SQL commands exist that read past the table buffer.
- Buffered items are held at the level of the application server and must be synchronized with one another. This means it can take some time until a database modification appears on another application server.

Suitability Based on experience, buffering is most suitable for small transparent tables that have only a few entries and are not modified very often, for example, Customizing tables or some types of master data.

You can define database indexes in the ABAP Dictionary. Because you need resources to manage these indexes, you should only create them for the relevant access paths. These are often known at design time; otherwise you should determine them using runtime analysis (Transaction SE30). For more information, see ABAP • ANALYSIS TOOLS • RUNTIME ANALYSIS in the SAP Library.

[!] | **Disadvantages of Indexes**

The time an index saves when reading is lost when writing. Inserting many individual data records is particularly intensive when you have to maintain the indexes each time. When you load data into SAP NetWeaver BI, you therefore delete the indexes before writing and create them again when all data is loaded into the system. Even if you use these strategies in application programming only in the rarest of cases, you should always consider this factor and define database indexes as economically as possible. You should also use bundling techniques, which we discuss in Section 3.3.1, Necessity of Database Access Layers.

Determining runtime gains These tools and Transaction ST30 (global performance analysis) are used to determine runtime gains on live systems. For example, you can store tables, which are often accessed in parallel, on different disks. However, you can generally only perform these types of optimization for a specific live system.

NULL Values

Transparent tables can contain NULL values. They can be tricky for the uninitiated because at first glance (for example, in Transaction SE16), they are difficult to differentiate from initial values. If you load a data record with NULL values into a working area using SELECT, initial values will also appear in the corresponding fields. You can only access NULL values in the WHERE condition using SELECT if you use IS NULL; the IS INITIAL check or the check for inconsistencies with another value will not work.

Before you learn how to create NULL values, we will explain the seman- **Semantics** tics of these values. A NULL value can represent an unknown value. For example, an object can have a certain characteristic but you do not know it at the moment. NULL values can map non-existing values. A typical situation is where you cannot use an attribute in a specific case.

However, a NULL value can also mean that you do not know whether a value exists. Every employee experiences the standard example of this situation when their company telephone system is being changed and their old number is no longer valid. There is a transition period where the employee may not know whether there is a new number or, if there is a new number, he may not yet know it.

How do you create NULL values? In the ABAP Dictionary, you can specify whether you want every column of a transparent table to be filled with initial values or NULL values. In the second case, NULL values are added when you create a new column or insert entries using a view that does not contain these fields.

There are limited benefits to NULL values for an ABAP programmer **Benefits** because they have no equivalent in ABAP. NULL values are implicitly converted into INITIAL values when loaded into working areas or internal tables so you cannot tell whether there was a NULL value. This is why these values are often used only temporarily after structural modifications in the ABAP Dictionary, when a new column has to be converted by a migration report that must decide between entries that have not yet been processed and entries processed by the initial content.

Archiving

Not many applications delete business data; for auditing and legal reasons, deleting data is not supported. Instead, deletion indicators are set for the business objects to be deleted and these objects will be excluded from future searches and processing. This increases the volume of data in the database, response times for database queries rise, backups take longer, and sometimes you have to get new hardware for the database server. The best way to prevent this is to avoid data and to delete temporary data. If you have exhausted these options, you will have to archive data. For more information, refer to the example given in the SAP Library under *CA-ARC Archiving*.

Archive
Development Kit

SAP provides an API for archiving functions with the *Archive Development Kit* (ADK). You can define archiving objects for an application object. You create write, read, and delete programs for these archiving objects, which write the data to be archived into an archive file, evaluate this data in a second process, and then delete it from the database. *Archive indexes are created in the process.* These are transparent tables that contain the object key of the objects to be archived, a reference to the archive file, and the item in the file, from which the object can be read. For the sake of completeness, we must mention that XML archiving is also possible. In this case, you create an XML document for each document to be archived and save it in a file. The scale of the data to be archived increases because of the XML markup. You can use methods of the standard SAP system to search in the archive index and look for corresponding data in a view similar to the Data Browser, that is, perform a direct access. It is unusual to restore data to the live system after it has been archived.

How to handle archiving in detail is beyond the scope of this book; therefore, we will only refer to the factors that can affect the data modeling of the application:

- **Archiving criteria**
  Are there simple criteria you can use to decide when you want an application object to be archived? You must ensure that there are no references of active application objects to archived objects. This could cause the program to behave incorrectly.

- **Archive search**
  What criteria should you use to be able to search for database entities in the archive? Should the most important attributes be displayed in the archive index to ensure that direct access to the object you are looking for is not necessary? Assuming that direct access is required, are the methods of the Archive Information System (Transaction SARI)

in the standard SAP system sufficient, or do the separate dialogs have to be archive-enabled?

▶ **Modifications to the data model**
Should you expect modifications to the data model? Can you make these modifications in such a way that you do not have to modify the archiving programs? Will you need to modify archived data?

3.3 Implementing Object Persistence

In the previous sections, you have seen how you can model application objects at the database level. Some developers question why additional development work is required. Is it not enough to access the database using Open SQL and manipulate individual table entries? Do additional wrappers not mean increased development effort, reduce performance and make programs more complicated? These arguments may apply in individual cases but generally turn out to be hazardous design errors. Specifically, the problem is that, in most cases, you can no longer reverse the conversion of Open SQL calls scattered in the application. This argument applies in particular when other applications access the database tables without access layers.

Design errors

In the following sections, we will first explain the need to encapsulate access to the application object. You will then implement an access layer for the modeled application object using Object Services. Finally, we will discuss when it makes sense to implement your own persistence mechanisms.

You need the following services to be able to use persistence mechanisms easily and efficiently:

Management service and search service

▶ **Management service**
You must ensure that several, possibly contradictory, runtime objects do not exist in the same internal session. This type of *management service* should also contain a cache to enable you to access the managed objects more quickly.

▶ **Search service**
A management service should also have a *Search service* that enables you to search for objects based on specialized criteria and load them

into main memory. A search should also be able to return only a constant number of objects to enable you to work in packages if you have large sets of objects.

3.3.1 Necessity of Database Access Layers

Database access layers are an old and established concept. They were previously implemented by BAPI interfaces, which you still require if you want data to be read by Remote Function Call (RFC) or Web services, or to be manipulated. However, there are also much simpler reasons for implementing database access layers:

▶ **Transaction mechanisms**
One important reason is the transaction mechanism itself. If you only work with Open SQL access without using update techniques, this means that the data is irreversibly saved to the database each time an implicit commit is performed. Where dialog applications are concerned, you are therefore not in command of transaction control and cannot guarantee data consistency. This also applies in batch programs. In a batch program, you cannot execute any more RFCs for accessing data in external systems or for the internal parallelization of the processing, because these implicitly perform a database commit.[2] This also makes it more difficult to enhance the programs. An implicit commit must not be performed in any enhancement by a BAdI implementation. To avoid these unwanted consequences, you would have to buffer the database modifications and persist them at the end of the LUW, which already very closely reflects a database access layer.

▶ **Subsequent processes**
Another problem with explicit database access is caused by the fact that you cannot implement any new subsequent processes for data modifications for the application system. If we assume that, for reasons of revision security, you want to write change documents for certain fields, replicate these changes by Application Link Enabling (ALE), or provide the delta queue when connecting to SAP NetWeaver

---

2 The same problem can occur when you debug, because database commits are also performed there. If you save data to the database without updates, the debugging of the application is risky because inconsistencies may occur.

BI, you must add these functions to all of the points in programs that conduct database updates. You must not include subsequent processes in the area of data replication. Loose event linkages (for example, for starting workflows) are also possible. These are presented in Section 5.5.3, Event-Based Interfaces, under the keyword Publish & Subscribe interfaces. In practice, you will no longer be able to perform a subsequent implementation into a live application, unless you perform a complete redesign.

► **Robustness**
Implementing a database access layer can also make an application more robust. For professional reasons, you are often not allowed to write any values into a table, but rather the programs must require minimum data plausibility in order to work. A typical example is a situation where certain fields are not allowed to contain any initial values; filling these fields with the wrong values equates to an error situation. You cannot assume that everyone who fills the database tables is fully aware of these conditions. Therefore, it is absolutely essential that you explicitly encode these conditions in one location and check them before the INSERT.

► **Modularization**
Hiding details about the data model is another important reason for creating an access layer. Developers often want to have the freedom to modify and optimize a data model in the future if performance problems were discovered in mass tests. If this means that you have to adjust SQL calls at every location where a database is accessed, you will find it very difficult to modify the data model because the application system is not sufficiently modularized.

► **Checking authorizations**
You may require specific authorizations to read sensitive data. For example, if a VIP indicator is set for customer-related master data, only users with special authorizations can have full access to this data. In such a case, data access modules must perform certain authorization checks and may not necessarily offer all data. You cannot currently avoid bypassing the programming of data access modules. However, by defining package interfaces, you can find out through the Code Inspector whether interfaces were bypassed in the program-

ming (see Chapter 5, Application Architecture). In Release 7.0 you can use dynamic SELECT statements or generated programs to avoid defined database access functions in package interfaces and access tables directly. You can use the Code Inspector to check the use of these potentially "dangerous" commands.

Alternatively, you have situations where you do not want to use a database access layer:

▶ You want to create a report for a user department that will determine entries according to specified criteria in one or more tables and output them in an ALV grid.

Migration ▶ As part of a migration you want to load a dataset into the SAP system in as short a time as possible.

▶ In some tables, you have to modify certain data records and fill additional attributes. You can do this using an XPRA program when making an ABAP Dictionary modification to a table structure.

▶ Within data archiving, you have to write large quantities of data into an archive file within a short time frame, and then delete this data in the database and create search indexes.

Even if the examples indicate that you often work directly with Open SQL tools in the database in mass process, you should not make this procedure the norm. There is also no reason to impose severe restrictions at the development phase of an application system already, simply because implementing a database access layer requires conceptual and implementation effort.

Are there reasons against Object Services? You can drastically reduce the implementation effort by using Object Services. Strangely, object-oriented access layers have a bad reputation that is entirely unfounded. This poor reputation is based on the fear that an object could be too finely detailed, resulting in lots of individual database operations in mass processes, drastically affecting performance. However, there are solutions to this problem in the form of bundling techniques.

Bundling techniques The standard SAP system's Object Services use bundling techniques using generic update tasks. The data to be modified is collected and transferred as a binary-formatted table to an update module that accesses the database dynamically. This procedure shows that you can perform mass modifications through a framework and completely hide it from the user.

If you use your own persistence mechanisms, you can save the modifications to be updated in an ABAP class or in the global memory of a function group and then execute the `PERFORM … ON COMMIT` command to implement them as mass inserts into a form routine of a function group. In this case, we specifically recommend that you use the non object-oriented `PERFORM … ON COMMIT` construction and not the modern variant by creating an `on_commit` method as the event handler for the `TRANSACTION_FINISHED` event of the `CL_SYSTEM_TRANSACTION_STATE` class using the `SET HANDLER on_commit` command. The reason for this is the following: Experience has shown that you cannot guarantee with certainty that updates started in the event handler are also executed in the same SAP transaction.

One problem with object-oriented access layers can be that the instancing of an object requires an overhead, which in some cases cannot be justified. This is the case, for example, if the user is searching for objects based on certain criteria and a number of attributes are displayed for this in an ALV grid. After the user selects an individual object, this is specifically loaded and shown in a display dialog. Another application scenario where instancing is not required is packaging as part of parallel processing. You want to determine packages of objects but do not need any time-consuming instancing to do this. A *search service*, that is, a class that can provide primary keys of object instances without instancing objects, can be useful in both of these application scenarios.

Complex search criteria

A search service can only consist of a static method of an application object that queries the database using direct `SELECT` statements. However, there are also application systems where you have to implement very complex search criteria that are required for controlling automatic processes. In the most complex case, these types of search services include objects that were instanced but whose status differs from the status in the database. You can even implement these techniques across sessions using *shared objects*, although the effort required to implement this type of object is usually too great. For more information about shared objects, refer to *ABAP – Shared Objects* in the SAP Library.

Object Search Services

Based on experience, search services are the basis of numerous application scenarios in business programming and guarantee high-performance, object-oriented programs. Their implementation will therefore also be the topic in the following chapters.

3.3.2 Object Services

No uniform persistence mechanism

In individual software development, either a lot of effort is invested in creating persistence layers, or commercial products are used. These software products implement mappings of objects to tables, of a database-independent persistence, and of caches and supported transactions. In ABAP development, a uniform persistence mechanism was previously not widely accepted. This was mainly because database updates occur predominantly in update modules and BAPIs that are developed individually. It was only relatively late in the game that the option of persistent ABAP classes was made possible with Object Services and an object-oriented framework made available for transactions. These functions are described in *ABAP Objects* by Horst Keller and Sascha Krüger, but also in the SAP Library under ABAP Object Services. The aim of the persistence layer is to be able to work with objects without having to worry about persistence. You instance objects and access their attributes using SET and GET methods. You then collect the modifications and write them to the database in separate update modules after the COMMIT WORK. The result of this procedure is that you do not need separate update modules. You can also use Object Services with classic update techniques, but you must take into account that, after a COMMIT WORK, a persistent object is invalidated and has an initial status. This means that accessing the object in an update module will fail if this object was already accessed in the LUW.

What must you keep in mind when using Object Services?

▶ **Mapping**
The options for mapping the application object to transparent tables are somewhat restricted. For special techniques such as deriving or mapping different classes to a transparent table, refer to the SAP Library.

▶ **Query service**

A query service using the methods of the IF_OS_CA_PERSISTENCY interface is available, but it always instances the objects found and is therefore not always suitable for mass processes.

▶ **Service interfaces**

The user must program different service interfaces such as lock management or creating change documents.

▶ **Transaction concept**

The Object Services were incorporated into the classic transaction concept. There are different transaction modes, including an object-oriented transaction concept that makes a transaction manager available in the form of an API. This lets you implement transparently complex scenarios such as nested transactions, however, there is no coexistence with the classic LUW concept: The COMMIT WORK or ROLL-BACK WORK commands will cause a runtime error. We present the aspects of transaction control in detail in Section 3.4.

Many developers have reservations about Object Services, due primarily to a perception of poor performance. The basic technique was optimized in this case. For example, rather than vast numbers of update modules being executed, the data to be updated is instead bundled and written into a generic update task, to which binary serialized data is transferred. This ensures that mass updates are implemented in a small number of database operations.

Reservations

An example of using Object Services in the sample application is shown in the text that follows. You create a persistent class called ZCL_VEHICLE in the ABAP Workbench, as shown in Figure 3.9.

Creating persistent classes

You then define the persistence mapping using the Persistence button (or Ctrl + F4). A dialog box called Add Table/Structure appears, where you enter the name of the ZVEHICLE transparent table you created earlier. Finally, you select all table fields sequentially in the lower Persistence Representation area. Each field then appears automatically in the middle drop-down box, where you can set the visibility. Select protected visibility for all fields, but only private visibility for the modification information because you want to be able to access the attributes of a class easily through a working area. This, however, is only one service function that you will develop in the following section.

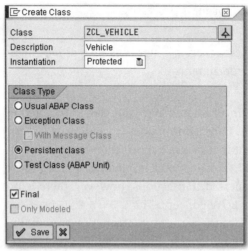

Figure 3.9 Creating a Persistent Class

Subsequently, two classes will be generated automatically: The ZCA_ VEHICLE class agent and its ZCB_VEHICLE basis class. The class agent is a singleton object and therefore only exists once in an internal session. The actual database access takes place in the basis class agent; as does the object-relational mapping using the MAP_LOAD_FROM_DATABASE_KEY( ), MAP_LOAD_FROM_DATABASE_GUID( ) or MAP_SAVE_TO_DATABASE( ) methods. The basis class agent is derived from the CL_OS_CA_COMMON class; therefore, you can redefine methods and also access the logic of a persistent class to define your own object-relational mapping, for example. The most important interfaces for the user are IF_OS_FACTORY, IF_OS_CA_ PERSISTENCY and IF_OS_CA_INSTANCE.

Implementing requirements

First, you will implement several requirements in the persistent class that will make it easier to work with the persistent class:

1. All equipment parts for a vehicle are to be automatically loaded from the database into an internal table when you instance objects. This means that you will be able to display these parts easily and save them using mass inserts when you save the vehicle data.

2. The change information (changed by, date, and time) should be determined automatically at the time of the COMMIT WORK.

The second item is easy to implement. You implement the IF_OF_CHECK interface in the ZCL_VEHICLE class and create an implementation of the IS_CONSISTENT( ) method. You execute this *checking agent* after COMMIT WORK and before you execute the update task. You normally use this to implement consistency checks for an object and, in the case of an emergency, prevent data from being saved. You use it to set the change information:

Using the checking agent

```
METHOD if_os_check~is_consistent.
  TRY.
      set_chdate( i_chdate = sy-datum ).
      set_chtime( i_chtime = sy-uzeit ).
      set_chuser( i_chuser = sy-uname ).
    CATCH cx_os_object_not_found .
*     The object has been deleted.
  ENDTRY.
  result = oscon_true.
ENDMETHOD.
```

To ensure the IS_CONSISTENT( ) method is executed, you must register it. You do this by redefining the INIT( ) method of the IF_OS_STATE interface (see Listing 3.2).

```
METHOD IF_OS_STATE~INIT.
**********************************************************
* Purpose       : Initialization of the transient state
*                 partition.
* Version       : 2.0
* Precondition  : -
* Postcondition : Transient state is initial.
* OO Exceptions : -
* Implementation : Caution!: Avoid Throwing ACCESS Events.
**********************************************************
* Changelog: 2000-03-07   : (BGR) Initial Version 2.0
**********************************************************
* Modify if you like
**********************************************************
DATA:
  lr_tm type REF TO if_os_transaction_manager,
  lr_t  type REF TO if_os_transaction.
```

```
    lr_tm = cl_os_system=>get_transaction_manager( ) .
    lr_t = lr_tm->get_current_transaction( ).
    lr_t->register_check_agent( me ).
ENDMETHOD.
```

Listing 3.2   Registering the Checking Agent

Transient attributes You can also use the initialization routine to load the equipment parts of a vehicle into a *transient attribute* that is not managed by the persistence service. Transient attributes are calculated at runtime and can be used to save data of dependent objects (see Section 3.3.4, Accessing Dependent Tables).

The source code from Listing 3.3 shows an example of how you create, modify, and delete a vehicle object in a transaction.

```
DATA:
  lr_vehicle_agent TYPE REF TO zca_vehicle,
  lr_vehicle       TYPE REF TO zcl_vehicle,
  lv_vehicle_id    TYPE        z_vehicle_id.

lr_vehicle_agent = zca_vehicle =>agent.
CALL FUNCTION 'GUID_CREATE'
  IMPORTING
    ev_guid_22 = lv_vehicle_id.
TRY.
    lr_vehicle = lv_vehicle_agent->create_persistent(
        i_id = lv_vehicle_id ).
    TRY.
       lr_vehicle->set_seats( i_seats = '2' ).
      CATCH cx_os_object_not_found.
*      Perform exception handling.
    ENDTRY.
 lr_vehicle_agent->delete_persistent( lv_vehicle_id ).
 CATCH CX_OS_OBJECT_NOT_EXISTING .
*  Perform exception handling.
ENDTRY.
COMMIT WORK.
```

Listing 3.3   Using Object Services

At the end of the transaction, the modifications are collected and written to the database by an Object Services update task. You can work with the object in this way, without having to worry about persistence factors. (Using Object Services in the update would also generally cause an exception.) In the example, you used Object Services in the classic transaction mode instead of using the object-oriented transaction service of the IF_OS_TRANSACTION interface. You can execute the Object Services within classic LUWs. In contrast, the END( ) method of the Object Services that completes an LUW implicitly calls a COMMIT WORK so that classic updates can also be performed in an object-oriented transaction. These aspects are discussed in Section 3.4.

> ### Deleting Persistent Objects
>
> When you delete persistent objects, note that deleting an object that does not exist or no longer exists does not trigger an exception, but instead only causes an update module to terminate.

[!]

3.3.3 Inheriting Persistent Classes

You use inheritance when there is a specialization relationship between a class and a number of subclasses. However, you should only use inheritance sparingly at the application object level, because there is a risk that you may link two business entities too closely together. If, in hindsight, your decision turns out to be incorrect, the cost of changing the program and database model of the database will in most cases be far greater than the benefits gained through reuse.

Use it sparingly

Nevertheless, inheritance is a powerful tool:

▸ **Polymorphy**
You can derive persistent classes and keep the mapping to achieve polymorphic behavior, for example, redefining methods: In the application sample presented here, you can avoid there being instances of coaches with standing room, define special checks, or implement display transactions.

▸ **Enhancing using additional attributes**
If you have to include additional attributes in a derived class that do not have meaningful semantics in the basis class, you can create them in an additional transparent table. This prevents transparent tables

from being enhanced in an uncontrolled manner in the development process.

Inheritance types Object Services support inheritance in the following way:

1. You can map *vertically*, meaning you can save data in the derived classes in additional, separate transparent tables that nevertheless must have the same primary key as the original table.

2. You can save the entire hierarchy in a table and define the type for an entry using a *type identifier* (OS_GUID data element).

3. You can map *horizontally*, which means that you redefine the mapping of the respective attributes and the basis class for each derived class and use another transparent table for this purpose.

Example of an inheritance for persistent classes You want to derive the ZCL_VEHICLE persistent class in such a way that all derived classes use the same ZVEHICLE table — this is an example of the second scenario in the list. To do this, you create an OS_GUID field in the table. Figure 3.10 shows the corresponding persistence mapping, with the type identifier selected.

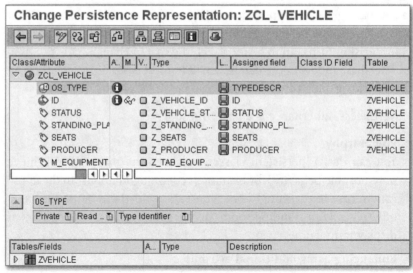

Figure 3.10 Persistence Mapping with Type Identifier

You can derive the ZCL_VEHICLE persistent class as shown in Figure 3.11. You only have to ensure that it is not final.

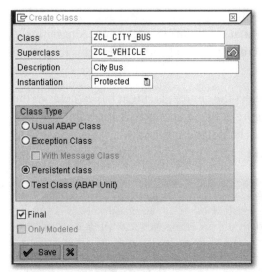

Figure 3.11 Deriving a Persistent Class

Both classes share the same tables, and the TYPEDESCR type identifier is automatically set by the Object Services and contains a GUID that displays the object type. Is it a ZCL_VEHICLE object or a derived class like ZCL_CITY_BUS, for example?

The class agent of the basis class works polymorphically. When you set an object using the query service (the details of which are described in Section 3.3.5, Query Service) and the I_SUBCLASSES parameter of the IF_OS_CA_PERSISTENCY~GET_PERSISTENT_BY_QUERY( ) method, the type descriptor is evaluated and a subclass object may therefore be returned. Other methods, such as GET_PERSISTENT( ) but also special methods of the IF_OS_CA_PERSISTENCY and IF_OS_FACTORY interfaces, behave directly polymorphically. The exact behavior is described in the SAP Library under ABAP – OBJECT SERVICES • INHERITANCE OF PERSISTENT CLASSES.

Polymorphy of the class agent for the basis class of an inheritance hierarchy

Thanks to polymorphy, you can work generically in your applications and in workflows. That is, you define a workflow with the basis class of a hierarchy of persistent classes but receive automatically derived objects through the Object Services, and the called methods behave polymorphically. In classic ABAP programming, you would explicitly define a type in the table in question and laboriously reproduce the polymorphy using comprehensive CASE commands. You can create this type of attribute with object-oriented methods; however, you would implement it as a non-modifiable attribute that is set during instancing. Alternatively, you could also return a constant in a method and redefine this in derived classes.

In derived classes, you can select the context menu in tables/fields in the persistence mapping (see Figure 3.11) to add exactly one table for each derivation that will also be included and must have a 1:1 cardinality to the table of the derived object.

Caution when Creating New Persistent Classes with Derivations

You cannot rename or copy persistent classes. If a persistent class is live in an application and has these derivations or is derived itself, under no circumstances should you delete and create them again. The reason for this is that a new GUID is selected for the type identifier. If you delete the ZCL_CITY_BUS class and create it again, the query service will no longer find the previously created object instances in the database.

3.3.4 Accessing Dependent Tables

In addition to its attributes (the vehicle data), the application object also has other data, such as assemblies, in dependent tables. In that case, methods that provide all dependent objects are made available.

Networks of persistent objects

If you also implement the associated objects with Object Services, simply extend the application object with a method that determines and returns the associated objects with the query service. The application then works with these objects as it does with normal persistent objects. In this case, you receive an object network where a transparent table generally corresponds to a class.

With runtime-critical applications, it makes sense to instance dependent objects only when they are explicitly requested by a method, not when the application object is already being loaded.

Separate persistence mechanisms for transient data of persistent classes

At this point, we will choose another strategy to show you that you can also load dependent data using the classic approach. For example, this is required for tables that do not have any persistent objects, and may only have BAPI interfaces. The techniques developed in this section are also used in Section 3.5.3, Service Functions for Persistent Objects, for creating change documents.

For this purpose, you load data into transient attributes at the time of initialization (which you have already learned about in Section 3.3.2, Object Services). The required source code for this is shown in Listing 3.4.

```
METHOD IF_OS_STATE~INIT.
***************************************************************
* Purpose        : Initialization of the transient state
*                  partition.
* Version        : 2.0
* Precondition   : -
* Postcondition  : Transient state is initial.
* OO Exceptions  : -
* Implementation : Caution!: Avoid Throwing ACCESS Events.
***************************************************************
* Changelog: 2000-03-07    : (BGR) Initial Version 2.0
***************************************************************
* Modify if you like
***************************************************************
DATA:
  lr_tm type REF TO if_os_transaction_manager,
  lr_t  type REF TO if_os_transaction.

  lr_tm = cl_os_system=>get_transaction_manager( ) .
  lr_t = lr_tm->get_current_transaction( ).
  lr_t->register_check_agent( me ).

  SELECT * FROM zassembly INTO CORRESPONDING FIELDS OF TABLE
    m_assembly WHERE VEHICLE = id.
ENDMETHOD.
```

Listing 3.4 Loading Dependent Data into Transient Attributes

It is also useful to delete transient data when you invalidate an object; you do this using the IF_OS_STATE~INVALIDATE( ) method (see Listing 3.5).

Deleting transient data

```
METHOD IF_OS_STATE~INVALIDATE.
***************************************************************
* Purpose        : Do something before all persistent
```

```
*                    attributes are cleared.
* Version         : 2.0
* Precondition    : -
* Postcondition   : -
* OO Exceptions   : -
* Implementation : Whatever you like to do.
**************************************************************
* Changelog: 2000-03-07   : (BGR) Initial Version 2.0
**************************************************************
* Modify if you like
**************************************************************
  CLEAR m_assembly.
ENDMETHOD.
```

Listing 3.5 Deleting Transient Data

You can persist transient data in the IF_OS_CHECK~IS_CONSISTENT( ) method by calling an update module that deletes the old equipment parts from the ZASSEMBLY table and adds new entries (if available), as shown in Listing 3.6.

```
METHOD if_os_check~is_consistent.
  TRY.
      set_chdate( i_chdate = sy-datum ).
      set_chtime( i_chtime = sy-uzeit ).
      set_chuser( i_chuser = sy-uname ).
*     Update equipment parts
      CALL FUNCTION 'Z_UPDATE_ASSEMBLY' IN UPDATE TASK
        EXPORTING
          iv_id       = id
          it_assembly = m_assembly.
    CATCH cx_os_object_not_found.
*     Vehicle has been deleted.
  ENDTRY.
  result = oscon_true.
ENDMETHOD.
```

Listing 3.6 Using the Checking Agent for Updating Tables

You need to set result = oscon_true here. Otherwise, a serious inconsistency will be reported as an exception.

To ensure that this procedure works, you must redefine the DELETE_ PERSISTENT( ) method in the class agent (ZCL_VEHICLE object) and delete the dependent tables, as in Listing 3.7. This procedure is required because the IF_OS_CHECK~IS_CONSISTENT( ) checking agent is not also automatically called when you call DELETE_PERSISTENT( ).

```
METHOD DELETE_PERSISTENT.
  DATA lt_assembly type z_tab_assembly.
  CALL FUNCTION 'Z_UPDATE_ASSEMBLY' IN UPDATE TASK
    EXPORTING
      iv_id          = i_id
      it_assembly    = lt_assembly.
  SUPER->DELETE_PERSISTENT( I_ID ).
ENDMETHOD.
```

Listing 3.7 Deleting Tables Not Managed by Persistence Service

For the sake of completeness, the source code of the update module used is as shown in Listing 3.8.

```
FUNCTION z_update_assembly.
*"----------------------------------------------------------
*"*"Update function module:
*"
*"*"Local interface:
*"  IMPORTING
*"     VALUE(IV_ID) TYPE  Z_VEHICLE_ID
*"     VALUE(IT_ASSEMBLY) TYPE  Z_TAB_ASSEMBLY
*"----------------------------------------------------------
  DATA:
    lt_assembly TYPE TABLE OF zassembly,
    ls_assembly TYPE          zassembly.

  FIELD-SYMBOLS:
    <assembly>  LIKE LINE OF it_assembly.
  DELETE FROM zassembly WHERE vehicle = iv_id.

  IF LINES( it_assembly ) > 0.
    LOOP AT it_assembly ASSIGNING <assembly>.
      MOVE-CORRESPONDING <assembly> TO ls_assembly.
      ls_assembly-vehicle = iv_id.
      APPEND ls_assembly TO lt_assembly.
    ENDLOOP.
```

```
      INSERT zassembly FROM TABLE lt_assembly.
   ENDIF.
ENDFUNCTION.
```

Listing 3.8 Update Module

3.3.5 Query Service

To load persistent objects, the persistence framework has a query service you can call using the IF_OS_CA_PERSISTENCY~GET_PERSISTENT_BY_QUERY( ) method of the class agent. Detailed documentation about this is available in the SAP Library under ABAP - Object Services • Query Service.

Query service
The query service enables you to easily search for objects using complex search and filter criteria, as illustrated by the example of a search for vehicles with an iv_license_nr vehicle indicator shown in Listing 3.9.

```
DATA: lr_query_manager TYPE REF TO if_os_query_manager,
      lr_query         TYPE REF TO if_os_query,
      lt_objects       TYPE        osreftab

lr_query_manager = cl_os_system=>get_query_manager( ).
lr_query = lr_query_manager->create_query(
        i_filter  = `LICENSE_NR = PAR1` ).

  lt_objects =
lr_agent->if_os_ca_persistency~get_persistent_by_query(
          i_query   = query
          i_par1    = iv_license_nr ).
```

Listing 3.9 Using the Query Service

As the result, the query service returns a number of object references you must cast for the persistent object.

[!]
Public Attributes

The query service can only search for public attributes of a persistent class. Keep this in mind when defining the attributes of a persistent class or when changing attribute properties.

The query service is a powerful tool. However, it is not suitable for mass processes. In many cases, rather than wanting to create an object, you only want to determine numbers of IDs and process these in parallel (see Chapter 8, SAP Business Partner). In that case, the query service is not lightweight enough and should be enhanced by a separate search service, examples of which are developed in Chapter 5, Application Architecture, and Chapter 6, Application Layer.

Unsuitable for mass processes

3.3.6   Developing a Separate Persistence Service

The following can be reasons for developing a separate persistence layer:

Reasons for a separate persistence layer

▶ **Ability to Process Mass Data**
The focus of the application is on performance and the ability to support mass data. In this case, you may need to develop a separate persistence layer that is not as powerful as the Object Services but is more lightweight. This type of service will only involve loading, saving, and buffering object instances.

▶ **Denormalization and modification-free extensions**
Complex requirements for a persistent application object represent a great challenge when you implement them using Object Services. An example of this is a modification-free extension, as known from applications like the Business Data Toolset that are controlled entirely through Customizing (see the section of the same name in the SAP Library). Another challenge is complex denormalization strategies, as discussed in Section 3.2.2, Data Modeling at the ABAP Dictionary Level. You must implement these using Object Services and you might need to redefine the methods of the class agent to define a separate object-relational mapping. You also need to have detailed knowledge of Object Services.

In most cases, you do not need to create a separate persistence service, which would involve a lot of development and testing. This applies in particular for generic solutions that are supposed to be more powerful than Object Services and provide additional methods of object-relational mapping.

Lightweight wrappers Lightweight wrappers of an application object are easier to implement with a separate database access layer. When you choose this type of development, the first design decision should be to what extent you want the persistence service to work transactionally. For example, do you want a ROLLBACK WORK to cause the corresponding object to be invalidated, or to get the status it had prior to being modified? Other decisions should include which memory techniques (with and without updates) and means of updating (for example, SET UPDATE TASK LOCAL) you can use.

Ultimately, however, lightweight wrappers are also a poor compromise, because they often do not provide the scope of functionality for Object Services. We therefore recommend that you use Object Services in situations where you have to perform mass operations (for example, updates, deletions after archiving, or aggregations), and to work directly on the database in specific encapsulated service functions.

3.3.7 BAPI Access Methods

You can use BAPI interfaces to exchange data between SAP systems — as well as in other integration scenarios — because they can call object methods as RFCs. Every SAP system has an RFC API (for example, librfc32.dll) you can use for integration scenarios. Many software modules have other APIs, which means that you can access composite applications, SAP NetWeaver Portal applications, .NET integration and generally most programming languages easily on the SAP system using RFCs.

Conventions BAPIs are standardized RFC-enabled function modules. Some of the conventions are as follows:

▶ An attempt is made to map ISO-standardized data types in ABAP.

▶ If possible, you use data types of the standard SAP system to be able to define the BAPI definition in basic software components as well.

▶ Individual fields in structures should be a maximum of 250 bytes in size to be able to generate IDocs from BAPI interfaces.

▶ There must be no COMMIT WORK commands within BAPIs; instead, the initiator controls the transaction and can use the RFC-enabled BAPI_TRANSACTION_ROLLBACK function module to end a transaction explicitly. A two-phase commit protocol is not possible, however. This means that you cannot implement any distributed transactions that are mutually synchronized.

▶ Errors are returned in a `BAPIRET2`-type `RETURN` parameter. Error messages and other notes are returned in this way as `T100` messages, that is, through ABAP message classes.

BAPIs have other advantages. They are more efficient than web services, and it has become acceptable to use `TABLES` parameters for mass data, which avoid implicit XML conversion. However, this procedure will be obsolete as of Release 7.1, because there will be a binary XML format for parameters in RFC calls.

Advantages of BAPIs

You can continue to generate IDoc interfaces for BAPIs. This is described in the SAP Library under *BAPIs for Mass Data Transfer (CA-BFA)*.

3.4 Transaction Concept

Every application system has a transaction concept. For example, a user expects that, after he has performed an action such as clicking on the Save button, modifications will be saved or actions executed, and that these modifications cannot be undone using the Cancel button. From the perspective of the application, a number of application object instances are involved in this type of transaction. Modifications to the application objects involved are made in a Logical Unit of Work (LUW or SAP LUW).

A LUW is a fixed sequence of operations that is regarded as a logical unit. It begins and ends with a `COMMIT WORK` command and is divided into several database LUWs. This is because implicit database commits occur for PAI/PBO modifications and RFC calls, for example, and database modifications are persisted for these commits. Because you cannot undo these data modifications using a `ROLLBACK WORK` statement, in ABAP programming you use the update techniques you already learned about in Section 3.3.1, Necessity of Database Access Layers. In most cases, a LUW will therefore be processed as follows:

LUW concept

LUW process 1. The application objects required for mass processing are determined first by user interaction, search services, or packaging strategies.

2. You then lock application objects you want to modify.

3. Next, you modify the application objects by calling methods.

4. You end the LUW using a COMMIT WORK. Although sometimes persisted directly, database modifications are then typically persisted by update tasks and locks are deleted.

Explicit and Implicit Commits

You trigger an *explicit database commit* by calling the DB_COMMIT function module or by executing the COMMIT WORK statement. The ROLLBACK WORK statement causes an explicit *database rollback*. An *implicit database commit* is triggered when the control passes to another work process or the SAP GUI:

▶ A function module is called in another work process (CALL FUNCTION ... DESTINATION, IN BACKGROUND TASK DESTINATION, STARTING NEW TASK, and so on)

▶ The WAIT statement is executed

▶ The function module called ends in another work process

▶ A dialog step is completed (end of PROCESS AFTER INPUT processing block)

▶ Error dialogs (MESSAGE statement) appear within dialog steps

Implicit database rollbacks are triggered by runtime errors and termination messages (MESSAGE statement with an A or X message type, and, in some situations, with an I, E and W message type). It is important for the programmer of data modifications to know that an implicit database commit (for example, after a screen is processed or a message is issued) permanently commits data modifications made using the INSERT, UPDATE, MODIFY and DELETE Open SQL statements after the database LUW is completed and that these data modifications can no longer be rolled back.

Figure 3.12 shows a possible SAP LUW process flow. A work process executes a number of implicit commits, which results in several database LUWs. The COMMIT WORK statement ends the third database LUW. The updates are performed in a database LUW in an update process.

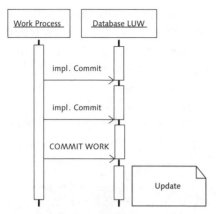

Figure 3.12 SAP LUW and Database LUW

When you design an application system, you must map the transaction concept of the application using LUWs. A minimum requirement is that you must perform this mapping in the application system without any errors, meaning that you must not create any inconsistencies, thereby guaranteeing transaction security and ensuring that the LUWs are automatic, independent of each other, and permanent. These properties are part of the *ACID properties* of a database transaction:

Transaction
security

▶ **Atomicity**
A LUW is either executed completely or not at all. However, you cannot strictly guarantee this because there is always the possibility that individual update tasks may terminate.

ACID properties

▶ **Consistency**
After a transaction ends, the integrity relationships are fulfilled at the database level. This condition is not generally important in SAP development, because transparent tables cannot have foreign keys at the database level — therefore referential integrity is always guaranteed.

▶ **Isolation**
Transactions do not influence each other. You can easily ensure this by using locks.

▶ **Durability**
The results of a transaction are saved permanently, even if the system crashes.

One extremely critical potential error in an application that is difficult to establish is when you can no longer retrace transaction control. For example, this occurs when any subroutine uses the COMMIT WORK command. As a result, the current LUW is split into two parts. This inevitably results in database inconsistencies if a ROLLBACK WORK statement is executed or if the program cancels, because one part of the database modification was performed and another was rejected. These disadvantages of the classic transaction concept are partially removed by the object-oriented transaction concept.

[+] | **Application Transaction Control**

We recommend that you conduct the transaction control of an application at a very high layer. Like BAPIs, the service functions called by this layer or deeper layers must not end or roll back any transactions. This is the only way to ensure that transactions are not split by inserted COMMIT WORK or ROLLBACK WORK commands.

Defining the size of a transaction (the number of business objects to be processed jointly) also only makes sense at a relatively high layer for mass processes. However, you can add a parameter to the service functions to specify whether you want database modifications to be performed directly or in the update. The first variant is useful if you want database modifications to be displayed for other service functions in the current internal session immediately after a service function is executed or if the initiator of the service function performs his modifications directly by Open SQL and does not execute explicit COMMIT WORK commands.

3.4.1 Special Techniques of the Classic Transaction Concept

The classic transaction concept is described in the SAP Library under UPDATES IN THE SAP SYSTEM (BC-CST-UP). Two types of update modules for updates exist: V1 module updates, which are executed first, and V2 modules, which are executed in a local transaction without any locks. The following recommendations have been proven:

Recommendations ▶ If possible, you should not execute any application logic in update modules. The reason for this is that you must, on all accounts, prevent update modules from terminating because otherwise the data will become inconsistent and postings will be lost.

▶ Use V2 update modules for less time-critical updates such as statistics updates, for example.

▶ However, you can also update locally using the SET UPDATE TASK LOCAL statement, in which case the update modules are executed in the same process as the calling program. This session is suitable for dialog applications where you save data for the screen's PAI event and want it to be read again for the PBO event.

Updating locally

▶ In some cases, you need to consolidate modification requirements, and therefore, update requirements, and not execute individual modifications in a process. If you call the update modules in a program shortly before the end of a LUW, in many cases you can work more flexibly.

▶ You can use the PERFORM … ON COMMIT command to write entries to be generated, modified, and deleted in the database by mass insert at the end of a LUW, after you have written the individual records into the module memory of a function group (rather than in an update task using a function module). Form routines registered in this way run exactly once per LUW, no matter how often they were registered.

▶ You can also enable updates to take place in a separate internal session. In this case, you create a separate internal session by calling a function module using CALL FUNCTION 'EXAMPLE_FUNCTION_MODULE' DESTINATION 'NONE'. This is how you create a separate LUW. You execute a COMMIT WORK by calling CALL FUNCTION 'BAPI_TRANSACTION_COMMIT' DESTINATION 'NONE', and a ROLLBACK WORK by calling CALL FUNCTION 'BAPI_TRANSACTION_ROLLBACK' DESTINATION 'NONE', each of which only affects the new internal session. This enables you to separate modifications from the current LUW and perform database modifications that do not have any influence on the current LUW.

Separate internal session

3.4.2 Object-Oriented Transaction Concept

There are two major disadvantages to the classic transaction concept:

- The classic transaction concept is not robust, because a ROLLBACK WORK can essentially cause a transaction to end unintentionally, anywhere in the program.

- Nested transactions can only be implemented with difficulty. You do this either using SUBMIT AND RETURN calls, or using an RFC call with DESTINATION 'NONE', as described in Section 3.4.1, Special Techniques of the Classic Transaction Concept, and used in Section 9.2, Parallel Processing of Applications (to implement parallel processing).

For this reason, SAP also provides an object-oriented transaction service together with the Object Services. Listing 3.10 shows an example where the CL_OS_SYSTEM class and the IF_OS_TRANSACTION interface are used.

```
LOAD-OF-PROGRAM.
* We use OO transactions
  cl_os_system=>init_and_set_modes(
    i_external_commit = oscon_false ).


START-OF-SELECTION.
  DATA:
    lv_tm TYPE REF TO if_os_transaction_manager,
    lv_t  TYPE REF TO if_os_transaction.

  TRY.
      lv_tm = cl_os_system=>get_transaction_manager( ).
      lv_t  = l_var_tm->create_transaction( ).
      lv_t->start( ).
*     Manipulate application objects
      lv_t->end( ).
    CATCH CX_OS_TRANSACTION.
  ENDTRY.
```

Listing 3.10 Object-Oriented Transactions

The example shows the advantages of the object-oriented transaction concept. You start a transaction explicitly using the CREATE_TRANSAC-TION( ) method and you end it with END( ), or you execute a rollback using UNDO( ). This procedure shows the beginning and end of a LUW more explicitly than the classic transaction concept. In this way, you can increase the transaction security of your applications. By calling

```
cl_os_system=>init_and_set_modes(
i_external_commit = oscon_false ).
```

you explicitly prohibit the use of COMMIT WORK and ROLLBACK WORK in the application and only allow the transaction service to still be used. You can also do this by selecting the OO Transaction Model checkbox in a transaction in the ABAP Workbench, or in Transaction SE93. However, this session is deactivated by default to ensure that you can also use the Object Services in the classic transaction concept.

Object Services with the classic transaction concept

The transaction service is just as powerful as the classic transaction concept:

▶ In the I_UPDATE_MODE parameter of the CL_OS_SYSTEM=>INIT_AND_SET_ MODES() method, you activate the update mode, which (like the class transaction concept) can be local, synchronous, or asynchronous.

▶ You can execute nested transactions more easily than in the classic transaction concept. For information about these functions, refer to the SAP Library.

▶ When working with persistent objects, you have seen that these are invalidated at the end of a transaction. If you want to avoid this, you must work with concatenated transactions, which you can use with the END_AND_CHAIN( ) or UNDO_AND_CHAIN( ) methods. The exact functions are described in the SAP Library.

Large parts of the standard SAP system — and possibly also of customer developments — use the classic transaction concept. Are there therefore risks involved in using it? Object-oriented transactions trigger an implicit COMMIT WORK to also enable update modules to be started that were created using classic techniques.

Classic and object-oriented transactions side by side

If you implemented the existing application with the recommended transaction control, problems are practically ruled out because the beginning and end of a transaction is controlled at a very high call level and service functions do not have any influence on the start and end of a transaction.

However, there are exceptions to every rule. In Chapter 7, Section 7.2, Table Maintenance Dialogs and View Clusters, you will see how you can write table entries on transport requests as an alternative to generated table maintenance dialogs. The `TR_OBJECTS_INSERT` function module used in this context is an example of a module that breaks the rule that a service module should never access transaction control. Such breaches usually occur only in very technical APIs, but they should always be investigated.

[+] | **Detecting Errors in Transaction Control**

You can use the `CL_OS_SYSTEM=>INIT_AND_SET_MODES( )` method call with the transaction service to identify hidden `COMMIT WORK` and `ROLLBACK WORK` commands that jeopardize transaction control. These cause runtime errors that can be detected during the software test.

How do you handle situations where service functions themselves end transactions with `COMMIT WORK` or `ROLLBACK WORK`? For this case as well you have learned about a solution in Section 3.4.1, Special Techniques of Classic Transaction Concept. Use the `DESTINATION 'NONE'` addition to start the function module — this enables you to activate a new internal session and execute the transaction separately.

3.5 Best Practices

It is difficult to specify general rules for modeling the application object. However, some procedures that have been proven are presented in this section.

3.5.1 Creating Primary Keys

In Section 3.2.2, we introduced different data modeling options and discussed the advantages and disadvantages of specialized keys, of using number ranges and GUIDs, and of composite keys. Object Services as a persistence mechanism support all of these strategies. However, this does not mean that these strategies correspond equally to each other.

Problems with specialized keys   Specialized primary keys can cause extensive problems in data migration projects, and integration projects in particular. The same problems occur if primary keys have components from number range objects and additional specialized components. We therefore recommend simply-structured number ranges or GUIDs. If the persons responsible frequently work with numbers, using number ranges will make more sense than GUIDs. Thorough data modeling is always required if you use complex number ranges with subobjects or group dependency.

However, you can also combine the strengths of number ranges and keys by selecting GUIDs as the primary key and another specialized key in an attribute that is not a key field, in order to support users. However, we generally advise against combining primary keys from number range components with specialized keys. This procedure will come back to haunt you if the specialization of a key component changes in any way. It is also cumbersome when you are setting up SAP systems for consolidation and QS purposes if you want number range interval statuses to be set or adjusted automatically.

Another alternative to specialized key components in primary keys created by number ranges is to choose disjunctive number range intervals. You can define the current interval in the Customizing of the application system. If you set the intervals for the application operators in a coordinated way, data merge projects will also be relatively easy to implement.

Disjunctive number range intervals

When you use number ranges, you must create the intervals in the target system. This is part of the initial Customizing of an application. You can transport intervals, but current statuses are transported also, which rarely makes sense. Even though you can directly create or modify number range intervals together with statuses using the NRIV table or an API[3], this is too risky in live productions and should be avoided.

Length of Primary Keys **[+]**

Note that the length of primary keys for number ranges is restricted. We also do not recommend long primary keys for two reasons: first, the indexes of the database tables are large and, second, the length is restricted in many generic APIs of the standard SAP system (for example, it is limited to 32 characters for objects that are used in workflows).

---

3 SAP provides some functions in the SZN package; particularly important are the function modules of function groups SNR0 to SNR7.

3.5.2 Modeling the Application Object in the ABAP Dictionary

Different layers
An application object exists at different layers of an application system. Its attributes are saved persistently in the database, it exists transiently as an application object when the program is being executed, and the user processes it at the presentation layer.

In most cases, it makes sense to use the same data elements for the application object, but not the same structures of the database. This enables you to separate the database representation of the application object from the specialized logic and from the presentation layer.

3.5.3 Service Functions for Persistent Objects

A powerful persistence service is available through Object Services. For most business applications, however, you need additional functions to create locks and change documents, for example. The aspects presented here will show you where you implement these functions.

Implementing functions on the persistent object
You can implement these functions directly as methods of the persistent object. It is useful to group the methods in interfaces to avoid complicating the method interface. For example, in each case you can create an interface for lock functions, for creating change documents, and so on. The advantage of implementing functions in the persistent object is that you can use polymorphy in a clever way. If necessary, you can redefine the corresponding methods in derived classes.

Implementing functions on a global utility class, such as the class agent
You can also extend the generated class agent of the persistent class. The additional methods will be able to take any necessary new generations that may be required after the mapping is changed, that is, after modifications have been made to the corresponding tables to be persisted. In this case, you work with static methods that contain an object reference as a parameter. However, there are disadvantages to this approach. You cannot use polymorphy because, first, you cannot redefine static methods and, second, there is a separate class agent for each persistent class (for derivations also).

You can also implement service functions on a persistent object and directly delegate them to a utility class, such as a local object. However, you must check whether the additional effort will be worthwhile because additional encapsulations do not automatically improve the application.

> **Implementing Service Functions** [+]
>
> You should define service functions that are associated with the life cycle of objects or at the database level — such as lock management and change documents — on the persistent object or class agent. If more specialization is involved, we recommend that you move them to a separate class. These aspects are the topic of Chapter 6.

We discuss typical service functions and their implementation in the following sections.

Typical service functions

Lock Management

Object Services do not provide any methods for setting and deleting locks. You saw how to create SAP locks in Section 3.2.2. You now want to implement these functions on the persistent object. To do this, you implement two methods, ENQUEUE( ) and DEQUEUE( ). Within the method, you must call one or more generated lock modules that have primary keys of database tables, and standardized lock parameters as parameters. You can determine the first ones within the persistent object, to enable you to provide a uniform interface for lock management through a uniform interface that is implemented by the different persistent classes.

Access to Attributes Using a Working Area

When you generate a persistent object, you automatically receive a comprehensive interface of setter and getter methods. It is often easier to provide all attributes in one ABAP structure and read and modify them using a single method. Implementation on the persistent object is obvious here.

Creating Change Documents

Business objects are subject to change. For reasons of revision security, it is useful to log these changes. A description of how to create change documents is provided in the SAP Library under BC EXTENDED FUNCTION LIBRARY • CHANGE DOCUMENTS. You create them in Transaction SCDO. You can generate an update module for a change document object, as shown in Figure 3.13. This function module, has working areas and internal tables as its parameters that contain the values before and after a change is made. The standard SAP system provides service functions for change documents in function groups SCD0 to SCD6.

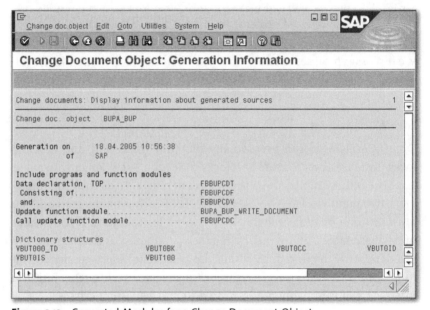

Figure 3.13 Generated Modules for a Change Document Object

Change documents for persistent objects

You can use some of the changes used in this chapter to use change documents with persistent objects. These changes are described in order here:

1. Provide the attributes of a class (the components of the table in question) linked to the persistence mechanism as a working area. You must implement this as a service function for the persistent object.

2. Define a structure as a transient attribute, the components of which contain the values to be logged in change documents before any changes are made. You can fill this transient attribute using the checking agent by implementing the IF_OS_STATE interface in the INIT( )

method. You have already learned about the checking agent in Section 3.3.2, Object Services.

3. Access the values after changes are made; this also occurs in the `IF_OS_CHECK~IS_CONSISTENT( )` method in the checking agent. In Section 3.3.4, Accessing Dependent Tables, you have already seen how to call update modules there.

4. In large transactions, it makes sense to bundle the changes, that is, to transfer tables to the update modules for change documents. You do this using the `PERFORM … ON COMMIT` bundling technique described in Section 3.4.1. Instead of calling the update task directly, you activate a function module that saves this technique for data for creating a change document in the top include of a function group, and at the same time registers a form routine using `PERFORM … ON COMMIT`. This form routine is called when you execute a `COMMIT WORK` (whether explicitly or implicitly for object-oriented transactions) to enable you to transfer quantities of data records in the form routine to the update task for change documents.

> Large transactions

3.5.4 Saving Unstructured and Semi-Structured Data

Some application systems must manage data that can only be mapped to transparent tables with a considerable amount of effort. Examples include:

- Complex data, such as the contents of nested internal tables
- Completely unstructured data, such as data from an external system in an external data format that must be saved to the database temporarily
- Semi-structured data, such as XML documents

XML documents are useful for complex specialized application objects that might frequently change over time because you will be able to assign additional attributes. Let's assume that you want to map a vehicle file for vehicle management in this sample application. This file can consist of structured and unstructured components, such as a workshop manager's notes, and there may be links to other documents, images, and files archived in the SAP system. This list clearly shows that modeling at the database level is too inflexible. At this point, you can model a file using

> XML documents

XML documents, but you can also use the standard functions of *SAP Records Management*. A description of this modeling would go beyond the scope of this book.[4]

In SAP Release 4.6C, unstructured and semi-structured data was saved in INDX-type tables for including data clusters, but this involves a large amount of administrative effort (see Chapter 9, Section 9.1.10, Saving Complex Data, for information about the business application log and data clusters). You can now save this data to the database directly, in STRING or XSTRING fields.

You can serialize unstructured and semi-structured data either in binary format using the EXPORT ... TO DATA BUFFER command or in XML and store it in the database. Binary format is useful for mass data, whereas XML is more flexible and can be converted and displayed using XSL Transformations. In addition, the syntax is standardized and there are numerous XML-based specifications you can use for encoding the data. You can therefore ensure that the data can be interpreted for longer periods and also be exchanged with other systems.

The following APIs are available in AS ABAP for processing XML documents:

XML Library
▸ The XML Library, with a DOM and a SAX API, as well as the option of DTD validation.

▸ An XSLT 1.0 processor integrated into ABAP using the CALL TRANSFORMATION command. This processor also supports important XSLT 2.0 commands and ABAP calls.

Simple Transformations
▸ Simple Transformations to quickly serialize and deserialize data.

XML clobbing
Saving XML documents as strings in the database is also referred to as *XML clobbing*. If you proceed in this way, it is useful to provide different utilities. This will pay off at development time and, at the latest, when assuring the quality of the software:

---

4 The SAP Records Management component is part of every AS ABAP (SRM main package). However, you still need a content server and TREX as a full-text search engine.

▸ You can use XSL transformations to transform XML documents into well-formed HTML and display them using the `DISPLAY_XML_STRING` function module.

▸ If you have large documents, it is worthwhile using the `CL_ABAP_ZIP` class to compress them.

To enable you to process XML documents reasonably, using automated processes, you must meet certain prerequisites in terms of their structure. You can check this either through the XML Library or specific XSL transformations using validation against a DTD, because AS ABAP does not support the standard W3C *XML Schema*. You can generate these types of check transformations from Schematron descriptions. *Schematron* (see *http://www.schematron.com/*) is a rule-based schema language you can use to encode structural properties and business rules. There are Schematron implementations that convert schemas into XSL Transformations that you can then execute on AS ABAP.

To search in XML documents, you generally have to access all documents saved in the database. Because the standard SAP system does not currently support XML database management systems, or special XML features of modern database management systems, you must ensure that the transparent tables contain the most important classification criteria so that you only have to check a small number of XML documents. XPath expressions, which you can use in XSL transformations, are useful for searching in XML documents.

Saving XML documents in relational structures is also referred to as *XML shredding*. XML shredding involves first deriving a database schema that corresponds to the XML schema from an XML schema (of a meta description using the content and structure of XML documents). This is not always easy, because recursive structures and extensive use of optional XML elements and attributes often make complex database structures necessary. In this case, transparent tables are often so wide that they have to be split, which results in denormalized database models. Another problem is that the element sequence is uniquely specified in the XML document, but this is no longer the case in the SQL database, which means that you may have to set up additional counters to avoid losing any information.

XML shredding

XML shredding is not supported by the standard SAP system; you have to program it yourself. Unfortunately, simple transformations are generally only suitable as a preparatory step because you can only convert tree-like XML structures with simple transformations into nested ABAP structures. This means further post-processing is required.

3.5.5 Further Considerations

In this chapter, you have learned how to design an application object, model it on the database, and implement persistence. However, some considerations that we did not previously discuss in this chapter include:

What is the life cycle of an object? Is it created in automated processes, in dialogs, or by external data — for example, by IDoc? Will you have to implement different CREATE( ) methods? Depending on the origin, will you be able to fill certain attributes?

Data quality   The last point raises the question of *data quality*. If customer relationship data is merged from different sources, you cannot assume that all have consistent quality. For example, with data from a call center, you cannot always assume that all input fields were filled. In addition, customers may intentionally enter incorrect information because they fear that companies will pass on their data and they will be plagued with unsolicited postal mail and emails in the future. Therefore, if the criteria you are forced to use when creating application objects is too strict, data may be rejected when you try to transfer it and, at worst, you may receive enormous amounts of business application logs (BAL) with more or less understandable error messages. There are two strategies you can use here. Either implement automatic error confirmation strategies that will send a confirmation to the sender to ensure that data can be consolidated at the source, or allow the consolidation in the SAP system. This means that a part of the specialized checks will not be hard-coded in the application object, but will instead be implemented in additional classes. Checks controlled by Customizing that customers can adapt to suit their needs may also be useful. We discuss these aspects in Chapter 6 in conjunction with application development techniques.

Channel and Data Quality
If the origin of the data is important in the life cycle of an object, or for other specialized checks, you can save this information as an additional attribute. You typically choose the channel (for example, telephone, Internet, fax, or mail). Although this procedure makes evaluations easier, it is not always suitable for describing data quality, because the quality of data from the same origin may change or be changed by subsequent processes. In this case, it makes more sense to include an attribute that explicitly describes which qualitative requirements the data must meet.

3.5.6   Key Transactions

The transactions shown in Table 3.1 are helpful for developing database models and for developing and monitoring database applications.

Transaction Code	Description
SARI	Archiving Information System
SCDO	Change Document Objects
SD11	Data Modeler
SE14	Database Utility
SE16	Data Browser (Table View)
SE93	Maintain transaction
SE30	ABAP Runtime Analysis
SM12	Select Lock Entries
SM13	Update Requests
SM14	Update Program Administration
SNRO	Maintains number ranges
SNUM	Maintains number range intervals
ST30	Global performance analysis

Table 3.1   Key Transaction Codes

"The object oriented paradigm, like any paradigm, embodies a set of architectural rules and guidelines. These rules constrain the activities of design and programming, but it is these constraints that keep design and long-term maintenance from going awry."
(James O. Coplien)

4 Classes, Interfaces, and Exceptions

In this chapter, we will deal with the smallest programming units of application development: classes, interfaces, and exceptions. We will describe the strengths of object-oriented language constructs and present guidelines for object-oriented design.

We will also discuss the basic principles of object-oriented programming and properties of the ABAP programming language. An application system is not only composed of application objects; it also consists of technical frameworks, an application core, and a presentation layer. Object-oriented techniques are also used to implement these software modules. Before we describe the techniques of application and dialog programming in detail in the following chapters, we will discuss the principles of object-oriented programming in some more depth in this chapter.

There is a great deal of certainty about object-oriented programming among many developers who have experience with purely procedural languages. When they are faced with object-oriented constructs, they often react defensively, questioning why they have to use them when they could instead use procedural techniques for the same purpose. They argue that, even worse, these language elements increase the complexity of ABAP, and as such can be a source of additional errors.

Uncertainty for developers

This assumption is based on a misconception. Object orientation is not practiced as an end in itself, because new language constructs have to be mastered or because it is fashionable to do so. Excellent programs can also be written without object orientation and object orientation does not and cannot solve all problems. However, using object orientation enables you to implement established basic principles of good system design and good programming better than before:

▸ Modularization separates components of *strong cohesion* from those of *weak cohesion. Explicitly defined interfaces* are used between different modules. The `INTERFACE` construct is useful for this.

▸ The principle of *information hiding* should be enforced. In addition to an interface, a module has an implementation. The user must not — or is not allowed to — know the details of this. You can differentiate between *public* and *private elements* in interfaces or classes.

▸ You can define *abstract data types*, that is, software modules that determine database access operations in addition to data structures. What are uses for these data types? In Section 4.2, Exceptions, you will be introduced to an example of this, using exception classes. In an error situation, for example, it makes sense to save other information, such as the location of the error in the source code, the call hierarchy, the content of certain variables, and so on, in addition to an error message. You also require functions to access this information. In error situations, this means that you can propagate detailed information about an error to a software layer that will evaluate the information and react accordingly.

Another misconception relates to the use of inheritance and polymorphy. Using a lot of inheritance is in no way an indicator of good object-oriented design. Inheritance always involves the risk of classes being coupled too closely with one another. There is also the risk that class hierarchies will be created that you will not subsequently be able to modify with reasonable effort. However, this does not mean that you should avoid these techniques. In Section 4.2, Exceptions, and Section 4.3.2, Open-Closed Principle, you will become acquainted with situations where inheritance and polymorphy are used successfully.

4.1   Advantages of ABAP Objects

Classic ABAP is no longer suitable for contemporary application development. ABAP Objects enables you to, at the level of language constructs, write programs that are more robust and more easily understood. This is demonstrated in the text that follows.

4.1.1 Defining Constants in Classes and Interfaces

In classic ABAP, you defined constants in global includes. A major disadvantage to this approach is that you cannot rule out naming conflicts.
Let's assume that you define a CON_OFF constant in the Z_VEHICLE_CON-
STANTS include as well as in the Z_CONTRACT_CONSTANTS include. If a program uses both includes, a naming conflict and an activation error will
occur.

Naming conflicts

The only sensible definition for constants is the one used in classes or
interfaces. In the situation presented here, you can differentiate constants
by referring to the interface, for example, Z_VEHICLE_CONSTANTS=>CON_
OFF and Z_CONTRACT_CONSTANTS=>CON_OFF. Another advantage of defining constants in classes and interfaces is that using this approach, they
are logically grouped. Based on experience, includes with global constants often degenerate into a large and confusing stockpile of data.

As an alternative, you can use constants in abstract and final classes. This
has the following advantages:

▸ You cannot implement the interfaces; this prevents aliases from being
created for the constants. Using aliases makes source code difficult to
understand, because the same constant appears with a different name
in the source code.

Constants in abstract and final classes

▸ In abstract classes, you can also implement service functions such as
conversions.

In Section 6.2, Customizing, you will find, in the context of developer
Customizing, a detailed discussion of constant definitions in interfaces.

4.1.2 Function Groups versus Objects

In principle, you can define a module memory in top includes of function groups and thereby simulate an object. However, if possible, you
should not use this technique:

Module memory

▸ An object implemented in this way can only have one instance
per internal session. You can save several objects using the classic
approach by saving the attributes as internal tables in the function
group's top include. The BAL or the Business Object Repository work

this way. If you decide to use this solution, you must develop object management, which, because of the complexity involved, will be time-consuming.

▸ Managing the module memory is extremely prone to errors. If you need the "function group object" a second time, you must ensure that all variables are initialized again. If you forget just one variable in an initialization routine, this will result in an error that will be difficult to reproduce. You do not have this problem with objects, because all attributes are automatically initial after instantiating.

▸ Function groups sort function modules based on thematic factors. It is not clear which function modules manipulate the module memory and which do not. In ABAP Objects, you can declare this uniquely by distinguishing instance and class methods and checking this at the time of activation.

4.1.3   Events

ABAP Objects provides other language constructs for events that you can use in GUI programming, in particular to react to events such as mouse clicks. This type of programming is easier and less error-prone than the procedural options with callback interfaces using function modules.

No exception interfaces

Note, however, that with events you cannot offer exception interfaces to react to system errors. Nevertheless, you can work with unchecked exceptions, which we will discuss in the following section.

4.2   Exceptions

You are confronted with the following challenges in every application system:

▸ How should the program behave in error situations?

▸ What error situations are there and what should the reaction to them be in the form of an exception?

▸ How do you return exceptions in method interfaces?

This section first deals with the term *exception*, followed by an explanation of the classic and object-oriented exception concept. Finally, it differentiates exceptions from assertions, and provides tips for creating exception concepts in a development project.

There are different definitions for the term *exception*. One thing, however, is certain: An exception, unlike a content-related error, represents abnormal program behavior. The example of an authorization check shows how difficult this classification is — a failed authorization check can be absolutely normal program behavior. One possible strategy is to separate exceptions in the same way as error events for business objects:

Definition

▸ **Temporary errors**
A resource is not available (for example, because of a database lock).

▸ **System errors**
A serious error has occurred – further processing is no longer possible.

You can also define *safety facades* using exceptions. To do so, you define a software layer that catches exceptions and decides how to proceed. Possible reactions include:

Safety facades

▸ Retry, for temporary errors

▸ Issuing a message for a dialog application

▸ Logging in the Business Application Log, for batch applications

4.2.1   Classic and Object-Oriented Exceptions

Classic exceptions provide user-friendly syntax. For example, the RAISE statement returns you to the calling code position and the SY-SUBRC system field is mapped to a certain value. If the program has been coded correctly, the other SY-MSG* fields are also filled, which enables you to use the MESSAGE statement to issue an error, or otherwise provide context-specific information. This is difficult to actually implement because you cannot guarantee that the SY-MSG* fields are filled with meaningful information.

This procedure also has major disadvantages if, because of an error situation, you have to return to a defined location in a large call hierarchy to decide about further processing, termination, or other ways of neutralizing errors. Problems occur at this point at the latest:

Disadvantages of the classic exception concept

▶ This course of action results in extremely illegible source code, because the SY-SUBRC value is regularly checked and the system must react to it.

▶ There is hardly any error information. Although there are different values from the system fields, they may be lost when you return to the call hierarchy. To enable you to log the location of the error, the system field values for the error, or the times when the error occurred and the call hierarchy, you must do this after an exception has occurred. Not only is this prone to errors and difficult, it also makes the source code completely illegible.

Advantages of object-oriented exception concept

You can solve or at least lessen all of these problems using object-oriented exceptions. Unlike a mapping mechanism resulting from an exception parameter in the interface of a modularization unit, an exception itself is a special object that provides a variety of information:

▶ The object has an error message and access methods for display as a string or through a MESSAGE dialog box.

▶ The location where the exception occurred, and that can be determined using the GET_SOURCE_POSITION( ) method, is saved in the object in the ABAP source code.

▶ You can define exception classes yourself using derivation and assign attributes to them that contain additional information about the error, such as data that describes the error situation in more detail or that you can use to implement troubleshooting strategies.

Object-oriented exceptions can be *checked*, *dynamically checked* or *unchecked*. The corresponding property affects how the exception must be handled. These concepts are known from other programming languages but there is no agreement on which exception types should be used.

Checked exceptions

Checked exceptions are derived from the CX_STATIC_CHECK class. If this type of exception occurs in the method, the initiator must deal with it using the CATCH command; otherwise, a runtime error will occur. However, such an exception can exit a modularization unit if the corresponding exception is declared in the interface; without a declaration, an error will occur in the extended program check. This approach means that you achieve a stable and transparent troubleshooting strategy. However, one disadvantage is that legibility may suffer in some parts of the program as a result of the troubleshooting-related code.

Dynamically checked exceptions are derived from the `CX_DYNAMIC_CHECK` class. Unlike checked exceptions, the initiator does not have to deal with these exceptions. If they happen nonetheless, a runtime error will occur, unless they are neutralized in the call hierarchy using `CATCH CX_SY_NO_HANDLER`. You can use these types of exceptions in frameworks you created for errors that occur as a result of improper use. In this case, the user receives a runtime error that he must correct, but at the same time — through the exception object — he has a meaningful description of the error. You can work with object-oriented exceptions easily within the framework, while not forcing the user to process errors caused by using the framework incorrectly as part of usual troubleshooting. For other framework error situations, you can use additional checked exceptions the user will neutralize as part of troubleshooting.

Dynamically checked exceptions

Unchecked exceptions are derived from the `CX_NO_CHECK` class. You do not have to declare these exceptions in interfaces; rather, they can occur without restriction. This feature is useful when you are troubleshooting errors that can occur at any time, such as a shortage of main memory. Ideally, you should let these types of errors occur unimpeded in the call hierarchy, and deal with them in a defined location. You can also use unchecked exceptions to cancel ABAP event handling, where the person performing the handling triggers such an exception.

Unchecked exceptions

The last example reveals two things in particular: Exceptions violate the principle of information hiding, because they disclose implementation details. They also result in drastic intervention in the control flow. Unchecked exceptions in particular can violate software layers easily, and, without a coherent troubleshooting concept, are often equivalent to a `GOTO` statement. If additional unchecked exceptions occur during event handling, this can easily result in inconsistencies. For example, part of the objects that handle an event may have changed their status because of the event, while others did not. Because transaction logic is not applied to transient objects, you also cannot usually restore consistency. You may subsequently be required to cancel the processing. If you are concerned about these types of effects, you should use unchecked exceptions only in error situations that are so serious that you have to cancel an entire processing step and restart it again.

4.2.2   Assertions

If a system error occurs, you do not always have to react by throwing an exception. Assertions are useful if you are not sure whether the cause of a system error is only a programming error you can identify through tests in the development system and correct. You can check a logical expression using the ASSERT command.

Checkpoint groups   You can assign assertions to a *checkpoint group* and, as shown in Figure 4.1, create the checkpoint group in Transaction SAAB or the ABAP Workbench. You can also define a behavior for assertions, for example, failed assertions can start the debugger, create a log entry, or cause a short dump.

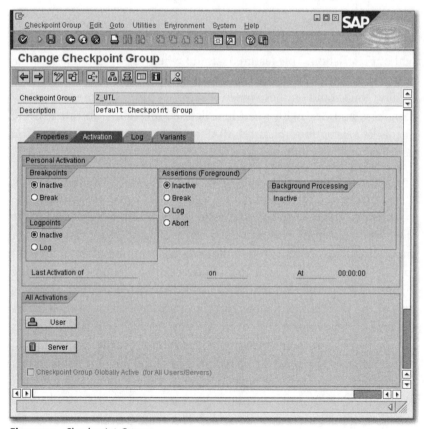

Figure 4.1   Checkpoint Group

In Figure 4.1, all breakpoints, log points, and assertions are set to inactive. You can also define the reactions for a user, and for certain servers. In that case, the syntax for an assertion is as follows:

Syntax for an assertion

```
ASSERT iv_paramater IS NOT INITIAL ID Z_UTL.
```

The procedure to make all breakpoints and assertions inactive is useful, because you want to be able to deactivate these in production (or for an important presentation) using Transaction SAAB. In this case, the assertions are ignored when you execute the program, which also means that the execution time is quicker.

Avoiding Side Effects

[!]

If you deactivate checkpoint groups, functional methods in assertions won't be executed during runtime. Functional methods have a returning parameter that performs the result of a complex and, possibly runtime-intensive diagnosis. To guarantee that this does not result in different behavior for activated and deactivated assertions, you must ensure that the methods do not have any side effects: You must therefore not change any variables in functional methods that are used within assertions.

It is useful to create a number of variants in Transaction SAAB that you can activate as required to analyze error situations in consolidation or live systems.

4.2.3   Exception Handling

Using object-oriented exceptions generally contributes to the quality of the source code, because you can reduce the scope of the source code for system troubleshooting and the behavior of the application system becomes more transparent when an error occurs.

At the same time, it is essential that you consider strategies for handling exceptions. It generally makes sense to react as early as possible to exceptions; however, deep layers cannot decide how the processing should proceed when an error occurs. Typical options include logging the error, executing a retry, or canceling the entire processing. This type of decision can usually only be made by a specific software layer, a security façade. This layer knows the processing mode (batch or online) and can select the appropriate logging method.

Strategies for handling exceptions

When designing exceptions, you can either throw an exception hierarchy for each subcomponent, or try to classify general error situations using exception classes such as ZCX_PROCESSING_ERROR or ZCX_CUSTOMIZING_ERROR, to which the system can then usually react. Error situations from incorrect Customizing usually directly result in terminations, because missing or inconsistent Customizing normally requires immediate intervention by application support staff. With processing errors, different strategies are often possible and further processing is not always ruled out. However, the difficulty is that you cannot always clearly decide whether the application data or Customizing are incorrect – consider tables with key values, for example.

Uniformity when handling exceptions does not do any harm, except that a large part of the source code consists of handling one particular exception type and the transformation into the exception type that is specified in the method interface. This can result in almost illegible source code.

Breadth and depth of the exception hierarchy
Typically, you should ensure that the breadth and depth of the exception hierarchy is not too comprehensive. This also applies for the method interfaces. It makes sense to define more than just one exception for the method interface, to ensure that approximate error classification is possible. If the interface is too broadly based, the source code for handling exceptions may be too comprehensive. You can benefit from this if the possible exception classes are derived from a basis class so that you can handle all together using a CATCH block.

Linked exceptions
If you are forced to convert an exception type into another type, we recommend that you use linked exceptions and provide a reference to the previous exception using the PREVIOUS parameter.

4.3 Basic Principles of Object-Oriented Design

The phrase "Basic principles of object-oriented design" is misleading because it suggests that new and possibly completely different principles apply for object-oriented design and object-oriented programming. You might also think that these principles must always be adhered to in every circumstance to achieve programs of satisfactory quality. This is not the case. Every design decision is in fact directed by a specific objective. Through your own experience, product vision, or discussions with the user department, you want to design the application system in such a way that you can extend it with regard to certain criteria. You also want to design it in a modular way, to enable other developers to quickly find code positions that have to be adapted when modifications are being made, and to ensure that any side effects of the modifications can be ruled out as much as possible, or at least can be controlled quickly. The principles presented in the following sections are used for this purpose.

4.3.1 Dependency Inversion

Academically expressed, the principle signifies the inversion of dependencies, whereby there should only be dependencies for abstract implementations, not for concrete implementations, because abstract implementations (for example, using interfaces) are not changed as often as concrete implementations. This means that a main program must only call interfaces, not concrete classes. You want to use this approach to ensure that you can re-implement functions better.

Programming against interfaces and not against classes

Figure 4.2 illustrates this principle. You have a business process that consists of different substeps. First, you must obtain data for a correspondence, then determine the sender and any additional recipients and, finally, generate the output. A prototype of everything that can change is presented here:

- ▶ Data retrieval does not access transparent tables, but must instead determine data that has not yet been saved from the dialog currently being displayed. However, this only applies for online printing.

- ▶ If a workflow takes place, the person responsible (as the sender) who is currently processing the business process should be determined. Otherwise, you should determine this information in an alternative way.

- ▶ Different procedures are also possible for generating output, for example, you can use SAPscript, SmartForms and, more recently, Adobe Interactive Forms as print technologies.

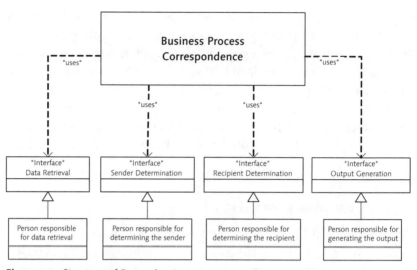

Figure 4.2 Structure of Dependencies

Control program not based on many details

These examples show that it is difficult to predict which modifications will be required for an application in the future. A sensible programming principle is therefore not to base a control program on many details. Figure 4.2 shows an ideal situation: All individual steps of the process are encapsulated by interfaces, which means that each function can be replaced with a new class.

In Section 5.5, Composition of Packages, we present more flexible interface techniques that you can use at runtime to determine the appropriate implementation.

4.3.2 Open-Closed Principle

Open for extensions, closed for modifications

The *open-closed principle* means that software must be open for extensions and closed for modifications. You are already aware of one aspect from non object-oriented development, where interfaces of function modules are difficult to change because, in this case, you also have to adapt each code position where you want to use the function modules. However, adding optional parameters is not critical.

Object-oriented technology has much more powerful techniques. The SAPlink tool by Edward Herrmann and Dan McWeeney, which you can download from *http://saplink.org*, is an established successful example of the implementation of this principle. This tool is an ABAP Open Source application that enables you to exchange SAP development objects such as classes, programs, and ABAP Dictionary elements in XML format. The architecture is displayed in Figure 4.3.

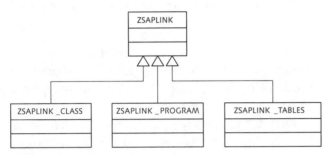

Figure 4.3 SAPlink Plug-Ins

To be able to (de)serialize a specific SAP development object using SAP- **Plug-in concept** link, you must create a plug-in for its object type. There are currently plug-ins for more than 20 object types. Each plug-in is derived from the ZSAPLINK class and redefines five object-type-specific methods, of which the most important are serialization (`CREATEIXMLDOCFROMOBJECT( )` method) and deserialization (`CREATEOBJECTFROMIXMLDOC( )` method).

The recipe of success for this approach is that the object-type-specific knowledge is completely encapsulated in the plug-ins. The list of available plug-ins is determined when you start the program, and the `VSEO-EXTEND` database view is used to search for classes that are derived from `ZSAPLINK`. You cannot implement this behavior with classic ABAP because the program flow is controlled using `CASE` constructs. This is too static for the purpose presented here because adding a new plug-in requires intervention in either the control program or Customizing.

This example also indicates a typical characteristic of a successful frame- **Generic concept** work, where the main program does not need to know which class the plug-in implements, but instead now works with the `ZSAPLINK` parent class. In this respect, this is a predominantly generic concept. Each subclass fulfills the same "contract" in terms of interface operations such as the parent class. This feature is the topic of the next section.

4.3.3 Inheritance and the Substitution Principle

Inheritance is the concept that probably causes the most problems for developers new to object orientation. There are two reasons for this: Most ABAP programmers are trained to develop flexible applications, which are controlled by tables, but have not yet faced the paradigm of inheritance.

Inheriting with business objects

The second reason is that, although inheritance is used in the SAP system for business objects,[1] developers often only use inheritance in the form of the SAP-specific delegation concept. You define a subtype for a business object in the customer namespace in the Business Object Builder (Transaction SWO1). This can have additional (often defined by the customer) attributes and methods. You select SETTINGS • DELEGATION to define a subtype with any new methods and events, which the parent object then "casts across" the system. Calls and events are automatically delegated to the subtype in workflows, workflow tasks, and event linkages. Note that this type of delegation is primarily useful only for customer developments for which an existing business object is extended without errors.

There is no equivalent to this delegation concept in ABAP Objects. In Section 3.3.2, Object Services, you saw how to derive persistent objects, but you cannot automatically instantiate objects of subclasses instead of the derived base class. However, when you encapsulate the object generation using a Business Add-In (BAdI), you enable customers to simulate this mechanism and have even greater control than for the procedure with classic business objects.

Substitution principle

The substitution principle means that a class can be replaced by each of its subclasses without the program behavior being changed. This guarantees that you can adhere to contracts during derivation. If we assume that the sample application has a class for transport requests, together with a method for cancelations that returns an indicator to specify whether the cancelation was successful, there will also be a derived class for special requests for which a cancelation is not always possible, but can instead occur only after a period of time. In this case, the cancelation is not

---

1 An example of a special accounting document is the accounts receivable document. The accounting document is therefore the basis class.

always possible for instances of the subclass. This kind of behavior is annoying because you no longer know whether a cancelation is possible or not. Imagine this type of behavior with an SAPlink plug-in. The main application would no longer be able to rely on the program working correctly for implementing serialization and deserialization. A method could reject the execution. This example clearly shows that violations of the *Liskov substitution principle* also imply violations of the open-closed principle.

> **Liskov Substitution Principle**
>
> The Liskov substitution principle states that a subclass must satisfy all contracts of the superclass:
>
> ▸ The preconditions of a method are not stricter than those of the basis class.
>
> ▸ The postconditions of a method are not less strict than those of the basis class.

How should you proceed when the substitution principle is violated? Obviously, this problem will not occur if you work with an abstract basis class, where you select the constructor "abstractly" for the instancing and thus prevent instances of an object from occurring. Alternatively, you can consider implementing the class hierarchy because, when using inheritance in a target-oriented way, you not only have to take into account the semantic aspect of specialization, or the addition of new attributes, but also the behavior of methods.

Substitution principle violations

4.3.4   Testability Using Unit Tests

It is difficult to name quality criteria for an object-oriented design. Therefore, we suggest a pragmatic criterion: Can you test a class or sub-application easily at the object level? The design raises the following questions:

▸ Can you instantiate basic objects with as little effort as possible?

▸ Can you test basic functions using simple test cases?

Advantages of module tests   Experience has shown that testable applications are usually modularized well. If you have a number of defined test cases for a class, you can work much more aggressively with modifications, because you have test data for a module that you can manage before and after a modification.

ABAP Unit   You can use ABAP Unit to create local test classes. You do so by generating a local test class for a class using the Class Builder or the ABAP Workbench, and selecting the UTILITIES • GENERATE TEST CLASS menu option (see Figure 4.4). The following methods are generated here:

▸ **Fixture methods**
You execute the SETUP( ) method before the test and the TEARDOWN( ) method after the test. Both are suitable for preparing and postprocessing a test case.

▸ **Test methods**
You create a test method for every method defined in Figure 4.4 and you can edit the methods by selecting the GOTO • LOCAL TEST CLASSES menu option. In this test method, you can call the corresponding method of the class to be tested and test the results using methods of the CL_AUNIT_ASSERT class.

ABAP Unit test cases are integrated into the Code Inspector (Transaction SCI) but you can also execute them directly by selecting CLASS • MODULE TEST, although not in the live system. You can also create test classes manually. By specifying the runtime category and the risk level, you ensure that only test classes that correspond to certain values will be executed.

Test-driven development   *Test-driven development* involves going one step further, where you create a test case before each new function to be programmed that will cover the new functions to be developed. Even if you do not follow this approach, we recommend that you include test phases in the development. In large development projects, you should integrate subapplications early on; otherwise you may not be able to implement any necessary adjustments and improvements with reasonable effort. If you create test cases in time, you have the chance to develop software modules that will be executable on time (even if not with all functions).

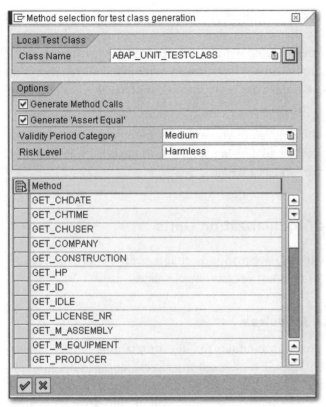

Figure 4.4 Generating Test Classes

Despite the fully developed framework, using module tests is often a challenge in the ABAP environment. ABAP Unit is the appropriate tool for module tests, but not for integration tests where many classes are involved. This also includes the test for asynchronous scenarios such as update techniques, and for asynchronous events. Including non object-oriented source code is also often complicated. This is also the case when one class is largely controlled by Customizing, which means that you do not know at the time of programming which values are allowed for a key value check. In this case, you can provide test Customizing that you also use in ABAP Unit classes. This approach has the added benefit that modules controlled by Customizing are regarded as an independent sub-application that is delivered with sample Customizing. This means that the subapplication can also be tested separately, and you can document how to use this application in the sample Customizing.

Test Customizing

One alternative is to encapsulate access to Customizing with an access layer in such a way that another class that uses its own record of (possibly hard-coded) values is used within the test code. This is common practice and you will find plenty of information in the standard references to the *JUnit Framework* under the keyword *Stub* or *Mock Objects* about how to implement this procedure.

General recommendation

Do not let these difficulties put you off using module tests. Instead, we recommend that you try to develop applications in such a way that they can be tested in part and as a whole.

4.4   Classic Modularization Units

Although ABAP Objects have many advantages over "classic" ABAP, non-object-oriented ABAP is not yet entirely obsolete.

4.4.1   Function Modules

You still require function modules for RFC programming, BAPI access layers (see Section 5.5.3, Event-Based Interfaces), and parallel processing (see Section 9.2, Parallel Processing of Applications). Because ABAP Objects classes cannot contain screens, you should create function groups.

4.4.2   Reports

You still also require classic report programming, even though you can only use it in a limited way for modularization because it is difficult to transfer report return values to the calling application. Reports should only be the entry point into a dialog or reporting application. In the latter case, the return data is contained in the list and evaluated directly by the user, or found (in addition to other information) in the job log (Transaction SM37) for background applications.

BAL

We recommend that you implement output in the form of Business Application Logs (BAL) and use a selection parameter in the report to decide whether you want these messages to be output in a print list or in the BAL. One of the many benefits of the BAL is that a callback concept enables you to interactively go to other applications — something you can no longer do with interactive lists if these are in the spool. You can also make quantities of logs available more easily to other applications; this either does not work with print lists, or works only in a restricted way. Although it is easy to make print lists available as HTML, other formatting and postprocessing options are limited. You should therefore avoid creating classic print lists and instead log data in the Business Application Log (see Section 9.1, Implementing the Application Log).

In dialog programming, you can easily define selection screens for reports, and transfer the input parameters to the application core. You can schedule batch programs per ABAP using Transactions SM36, SA38 or SE38[2] or start them from external schedulers. Some rules have been established for creating batch programs:

Creating batch programs

- There should be a "simulation mode" parameter that you can use to test the execution without updating the results; the results are displayed nevertheless. This type of parameterization helps developers when they are testing and troubleshooting in live environments, and it also helps users, who, before they start archiving or deletion reports, can test which datasets are affected in which combination with other input parameters.

- If you process large datasets in batch programs, a COMMIT counter is useful as a selection parameter because you will be able to use it to specify how many objects you want to be processed together in a LUW. This lets you reduce the number of individual COMMIT WORK statements and ensures that individual database transactions do not become too big, which can cause problems in some database systems.

- Ideally, use reports only as a kind of entry point that uses other modularization units such as classes or function modules. You can then also use these modularization units outside of the report. This means that reports will usually be very short and concise.

---

2 A wide range of programming interfaces are available, such as the BP_JOBVARI-
ANT_OVERVIEW and BP_JOBVARIANT_SCHEDULE function modules. These are
described in detail in the section "Programming with the Background Processing
System (BC-CCM-BTC)" under "Background Processing" in the SAP Library. This also
relates to calling batch programs using SAP events, which can be done in ABAP using the CL_BATCH_EVENT class.

▶ Arguably the most practical feature of reports is the option that enables you to save the contents of the reports' selection screens as variants. When you deliver these variants, the users will directly be able to use them. You process and transport variants by selecting the GOTO • VARIANTS menu option in Transaction SE38.

Parallel processing The SAP Library contains comprehensive documentation about *background processing* in the section *Background Processing*. If you want to use this approach to process large datasets, you often rely on parallel processing. Because this topic is important for applications capable of supporting mass data, we describe different strategies in detail in Chapter 9, Section 9.2, Parallel Processing of Applications.

4.5 Best Practices

In this chapter, you have learned some basic principles of object-oriented design. Should you always follow them? We recommend that you do because the principles are based on experience and developer community conventions. In individual cases there may be reasons not to adhere to them, but at the very least, you should document the reasons why. We conclude this chapter with some useful questions and tips.

4.5.1 General Considerations for Object-Oriented Design

If you, as a software architect or developer, have experience with object-oriented techniques, you will know the typical questions and have solutions for the following:

▶ How finely detailed are the objects? Should the classes correspond exactly to the classes from the object-analyzed analysis?

▶ Should I use inheritance or composition?

Procedure If you are not familiar with these questions, we recommend the following course of action:

▶ First develop the central application objects in an object-oriented way. If your application works with large datasets, you should try not to design the object model too fine-grained because this will result in large overhead through initializations.

▶ Use object-oriented techniques to modularize your application.

▶ Avoid deep inheritance hierarchies.

▶ Always use ABAP Objects because these language constructs have syntactic advantages.

An object-oriented design should be specific. This means that the objects in question should at least have meaningful names. For example, if a class has the task of retrieving data for a process or of controlling a process, its name should reflect this.

Specific design

Names that Are Easy to Remember   **[+]**

In an object-oriented design succinct object names that are easy to remember are a type of litmus test for quality. If you cannot assign an object name that is easy to remember, you will also often not be able to define the exact responsibility of a class. In addition, a useful name makes communication easier between designers and developers.

With each object-oriented design, there is a basic risk of creating comprehensive frameworks for simple tasks. The problem is that a framework only helps if users understand it and can call the service functions easily, and if the framework can also be extended. If it is designed incorrectly, it will either be too general or too specific for a problem or, in a worst case scenario, both features will each apply to other parts of the framework. To prevent this, you should make the framework available to users as early as possible to ensure that practical testing can be conducted. You can do this by making basic functions available, releasing them, and then successively creating other functions. You cannot always achieve this ideal situation with a feasible amount of effort, but it is an ideal you should strive for. Otherwise, there is a risk that you will discover at a well-advanced stage of the project that the basic service functions have been designed and implemented incorrectly.

Risks of frameworks you create yourself

4.5.2 Key Transactions

In this chapter we used the transactions shown in Table 4.1.

Transaction Code	Description
SAAB	Checkpoint that can be activated
SAUNIT_CLIENT_SETUP	ABAP Unit Configuration
SE24	Class Builder
SE38	ABAP Editor
SM36	Schedule Background Job
SM37	Job Selection
SCI	Code Inspector

Table 4.1 Key Transaction Codes

"Architecture has nothing to do with art; it constitutes a pure form of reasoning. Today, architecture is determined by economic, technical, and functional factors." (Egon Eiermann)

5   Application Architecture

Software technology demonstrates that an application system can be broken down into functional units. Dependencies between these units should be kept to a minimum to avoid unwanted side effects. Furthermore, existing dependencies must be explicitly documented.

Software structuring

This chapter begins by outlining the criteria that can be used to structure an application system. Next, it introduces you to possible implementations in the ABAP development environment. This environment allows you to use a *package concept*, which in fact is the cornerstone of this chapter and you will learn exactly how this concept can be applied. In addition to the splitting of a system into various packages, the *composition* of a system is also described: How can all of the parts in a software system be put together to form a whole? You will become familiar with callback interfaces, enhancements, and Publish & Subscribe interfaces. The chapter closes with tips for development leads.

5.1   Requirements for Application Architecture

In discussions about software architecture, famous architects are frequently quoted, and quotations emphasizing aesthetic considerations are chosen. For example, architecture may be described as "frozen music" (F.W. Schelling), which is only complete when nothing more can be taken away from it (Saint-Exupéry). However, if we examine these characterizations in the cold light of day, they seem to jar with reality. Software designers rely on such criteria to assess and compare architectures because, in practice, metrics and evaluations have not yet been

Aesthetics

implemented for software architectures. Therefore, there are no reliable alternatives to the aesthetic perspective, which is naturally prone to subjectivity.

But, if we take this approach, we are bound to judge software architecture on the basis of aesthetics alone. Is this really a sound approach? Do we not run the risk of pursuing an aesthetic ideal to the exclusion of all other aspects? Is it not possible that less obvious elements may actually be more important? Should we not, in fact, place special importance on a number of different aspects in the SAP development environment?

There are two possible reactions to this stream of questions. Theorists will view the questions as a challenge and as stimulus for further research with a view to formalizing the architectural concept to a greater degree.[1] Those with more practical leanings will look to their own experience, compile a list of functional and non-functional requirements for the application system that is to be developed, and use this as a foundation for the software structure. As pragmatists, this is the course they must follow.

Software-specific technical considerations

The following software-specific technical considerations must be addressed during the design phase:

▸ How can development objects be usefully grouped together in larger units to limit dependencies to local sub-areas of the application and facilitate maintenance?

▸ What are the dependencies between these units?

▸ How can these dependencies be documented in the system? How can we ensure that these units correspond to useful sub-applications?

Product idea

The *product idea* also plays a key role in shaping the structure of the application system and gives rise to implicit requirements for the architecture:

▸ How can the application be given a modular design, so that sub-applications can also be used independently of the overall application?

---

1 A number of theoretical approaches exist for formalizing the software model and architecture concept.

- Should development be organized according to various releases, which can run in sequence?

- Should the customer be able to connect a third-party application to the existing application?

- Is it necessary to provide the option of customer-specific development to enhance the application?

- Should the customer be able to replace sub-applications with proprietary applications?

Additional questions arise in the SAP development environment in relation to the *dependency of the application on SAP standard components*:

Dependency on SAP standard components

- Which SAP software components should be used?

- How can the application be modularized so that it can run with or without specific SAP software components?

- How can a custom application be "coupled" to the SAP standard components?

The primary task of a software architect is to find answers to these questions, to develop a vision of the application system that is supposed to be implemented. Software architects need to be very familiar with the exact customer requirements, and need to know which options for customizing the product should be made available to customers. Software architects also require a clear picture of how a product can be developed further in the future, and they must be able to envision an architecture that enables such development. Provisions must also be made to ensure that the structure of the software cannot be impacted by distributed maintenance to the extent that further development is necessarily costly and therefore not economically viable.

Primary task of a software architect

5.2 Software Structuring from a Technical Perspective

Classes and interfaces modularize an application at the lowest level. The challenge in application development is to manage the dependencies between the individual elements of the software by grouping them together in structures called packages. This approach lends transparency to a software system, which then comprises components with clearly defined interfaces. A package structure also makes the software more robust because changes made in one part of the program have only a local effect and the cost of implementing changes is low.

Package structure of the application
It is useful to use packages in this way because function modules, function groups, and classes are all too small to be used as modularization units. Several of these modules are often required to implement a function and thus have to be grouped together in one software component.

The package concept extends the familiar concept of development classes. It allows these to be nested hierarchically, and to have interfaces assigned to them (this is all explained in detail later in this chapter).

The Package Concept

The package concept provides the following options:

► Declaration of public interfaces
► Implementation of the principle of information hiding
► Documentation of usages
► Restriction of usages

Software structuring does not play a special role in cases where ABAP development is limited to the creation of user exits, or if a small number of reports need to be written for special evaluations. For the development of large applications, on the other hand, it is absolutely essential.

Alternatives to using packages
Some alternatives to using packages are described in the list that follows. Note, however, that these are not recommended.

► **Development classes**
If you completely avoid using packages, you run the risk of development classes becoming unwieldy in terms of size and complexity. Primarily, this is because it is impossible to keep stock of the interdependencies between development objects.

A programmer using these development classes will be unable to tell functions that are available as a public interface from those that are not.

▶ **Documentation effort**
The effort involved in documentation increases because the structure of the software has to be recorded outside of the SAP system in separate design documents. In the SAP system, the only way to group development objects thematically is to use the same naming conventions. This results in follow-on problems: Are these conventions easily understood? Will they be retained during maintenance?

Much more serious is the problem that may occur when a change is made to the software where it is moved to a different area defined by different naming conventions. The result is that the development objects must be renamed. Often, a considerable amount of effort is required to rename a large number of development objects and adjust the relevant objects. For example, if a module was developed for a specific scenario but it then emerges that the module can be reused, the naming convention must be changed because of this general use. This happens on every single software development project. The same applies to the SAP standard system. The parallelization framework described in Chapter 9, Section 9.2.5, Parallelization with the Parallel Processing Tool BANK_PP_JOBCTRL, is a good example of this.

Renaming development objects

▶ **Maintainability**
If public interfaces—and thus the principle of information hiding—are violated, it will seriously impair maintainability. Specifically, if too many modules that were designed as internal service functions are used in other parts of the application, software changes will necessitate a considerable effort in terms of implementation and testing.

▶ **Further development and release planning**
If you do not use clearly defined interfaces, you will be confronted with restrictions in relation to further development of the software and release planning. SAP developers have a shared repository of development objects, and changes are assigned to various tasks using

the SAP transport system. In a product release, an effort is made to both eliminate errors and enhance the product.[2]

Package concept ► The package concept is an important concept because it allows you to deliver development objects with a consistent status. You can deliver parts of the software in advance, and identify these as provisional by restricting the package interface to objects that already have a stable development status. Using the package and interface concept, you can also separate sub-applications to minimize the risks associated with development and maintenance. If delivery of the release of a sub-application is delayed, this does not automatically delay the delivery of the entire product, and sub-applications can be tested—or even rolled-out—before the entire product is delivered. If this is not done, a delay in the implementation of a sub-component will have a negative effect on the complete product.

[!] **Why Using Packages is Necessary**

Failure to use the package concept necessitates planned distributed maintenance when you start to develop an application system, and the basic principles of software engineering will be continuously violated. In addition, the design of the application will not be sufficiently modular. Even in a modular application, the principle of information hiding must apply; in other words, the implementation of a module must not be externally visible. Because of the lack of an interface concept in development classes, it is impossible to tell which development elements are public and which are private.

In large development projects, software structuring is not an aesthetic end in itself. Rather, it is a useful way to ensure that the application can be understood and maintained, and to enable flexible release planning. This has a direct effect on the effort involved in testing and documentation, and on the possibility of further development of the product.

---

2 The distinction made between "technical" and "concept" releases when developing proprietary software also applies, in part, to SAP development. Purely technical releases (for example, modification of the graphical user interface with new technology, such as Web Dynpro) should not also contain an excessive number of content changes. However, it is difficult to explain why technical changes should not be included in concept releases. Other release strategies distinguish between "errors" and "change requests". This approach stretches the limits of product development if the customer does not understand the difference.

5.3   How To Structure a Software System

At the start of any development project, once the central application objects have been identified, the software architect must begin the task of structuring the overall application. Books about software architecture often discuss heuristic issues. Typical approaches include structuring by business objects and business processes, and the isolation of purely technical components.

Software structuring is not a task that can be automated, and ultimately requires that a whole range of basic conditions are taken into account, for example:

Taking account of the basic conditions

- ▶ Integration into the company's IT architecture
- ▶ Communication with external systems
- ▶ Dependencies on other SAP modules and proprietary developments in the production environment

The following sections describe the main options available for software structuring.

5.3.1   Taking Account of the Business Structure

Structuring based on business objects and business processes is useful because it allows you to focus on the business structure. Structuring by business processes may mean that business rules will be implemented in a package. This reflects the need to separate processes from the business rules they use. This separation allows not only for greater flexibility, but also lets you make business processes available in the form of web services, which can be used by other applications.

It is also useful to define a separate package for each complex application object, in which the basic inventory functions are implemented.

Figure 5.1 shows one possible structuring: A *main package* is defined for an application object, and contains four sub-packages:

Structuring by business objects and business processes

- ▶ **Inventory**
  Object administration and object persistence.

▶ **Business rules**
What are the business requirements an object instance must fulfill, and when will anomalies be seen?

▶ **Processes**
Workflows, for example.

▶ **External interface**
For example, do you require BAPIs for the selection and manipulation of individual object instances or programs to create the opening inventory as part of a migration?

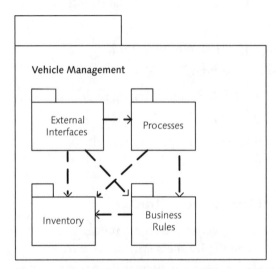

Figure 5.1 Sub-Packages of a Business Object and Their Dependencies

Visualizing the package structure with UML diagrams This section explains how the packages in an application system are visualized using UML diagrams. The usage dependencies between packages are indicated by the dotted arrows shown in Figure 5.1. Each arrow points from a user of services (client) to a provider of services (server). If such a relationship exists, elements of the server package that are declared in an interface may be used in the ABAP code or in ABAP Dictionary elements of the client.

The structure of the sample application shown in Figure 5.1 ensures that consolidated inventories of business entities can be managed. These may be application entities (such as vehicles or contracts), or links to inventory data in the SAP standard system, such as business partners etc. Processes and business rules operate on this inventory, which means that companies can map their specific business processes in the system. Making the inventory dependent on specific business processes, on the other hand, would be unnecessary and would restrict flexibility because these processes are usually customer-specific.

Package Responsibilities	**[!]**
When defining packages, software architects must ensure that each package has clearly defined *responsibilities*: The functions defined and implemented this way are executed wholly and exclusively in this package. Exceptions to this principle are discussed in Section 5.5, Composition of Packages.	

Experience has shown that it is best to avoid *cyclical dependencies* in relation to usages. In our example, both the processes and external interfaces have access to business rules, which can in turn access the inventory and therefore determine and check the required properties of business objects. This type of access is useful, for example, when performing checks against the entire inventory (for instance, duplicate checks).

Avoiding cyclical dependencies

To determine whether a cyclical dependency would be useful in this case, we must look at how the package responsibilities are defined. If the inventory does not have direct access to business rules, responsibility for the selection and usage of business rules falls to the processes or external interfaces. This may be useful. In certain use cases, such as migration, you can use specific business rules (such as less strict content checks for application objects) to copy a large portion of the dataset and have poor-quality data post-processed later, either automatically, or by the person responsible. Of course, stricter business rules can be applied during normal use of the application.

Figure 5.1 shows an architecture in which the inventory has no access to content. If cyclical dependencies exist at the level of module calls (as shown in Figure 5.2), this makes the application more complex. Consider, for example, a scenario where an inventory object uses a business rule, which in turn manipulates the same inventory object. These kinds of cycles are often responsible for errors that are difficult to trace. You can define interfaces with a high degree of granularity to avoid these errors. The package containing business rules may only use existing interfaces that provide read-only access.

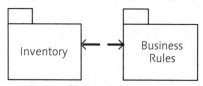

Figure 5.2 Cyclical Dependency

Mutual use of data elements The mutual use of data elements is less critical but may indicate an error in the design. This is because packages are coupled at the ABAP Dictionary level and therefore cannot be replaced by another package. If a package offers a service in its interface, ideally it must also offer the data elements in the interface structure, or use generally known data elements that were, for example, defined in packages that can only include ABAP Dictionary objects (see Section 5.4, The Package Concept).

To avoid cyclical dependencies, you can either define additional encapsulations at the package level (which may impair performance and make the application unnecessarily complex), or use special techniques for the flexible composition of packages. The latter are introduced in Section 5.5, Composition of Packages.

5.3.2 Identification of Layers

A *layer* can be defined as a set of classes and programs that offer similar services. In AS ABAP, for example, the layers GUI, application server, and database server are immediately identifiable. This chapter only discusses layers within the application system.

Layer model Figure 5.3 provides a view of the package structure that is different from the one shown in Figure 5.1. Here, because they both contain content, only the packages for processes and business rules are grouped together in an application layer. While the option of direct access to the inventory using external interfaces may immediately strike you as incongruous, it is not all that unusual in practice.

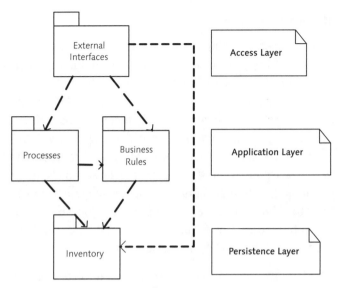

Figure 5.3   Structuring According to Layers

5.3.3   Dividing Applications into Sub-Applications

Section 5.3.1, Taking Account of the Business Structure, described the composition of the system using business objects and business processes. A division of the application into sub-applications is closely associated with this type of structuring. In this case, software architects must answer the following questions:

▶ Which sub-applications should be able to run completely independently?

▶ What are the dependencies between the sub-applications? Which sub-applications cannot run without others?

▶ Should the customer be able to decide that only certain sub-applications will be used?

In this way, the product design may have a significant influence on software structuring. These criteria are applied to the structuring of the application that is used as an example in this book, and which is described in Section 5.3.6, Structuring of the Sample Application.

Product design and software structuring

145

5.3.4 Creating Basic Components

The isolation of purely technical components as part of software structuring is a familiar concept from proprietary software development. In that context, it is often seen as necessary to ensure independence from the underlying database or application server. However, AS ABAP already ensures the independence of the database, while independence from a specific application server has no significance in the proprietary ABAP environment. However, it is useful to have purely technical components that can be reused within the application as *cross-sectional functions*, or that can even be used in future applications. If you create basic technical components, you can achieve a consistent implementation and use of these cross-sectional functions. This reduces development costs and the likelihood of random proliferation of various solutions.

Encapsulating unstable basic functions

Purely technical basic functions can also be used to encapsulate unstable basic functions. A typical example of this is access to the file system. Unlike the database connection, the file interface of AS ABAP is dependent on the underlying operating system. This has implications, for example, for the structure, case-sensitivity of the file names and paths, behavior during parallel access, codepage and line breaks, and so on. In addition, many changes were made to this interface as part of the latest release, and new middleware functions were added. Unified file access modules ensure a robust, and tested file interface for the complete application, and therefore also flexibility in the face of changes to functionality as part of release changes.

If a package is based only on SAP_BASIS (SAP Basis component) and SAP_ABA (cross-application component), it can be used in any SAP system and is therefore ideally suited for reuse.

[+] | **Declarative Packages**

Basic components are not necessarily of an entirely functional nature. They may also define purely declarative elements, such as data elements, which form an underlying set of data types. They can therefore be used, for example, for consistent and homogenous dialogs, and in interfaces.

This type of package can be used both for an add-on development in HR (SAP_HR component) and, for example, for CRM (BBPCRM component). The reverse is also true; that is, the more dependencies that exist in relation to SAP software components, the less frequently a package can be reused.

5.3.5 Dependency on SAP Standard Components

In Section 5.3.4, Creating Basic Components, we looked at package dependencies on SAP standard components from the point of view of reuse. However, it is useful to make the dependency on SAP basic packages a general structuring criterion. Modularization based on these criteria is useful, assuming that part of an application uses the BBPCRM component and another doesn't. When it is time to upgrade the release of the SAP standard component, only part of the application system needs to be modified and tested. This lets you design separate release strategies for the sub-applications, which gives you greater flexibility in the design of the overall application.

General structuring criterion

5.3.6 Structure of the Sample Application

Figure 5.4 shows one possible package distribution for our sample application. Here, structuring is based on business objects, where two main packages are created: VEHICLE MANAGEMENT and CONTRACT MANAGEMENT.

The VEHICLE MANAGEMENT package contains two sub-packages for vehicle inventory and vehicle procurement processes. The CONTRACT MANAGEMENT package implements contract management functions and is based on the VEHICLE MANAGEMENT package. All packages may use a package with utilities.

Package splitting

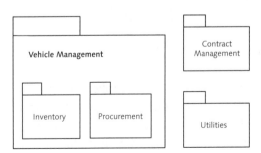

Figure 5.4 Package Structure of the Sample Application

The distribution of packages is based on the following product decisions:

▸ Vehicle Management is capable of running as an independent application.

▸ Contract Management, including the assignment options for vehicles, is based on Vehicle Management.

Contract Management is independent because it only represents the management of assignment options for vehicles. An independent vehicle scheduling application is not defined because it is conceptually integrated into round trip planning.

[+] **Analysis of Dependencies**

Individual sub-applications should be separated at the package hierarchy level within the overall application. This process requires an analysis of dependencies, which may be either one-sided or symmetrical.

Principle of information hiding

When you separate software modules (at the level of packages or classes), you must take into account the dependencies between the modules. In the case of our sample application, Vehicle Management is independent of Contract Management, but Contract Management depends on Vehicle Management. Therefore, the principle of information hiding must also be ensured: A vehicle is not aware of the existence of a contract, but a contract can access the properties of the assigned vehicles. There are several reasons why it does not make sense here to have a generally accessible Contract Management module (for example, the product design of the sample application, implementation costs, etc.). Therefore, a complete mutual decoupling is not required.

5.4   Package Concept

Following the general considerations regarding the application architecture, this section deals with the implementation of software structuring in ABAP. For this purpose, SAP has enhanced the concept of development classes with the package concept. We will now introduce you to this concept and discuss package checks, dependencies on SAP software components, and namespaces.

The basic properties of packages are as follows:

Package properties

- A development object can only be contained in one package.
- A package, on the other hand, may contain development objects or other packages.
- A package may not be directly contained in more than one other package.

The following package properties distinguish packages from development classes:

Package interfaces

- A package may specify various package interfaces, which define the visibility of package elements.
- All packages can be nested. To ensure improved structuring options, SAP introduced *main packages and structure packages*.

Use accesses

- You can define the visibility of package elements and restrict their use to certain packages via *use accesses*. You do this on the tab provided in Transaction SE21, or in the ABAP Workbench (see Figure 5.6).
- Unlike UML packages and Java packages, ABAP packages do not have their own namespace. As is the case for the names of development objects, package names must be unique. You do have to ensure that the packages in a namespace can only contain objects from that namespace. These aspects are discussed in more detail in Section 5.4.5, Excursion: Naming Conventions and Namespaces.

You create packages in Transaction SE21 or SPACKAGE (see Figure 5.5).

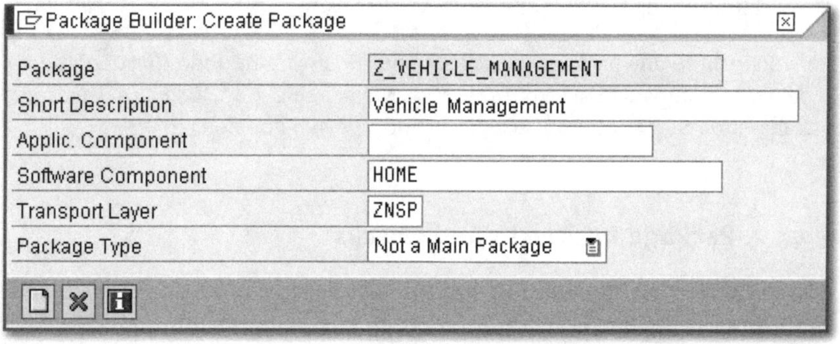
Package Builder: Create Package
Package
Z_VEHICLE_MANAGEMENT
Short Description
Vehicle Management
Applic. Component
Software Component
HOME
Transport Layer
ZNSP
Package Type
Not a Main Package

Figure 5.5 Creating Packages

Including packages This transaction lets you include existing packages in another package, as shown in Figure 5.6.

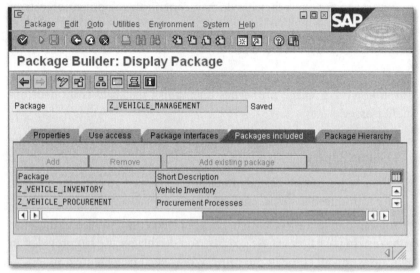

Figure 5.6 Including Packages in a Main Package

Both main and structure packages can contain other packages. You can also define a package type for each package. This determines whether there are any restrictions on the objects a package can contain. If a package can only contain descriptive objects, this means it can only contain ABAP Dictionary elements (such as domains, data elements, structures, search helps, table types or package interfaces).

[!] **Changes to the Package Hierarchy**

If you include one package in another and then want to undo this operation, follow the steps in SAP Note 636704. Never remove included packages in Transaction SE80 or SPACKAGE; if you do, they will be deleted.

5.4.1 Package Interfaces and Checks

Implementing the principle of information hiding The principle of information hiding has already been referred to several times in this chapter but how do you implement it in practice? You define package interfaces and create use accesses for these interfaces in the packages. You also perform package tests to identify any possible interface violations. This section discusses the following two check switches in detail:

▶ You can use a system-wide check switch to activate package checks and configure a mode.

▶ You can configure an additional check mode at the level of individual packages. Do you only want to ensure that you, as the user, define the required interfaces? Or, do you also want to commit the users of the services defined in the package to the interfaces you defined?

To define package interfaces for a package, create the interfaces in the Package Builder (see Figure 5.7). If you then navigate forward, data can be added to the interface. The simplest way to do this is using drag and drop in Transaction SE80.

Creating package interfaces

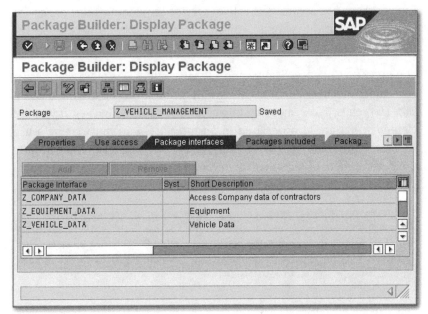

Figure 5.7 Defining Package Interfaces

Transaction SPACKAGE has a tab with the same name, where you can define user package restrictions for package interfaces. You can similarly define error responses to use accesses. In this way, you can, for example, make useful functions available to only certain packages such as those used exclusively for testing purposes during development.

The check for violations of the package interfaces in programs produces an error in the extended syntax check. A violation within the ABAP Dictionary results in an activation error, but the object can still be activated.

[!] **Activation Error When Interfaces are Violated**

To allow the user to decide whether activation errors should become warnings after confirmation, the user master must contain the S_DEVELOP authorization object with activity 94 (overwrite) in reference to the DEVC authorization field for the user's development class (and with the name of this development class as an object name).

Each package can assume the role of service provider (server) or service user (client). For our sample project, select the Package Check as Server setting (see Figure 5.8).

Check modes for different levels of strictness

The PACKAGE CHECK AS SERVER and PACKAGE CHECK AS CLIENT settings let you configure check modes with two different levels of strictness. With *loose check mode*, you can program across interfaces. However, if you use elements that are also declared in an interface, you must create a use access for this interface. With PACKAGE CHECK AS SERVER, you can only use development objects that are declared in the interface, and for which you have also created a use access.

RESTRICTED Check Mode

RESTRICTED check mode in the transparent table PAKPARAM increases the strictness of the checks described above. To activate RESTRICTED check mode, refer to SAP Note 792058.

You can display use accesses with the RS_PACKAGE_TREE report. This report makes it easy to display the packages, as well as user packages used for a specific package or for a set of packages.

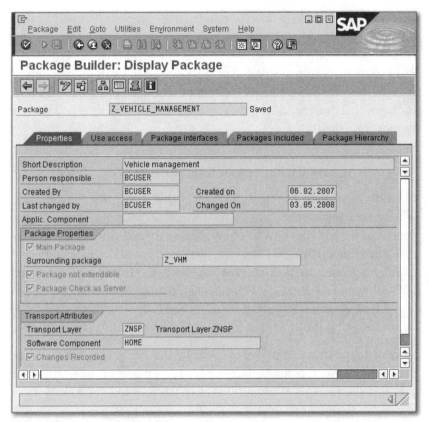

Figure 5.8 Package Check as Server

5.4.2 Visibility of Package Interfaces

In our sample application, the Z_VEHICLE_MANAGEMENT main package contains two sub-packages: Z_VEHICLE_INVENTORY and Z_VEHI-CLE_PROCUREMENT. If you want these packages to be visible outside of the main package, you must define new interfaces for the main package, and include the package interfaces from embedded packages.

Extending visibility

In this way, you "extend" the visibility of interfaces. If, on the other hand, you want to create use accesses for packages outside of the Z_VEHICLE_MANAGEMENT main package in the Z_VEHICLE_INVEN-TORY package, the main package must also have these use accesses, as well as the Z_VEHICLE_INVENTORY package.

The visibility of package interfaces is a "local property" of packages at the same package level. Nesting allows you to define packages that can only be used locally in a main package. If you want interfaces to be visible externally despite nesting, you must extend them from the point of view of the provider package. You might also need to include them in packages that "surround" the user package, so that package boundaries are not "breached".

5.4.3 Structure Packages and SAP Software Components

Structure packages

In addition to main packages, SAP has introduced structure packages, which may contain structure packages and main packages. Usage dependencies at the level of software components can be defined at the level of structure components. SAP delivers two structure packages with the AS ABAP: ABAP and BASIS. These correspond to the software components SAP_ABA and SAP_BASIS. When you analyze usage dependencies, BASIS is visible in all packages. ABA is based on BASIS and can use objects from both ABA and BASIS.

You can define structure packages to ensure that an application uses only these software components, but is not independent of other structure packages such as SAP_HR or APPL (the classic SAP ERP modules).

> **Software Components and Structure Packages**
>
> Recall at this point the difference between a software component and a package. A software component is a concept from software logistics. It contains a set of ABAP development elements (including packages) that belong together and can only be implemented usefully as a whole. A package, meanwhile, is a concept from software architecture, which structures development elements (hierarchically if necessary) and assigns them clearly defined package interfaces.

Figure 5.9 shows you how to create a structure package called Z_VHM and include the packages Z_CONTRACT_MANAGEMENT, Z_UTILITIES and Z_VEHICLE_MANAGEMENT in this new package. You do this after creating the packages in the Package Builder by clicking on Add existing package on the Packages included tab.

Package Builder: Create Package   ⊠

Package	Z_VHM
Short Description	Vehicle- and contract management
Applic. Component	
Software Component	HOME
Transport Layer	ZNSP
Package Type	Structure Package

Figure 5.9 Creating a Structure Package

Next, define use accesses for the SAP_ABA and SAP_BASIS software com-   Defining use
ponents by creating use accesses for the package interfaces of the ABA   accesses
and BASIS structure packages (see Figure 5.10). These use accesses must
be entered in all packages that use SAP_ABA and SAP_BASIS, not only in
structure packages. You can also define a specific error severity for a use
access. This value is set by default to No response, but you can change it
at any time to Error or Warning if you want the package check to determine which interface elements are used where.

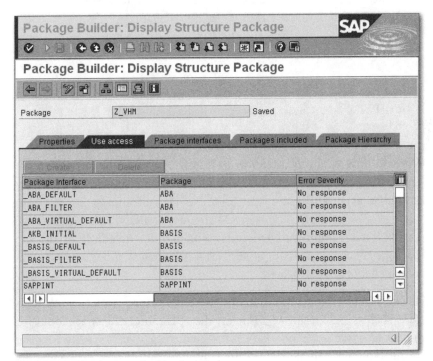

Figure 5.10 Use Accesses for Structure Packages

Error severity | You can use the error severity to display the use of interface elements with the Code Inspector (Transaction SCI). This can be used as part of the reengineering of an application system to gradually assign an increasing error severity to certain elements, until they are replaced with other functions. This procedure is described below:

1. Create use accesses (if they do not already exist) for a defined package interface.

2. Next, find the user packages with the RS_PACKAGE_TREE report.

3. In the packages you find, configure the error severity in the use accesses so that warnings, or even errors, will appear when the interface is used in the future. A code inspection then allows you to identify where you need to make changes.

4. If the elements of the interface that will be replaced are no longer used, before deleting the elements themselves, you can delete their use accesses. The replacement is then completed.

For a description of how the check works at the structure level, refer to the SAP Library under ABAP WORKBENCH: TOOLS • PACKAGE BUILDER. The check follows the package check described previously, and is only relevant for objects that are found in various structure packages.

Activating the Structure Package Check

SAP Note 648898 describes how to activate the R3ENTERPRISE check mode.

Interface types | We will now turn our attention to interface types, some of which are shown in Figure 5.10. An interface type is defined in the INTF transparent table, as an attribute of the interface. Default interfaces (for example, _ABA_DEFAULT or _ABK_DEFAULT) are queried first during the package check. If a development element is contained in a default interface, the package check is successful in R3ENTERPRISE check mode and no additional checks are performed.

If a default interface is not used, the check looks for a *virtual default interface*, such as _ABA_VIRTUAL_DEFAULT. If one is found, the check looks for a *filter interface* (such as _ABA_FILTER), which may only specify a subset of development elements. In this way, you can ensure that elements that are globally visible within the structure package are not released for external use. However, use accesses must be created for virtual default interfaces (as opposed to default interfaces) in the package hierarchy as a whole.

So, which interface types should you use? Note, first, that this problem often does not occur with the SAP structure packages, but rather depends on the package check mode you selected in the system:

▶ The MANDT data element is only contained in the _ABK_INITIAL default interface. You will have to include this interface if you select the R3ENTERPRISE check mode. As described earlier, a single use access at the top of the package hierarchy is sufficient. This also applies to the FIMA_DECIMAL_MONTHS_AND_YEARS function module – in this case you also need to use the _ABA_DEFAULT default interface. This interface usage is sufficient in the R3ENTERPRISE check mode. In this example, it is not helpful to use _ABA_VIRTUAL_DEFAULT and _ABA_FILTER.

R3ENTERPRISE package check mode

▶ In RESTRICTED package check mode, the use of structure package interfaces is not useful. However, the function module is contained in the FIMA_GEN_DEF interface and in the next-highest hierarchy of the FS_FIM_INTERFACE_MAIN interface. Both interfaces belong to packages with the package check as server, that is FS_FIM and the FIMA it contains (with functions for financial mathematics). The higher-level packages do not have these check properties. Accordingly, you must also use the FS_FIM_INTERFACE_MAIN package interface to avoid a package check error.

RESTRICTED package check mode

| **Structure package checks require structure packages** | **[!]** |

If you want to use structure package checks in R3ENTERPRISE mode, you must also include the packages of the application system in a structure package to ensure correct package results. If you define several structure packages and dependencies between these, you must also specify default interfaces, or virtual default interfaces and filter interfaces, for your own structure packages to avoid error messages when they are used.

5.4.4 Excursion: Compatibility Problems

Even though the package concept and the use of package interfaces are part of software structuring, they also indicate how compatibility prob-

Bad habits among ABAP developers

lems can be avoided. Many ABAP programmers have fallen into the bad habit of indiscriminately using data elements and function modules from the SAP standard components, even when there is no need to do so. This habit originated in conventional report programming in the SAP R/3 environment. With this type of programming, you simply search for a data element with the required type properties and use it in the source code.

▸ Because SAP R/3 is very stable, this often works—but this is not the case with other software components, such as SAP_ABA, SAP_BASIS or BBPCRM. AS ABAP has changed significantly in this regard in releases 6.10 to 7.0. If a package defines interfaces, the declared package components are preserved, but the same does not apply to other packages. Because even SAP consultants with experience in the SAP R/3 environment often mistakenly assume a certain level of stability in the SAP standard, some instructive examples are provided here as a caution against making this assumption. The BBPCRM software component contains the `BU_SYSUUID_C`, `BU_DATEFROM`, `BU_DATETO` and `WFM_BAS_LTEXT` data elements. Many developers do not heed the short text warnings against their use. As a result, programs contain activation errors after the software component is updated. SAP also deletes APIs marked as obsolete, for example, `BAPI_BUSINESS_PARTN_GET_DETAIL`.

▸ Just because an object is object-oriented and is therefore "new", it will not necessarily survive a release change. This is illustrated by the static attribute `CL_DB6_TOOL=>DIGITS`, which is misused by developers to test numeric content, even though—thematically speaking—it belongs to a completely different area (DB2 database connection). A local constant should be defined instead:

```
CONSTANTS: lc_digits type c length 10 VALUE '0123456789'.
```

▸ In the SAI package contained in SAP_BASIS, which is used for web development and SOA functions, major changes were made between Releases 6.20 and 7.0 while the interface remained constant. A proprietary development that only uses elements of the SAI package from package interfaces that SAP has specified as being "supported" avoids all of the release problems discussed in the previous sections.

Another irritating bad habit is the violation of interfaces through simple carelessness. For example, if a character field with eleven places is
required in an ABAP report, some programmers use the TEXT11 data
element, overlooking the fact that it originates in a package (SVER) with
SAP-internal verification code and is not released by an interface. This
results in unnecessary package errors during the package check.

[!]

> **Compatibility problems are often quality problems**
>
> If developers complain of compatibility problems, these should become the responsibility of the person in charge of quality on a development project. In most cases, the error is a result of the developer's methods, rather than of the SAP software. The same applies to problems with syntax errors after a release upgrade. In this case, a warning in the extended syntax check may become an error in the subsequent release. It is therefore advisable to take note of warnings that occur during activation, and to use tools such as the extended syntax check (Transaction SLIN) and the Code Inspector (Transaction SCI).
>
> If you limit yourself to using the package interfaces in the SAP standard components, there is a good chance that the functions used will continue to be available in future releases, but this is not guaranteed. By default, most interfaces have the attribute "not supported". SAP provides the following explanation in the SAP Library documentation: "Every element is assigned this value by default. This value reveals nothing about the future availability or compatibility of the element, which may remain unchanged for several releases, but which could become incompatible at any time. "

5.4.5 Excursion: Naming Conventions and Namespaces

In legacy applications, naming conventions are often the only means for software structuring. They can also be used for this purpose in SAP development. However, they were originally intended for a different purpose, and should be used first and foremost to keep SAP developments separate from customer developments to avoid naming conflicts in relation to development objects.

Avoiding these conflicts is essential to the coordination of large development projects where many packages are developed in different systems. You can use naming conventions for this purpose, as described here.

SAP solves the problem of naming conflicts with a global directory of object catalog entries. This type of repository could, in theory, be set up by implementing user exists for the development and transport system. However, this method is not suitable for large customer development projects, and is not discussed in this book.

You must be very clear about your objectives when defining naming conventions. A range of strategies are described here, all of which ensure that naming conflicts cannot occur in relation to development objects, even if these have been developed in different systems. To keep things simple, it is assumed that all objects were created in the same namespace:

▶ All objects in a subpackage have the same prefix, which is unique to the package. This allows you to move packages from one structure package (or software component) to another. The disadvantage of this naming convention is that it is very restrictive in that you cannot move a development object to another package. Packages can be moved into any other structure packages or systems at any time without the risk of naming conflicts.

▶ All objects in the subpackages of a main package have the same, unique prefix. This naming convention ensures that "neighboring" elements have similar names. Development objects can only be reassigned within the main package, and packages cannot be moved.

▶ All objects within a structure package or application component have the same prefix. In this case, an object can be assigned to another package within the structure package (application component), but cannot be moved to another structure package or application.

It is recommended that naming conventions should not be excessively restrictive. During development, it should be possible to reassign data elements between packages, and move packages within the hierarchy of a structure package. In most cases, if major software structuring errors were made, you only need to move a package from one structure package to another. If you follow the recommendation that basic technical components should be kept in a separate structure package, and if you use naming convention No. 3 from the previous list, you should not need to move structure packages. Instead, you can simply transport the structure package to other systems if the functions it contains are required there.

You need to apply for a separate prefix namespace for product developments, to exclude the possibility of naming conflicts in the customer namespace. For more information, refer to the SAP Library under SOFT-WARE LOGISTICS • CHANGE AND TRANSPORT SYSTEM.

5.5 Composition of Packages

A software system can be divided into classes and packages. This section describes how, conversely, classes can be flexibly combined into a software system. You can do this simply and transparently using defined package interfaces and use accesses.

It becomes more difficult if services are called that are only recognized at runtime, or if "loose couplings" exist. However, if an application has a modular design, specific challenges arise, which are described as follows, using our sample application:

Challenges

▶ If a vehicle is decommissioned, this affects assignment planning in Contract Management, which Vehicle Management knows nothing about. In this case, you require a message service.

▶ The design of the applications should be sufficiently flexible that various functions (such as search services) in Vehicle Management can also return data from other modules, such as Contract Management.

This type of flexible architecture may be an explicit requirement for the product but, in any case, it should be considered as a fundamental implementation method. It means that the product can be developed further, with customer developments, or by integrating third-party products, if necessary. Even if these kinds of functions are not envisioned in the first release, each product designer should consider whether the software will be a "monolith", or whether customers will be able to adapt it to their needs (for example, by using plug-ins to enhance functionality). Using object-oriented methods often allows you to implement flexible interfaces without much additional effort. On the other hand, major effort is required to subsequently configure flexible interfaces in an existing, poorly structured software system.

The following technical sections deal with services whose implementation cannot be detected and called until runtime, enhancements implemented with SAP BAdI technology, and Publish & Subscribe interfaces based on the event linkage function in SAP Workflow. We will demonstrate that object-oriented methods greatly simplify the creation of such interfaces and contribute to robustness.

5.5.1 Runtime Configuration of Software Components

Search service This section discusses the implementation of the following requirements: A general search service to search for and display vehicles will be developed for our sample application. The selection of search criteria should be sufficiently flexible that search criteria and search strategies exist for objects that are defined outside of the Z_VEHICLE_MANAGEMENT package and that are unknown in Vehicle Management.

The class structure and call of the search service are described first, followed by a discussion of the implementation details. Finally, this section identifies the strengths of object-oriented approaches.

Class Diagram and Calling the Search Service

This design problem is solved by defining a shared interface for search functions. Conceptually speaking, this means that all search functions are used the same way. Access is via a FIND( ) method, which receives an object with search criteria and returns a set of object references. The search strategy can be implemented in any package, and data outside of the visibility of the Z_VEHICLE_MANAGEMENT package can therefore be accessed. There are two strategies used in this example (see Figure 5.11). The first strategy searches only in the vehicle fleet, while the second can also access the assignment options in Contract Management.

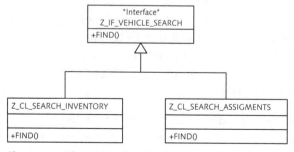

Figure 5.11 Shared Interface for Search Functions

Using Polymorphism

Polymorphism allows you to have various implementations of the same interface. In Customizing, you can control which implementation is selected, by encapsulating the instantiation of a class using a factory method and defining the name of the class to be instantiated in a Customizing table.

Figure 5.12 shows how the search service is called. The user or application program instantiates an object with search criteria and transfers this object to the search service, together with the search strategy. This generates a search object and, together with the search strategy, transfers it to the search service. This instantiates the search objects, transfers the search criteria, and returns the search results.

Calling the search service

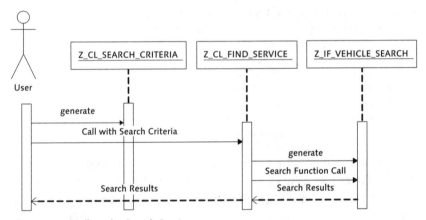

Figure 5.12 Calling the Search Service

The FIND( ) method is defined as static, which means it has no object memory. This is sufficient for our purposes here, but other options are also possible: A method saves information about the last search processes in the object so that it can, for example, return search results on a package basis. The interface is defined in Listing 5.1:

```
INTERFACE z_if_vehicle_search
  PUBLIC .
  CLASS-METHODS find
    IMPORTING
      iv_strategy TYPE z_search_strategy
      ir_criteria TYPE REF TO z_cl_search_criteria
```

163

```
  RETURNING
    value(rt_vehicles) TYPE z_tab_vehicle
  EXCEPTIONS
    z_cx_internal_error .
ENDINTERFACE.
```

Listing 5.1 Interface for a Search Function

Implementing a Search Service

Strategies The search service Z_CL_FIND_SERVICE operates with various strategies. The strategy determines a search object, which implements the Z_IF_VEHICLE_SEARCH interface. The implementing class is defined in a Customizing table called ZCSEARCH_SERVICE.

The Z_CL_FIND_SERVICE class is called by the FIND( ) method, for which an alias is defined to shorten the method name:

```
CALL METHOD z_cl_vehicle_search_service=>find
  EXPORTING
    iv_strategy = lv_strategy
    ir_criteria = lr_criteria
  receiving
    rt_vehicles = lt_vehicles.
```

You define the method as follows: First, the entry that corresponds to the search strategy is read from Customizing. The Customizing table is called ZCSEARCH_SERVICE, and its primary key is the search strategy. The search service implementation to which the call is delegated is in the CLASS field. The search service is thus called with the source code shown in Listing 5.2.

```
METHOD z_if_vehicle_search~find.
  DATA:
    ls_service TYPE          zcsearch_service,
    lr_error   TYPE REF TO cx_root.
* Determine implementation for transferred strategy
  CALL METHOD z_cl_tablebuffer=>facade_get_entry
    EXPORTING
      iv_key     = iv_strategy
      iv_tabname = 'ZCSEARCH_SERVICE'
    IMPORTING
```

```
      es_entry   = ls_service.

  TRY.
*     Call search service.
      CALL METHOD (ls_service-class)=>find
        EXPORTING
          iv_strategy = iv_strategy
          ir_criteria = ir_criteria
        RECEIVING
          rt_vehicles = rt_vehicles.
    CATCH cx_root INTO lr_error.
      RAISE EXCEPTION TYPE zcx_internal_error
        EXPORTING
          previous = lr_error.
  ENDTRY.

ENDMETHOD.
```

Listing 5.2 Implementing the Search Service

Here, the Z_CL_TABLEBUFFER=>FACADE_GET_ENTRY( ) method implements a generic access to a transparent table, i.e. ZSEARCH_SERVICE. It is advisable to create these kinds of auxiliary functions for accessing Customizing tables in each development project. They can also be enhanced with additional mixed strategies, which implement strategies such as "Override standard Customizing with customer Customizing," for example. In Chapter 7, Section 7.2, Table Maintenance and View Clusters, we explain how table maintenance is defined for this Customizing table.

The functions of the search object are defined by the interface construct. But could a base class be used instead? In principle, yes – however, the interface is a better option because it explicitly defines the methods a search function must implement. If you use and extend a base class, you need to determine whether these functions must also be redefined by the search objects.

Interface or base class?

However, it is also possible to define a base class in addition to the interface, where you specify basic functions that can be used by all search services. This approach is used to implement the search service in Chapter 6, Application Layer.

Superiority of Object-Oriented Methods

The example of the search service illustrates the advantages of object-oriented methods. How could the same problem be solved with conventional methods?

Solution based on conventional methods

First, you would need to be able to transfer the search criteria from the parameter string, which is an awkward procedure and not at all flexible (Chapter 6, Application Layer, provides details on the class containing the search criteria and on the search service). If interfaces were not used, the search functions would be implemented as function modules and defined in Customizing tables, for example. However, this presents the following difficulties:

▶ Without Customizing, you cannot tell which function modules are part of a search service and which aren't. When you use interfaces, however, you can determine the implementing classes using the where-used list in the ABAP Workbench directly.

▶ The search service can also be extended by giving the FIND( ) method an optional additional parameter, for example. A change to the interface results in a change to the implementing classes, even if they are defined in other applications, for example. The parameter strings of function modules do not have this flexibility. If a new parameter is added, a runtime error occurs when it is called. Admittedly, this runtime error can be caught, and an analysis of the parameter string at runtime will detect which parameters actually exist. However, this is laborious procedure that would have a negative impact on performance.

Scope of the interface

▶ Another problem with function modules is the scope of the interface. A search service may offer several methods, for example, methods that only return IDs, find additional information for quick display, or return results for a specific package. If you want to use conventional methods to achieve this, you need to use a range of function modules, all of which must be maintained in Customizing. Alternatively, you could enter main programs in Customizing and work dynamically with form routines, but this is an involved procedure. (If you require evidence of this, search for archiving classes in Transaction ACLA and analyze how these are integrated into the Development Kit.)

▶ It is even difficult to create the function modules in the first place because they can only be copied because of the constancy of the parameter string. Otherwise, you run the risk of runtime errors. However, when you copy a function module, the function module documentation (if it exists) is copied too. If you use function modules, you must therefore ensure that the copy templates have reliable documentation. The object-oriented approach provides a much better solution. In this case, you describe the method documentation in the interface, and you can display it directly by navigating forward from the implementation. Additional information can be created in the documentation for the implementing class.

Object-Oriented Constructs   [+]

The use of object-oriented constructs has a positive effect on transparency and enhanceability.

5.5.2 Using Enhancements to Implement Interfaces

The SAP enhancement concept can also be used to implement flexible interfaces. The procedure is as follows: First, define an interface. Then create a Business Add-In (BAdI) that permits one or more implementations. Some examples of scenarios in which the use of BAdIs is recommended are as follows:

▶ **Callback interfaces**   Sample scenarios
Here it is assumed that you are implementing a cross-sectional function (for example, the display of error messages or the generation of print output). These functions require additional information; this information, however, is only known to the calling application and was not transferred in the interface. In this case, implementing the callback as a BAdI is a handy way to solve the problem. The cross-sectional function does not require specific information about data elements, classes, or functional modules. Instead, these implementation details are hidden in the interface.

▶ **For SAP cross-system development of callback interfaces, BAdIs are virtually indispensable**
Some development landscapes have development systems in which cross-sectional functions were developed and transported in other

development systems for reuse. If these functions require callbacks that were implemented in other systems, conventional approaches (such as dynamic function module calls) are not sufficient. There are two reasons for this: the programs are not executable in the legacy system, and you must ensure that the calling function implements the same interface as the calling function.

- ▶ **Encapsulating a service to enable re-implementation**
  If you want to allow for a cross-sectional function (for example, the forwarding of print requests to an output management system), changing the external system may also necessitate additional access functions. In this case, all you need to do is re-implement the BAdI.

- ▶ **Providing for customer enhancements and navigational jumps to other applications**
  This approach replaces conventional user exits with a technology that provides for explicit interface definitions — filters and multiple implementations, for example. You can use this technology to provide jumps for other sub-applications at defined times.

New BAdI technology

An example of this last approach is described in the text that follows. The new BAdI technology in the AS ABAP 7.0 is used in this case. This technology replaces conventional BAdIs and has numerous advantages over these. For example, the selection of implementations with a new GET BADI ABAP command is integrated into the kernel, which improves performance significantly. You can configure BAdIs in the ABAP Workbench context menu under CREATE • ENHANCEMENT • ENHANCEMENT SPOT, as shown in Figure 5.13.

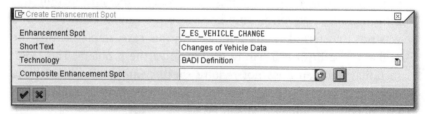

Figure 5.13 Creating an Enhancement Spot for a BAdI

You want to create a Z_BADI_VEHICLE_CHANGE BAdI for the enhancement spot, which will allow other applications to implement follow-on actions when a vehicle is changed or deleted (see Figure 5.14). Therefore, enable the MULTIPLE USE option for the BAdI.

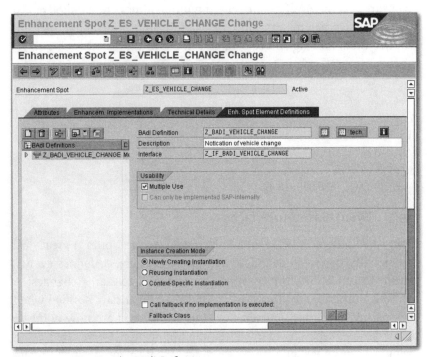

Figure 5.14 Creating the BAdI Definition

Select Z_IF_BADI_VEHICLE_CHANGE as the interface.

```
INTERFACE z_if_badi_vehicle_change
  PUBLIC .

  INTERFACES if_badi_interface .

  CLASS-METHODS notify_change
    IMPORTING iv_id TYPE z_vehicle_id .
  CLASS-METHODS notify_delete
    IMPORTING iv_id TYPE z_vehicle_id .
ENDINTERFACE.
```

The Z_IF_BADI_VEHICLE_CHANGE interface must comprise a tag interface called IF_BADI_INTERFACE so that you can use it in a BAdI. This makes

BAdI interfaces easily identifiable (for details of other uses of tag interfaces, refer to Chapter 6, Section 6.2.2, Technical Customizing).

To ensure that the BAdI can be reused multiple times, the methods must have no return parameters. However, CHANGING parameters are permitted. Use the following source code to call the BAdI:

```
DATA:
  lr_badi    TYPE REF TO z_badi_vehicle_change,
  lv_vehicle TYPE        z_vehicle_id.

GET BADI lr_badi.
CALL BADI lr_badi->notify_change
  EXPORTING
    iv_id = lv_vehicle.
```

5.5.3 Event-Based Interfaces

Event-based interfaces or *Publish & Subscribe interfaces* offer a great deal of flexibility thanks to complete decoupling. An object defines events, which, in our application example, correspond to status changes. A receiver "subscribes to" these events and is automatically notified when they occur. To see for yourself how this works, you are now going to define an event-based interface for the application we've used as an example in this book, and couple Contract Management to vehicle inventory. However, loose coupling hampers error handling because it is not possible to send confirmations to the application that reports the event. Therefore, we will begin by providing the details of this interface technology, before turning to the subject of managing the events and error handling strategies.

Implementing an Event-Based Interface

Event-based interfaces originated in SAP Business Workflow. In response to an event (such as the writing of a change document), a business process is started in which a user must execute a set of processing steps in a defined sequence.

ABAP Objects supports this concept with events. This form of event linkage is not suited to asynchronous processes or general, cross-mode scenarios. Two examples of this type of communication are as follows:

▸ You create business objects, use the familiar event linkage from SAP Business Workflow with conventional BOR events, and generate receiver function modules that trigger follow-up actions.

▸ You use ABAP Objects to define event coupling. This approach is recommended, even for syntactical reasons alone, because you must implement an interface method. The input and output parameters are defined, and you can find all implementing classes and interface types in the ABAP Workbench.

Implement the second variant and define an IDLE event for a vehicle, which is triggered when a vehicle is decommissioned. You can define type linkages for this event, that is, a receiver class that subscribes to this event for all instances of the sending class. When a vehicle is decommissioned, we want the resource assignment options in Contract Management to be invalidated. For this purpose, define a manager class called Z_CL_ASSIGNMENT for the assignment options defined by the BI_EVENT_HANDLER_STATIC interface. The ON_EVENT( ) method is called when the event is triggered. In our example, this method finds and invalidates all contracts to which the vehicle in question is assigned. The sequence diagram is shown in Figure 5.15.

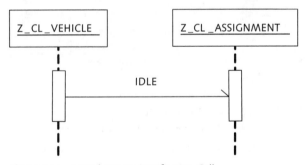

Figure 5.15 Asynchronous Notification Call

You define event linkages in Transaction SWETYPV, which is shown in Figure 5.16. The RECEIVER TYPE usually specifies a workflow that should be started. In this case, you can select any character string. You use the event queue, which has a positive effect on system load because events are slightly delayed but are delivered on a package basis.

Event linkage

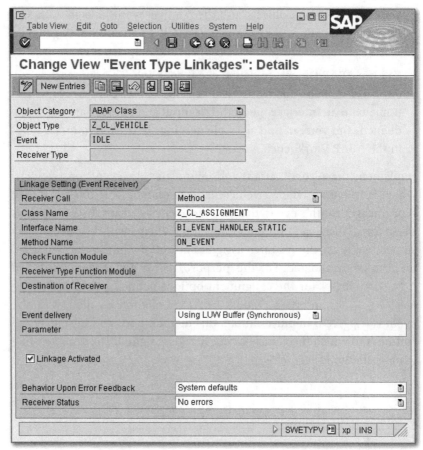

Figure 5.16 Creating an Event Linkage

In this case, the Z_CL_VEHICLE class must implement the IF_WORKFLOW interface and the Z_CL_ASSIGNMENT class must also implement the BI_EVENT_HANDLER_STATIC interface. You can use the following source code to trigger the event:

```
DATA:
  lv_objkey TYPE sibfinstid,
  lv_id     TYPE z_vehicle_id.

  lv_objkey = lv_id.
```

```
TRY.
    CALL METHOD cl_swf_evt_event=>raise
      EXPORTING
        im_objcateg = cl_swf_evt_event=>mc_objcateg_cl
        im_objtype  = 'Z_CL_VEHICLE'
        im_event    = 'IDLE'
        im_objkey   = lv_objkey.
  CATCH cx_swf_evt_invalid_objtype.
*   Execute error handling
  CATCH cx_swf_evt_invalid_event .
*   Execute error handling
ENDTRY.
```

Listing 5.3 Triggering a Workflow Event

Readers with eagle eyes will immediately detect the following weaknesses in this source code for triggering an event:

Weaknesses in the source code

▶ **No exception handling**
The CATCH blocks are not implemented, which means that possible exceptions of the CX_SWF_EVT_INVALID_OBJTYPE and CX_SWF_EVT_INVALID_EVENT classes are not handled. So, how should exceptions be handled? First, keep in mind that these errors can only occur if the Z_CL_VEHICLE class or IDLE event does not exist. However, this is only the case if the class was renamed, has an incorrect version, or was not delivered. You can check this statically, for example, by creating an ABAP unit test that triggers this type of event, or that statically checks whether it can be triggered. If this way you can ensure that the event is triggered, you don't need exception handling and you can simply cancel it with an ASSERT, for example.

▶ **No where-used list**
You cannot tell from this section of code that the Z_CL_VEHICLE class is used, because the name of the class is transferred as a character string. You can force this by creating a variable that refers to this class.

▶ **No error message from the event linkage**
The CL_SFW_EVT_EVENT=>RAISE( ) method does not return an error message from the event receiver. In part, this is because of the asynchronous nature of the event linkage. Note that this is the first prob-

173

lem we have encountered that does not have a simple solution; there-fore, event linkage—and the possible error scenarios—are discussed in detail in the following sections.

To receive the event, implement the `BI_EVENT_HANDLER_STATIC~ON_EVENT( )` method in the `Z_CL_ASSIGNMENT` class. In the application in our example, it is useful to find all assignment options of the decom-missioned vehicle, and then mark the assigned contracts as "to be re-planned". Additional parameters can also be passed to events in a con-tainer class. These methods are explained in the context of workflow development in Chapter 6.

The question of error handling becomes immediately relevant if you use the loose coupling of applications described here. Three factors play a role:

▸ The error message from the event receiver

▸ The type linkage settings

▸ The system settings for the error message

For event receivers, you can classify system errors as follows:

▸ **Type 1: A temporary error has occurred**
For example, the person responsible for a business object that needs to be updated has just locked it.

▸ **Type 2: A potential error occurs**
You want to perform an update but are unable to do so. In this case, it is possible that an assignment that should be deleted by the event receiver (for example, by the person responsible) was deleted by another process.

▸ **Type 3: An unexpected error has occurred**
A program or Customizing error has occurred, or the database reports a problem.

Type 1 errors are the easiest to handle. When these occur, the event needs to be re-delivered, but you do not need to assume that a type 2 error will occur also. The `CX_BO_TEMPORARY` class is provided for these temporary errors. For type 3 errors, use the `CX_BO_ERROR` exception class.

We will now demonstrate how errors that occur in relation to events are handled in the SAP standard components, and we will cover the tools provided before describing the error handling strategies used.

Administration and Monitoring Tools

If a temporary error occurs, you can specify in Transaction SWEQADM how the system should respond (see Figure 5.17). On the BASIC DATA tab, you can specify whether the event linkage should be deactivated in the event of an error (temporary or other error). On the ACTIVATION tab, you can specify how many repeated attempts should be made when a temporary error occurs.

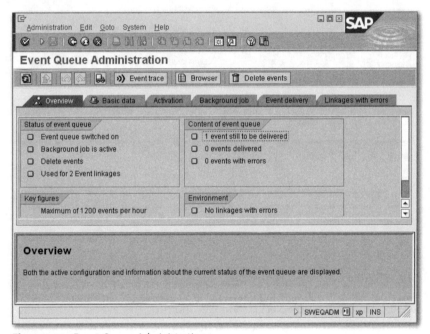

Figure 5.17 Event Queue Administration

The Event trace (Transaction SWEL) allows you to trace how an event of a certain object type was handled. In the example shown in Figure 5.18, there were two repeat attempts at delivery; a third attempt was followed by the response defined in Figure 5.16, that is, the default system

Event trace

settings were applied and the event linkage was deactivated. The event trace also shows which method of the event receiver was called. If the BI_EVENT_HANDLER_STATIC~ON_EVENT( ) method had not been implemented, this would not be shown in the trace, but the event would still have been executed.

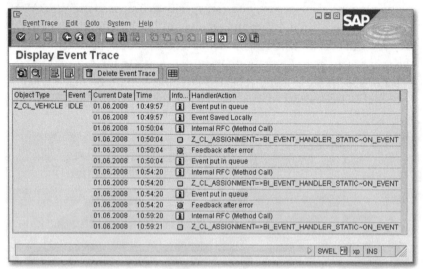

Figure 5.18 Event Trace

[+] **Event Trace in the Production System**

Typically, the event trace should be deactivated in the production system. It should be activated only temporarily to trace errors, because it has a negative impact on system load.

You can activate and deactivate the trace in Transaction SWELS, and select it in Transaction SWEL. You can monitor the events to be delivered in the event queue browser (Transaction SWEQBROWSER), which is shown in Figure 5.19.

[+] **Event Queue Browser**

The event queue browser allows you to re-deliver incorrect events and to navigate directly to the event trace. Both the event trace and the event queue browser are primarily tools for workflow administrators and developers.

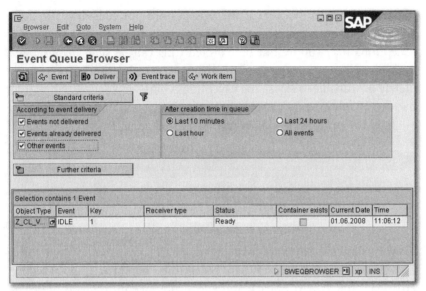

Figure 5.19 Event Queue Browser

Error Handling Strategies

How system errors are handled must also be taken into account in relation to software structuring. There are several reasons for this:

▶ Exceptions necessarily violate the principle of hidden information because they often reveal implementation details. You require a pragmatic strategy so that information about an error is revealed only if it is essential for the error to be neutralized by the calling layer. Neutralization means that the application system ensures that its status does not become inconsistent or unpredictable (where it could even begin to respond incorrectly).

▶ You need to define how this neutralization will be performed. A range of strategies can be used, the simplest of which are logging and termination of processing. However, more sophisticate responses are frequently required, including the following: retry for a temporary error, abandon a substep and continue with the remaining processing steps, and so on.

If you define these strategies, you must also specify a software model or layer in which error handling occurs.

Preprogrammed
disaster Experience has shown that if these issues are not considered in software structuring, a "preprogrammed" disaster is inevitable. For example,
exceptions may simply not be handled (this can be seen in programs
with empty `CATCH` statements) or the source code may become completely unreadable (because the exception is handled, logged, and passed
back and forth at every turn, with the result that you can no longer even
tell how the program responds when an error occurs).

[!]

Handling System Errors
Of course, the handling of system errors is the hardest source code to test in an application system. It is also the most poorly tested and has the lowest quality.

Even during the software structuring phase, you should give some
thought to how system errors are going to be handled. This is because
error handling is part of each and every interface in terms of the composition of the application system. This section discusses the relevant
considerations, based on the event-based interface of our sample application system.

First, it is important to consider that this interface is an asynchronous
interface for Contract Management, which should be flexible enough to
allow another application (for managing vehicle assignment options) to
be coupled to Vehicle Management. But this flexibility comes at a price:
Errors cannot be reported to the calling application, and an error concept
must be created for this type of interface.

Error types A distinction was already made in this section between temporary,
potential, and unexpected errors:

▶ **Temporary errors**
You can use a repetition mechanism to avoid temporary errors (such
as locks by SAP lock objects). You may need to specify in the event
linkage that an error must not result in deactivation (see Figure 5.16).
You must also set up the runtime system (Transaction SWEQADM)
with a sufficiently high number of repeat attempts at delivery.

▶ **Unexpected errors**
In online processes, unexpected errors can be reported to the person
responsible via an express message. In batch processes, you can log

the error in the Business Application Log, which is described in Chapter 9, Section 9.1, Implementing the Application Log. In this case, you must ensure that the Contract Management application has a function for validating assignment options, so that vehicles that are decommissioned are also deleted from the assignment options.

► **Potential errors**
In the case of potential errors, you need to investigate the error handling options and decide whether to ignore errors, or, as in the case of unexpected errors, log an error message as a warning. However, you always have to ensure that logging of this error type is possible during development and QA, and for the purpose of troubleshooting during production.

5.6 Best Practices

In this chapter, the basic considerations for software structuring were introduced, illustrated using our sample application, and, finally, implemented using the ABAP package concept. Package composition and specific interface technologies were then discussed. We will now evaluate these concepts and provide some practical tips. It is the *role of the software architect to develop a new application system*. A software architect is responsible for ensuring that the software is flexible enough to have the following properties:

Flexible architecture

► It can be integrated into the company-internal application landscape.

► It can be adjusted flexibly to suit customer requirements.

► It can be maintained.

► It offers sufficient scope for further development of the product.

5.6.1 Architecture Documentation

The structure of the software must be documented. A key objective in this regard is to ensure that developers can understand the architecture of the software structure. If this is not the case, you run the risk of the structure being damaged during development. The package hierarchy is usually visualized with a hierarchical display in box form, in which you need to specify whether a package can use all packages at the same or lower level. At the very bottom of the hierarchy, you need to specify the SAP Basis packages on which the application system is based.

This visualization can be supplemented by detailed representations, for example, in UML. UML has the elements package, component, and interface, which can be used to visualize interface usages.

However, it's not enough to document the architecture. You also need to guarantee that it is understood by the developers so that it is not subjected to distributed maintenance during development.

The software structure may need to be changed during development because the assumptions on which the architecture is based may subsequently change, or design decisions may prove to be unsustainable. In this scenario, it is essential that the new architecture also fulfills the original requirements.

[!] | **Rotten Software Architectures**

Many architectures begin to degenerate even during development. This is because developers understand neither the strengths and weaknesses of the architecture, nor the functional and non-functional requirements and quality goals that need to be achieved. Instead, the architecture is regarded as a source of guidelines that interfere—to varying degrees—with their work. If weaknesses are detected in the architecture and it needs to be improved, but is instead chock full of code, this marks the beginning of distributed maintenance. You can counteract this by documenting the cornerstones on which the architecture was originally based.

5.6.2 Characteristics of Package Splitting

The following requirements apply to package splitting:

- Packages should not be too large. Otherwise, you will be unable to decouple dependencies to a satisfactory degree.

- Package must not be too small either, because a large number of packages makes for an unwieldy system.

- Packages should have as few SAP basis component dependencies as possible. Otherwise, they will be unsuitable for reuse, and you will run an increased risk of needing to make adjustments after release changes.

▶ Ideally, all packages should be of similar size. Exceptions to this rule should be justified (for example, in the case of basic technical functions).

The *layer model* is a clear and simple structure concept that, in most cases, allows you to minimize dependencies. An added benefit of using this model is that, as a rule, it strictly regulates callback interfaces, which are frequently only supported in BAdI form. As a result, implementations are easily changed and package coupling is not too tight (as is the case, for example, with reciprocal function module calls). However, a layer model cannot replace package interfaces. This is because only package interfaces can effectively prevent a higher-level package from accessing lower-level packages.

Layer model

From a software technology perspective, cyclical usage of packages is always problematic because package are always coupled too tightly:

Cyclical usage of
packages

▶ Often, it is not possible to subsequently replace an individual package with another, re-implemented package.

▶ Complex error scenarios may occur as a result of chains of reciprocal calls.

The solution to cyclical dependencies is often to introduce a third package that provides both user packages with basic functions. This solution has the added benefit of facilitating re-implementations. As we saw in Section 5.4.5, Excursion: Naming Conventions and Namespaces, ABAP packages differ from Java packages in that they do not have their own namespaces. As a result, they cannot be fully replaced by another package if the development objects they container are used by the user package.

Shared Functionality Versus Cross-Sectional Functionality	**[+]**
If basic packages are used by other packages, the shared basic functions will also be used for cross-sectional functions. However, this results in dependencies that, at best, are encapsulated by technologies similar to BAdIs and, at worst, make usages impossible to control. You can avoid this problem by developing cross-sectional functions in separate packages, which then appear at the top of the usage hierarchy.	

However, the possibility of cyclical usages can never be completely removed. If a package uses a service from another package, this package may require additional information that is not available at the time of the call or could not be mapped adequately in the interface. In this scenario, a callback using a BAdI is often a practical solution. In some cases, you can use dynamic interface technologies, as was done in the example of the search service in Section 5.5.1, Runtime Configuration of Software Components.

5.6.3   Interface Design

Structuring begins with the division of an application into packages. The next step involves the software architect defining interfaces between the packages.

Risk   A major risk for software development projects is that the component structure will be violated by cross-sectional calls. In this case, the architectural concept degenerates in proportion to the degree of violation. Furthermore, the software can no longer be maintained and can only be enhanced at a significant cost, if at all. It is possible to recover from such an outcome if the planned life expectancy of the application system is just a few months, but not in the case of product development.

[+]   **Combating Architectural Degradation**

There are effective ways to combat architectural degradation. To prevent the creation of too many packages during development, you can specify that this is the exclusive task of the development lead. If you use package interfaces, and make regular use of the Code Inspector, you can be sure that unwanted dependencies within the application can be detected and eliminated.

If a package offers several services, it is useful to have a separate interface for each service because this makes it easier to monitor use of the services. It is therefore recommended that you provide functions for manipulating application objects in an interface, as well as an interface for reporting functions. If necessary, you should also provide an interface for development objects that are not released, which may only be used in specific packages with test functions released exclusively for these objects.

Package hierarchies allow you to "hide" subpackages by not passing the interfaces on to the transferred packages.

The package hierarchy and interface concept give rise to a natural composition of the modules in the application system. In some cases, however, you require other coupling mechanisms, such as BAdI interfaces. Never use these lightly just to avoid using package interfaces.

Composition of packages

A key consideration for the selection of a suitable interface technology is the handling of system errors. In the case of direct calls of functions in another package, exception handling is a suitable tool for neutralizing system errors. More flexible interface technologies come at a price. For example, the Publish & Subscribe interface described in Section 5.5.3, Event-Based Interfaces, decouples applications but hampers error reporting and monitoring. The same applies to BAdI interfaces, which permit multiple implementations, as illustrated in Section 5.5.2, Using Enhancements to Implement Interfaces. The only technologies that are flexible enough to be adapted to any neutralization strategy for system errors are the generic technologies that can be set up with only a little more effort, as in the example of the search service in Section 5.5.1, Runtime Configuration of Software Components.

Certain criteria must also be fulfilled for BAdI interfaces, as follows:

Criteria for BAdI interfaces

- ▶ BAdI interfaces should be used if the emphasis is on the possible replacement of an implementation. In the future, an external system connected in this way may be replaced by another.

- ▶ The process that calls a BAdI should also be executable with an empty BAdI implementation. The BAdI should therefore have the character of an "enhancement". Typical applications of BAdIs include a BAdI for finding additional data or calls of an autonomous subprocess.

5.6.4 Package Check Mode

If you activate the package check, error messages occur as soon as you violate package interfaces when using SAP standard components. You should therefore activate the package check switch as soon as possible and create use accesses for the required interfaces as part of development. Note that as soon as you do this, the use of SAP standard ABAP

Dictionary elements in your own ABAP Dictionary is subject to restrictions. As a rule, it does not make for good programming style to indiscriminately add elements of the SAP standard to your own ABAP Dictionary. In proprietary data types, you have a lot of freedom with regard to output characteristics, short and long texts, and F1 and F4 help. If you also use standard ABAP Dictionary elements in your own ABAP Dictionary without due consideration, you may save some implementation time in the short term but you also introduce risks for future release upgrades.

Define the
objective of
package checks

First, you need to decide what purpose the package checks should serve:

▶ If you want to structure the software in the application system, and restrict cross-sectional usages or make these transparent, the packages should use the PACKAGE CHECK AS SERVER option, and the package check switch should have the value RESTRICTED. However, you may also have to create use accesses for SAP standard packages.

▶ If you want to monitor the dependency of standard structure packages, the RESTRICTED setting is not sufficient. This is because, in many cases, no interfaces are created, or not all packages have the PACKAGE CHECK AS SERVER property. If you use R3ENTERPRISE mode instead, you can either add default interfaces in the package's use accesses, or virtual default and filter interfaces. In the first scenario, you can minimize the number of use accesses required. In the second, you need to create additional use accesses, which explicitly document the SAP standard dependencies. In both cases, you must create use accesses for the SAP standard package interfaces, starting at the top of the package hierarchy.

[!] **Creating Structure Packages**

If you want to use the R3ENTERPRISE package check mode, you must assign each of your packages to a structure package, as in the SAP standard. The package check will return incorrect results if you fail to do this.

Activating the package check switch has an effect on all customer applications in a development system. This means that new errors may occur in the extended syntax check in existing applications, although these do not prevent transport. However, activation errors may occur in ABAP Dictionary elements, which you can eliminate in most cases by creating use accesses. These postprocessing tasks can be performed after a release upgrade. With a release change, you should, as a rule, check whether some basic functions were obsolete and replaced with new ones, or whether you can expect this to occur during the next upgrade. You can check this quickly and easily by analyzing the package interfaces. This approach also allows you to detect any programming outside of existing APIs, and to determine whether changes are required.

5.6.5 Outlook

An enhancement of the package concept was announced for Release 7.1. Packages can now be *strongly encapsulated*. A package can therefore prevent the use of elements that were not defined in the interface, provided that the `abap/package_check` system parameter is activated. The check options are much more restrictive than in the previous package concept because the checks are also performed at runtime. It is therefore possible to monitor circumventions of interfaces, with, for example, dynamic calls or transient programs. You can even protect transparent tables containing sensitive data by only allowing them to be accessed via defined service interfaces.

Strong encapsulation

5.6.6 Key Transactions

The transactions shown in Table 5.1—for software structuring and to implement interfaces—were used in this chapter.

Transaction Code	Description
SCI	Code Inspector
SLIN	Extended syntax check
SPACKAGE	Package Builder
SWEQADM	Event queue administration
SWEQBROWSER	Event queue browser
SWETYPV	Definition of event type linkages

Table 5.1 Key Transaction Codes

185

"It is not the strongest of the species that survive, nor the most intelligent, but the most responsive to change." (Charles Darwin)

6 Application Layer

One of the biggest challenges in software development is to create software that is as flexible as possible. Enterprises must be able to modify business rules, or even entire business processes, to adapt them to new organizational or statutory circumstances.

Experience has shown that the first thing to be affected by these modifications is the application logic of a software system. Long-term changes to the ABAP Dictionary structure of master data or transaction data, on the other hand, can in many cases be completed only by the administrator, or as part of a migration or data integration project. For their part, business rules such as the classification criteria for customer creditworthiness, must be easily adaptable. In Section 5.3 (in Chapter 5), How To Structure a Software System, we already showed you that these processes are implemented in their own layer: the application layer. The focus of this chapter is on programming techniques for this layer. These techniques comprise the following:

- Implementing specialized logic in the application object
- Mapping business rules in Customizing
- Solving typical problems, such as search services
- Workflows

First, we will describe techniques for adding specialized logic to a persistent object that was created using, for example, the techniques described in Section 3.3 (in Chapter 3), Implementing Object Persistence. Next, we will look at how to structure the application system more flexibly in the context of Customizing. Here, we will again use the example of a search service developed in Section 5.5.1, Runtime Configuration of Software

Components. This chapter ends with a few comments on the process layer, and the development of a workflow using a simple resubmission scenario.

6.1 Application Logic

Implementing the application core is a developer's most difficult task, because this area shows whether he really understands and can implement the business processes and business rules.

Identifying and implementing application objects

One essential preliminary step in modular applications is to identify and implement appropriate application objects. In Chapter 3, Section 3.3, Implementing Object Persistence, you learned how to implement the persistence of an application object very quickly using Object Services.

The following functionality needs to be added to a persistent object to make it a business application object:

▶ **Business functions**
Special methods have to be implemented for the business logic of an application object.

▶ **Status management**
Several application objects have a status concept, which specifies the objects' lifecycle and processing status. You are sure to be familiar with statuses such as "Error reported" and "Processing error", or end statuses such as "Duplicate error reported" and "Error resolved" from typical bug-tracking applications. The application system can use status information messages to decide which application objects should be processed by the user or by automatic processes, and which objects have reached their final status and no longer need to be taken into account.

Finding duplicates

▶ **Comparison methods**
Objects need to be compared so that duplicates can be found. You may want to use the existing functionality in the SAP standard to do this (for example, see AVOIDING DUPLICATES in the SAP Library). In practice, it is usually easy to find similar data records by searching the

main key fields. However, detailed comparisons and automatic duplicate merging often require detailed comparison functions.

▶ **Validity check**
In many cases, it makes sense to implement certain minimum prerequisites for data quality and inspection methods because subsequent processes, for example, cannot take place without a minimum level of correctly-maintained attributes.

▶ **Object methods for workflows**
In Section 6.4.1, Sample Scenario: Resubmission on a Specific Date, you will use object methods for workflows. These methods provide the workflow information about the object and can also call processing transactions for the administrator.

Several years ago, it was common practice to directly include authorization checks in screen flow logic. With this approach, authorization checks were part of the dialog layer of the application in question. However, this meant that it was easy to bypass authorization checks and to manipulate business objects by calling function modules.

Authorization checks

Today, several different channels are used to access applications: the SAP GUI dialog, Web Dynpro, direct input, ALE/IDoc, BAPI, RFC, and Web services are just a few examples. All of these channels carry out the same authorization checks. Needless to say, it does not make sense to program them individually—and therefore redundantly—for each channel.

A better approach is to use authorization checks to protect all public specialized methods of a business object from unauthorized access. The authorizations are checked in the interface methods by the business object and application.

The authorization object protects the application and all of its transactions, reports, and services from unauthorized access. With every action the user executes, the system checks that the user is permitted to take this action. The profiles assigned to the user master record contain authorizations. Every authorization is a specific instance of an authorization object. An authorization object consists of up to 10 fields, which are used jointly in an authorization check. In every call, the application checks a specific combination of values against the authorizations contained in the user master record. The check is completed successfully if at least

Authorization object

one authorization in the master record satisfies the requirements of the request. For further information on this topic, see the *Identity Management* section in the SAP Library and the documentation for the AUTHOR-ITY-CHECK ABAP command.

Authorization Concept

Only rarely does an application manage to map all of its authorization checks using a single authorization object. The more typical approach is to create a small number of authorization objects with different authorization fields. You should consider the following questions when structuring authorization objects:

▶ How does the user describe the groups of people who should have specific authorizations?

▶ Will the activities that will be carried out be divided into different categories?

▶ How important will the regional and organizational assignment of users be?

▶ Are there different, clearly separate activity profiles, such as administration and reporting?

6.1.1   Implementing the Application Object

In Chapter 3, Section 3.3, you learned how to create persistent classes for application objects and thus how to implement database access. Now, how do you implement the more specialized application object methods? One option is to add them to the persistent object. However, this creates the problem of overly-extensive method interfaces. Because of the automatically-generated SET and GET methods, persistent objects already have an extensive method interface, and more methods are added by service functions for locking and identifying associated objects, and so on.

Single-step tasks   It is also possible to use interfaces to group additional methods; however, if you do this, you will have to create aliases for these methods. This is because what are known as single-step tasks in workflows (see Section 6.4.1, Sample Scenario: Resubmission on a Specific Date), which, for example, enable processing dialogs to be called, cannot use methods from interfaces.

Another alternative is to place persistent objects in a wrapper. This is explained in more detail below.

Wrapping a Persistent Class

A simple approach is to create a special ABAP class for the application object. This class contains the persistent class as a private attribute and the newly-created class delegates to the persistent class. The following methods are suitable for use as an interface:

Interface

▶ **CRUD methods**
CRUD functions are methods that manage the "Create, Read, Update, Delete" lifecycle. Most of the methods for creating and reading are static; the reading methods, for example, allow you to use search services.

▶ **Specialized methods**
An application object possesses a number of methods that can be called directly by the application layer. These could be methods to call processing dialogs for administrators, for example.

In the wrapped application object you can also implement event-based interfaces (see Section 5.5.3, Event-Based Interfaces), such as the BI_ EVENT_HANDLER_STATIC interface, or workflow integration, using the IF_ WORKFLOW interface (see Section 6.4.1).

This procedure is an alternative to the usual decorator pattern, which, for two reasons, is not recommended in this case. First, it uses a derivation of the persistent object, which in ABAP is possible only by means of a non-required persistent object. Second, with this object, all public methods of the persistent class would be accessible, which is not always desirable.

Alternative to the decorator pattern

Decorator Pattern

The *decorator pattern* is a design pattern that enables you to add functionalities to an object by enclosing it in another object known as a wrapper. To do this, insert a reference to a derived object into the object in question that redefines the methods of the base class. You then work with the derived class and, if necessary, delegate calls to the base class.

Creating Your Own Business Objects

At a very early stage, SAP defined business application objects as business objects (or *Business Object Repository (BOR) objects*) using the Business Object Builder (Transaction SWO1). This made it possible to implement Publish & Subscribe interfaces and workflow integration. Today, there are new techniques for doing this. You have already learned about how to implement event-based interfaces in Chapter 5, Section 5.5.3, Event-Based Interfaces. Workflow techniques are discussed in Section 6.4.1.

Weaknesses of business objects
Today, the goal is to avoid implementing too much functionality in business objects. The development environment (editor and debugger) is not convenient to use, and programming with it involves cumbersome macros that developers first have to learn.

Wrapping application objects in business objects is also cumbersome, because method calls and event consumption are different from the concepts implemented in ABAP objects.

Benefits
Nonetheless, there are good reasons for creating business objects:

▶ **Data model documentation**
Application objects are often complex and use combinations of objects and associations with other objects. You can identify these object networks with business objects and assign data models to them that you created with the Data Modeler (see Chapter 3, Section 3.2.1, Structured Entity Relationship Model).

▶ **Use of SAP standard APIs**
The SAP standard contains a wide range of interfaces you can modify for your own development work. One example is the interface IFARCH21, which can be used in conjunction with ArchiveLink. If you include this interface, you can use what are known as *generic object services* to display archived documents of an application object in SAP standard transactions.

Creating a BOR object
Business objects are created using Transaction SW01. When doing this, you have to specify the name of a program in which the application logic is implemented as a special include. The dialog shown in Figure 6.1 then opens. Here, you can select a sub-item such as KEY FIELDS and define

the business object key by clicking on Create ⌷F5⌷. You can include the IFARCH21 interface in the same way.

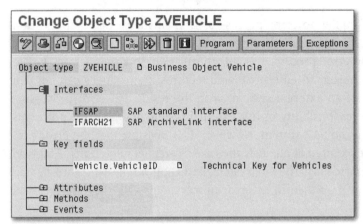

Figure 6.1 Business Object

You can now use function modules of the function group OPTD to store documents (such as images or PDF documents) with a business object. You may have to customize ArchiveLink to do this. After archiving, an entry is created for the business object in table TOA01, which lets you access the stored documents using appropriate APIs; however, this can be done for classic BOR objects only. For more information on document archiving, see the ARCHIVELINK (BC-SRV-ARL) • ARCHIVELINK section of the SAP Library. For more information on generic object services, see the GENERIC OBJECT SERVICES (BC-SRV-GBT) section of the SAP Library.

ArchiveLink integration

6.1.2 Separation of Object and Process

The lifecycle of an object can change if a new use case arises. Initially, in many cases, only one transaction is required to create or change an object. Later on, new use cases may arise – for example, the object may need to be used in a workflow, a processing step may need to be simulated, or correspondence may need to be created in the form of print processes that contain object data, and so on. You cannot and should not attempt to anticipate all of these use cases in your design and programming; simply keeping the various responsibilities separate will give you

the flexibility you require. If, for example, you implement print requirements that arise in a use case as independent objects, you may be able to
discard these in the process control stage, if necessary.

Error processes This also applies to error processes. If an instance of an application
object is changed, and a business rule is violated, it is often necessary
to start the error processes — this means that an administrator has to
check the object. In enterprise architectures, the changes can happen
by means of an external system, with the result that error processing
is also the responsibility of this external system and no error process is
required in the SAP system. However, it is possible that the error process is not required at all, as is the case in archive migrations. Archived
data is imported into the SAP system, and application objects are created
that are not processed in an error process – instead, they are archived
immediately.

These examples demonstrate that subsequent objects and subsequent
processes can arise in processing, and that it often makes sense not to
associate these too closely with the application object and to instead
implement an extra layer for process control. When you do this, how
subsequent objects and subsequent processes are handled is decided at a
high hierarchical level, instead of the objects and processes being created
individually at a lower level in the call hierarchy which causes knowledge of the subsequent process to be scattered throughout the code.

Separation of We recommend that you locate the application logic in its own service
objects and class, rather than overloading it with too much application logic. This
business rules service class then contains the implementation of the business rules;
that is, when a service object is regarded as consistent, when something
unusual is identified that needs to be checked by an administrator, and
so on. It is impossible to provide specific guidelines on which functionality should be located in one class or another. Nonetheless, the criterion
of cohesion – that is, the association of individual methods with each
object in question – is an orientation point for assigning functionalities
to classes. In this case, cohesion is meant in the sense of something that
is self-contained and functionally cohesive. In other words, a certain task
is completely implemented in a class. Conversely, all tasks in a class can
be assigned to the same thematic area.

For example, you may define that the application object has methods that allow only read and write access to its attributes and associated objects to ensure both persistence and the consistency of the object. The requirement for consistency can also comprise certain specialized checks that must be guaranteed as minimum requirements of the object. The tasks of the service class, meanwhile, are functions that go beyond the minimum:

- Checks of the currently valid business rules

Service class tasks

- Checks of attribute changes to an object that are different from the database, such as status changes to an object

After the responsibilities (functional scope) of each class have been clarified, the next step is to define the usage relationships between the classes. It is difficult to define general rules for this purpose; therefore, we will present two different scenarios.

Figure 6.2 illustrates the design decision that application object Z_CL_VEHI-CLE will contain the entire method interface for the specialized functions. These functions are moved to the service class Z_CL_VEHICLE_SERVICE.

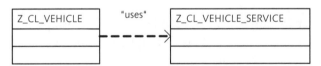

Figure 6.2 Application Object Delegates to Service Class

In this scenario, the application object delegates the specialized checks to the service class. You can then use this class as an external location — for the implementation of specialized processes, for example.

However, another scenario is also possible, as shown in Figure 6.3. In this alternative scenario, access to the service object can be obtained via the service class only. In this type of architecture, the service class takes over the management tasks and can provide proxy objects that function as proxies to represent the object in question, for example, in dialogs.

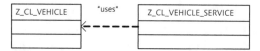

Figure 6.3 Service Class Delegates to Application Object

Pragmatic solution

We recommend a pragmatic solution: you should ensure in all cases that the portion of the content that is likely to undergo the most change is not too closely linked to the application object; instead, it should be configured flexibly. Customizing is one way of achieving this flexibility.

6.2 Customizing

Customizing makes application configuration possible. It does this by storing parameters, such as key values (possibly along with meta-information such as validity periods and Help texts), in transparent tables. This approach has the following benefits:

Benefits

- The application is transparent. A user or system consultant can always check which values have been maintained and are therefore permitted.

- The system is user-friendly. Thanks to foreign key relationships and search helps, input help (also known as F4 Help) can be implemented with a minimum amount of development work.

- The application can be maintained and adjusted. The provision of table content makes it possible to modify the behavior of the system. Likewise, customers can set up Customizing projects to adapt the system to their individual requirements.

A prerequisite for successful Customizing is that you are already familiar with Customizing tables at the ABAP Dictionary level and with the maintenance interfaces. In this section, we first present a few tips for using Customizing. We then take a look at a typical technical Customizing problem: the duplication of values defined as ABAP constants that also appear in Customizing tables. Last, we will use object-oriented techniques to illustrate a solution.

6.2.1 Basic Principles

One way of classifying Customizing is to look at the maintenance responsibilities: should the developer or the customer be able to modify table
content? That is why we speak of developer Customizing and customer
Customizing, depending on responsibility. It is also possible to classify
based on how frequently changes occur; if Customizing activities are
required only when the SAP system is installed, or when a major release
upgrade occurs, this is called initial Customizing.

What is the difference between Customizing and control parameters in
master data tables? The answer is: master data can be changed in production whereas because of unpredictable side-effects, it is not usually
possible to change Customizing in production. Every experienced SAP
consultant knows of examples where there is a gray area between Customizing on the one hand, and master data and processing parameters
on the other. Consider for example posting period locks in the SAP ERP
modules Financial Accounting (FI) and Controlling (CO). In special periods and at year-end closing, these have to be set and locked several times
a day – in many cases, it is simply too time-consuming to transport the
Customizing.

What are the reasons for allowing Customizing to be carried out only
by developers? One reason is the robustness (freedom from errors) of
the system. If the user has too many ways to modify the configuration,
the complexity of the application increases and so does the time and
effort required for testing and support. Also, there can be entries that
are essential for the correctness of a program and should on no account
be modified. Another reason for developer Customizing is the technical
nature of table entries. In Chapter 5, Section 5.5.1, Runtime Configuration of Software Components, we created names of development elements (to be more precise, ABAP classes) to implement flexible interface
strategies, thus ensuring that the decision which implementation of a
functionality is executed is made at runtime.

This separation of developer and customer Customizing is also reflected
in the table properties. Developer Customizing can be delivered in system tables that are unsuitable for customer Customizing, because certain
modifications are not permitted.

[+]

> **Customizing Access Layers**
>
> It is good practice to implement an extra software layer to enable the application to access Customizing tables and tables with control parameters, rather than allowing the application to do this directly. In this kind of module, the content of Customizing tables can be buffered in main memory. This has two advantages: improved speed, and a positive effect on the application system's software structure.

Multitenancy

In a development project, aside from categorizing the Customizing, you have to clarify whether the developer Customizing will be delivered in Customizing tables or system tables. The client dependency of the tables also needs to be specified. It is difficult to make general recommendations on these issues; nonetheless, what we do recommend is that you use client-specific Customizing tables. That way, the application is automatically client-capable. For example, a test client or a second production client can be set up with its own Customizing. Of course, the disadvantage of this flexibility is that the customer Customizing has to be adapted multiple times.

Basis component

Last, we also have to consider the case where the SAP application to be developed is itself a basis component used by other SAP applications. In this case, you have to ensure that name conflicts do not arise in the application-specific Customizing. For this purpose, SAP has created customer namespaces that start with a prefix. The sample application in this book is located in the "Z" namespace.

You can set up your own similar naming conventions and you can also explicitly store them in the ABAP Dictionary with table property E. It is likewise possible to include an additional application ID in the primary key of the Customizing table or to specify special naming conventions for Customizing entries.

6.2.2 Technical Customizing

Storing the names of classes or function modules in Customizing, as described in Chapter 5, Section 5.5.1 in the context of creating a search service, has one disadvantage: it is not possible to recognize which class names are permitted in the table maintenance process.

One way of creating transparency in this sense is to create search helps that simplify Customizing maintenance and make the application more transparent in general. Figure 6.4 shows a simple and pragmatic approach. An elementary search help provides classes that implement the Z_IF_VEHICLE_SEARCH interface. The transparent table, SEOMETAREL, is accessed for this purpose.

Elementary search help

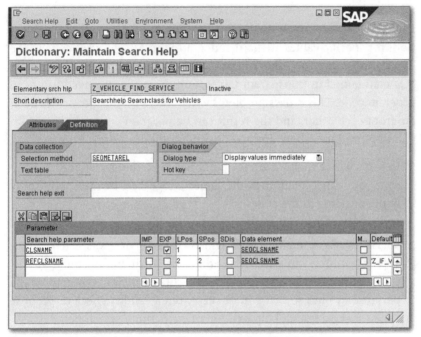

Figure 6.4 Search Help for Classes That Include a Specific Interface

In some cases, complicated validity checks are necessary. For example, it may not be enough to include an interface – you may also have to implement additional methods. Check routines will be necessary in such cases. In Chapter 7, Section 7.2, Table Maintenance Dialogs and View Clusters, you will see how maintenance dialogs are created and check functions included for Customizing purposes. Check reports, which carry out checks on the Customizing, are also a good alternative. These can be used by developers and also by consultants who are rolling out the application.

The example shows the benefits of using object-oriented constructs. To check the interface of a function module involves more time and effort.

An essential part of any set of rules is to define the permitted value quantities of data types for program-specific reactions to specific values. Ideally, the program is purely an interpreter of the Customizing and controls the program flow in accordance with the particular instance of the data type.

However, this ideal case is rarely reality. Often, queries and case distinctions for specific values are hard-coded into the ABAP source code in the application logic. The result of this is that the Customizing is duplicated: it is maintained in transparent tables, and there are also fixed values in program code. This causes problems when the two value quantities deviate from each other, and the result can be program errors that are difficult to reproduce. There are two possible solutions to this problem:

1. In cases where Customizing content has to be duplicated in the ABAP code, omit the creation of the tables altogether. Instead, work only with constants in the code.

2. Allow permitted values to be defined by constants in the code only. Specify in Customizing tables which of these values is active in the application. You can also define additional attributes for them. In this case, you have to be able to make available a function that returns the permitted values so that you can carry out a validity check or propose values using a search help exit for an elementary search help.

We will now develop a generic solution for the second option. In Chapter 4, Section 4.1.1, Defining Constants in Classes and Interfaces, you saw why it is preferable to use include programs to create constants in classes and interfaces. This approach also has another benefit: *run time type information* (RTTI) enables access to values determined this way. This means that you can define search helps for data elements that return precisely these values. You can also write check programs that check the content of Customizing tables against the values defined in class constants and interface constants.

An example of this method is shown in Listing 6.1. The code determines all public constants of the LVC_STYLE type of the CL_GUI_ALV_GRID_BASE class. For this purpose, it defines a l_typ_shlp type for the values you want to display in the search help. The values are returned by the Z_CL_ SHLP=>GET_VALUES_FROM_INTERFACE( ) method.

```
TYPES:
  BEGIN OF l_typ_shlp,
    value TYPE LVC_STYLE,
    text  TYPE string,
  END OF l_typ_shlp.

DATA:
  lv_datatype        TYPE          LVC_STYLE,
  lt_values          TYPE TABLE OF l_typ_shlp.

CONSTANTS:
  con_if_name type string VALUE 'CL_GUI_ALV_GRID_BASE'.

CALL METHOD z_cl_shlp=>get_shlp_from_interface
  EXPORTING
    IV_IF_NAME   = con_if_name
    iv_datatype  = lv_datatype
  CHANGING
    ct_datatype  = lt_values.
```

Listing 6.1 Implementing Constant Evaluation

Listing 6.2 shows how the Z_CL_SHLP=>GET_VALUES_FROM_INTERFACE( ) method is implemented.

```
METHOD get_shlp_from_interface.
  DATA:
    lr_descr     TYPE REF TO cl_abap_objectdescr,
    lr_datadescr TYPE REF TO cl_abap_datadescr,
    lv_dataname  TYPE        string,
    lv_attribute TYPE        abap_attrdescr,
    lv_key       TYPE        seocmpkey,
    lv_attrib    TYPE        vseoattrib,
    lr_data      TYPE REF TO data,
    lv_content   TYPE        string,
    lv_length    TYPE        i.

  FIELD-SYMBOLS:
    <fs_struc>   TYPE ANY,
```

```
       <fs_value>    TYPE simple,
       <fs_text>     TYPE ANY.

* Generate a work area for the return table
  CREATE DATA lr_data LIKE LINE OF  ct_datatype.
  ASSIGN lr_data->* TO <fs_struc>.

* Generate a RTTI object of the class/interface
* to be examined
  IF ir_object IS BOUND.
    lr_descr ?= cl_abap_typedescr=>describe_by_object_ref(
                ir_object ).
  ELSE.
    lr_descr ?=
      cl_abap_typedescr=>describe_by_name( iv_if_name ).
  ENDIF.

* Generate a RTTI object of the data type to be found
  lr_datadescr ?=
    cl_abap_datadescr=>describe_by_data( iv_datatype ).
* Determine name
  lv_dataname = lr_datadescr->get_relative_name( ).
* Delete return table
  CLEAR ct_datatype.

  IF lr_descr IS BOUND.
*   Loop at public constants
    LOOP AT lr_descr->attributes INTO lv_attribute
      WHERE visibility  = cl_abap_objectdescr=>public AND
            is_constant = abap_true.

*     Determine attribute properties
      lv_key-clsname = lr_descr->get_relative_name( ).
      lv_key-cmpname = lv_attribute-name.
      CALL FUNCTION 'SEO_ATTRIBUTE_GET'
        EXPORTING
          attkey    = lv_key
        IMPORTING
          attribute = lv_attrib.

*     Does the constant have the required type?
      IF lv_attrib-type = lv_dataname.
*       Copy constant text without apostrophe
```

```
      lv_length = STRLEN( lv_attrib-attvalue ).
      lv_length = lv_length - 2.
      MOVE lv_attrib-attvalue+lv_length(1) TO lv_content.
      ASSIGN COMPONENT 1 OF STRUCTURE <fs_struc>
        TO <fs_value>.
      <fs_value> = lv_content.
*     Copy short text
      ASSIGN COMPONENT 2 OF STRUCTURE <fs_struc>
        TO <fs_text>.
      IF <fs_text> IS ASSIGNED.
        <fs_text> = lv_attrib-descript.
      ENDIF.
      APPEND <fs_struc> TO ct_datatype.
    ENDIF.
  ENDLOOP.
  ENDIF.
ENDMETHOD.
```

Listing 6.2 Determining All Constants in a Class

This method has two optional parameters: `ir_object` as a reference to a class, and the `iv_if_name` string with the name of an interface or class whose attributes should be checked. In terms of a where-used list, it makes more sense to transfer a reference to a class. However, abstract classes and interfaces cannot be instantiated, while in other cases, instantiation is not desirable. RTTI techniques enable you to identify the description object `CL_ABAP_OBJECTDESCR`. You use this to identify all public constants of the same type, such as the transferred parameter `iv_datatype`. Once you have identified its value and the short text, you add both to the `ct_datatype` table.

Tag Interfaces   [+]

If you want to use interfaces for value quantities, it makes sense to use tag interfaces to identify these interfaces. Tag interfaces are empty interfaces that are used by other interfaces to uniquely identify themselves. One example is the interface `IF_SERIALIZABLE_OBJECT` in the SAP standard, which is used only to identify serializable objects and is evaluated only by the `CALL TRANSFORMATION` command. The benefits of the tag interface approach are twofold: it enables you to identify which interfaces correspond to constant Customizing content by means of the where-used list, and it allows you to explicitly identify them.

6.3 Search Services

Almost every business application uses search services for business objects. They are used in dialog functions and in the application logic, where a quantity of relevant objects must first be determined and evaluated before a specific function can be executed.

In Chapter 5, Section 5.4.1, Package Interfaces and Checks, you saw an example of a search service in which the implementation is determined at runtime. This means that a search can be run on the basis of search criteria known to another application that is only loosely associated with the fleet management application.

Problems with implementing search services

When implementing search services, you are always going to face several problems:

- How do you enable the application to support different search strategies?
- How do you create screens in which you can maintain selection options, and how do you include these in your application?
- How do you create database queries from the values entered?

The GUI programming aspects mentioned here are discussed in more detail in Chapter 7, Section 7.4, Object-Oriented Screen Programming, in the context of object-oriented screen programming using the BUS Screen Framework. Chapter 8, Section 8.2, Business Partner Extension, builds on this and develops these GUI programming aspects using the locator framework. However, you can still develop GUIs for search services in a pragmatic way, without these advanced techniques. In this section, we present search services for our sample application.

Dynamic selections

To do this, we use object-oriented encapsulation of what in the SAP standard is known as dynamic selections (function group SSEL), and which belongs to package SLDBV (selection criteria). The Z_CL_SEARCH_CRITE-RIA class helps you manage any quantity of RANGE OF selection parameters for any number of flat ABAP Dictionary structures. Also, the encapsulated function modules can be used to enable the user to dynamically maintain selection criteria for these ABAP Dictionary structures without the need to program graphical functions. This input screen is shown in Figure 6.5.

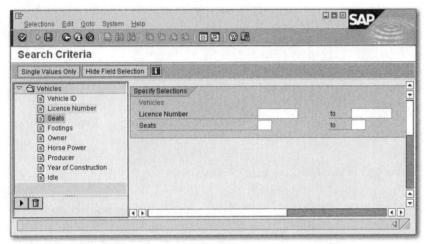

Figure 6.5 Dynamic Input of Selection Criteria

Create a Z_CL_SEARCH_CRITERIA class that encapsulates a quantity of search criteria. These criteria exist in the form of the private attribute mt_ranges of the RSDS_TRANGE type, which contains a set of generic RANGE parameters for components of a transferred, flat structure. You can use this object in your search service. Create the object with the search criteria using the factory method GUI_FREE_SELECT( ), which dynamically generates a selection screen for the transferred structure, enables the user to enter input in the form of selection parameters, and then encapsulates these in an object instance (see Listing 6.3).

```
DATA:
  lr_search_criteria TYPE REF TO z_cl_search_criteria,
  lt_vehicles        TYPE        z_tab_vehicle,
  lt_tables          TYPE        tttabname.

APPEND 'ZVEHICLE' TO lt_tables.

TRY.
    CALL METHOD z_cl_search_criteria=>gui_free_select
      EXPORTING
        i_tablenames    = lt_tables
        i_as_popup      = abap_false
```

```
        RECEIVING
          r_search_criteria = lr_search_criteria.
      IF lr_search_criteria IS BOUND.
        CALL METHOD z_cl_vehicle_search_service=>find
          EXPORTING
            iv_strategy = 'VEHICLE'
            ir_criteria = lr_search_criteria
          RECEIVING
            rt_vehicles = lt_vehicles.
      ENDIF.
    CATCH zcx_internal_error .
*     Handle errors
  ENDTRY.
```

Listing 6.3 Implementing the Search Service

Calling function
modules The gui_free_select( ) method dynamically creates a selection screen like the one shown in Figure 6.5, in which the function module FREE_SELECTIONS_DIALOG is called (see Listing 6.4). Calling function module FREE_SELECTIONS_INIT is a prerequisite for this.

```
METHOD gui_free_select.
  DATA:
    lt_sel_tables TYPE TABLE OF rsdstabs,
    ls_sel_tables TYPE            rsdstabs,
    lt_fields     TYPE TABLE OF rsdsfields,
    ls_dummy      TYPE            string,
    ls_msg        TYPE            scx_t100key,
    lv_title      TYPE            sytitle,
    lv_sel_id     TYPE            dynselid,
    lv_key_where  TYPE            rsds_twhere,
    lt_sel_range  TYPE            rsds_trange,
    lv_where      TYPE            rsds_where.
  FIELD-SYMBOLS:
    <fs_range> LIKE LINE OF lt_sel_range.

  LOOP AT i_tablenames INTO ls_sel_tables-prim_tab.
    APPEND ls_sel_tables TO lt_sel_tables.
  ENDLOOP.
* Initialize selection function
  CALL FUNCTION 'FREE_SELECTIONS_INIT'
    IMPORTING
      selection_id              = lv_sel_id
```

```
          where_clauses          = lv_key_where
          field_ranges           = lt_sel_range
       TABLES
          tables_tab             = lt_sel_tables
       EXCEPTIONS
          OTHERS                 = 20.

   IF sy-subrc = 0.
     IF lv_title IS INITIAL.
        lv_title = 'Search criteria'(001).
     ELSE.
        lv_title = i_title.
     ENDIF.
*    Show selection dialog
     CALL FUNCTION 'FREE_SELECTIONS_DIALOG'
        EXPORTING
          selection_id    = lv_sel_id
          title           = lv_title
          frame_text      = 'Limit selection'(002)
          as_window       = i_as_popup
          tree_visible    = space
          start_row       = 1
          start_col       = 1
          no_frame        = abap_true
        IMPORTING
          where_clauses   = lv_key_where
          field_ranges    = lt_sel_range
        TABLES
          fields_tab      = lt_fields
        EXCEPTIONS
          internal_error  = 1
          no_action       = 2
          selid_not_found = 3
          illegal_status  = 4
          OTHERS          = 5.

     CASE sy-subrc.
       WHEN 0.
*        Return input.
         CREATE OBJECT r_search_criteria
            EXPORTING i_ranges = lt_sel_range.
       WHEN 2.
*        Returning a non-initialized
```

```
*        object.
     WHEN OTHERS.
*        Execute system error handling
     ENDCASE.
   ELSE.
     RAISE EXCEPTION TYPE zcx_internal_error.
   ENDIF.
ENDMETHOD.
```

Listing 6.4 Object-Oriented Encapsulation of Dynamic Selection Criteria

Note that for reasons of clarity, in the code shown in Listing 6.4, not all EXCEPTIONS of the function modules are evaluated. In a production application, it makes sense to return the value sy-subrc in an exception. The current exception object contains an error test in a message class that, together with the return value, logs the name of the function module in an error message.

For these selection parameters service functions that contain WHERE clauses for SELECT statements are also provided. A search service such as the one presented in Chapter 5, Section 5.5.1 can use the search criteria managed in this way for either BAPI calls or direct database selections. You can implement this using the method shown in Listing 6.5.

```
METHOD get_condition_from_selection .
  DATA:
    lt_conditions TYPE rsds_twhere,
    lv_statement  TYPE STRING.

  FIELD-SYMBOLS:
    <fs_statements>  TYPE rsds_where.

* Build WHERE clauses
  CALL FUNCTION 'FREE_SELECTIONS_RANGE_2_WHERE'
    EXPORTING
      field_ranges  = mt_ranges
    IMPORTING
      where_clauses = lt_conditions.

  IF lt_conditions IS NOT INITIAL.
*    Find WHERE clause for required table
    READ TABLE lt_conditions with key tablename = i_tabname
```

```
      ASSIGNING <fs_statements>.
    IF sy-subrc = 0.
      rt_where = <fs_statements>-where_tab.
    ENDIF.
  ENDIF.
ENDMETHOD.
```

Listing 6.5 Dynamic WHERE Condition from Selection Criteria

The rows of the returned data `rsds_where_tab` can be used directly as a dynamic WHERE condition in a SELECT statement.

Because the `mt_ranges` (RSDS_TRANGE type) attribute of the Z_CL_SEARCH_ CRITERIA class encapsulates data types to which you can assign TYPE RANGE OF parameters defined in ABAP using MOVE-CORRESPONDING, methods can also be defined that you can use to set search criteria for a search service without a user dialog.

6.4   Workflows

A workflow is a range of activities required to complete a business process. These activities can be carried out by one or more end users. An example of the latter is authorization processes.

Workflows are especially useful when a series of transactions or programs has to be called to complete a business process that will process a defined set of business objects, or if you want to use an appointment management application. When workflows are used, the goal is to improve process management and transparency, and to shorten lead times.

Before we get started with the actual programming, let us take a look at the central technical components that are described in this section:

Central technical components

▶ **SAP Web Flow Engine**
The SAP Web Flow Engine contains definition tools and runtime tools for workflows. Over time, the distinction between SAP Business Workflow and SAP Web Flow has become obsolete, as the classic SAP workflow provides several interfaces that enable it to be easily integrated into Web scenarios. Thus, from SAP NetWeaver release 6.40 on, ABAP applications can be accessed in the SAP GUI for HTML,

using a Web browser. Also, the administrator's inbox (Transaction SWBP) is available as a universal worklist. The universal worklist is described in SAP Note 794439. It is integrated into the SAP Enterprise Portal and has a Java API. SAP Web Flow Engine also supports the Wf-XML standard and is thus suitable for cross-system collaborative workflow scenarios. In the SAP Library, the Web Flow Engine is described under SAP BUSINESS WORKFLOW • INTEGRATION WITH SAP BUSINESS WORKFLOW.

► **SAP Business Workplace**
The SAP Business Workplace (Transaction SBWP) is an integrated inbox for worklist and email documents. It provides automatic task grouping, a work item preview, and a task description function which is set for our sample application. The SAP Business Workplace contains several other functions, such as access to technical workflow data, and the workflow log. It also allows you to forward and resubmit an activity, access work item attachments, specify substitute rules via the menu path SETTINGS • WORKFLOW SETTINGS • MAINTAIN SUBSTITUTE/ACTIVATE SUBSTITUTE, and actively transfer substitutes via the menu item Transfer substitutes/End substitutes.

For more information on SAP Business Workplace, see BUSINESS COMMUNICATION SERVICES • BUSINESS WORKPLACE (BC-SRV-GBT) in the SAP Library.

► **Organizational management**
Organizational management maps the organizational structure of an enterprise. Even though this is normally done in an HR system, and the organizational data is then replicated to other production systems, organizational management is part of every SAP NetWeaver Application Server. You can maintain organizational units, positions, and links to personnel master records and user master records in Transaction PPOME. In workflow steps, you can use Transaction PFAC to define rules for agent determination. For more information on this topic, see the ORGANIZATIONAL MANAGEMENT (BC-BMT-OM) section of the SAP Library.

► **Single-step tasks as methods of business objects**
Among other things, workflows consist of a set of business activities known as single-step tasks. These are usually methods of application objects, which can be BOR objects or ABAP Objects classes.

In this section, you will develop a sample scenario with a particular focus on object-oriented workflow techniques. We will concentrate on the technical aspects of the SAP Business Workflow.

A workflow project has several other challenges, such as process model-ing, managing organizational risk, user assignment, and administrating the SAP Web Flow Engine. If you are not familiar with these aspects, aside from reading the sections of the SAP Library mentioned in this text, we also recommend that you read the specialist literature on the subject, such as *Practical Workflow for SAP* by Rickayzen, Dart, Brennecke and Schneider (SAP PRESS 2002).

Other challenges

6.4.1 Sample Scenario: Resubmission on a Specific Date

We will now create a simple workflow in our sample application. When you are working on a vehicle service contract, a date is calculated on which a request for the vehicle requirements planning to be executed appears in the inbox (Transaction SBWP). The functionality of the vehicle service contract is not significant for our purposes – it could involve exporting contract and order data to an external application, for exam-ple. In this section, we will look in detail at process management and scheduling, and demonstrate how you can implement these using the tools in SAP Business Workflow. Specifically, we will implement the fol-lowing functional requirements:

Simple workflow

- If the start date of the contractual service changes, the resubmission date should automatically change accordingly.

- If the contract is deleted, the work item also disappears from the user's inbox or is not displayed at all.

- If vehicle requirements planning is carried out, the corresponding work item disappears from the user's inbox or is not displayed at all.

To do this, you define a workflow as shown in Figure 6.6.

While this scenario uses only a fraction of the functions provided by SAP Business Workflow, it is still a useful one for learning purposes:

- **Routine tasks**
  Almost every application system has functions for resubmitting objects in a specific business process. In such cases, you should use

the workflow functions in the SAP standard to set up unified access for the user via the inbox. You can implement flexible absence and substitute rules by linking to the organizational management functions in this way.

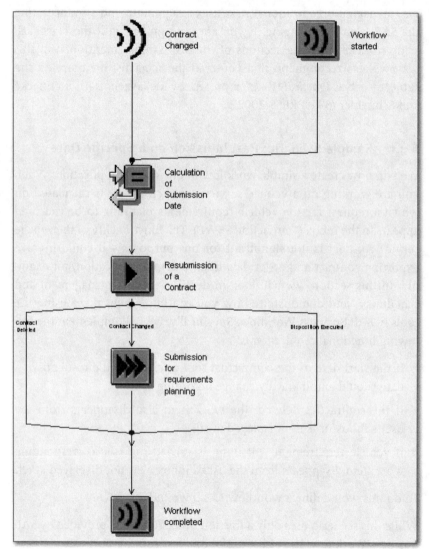

Figure 6.6 Workflow for Contract Submission for Materials Planning

▶ **Asynchronous event linkage**
You are already familiar with event linkage in the context of Publish & Subscribe interfaces from Chapter 5, Section 5.5.3, Event-Based Interfaces. In this section, we present other potential uses of event linkage. The benefit of event linkage is that the workflow does not have to evaluate any synchronous confirmation from the applications; also, it can react if the link to the application happens via a direct transaction call, for example, instead of in the workflow.

▶ **Use of object-oriented workflow techniques**
Conventional workflow programming uses objects of the SAP Business Repository – that is, BOR objects. In most cases, however, BOR programming has become obsolete. In Section 6.1.1, Implementing the Application Object, we already discussed the situations in which it makes sense to define a BOR object.

Using ABAP Classes in Workflows

Using ABAP Objects in workflows is the right choice for a number of reasons:

▶ **Better ABAP Workbench support**
The editor for creating and editing BOR objects is not very usable or convenient. ABAP Objects has better tool support – accessible via the Memory Inspector, for example (see Appendix A) – that you can use to analyze the memory usage of an object instance. Method calls of BOR objects cannot be tracked using the where-used list.

▶ **No specialized programming knowledge required**
BOR objects are accessed in the workflow using a range of special macros that do not belong to the ABAP language world and have to be learned separately.

▶ **Simple programming**
If you use persistent classes to develop your application object in ABAP Objects, you have a method interface. If you transfer this to your BOR object, double maintenance will be necessary, which is very time-consuming.

If you want to use application objects in workflows, include the IF_ WORKFLOW interface. This comprises the two interfaces BI_OBJECT and BI_

PERSISTENT. To properly use the application object in a workflow, you should implement the methods of this interface; the sections that follow show you an example of how to do this.

Local persistent object reference

Internally, the workflow uses a generic method for referencing objects: it uses the data element SIBFLPOR to store a local persistent object reference. This kind of structure has three components. The first is the TYPEID, which contains the object type – that is, the name of a business object or an ABAP class. The CATID component specifies whether an ABAP class ("CL") or a business object ("BO") is stored in the TYPEID field. Last, the INSTID field contains the object key. This field is 32 characters long and specifies an upper limit for the size of the object key or the primary key of the database table that represents the object.

To ensure that the workflow can instantiate an application object, implement the method BI_PERSISTENT~FIND_BY_LPOR( ) by evaluating the content of the component INSTID and loading the associated object of the persistent class ZCL_CONTRACT (see Listing 6.6).

```
METHOD bi_persistent~find_by_lpor.
  DATA:
    lv_id        TYPE          z_contract_id,
    lr_contract TYPE REF TO zcl_contract.

  lv_id = lpor-instid.

  TRY.
      lr_contract =
  zca_contract=>agent->get_persistent( i_id = lv_id ).
      result = lr_contract.
    CATCH cx_os_object_not_found .
      CLEAR result. "Work item contains errors
  ENDTRY.
ENDMETHOD.
```

Listing 6.6 Instantiating the Application Object in the Workflow

If the object cannot be loaded – because it has been deleted from the database, for example – you need to return an initial object reference that causes the workflow to terminate with an incorrect work item. In this kind of scenario, you can use the LOGPOINT statement to return a message about the cause of the error, for example.

The next method you have to implement returns the local persistent object reference. Because we have already explained the structure of the SIBFLPOR data element, this is easy to do:

Returning local persistent object reference

```
METHOD bi_persistent~lpor.
  result-instid = me->id.
  result-typeid = 'ZCL_CONTRACT'.
  result-catid  = 'CL'.
ENDMETHOD.
```

The BI_PERSISTENT~REFRESH( ) method stays empty when you implement it because you do not need any reload scenarios after instantiation:

```
METHOD bi_persistent~refresh.
ENDMETHOD.
```

Finally, implement the BI_OBJECT~DEFAULT_ATTRIBUTE_VALUE( ) method, which returns a preview text that is displayed in the workflow inbox:

Preview text

```
METHOD bi_object~default_attribute_value.
  TRY.
      DATA lv_id TYPE z_contract_id.
      lv_id = get_id( ).
      GET REFERENCE OF lv_id INTO result.
    CATCH cx_os_object_not_found .
*     Preview text cannot be displayed.
  ENDTRY.
ENDMETHOD.
```

> **Implementing the Preview in the Inbox "Lightly"**   **[+]**
>
> The preview in the inbox should be programmed "lightly". It must be possible to determine the preview texts while maintaining good performance. Otherwise, several inbox entries have to be displayed, which is very time-consuming and causes unacceptable wait times when users are working with the SAP Business Workplace.

Your preparations are now complete and you can call methods of the class ZCL_CONTRACT in the workflow.

Creating a Workflow Template

In the ABAP Workbench, create a workflow template called ZCON_SUBM using the menu path EDIT OBJECT • BUSINESS ENGINEERING • WORKFLOW TEMPLATE. Later, we will add the three workflow standard tasks shown in Figure 6.7.

After creating the workflow template, enter the description "Submission for requirements planning". In this screen, use the menu to select ADDITIONAL DATA • AGENT ASSIGNMENT • MAINTAIN. Use the AGENT ASSIGNMENT menu and the PROPERTIES button to set the workflow template to GENERAL TASK. This ensures that all SAP users can be agents. This is a practical approach for the purposes of our sample application; however, it may not always be realistic in a production application.

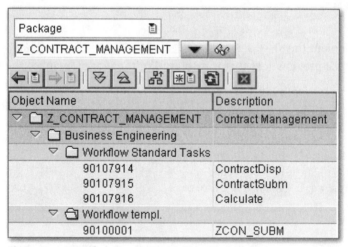

Figure 6.7 Workflow Template with Three Tasks

Workflow container

Next, open the CONTAINER tab title and define a workflow container. The container contains references to the object to be processed, the workflow itself, and local variables you can define. Use the CREATE button to create a container element called CONTRACT with the object type ABAP CLASS, and select the ABAP Objects class ZCL_CONTRACT as the object type. For the second workflow variable, create a container element called "Submission date" as an ABAP Dictionary reference with the structure SYST and the field "Date". Alternatively, select an ABAP DICTIONARY DATE data type. Both variables are now visible on the CONTAINER tab title as shown in Figure 6.8 and can be used in the workflow.

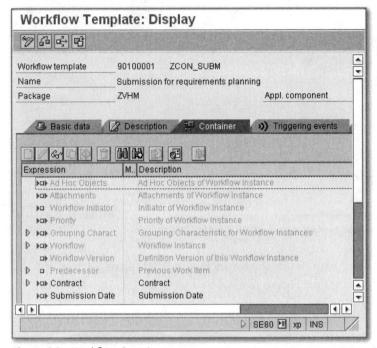

Figure 6.8 Workflow Container

Now, return to the BASIC DATA tab title and use the WORKFLOW BUILDER button to go to the application of the same name. Our goal here is to use the graphical editor to create the workflow shown in Figure 6.9.

First, the graphical editor opens an initial workflow consisting of the start of the workflow, an unspecified step, and the end of the workflow. Double-click on the unspecified step to open a window called SELECT STEP, in which you create a container operation, as shown in Figure 6.10. In this operation, you assign a value to the SUBMISSION DATE element of the workflow container by calling the `CALCULATE_SUBMISSION_DATE( )` method of the contract object.

Creating a container operation

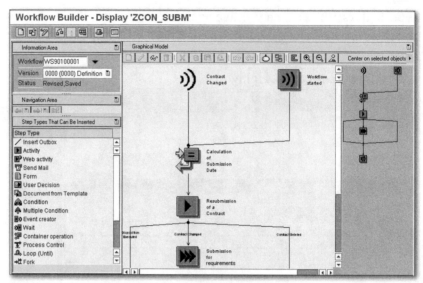

Figure 6.9 Creating a Workflow With the Workflow Builder

To create the expression shown in Figure 6.10, press F4 to open the relevant dialog (see Figure 6.11). Then click on the TRANSFER AND TO GRAPHIC button.

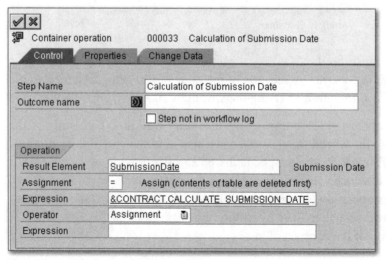

Figure 6.10 Calculation of Submission Date Using a Container Operation

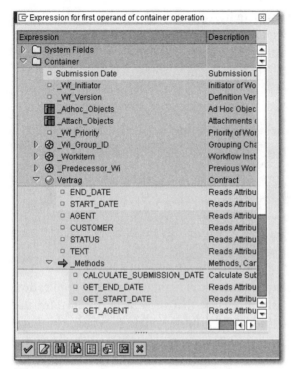

Figure 6.11 Selecting the Calculation Method

Next, use drag and drop to create an activity after the container operation, as shown in Figure 6.12. Select WORKFLOW INITIATOR as the agent for the workflow.

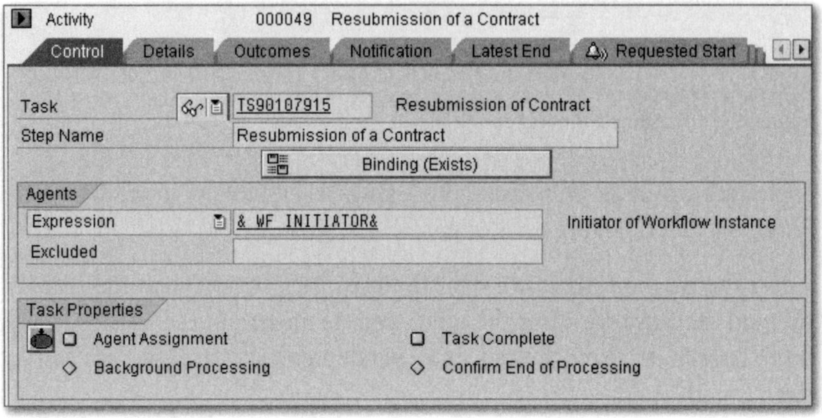

Figure 6.12 Creating an Activity

Submission date

To specify a start date for an activity, open the tab title REQUESTED START, and select the container element SUBMISSION DATE as the execution time (see Figure 6.13). Calculating the submission date in advance this way ensures that the single-step task is executed at the defined time.

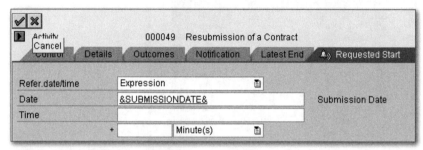

Figure 6.13 Defining a Start Date

We want the resubmission itself to call a method of the application object in a single-step task. To ensure that the object instance for the object ZCL_CONTRACT can also be used in the single-step task, you have to define a binding from the workflow container to the single-step task. You do this by clicking on the BINDING (EXISTS) button (see Figure 6.12) and specifying the binding as shown in Figure 6.14.

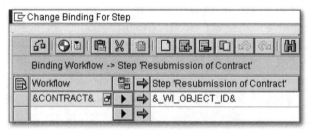

Figure 6.14 Defining a Binding to the Task

Creating a single-step task

Next, create a single-step task by selecting EXPRESSION • CREATE TASK. The dialog shown in Figure 6.15 opens.

Select the method DISPLAY( ) of the class ZCL_CONTRACT as the display method. Because we want the work item to appear in the agent's inbox on the start date, leave the execution parameter BACKGROUND PROCESSING deactivated.

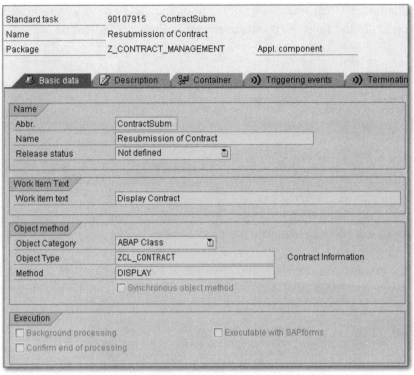

Figure 6.15 Creating a Standard Task With Asynchronous Object Method

You also leave the SYNCHRONOUS OBJECT METHOD option unchecked; this means that flow control is not returned to the workflow system after the method is called. The reason for not selecting the synchronous option is that the method to be executed in this case will also be called outside the workflow system. We want the workflow to react to a range of external events, and to proceed only once these events have taken place. This is the same object event-triggered event linkage we encountered in Chapter 5, Application Architecture, in the context of Publish & Subscribe interfaces.

Asynchronous method

The flow logic of the workflow was illustrated in Figure 6.6. Now, in the single-step task, you need to define a series of terminated events. If the event of the class ZCL_CONTRACT was changed or deleted (event CHANGED or DELETED), the workflow proceeds. This also applies to cases where the event DISPOSED is triggered; that is, cases where the vehicle requirements

Defining terminated events

planning process was carried out. You define these events as terminated events in the single-step task, as shown in Figure 6.16.

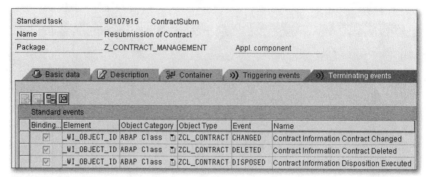

Figure 6.16 Defining Terminated Events of the Activity

Three outcomes If you now look at the activity for which you created the single-step task, you will see that three outcomes have been created (see Figure 6.17).

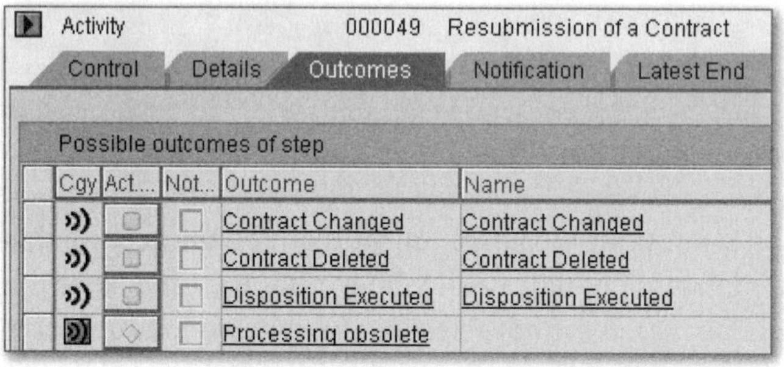

Figure 6.17 Outcomes of a Single-Step Task

Workflow calls itself You have now created the structure shown in Figure 6.18 using the Workflow Builder. You can identify the outcome that corresponds to each of the three asynchronous events. Next, use drag and drop to assign an activity to the CONTRACT CHANGED outcome, and select the task that corresponds to the workflow you just created (these kinds of tasks are also known as multistep tasks). It is in this way that the workflow recursively calls itself if the instance of the ZCL_CONTRACT class is changed. In such cases, a new resubmission date has to be determined, and the work item has to be re-created.

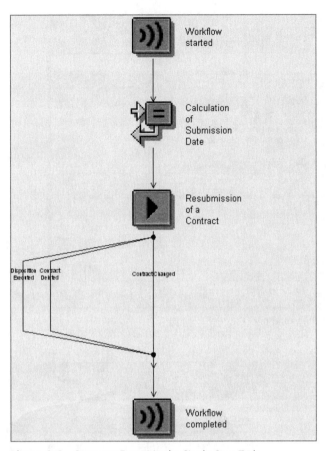

Workflow
started

Calculation
of
Submission
Date

Resubmission
of a
Contract

Disposition Contract
Executed Deleted

ContractChanged

Workflow
completed

Figure 6.18 Outcome Events in the Single-Step Task

You can now test the workflow using Transaction SWUS and, in this transaction, determine the content of the workflow container; in other words, create an instance of the class ZCL_CONTRACT, and a submission date, and use these to start the workflow, as shown in Figure 6.19.

Testing the workflow

If the submission date is correct, a work item appears in the inbox on the specified date. The inbox in Figure 6.20 shows the information on the task to be carried out, and the object to be processed. You can use Transaction SWU0 to simulate the events, and thus to test the processing of the asynchronous method.

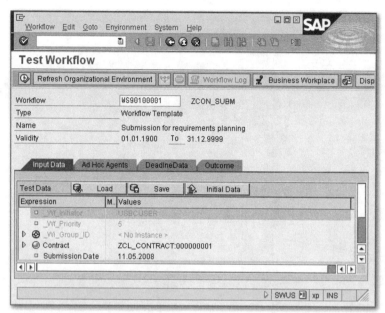

Figure 6.19 Testing the Workflow

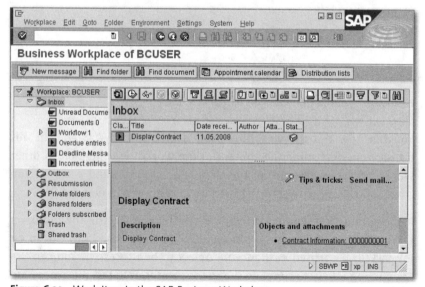

Figure 6.20 Work Item in the SAP Business Workplace

From the inbox, you can also access the workflow log (see Figure 6.21) **Workflow log** and see the recursive call structure.

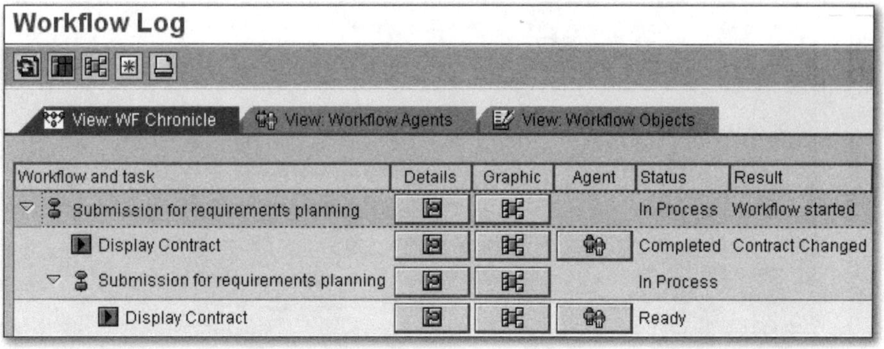

Figure 6.21 Recursive Call in the Workflow Log

As you know, workflows are started by means of events. Therefore we **Triggering event** create a new event SUBMITTED_FOR_PLANNING of the class ZCL_CONTRACT and define it as a triggering event. You do this on the tab title TRIGGERING EVENTS (see Figure 6.22).

Figure 6.22 Activating the Triggering Event

By doing so, you cause an event type linkage to be automatically created, as shown in Figure 6.23.

Figure 6.23 Event Type Linkage

Starting workflows
by means of events You saw in Section 5.5.3 how you can trigger events. Alternatively, you can use the function module SAP_WAPI_START_WORKFLOW. What is the benefit of using events? One is that events can be re-assigned if errors occur; another that the event queue has a positive effect on the system load. The most important reason for using events, however, is a principle we mentioned at the start of this chapter: the separation of application object and process. You can activate and deactivate this separation at any time using event linkage, and you can use Transaction SWETYPV to specify whether a workflow is started after an event.

6.4.2 Key Transactions

The transactions shown in Table 6.1 are used in the context of the SAP Business Workflow.

Transaction Code	Description
SBWP	SAP Business Workplace
SWDD	Workflow Builder
SWETYPV	Definition of event type linkages
SWI2_DEAD	Work items with monitored deadlines
SWI2_DURA	Work items by processing duration
SWI2_FREQ	Work items per task
SWI6	Display workflows for a business object
SWPR	Restart workflow after error
SWU0	Event Simulation
SWO1	Business Object Builder
SWUD	Workflow Diagnosis
SWUS	Test workflow
PPOME	Organization and Staffing

Table 6.1 Key Transaction Codes

"Radically simplify the user interface, reinvent it, enough face lifts! You can put as much lipstick on a chicken as you want; it's never going to look good!" (Philippe Kahn)

7 GUI Programming

The SAP system includes different technologies for creating graphical user interfaces (GUIs). They range from classic screens to controls such as the ALV grid, to modern technologies such as Business Server Pages (BSP) or Web Dynpro. Special technologies for displaying business graphics[1] also exist. From a software point of view, we believe that Web Dynpro is the most fully developed technology and it has the advantage that it only requires an Internet browser and can be integrated well into portal applications.

Does this mean that classic screen programming has become obsolete? The answer is no, because not all parts of the standard SAP system are available as web technology. Although most applications have SAP Business Partner as the central component, they also have many small dialogs such as the Business Application Log (see Section 9.1, Implementing the Application Log). For this reason, classic technologies like Web Dynpro ABAP or Custom Controls are also required when developing add-ons for the standard SAP system. These add-ons have comprehensive frameworks such as the *Business Data Toolset* (BDT), where you can add your own views, application logic, and data models to standard SAP applications without any modifications.

Is classic screen programming obsolete?

Even if you decide to develop an application using technologies such as Web Dynpro or BSP exclusively, we would advise you to use classic tools

Dialog standards

---

1 A sample dialog for the oldest and now obsolete technology is Transaction GRAL. A more modern technology is controls that are provided by the Internet Graphics Server (IGS) and can be integrated into screens. For more detailed information, see the SAP GRAPHICS (BC-FES-GRA) topic in the SAP Library.

to program the maintenance of your own Customizing tables, as well as enhancements of SAP Organizational Management. If you do so, you should adhere to tried and tested dialog standards.

This chapter first explains ergonomic standards in SAP programming, before it discusses problems of classic screen programming in detail. Using modern methods, you will learn how to design screens transparently, robustly, and so that they are easy to maintain. This chapter concludes with an introduction to Web Dynpro programming, where you will learn that modern SAP technologies are just as good as their predecessors. For example, Web Dynpro components can also be enhanced without modifications; however, in this case, the software is much more fully developed than BDT programming.

7.1 Ergonomic Examples and Dialog Standards

Consistency of user interfaces

One great strength of SAP applications is that there is a dialog standard that provides consistency. This helps users familiarize themselves quickly with new applications because they can transfer their knowledge about one application to another. Rules that cause functions to be executed in the same way in the entire application help to create a consistent user interface.

What does this mean, exactly? Users are familiar with a typical screen layout and know key settings, such as the F1 and F4 help buttons for input fields. They are also accustomed to working with the Business Workplace (Transaction SBWP) or using the Locator Framework.

We present a number of proven dialog types here and discuss how you can achieve consistency. Other topics include self-descriptiveness, error tolerance and suitability for individualization.

7.1.1 SAP R/3 Style Guide

Whoever works as a developer in the SAP environment and has, as a result, learned about specialist applications in addition to the development environment is familiar with the look and feel of the standard SAP system. Fortunately, other more explicit sources are also available. The *SAP R/3 Style Guide* is a comprehensive document that explains in numerous examples in more than 200 pages how you should design user interfaces in the SAP system to ensure that they are easy to understand, user-friendly and consistent.

The Style Guide covers all topics you should be aware of when designing user interfaces in the SAP system. These range from screen layout and function key settings, to the exact semantics of functions such as *Back*, *End*, *Cancel*, to best practices for using terminology. This makes the Style Guide essential reading material for dialog programmers and designers. In particular, the document contains guidelines for modern screen design, in which not static sequences of dialogs but intricately structured screens with several areas are used. The Style Guide is available in the section R/3 / ERP OUTDATED – MOST RECENT VERSION at *http://www.sap-designguild.org/*.

Screen layout and function key settings

7.1.2 Ergonomic Examples

Another valuable source of information is directly integrated into the development environment and can be accessed in the ABAP Editor using the menu path ENVIRONMENT • EXAMPLES • ERGONOMIC EXAMPLES • SCREENS (or Transaction code BIBS). The ergonomic examples are not as up-to-date as the recommendations of the *Style Guide*; however, they do contain a lot of important information in compressed form, as shown in Figure 7.1 and Figure 7.2.

For each topic, we provide some dos and don'ts as well as tips that make the ergonomic examples a quickly available reference with high usage value. Here, you will also find control programming examples that demonstrate the use of modern design elements from a programming perspective (more so than from an ergonomic perspective).

Control programming examples

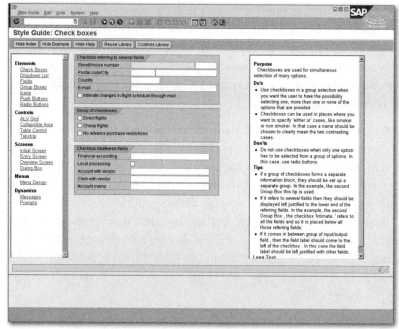

Figure 7.1 ABAP Ergonomic Example for Checkboxes

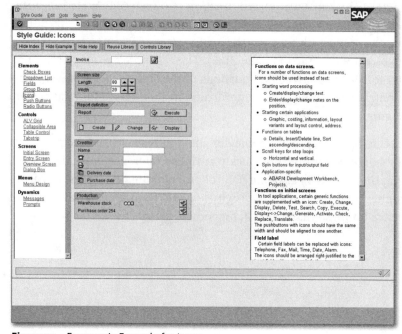

Figure 7.2 Ergonomic Example for Icons

7.1.3 Menu Standards

The system has standards for designing menu bars and other subobjects of an interface status that can be transferred as a template when you create a new menu. Function key settings, shortcuts, and texts for frequently-used functions also have standards that you should adopt as much as possible to make orientation easier for users. The standard settings are available in the *Menu Painter* under UTILITIES • HELP TEXTS • STANDARDS/PROPOSALS.

Interface status

7.1.4 Screen Layout and User Guide

We will use an example to illustrate a few standards for screen layouts and user guides. We have selected *SAP Business Partner* for this purpose, because this is part of the application basis and is available in every system type, including mini-SAP systems. You access SAP Business Partner using Transaction code BP.

Object Selection

The initial screen (see Figure 7.3) shows how you can design object selection in an application. Here, the user selects the object to be edited – in this case, a business partner. The *Locator*, which allows you to enter search criteria, is on the left of the screen. The user can select which fields he wants to use to conduct a search from a list of available search strategies. The objects found are displayed in a results table in the lower screen area and can be selected by clicking on them. A list of the last objects edited, or of objects selected as favorites, is also available.

Locator

Alternatively, you can enter a business partner number directly into the header area. This function is supported by a comprehensive F4 search help with several included search helps that provide different search fields. The search help for the business partner is shown in Figure 7.4.

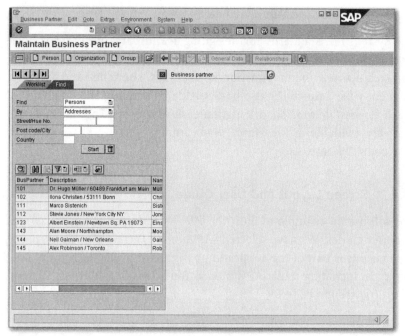

Figure 7.3 Initial Screen with Locator and Search Results

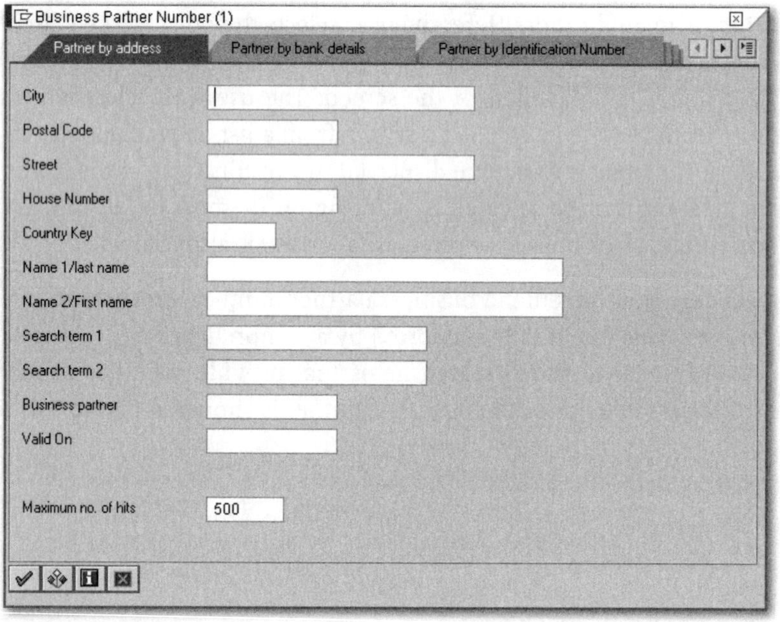

Figure 7.4 Search Help for Selecting a Business Partner

Displaying and Editing Objects

Unlike with older applications, the object editing of modern standard applications such as SAP Business Partner does not use separate screens for the *Create, Display* and *Enter* editing modes. Instead, it is always the same screen, and the different editing modes have different ready-for-input fields and different available functions.

No separate screens for editing modes

You can use the CREATE and SWITCH BETWEEN DISPLAY AND CHANGE MODES functions (see Figure 7.5) to change from one editing mode to another at any time without selecting an object again.

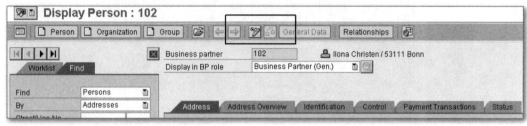

Figure 7.5 Icon for Changing the Editing Mode

Tabstrips

A business object frequently contains more data fields than can fit on a screen. This is also the case with the business partner object. Static dialog sequences were previously used in such cases, whereby the user was guided from screen to screen and could change between the screens using the NEXT SCREEN/PREVIOUS SCREEN functions, as well as the menu.

Previously: static dialog sequences

In newer applications, you typically work with tabstrips, provided the data to be placed on the tabs can be entered and checked independently. This means that you can have all data for a complex business object or business process available within one screen (see Figure 7.6).

Icons

Icons are a powerful design tool you can use to make application transactions intuitively accessible. From the Windows world, users will already be familiar with numerous standard SAP system icons, while other icons have a meaning that is valid across applications in the SAP world.

235

Some icons belong exclusively to specific applications such as Human Resources Management, SAP NetWeaver BI or the Workflow, and must not be used in other contexts.

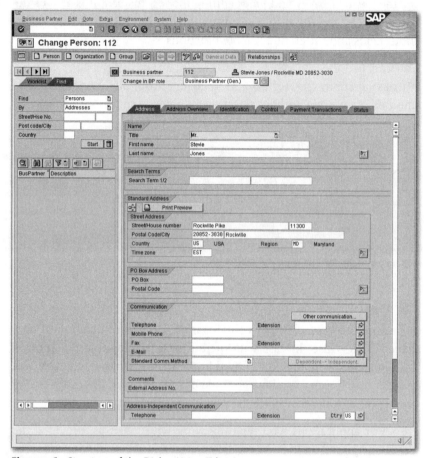

Figure 7.6 Structure of the Dialog Using Tabstrips

False friends   When icons are selected for a new application, particular care needs to be taken to avoid the effect of "false friends". *False friends* are icons the user is familiar with, but that end up having semantics that differ from the semantics expected by the user. These types of faux pas when designing the user interface can lead to users being mistrustful of your application.

The icons available in the system are assigned to different classes that describe their application area:

Classes

▶ The *general icons* class contains generic, frequently-used icons for standard functions, such as Copy, Next Screen, Approve, Information, and so on.

▶ The *special icons* class contains icons that are generally available for specific functions that are not used very often (for example, adding a relationship, unfreezing columns, and transferring goods).

▶ *Other icon classes* contain icons that must only be used in the development environment, icons for special applications such as Workflow or Human Resources Management, specific icons for SAP industry solutions, and icons for GUI system functions.

You will find the latest, publically available version of the *SAP R/3 Icons* guide under Resources • Archive • Visual Design • SAP R/3 Icons in the resource area of the SAP Design Guild (see *http://www.sapdesignguild.org*). In addition to the complete taxonomy of icons, each icon is listed in this guide with a short text, function description, and allowed usage as a button, function, status, or text field.

SAP R/3 icons

Collapsible Data Areas

Another technique to display a lot of information in a single dialog is using collapsible and expandable data areas, as shown in Figure 7.7 and Figure 7.8. A standard icon signifies that a data area contains additional fields that you can display if required. When you click on the icon, the data area expands. You use another icon to collapse the area. The normal scenario is for non-empty fields to always be displayed; however, in individual cases a different design decision may also make sense.

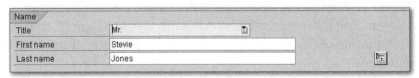

Figure 7.7 Collapsible Data Area in Collapsed State

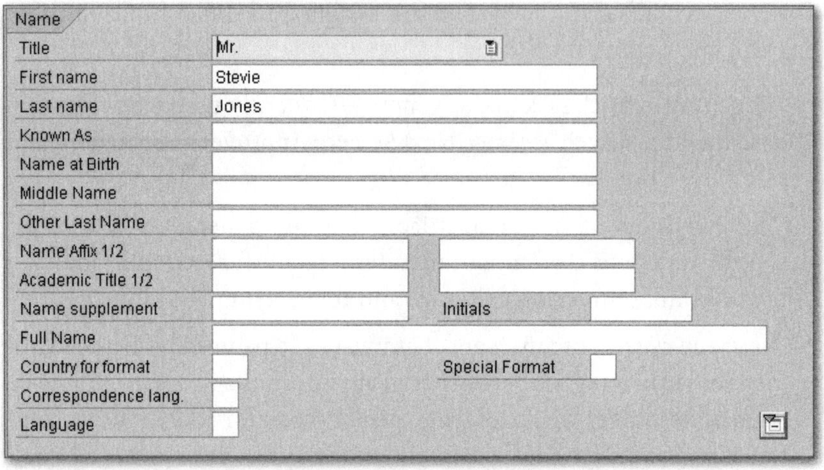

Figure 7.8 The Same Data Area as in Figure 7.7, Expanded

7.2 Table Maintenance Dialog and View Cluster

Minimum effort To maintain Customizing and basic master and transaction data, you can use generated table maintenance dialogs and view clusters because you can create them with minimum effort. They also support numerous functions such as setting locks, rejecting changes, automatic positioning, as well as connections to the transport system for Customizing tables. In this section, you will learn how to create maintenance views, how to add your own functions to them, and how to call them.

Example You create a transparent table called ZTDCLASS that contains time-dependent application classes for a class (we are referring to business objects here) and these classes contain, for example, certain specialized checks. The principle of encapsulating specialized checks in separate classes and determining the implementation at runtime was discussed in detail in Chapter 6, Application Layer. You will now learn how to generate a user interface for this purpose, which is displayed in Figure 7.9. This type of dialog can be a component of the developer Customizing for an application.

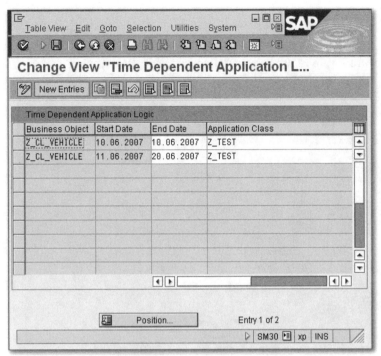

Figure 7.9 Table Maintenance

However, this situation also illustrates a problem: If you want to manage time-dependent implementations, you will also want to exclude inconsistent entries, to prevent two implementations or no implementation at all to be active at a given time.

Excluding inconsistent entries

The next section deals with generating table maintenance dialogs and how to enhance them.

7.2.1 Generating and Enhancing Table Maintenance Dialogs

You will now create a maintenance view for a ZTDCLASS table in the ABAP Workbench. Start by selecting UTILITIES • TABLE MAINTENANCE GENERATOR. Alternatively, you can use Transaction SE55, as shown in Figure 7.10.

Creating a maintenance view

239

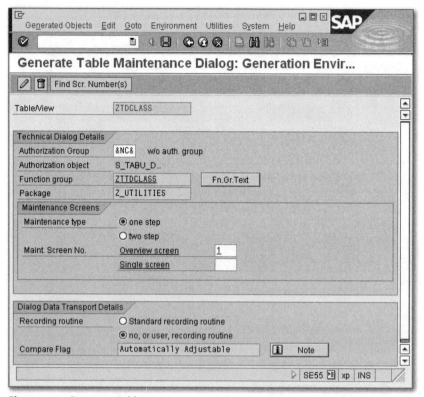

Figure 7.10 Creating a Table Maintenance Dialog

Setting a table maintenance dialog

You can implement the following setting when you create a table maintenance dialog: By specifying an authorization group, you can force an authorization check. You create the source code for the maintenance dialog in a function group for which you have selected ZTTDCLASS. You can generate the complete source code in one function group for a number of tables in a function group. There are two reasons not to do this, however: If you change a table, a maintenance dialog may be syntactically incorrect and no longer executable, and along with it, the entire function group and therefore all dialogs. In addition, you will not be able to identify as quickly the function group in which the maintenance dialog was generated. If you choose suitable naming conventions, you can quickly identify which table maintenance dialog a certain function group represents. In the case here, a "T" and then the name of the table in question were written after the namespace. This means that you can ensure that all maintenance dialogs are excluded from all automatic checks by the Code Inspector (Transaction SCI), to reduce the number of error messages.

In the MAINTENANCE SCREENS subdialog, you can specify the maintenance type and also select maintenance screen numbers. You can have either one-step or two-step maintenance dialogs. Two-step maintenance dialogs also have a detail view for a record to be edited, which makes it easier to work with transparent tables with many columns.

Two-step maintenance dialogs

When configuring specifications for transferring data for the dialog, one of the many things you can do is define the connection to the transport system. We recommend that you choose the standard recording routine for Customizing tables.

To enable you to use the maintenance view in Transaction SM30 for maintaining tables, the table in question must have the DISPLAY/MAINTENANCE ALLOWED mode. If RESTRICTED MAINTENANCE is set, you can perform the maintenance in the development system only.

Creating Maintenance Views [+]

Instead of directly creating generated table maintenance dialogs for transparent tables, we recommend that you create them for ABAP Dictionary maintenance views. This approach has the following advantages:

▶ You can maintain other tables (for example, text tables) simultaneously using a join or, for purely informational purposes, also display tables that cannot be maintained.

▶ You can prohibit certain fields from being modified, or remove them completely from the display.

▶ You can define selection criteria to restrict the display to different areas.

Enhancing Maintenance Dialogs

Generated table maintenance dialogs are useful for maintaining Customizing and basic master and transaction data; however, other functions may often also be desirable, such as the following:

▶ Checking the plausibility of a new or changed table entry

▶ Checking the plausibility of all table entries

> ▸ Automatically filling of table fields that are not displayed and cannot be changed

> ▸ Creating special primary keys (for example, GUIDs)

Services for plausibility

We will now present a service for checking the plausibility of entries. You will be able to check single records, entire tables, or even entire view clusters. You enable that a plausibility check will take place for a record by integrating a suitable method call into the event maintenance of the generated table. To do this, follow the menu path ENVIRONMENT • MODIFICATION • EVENTS from the table generator, the result of which is shown in Figure 7.11. In each row, you can store a separate form routine for a *table maintenance event and t*his form routine will be called during processing.

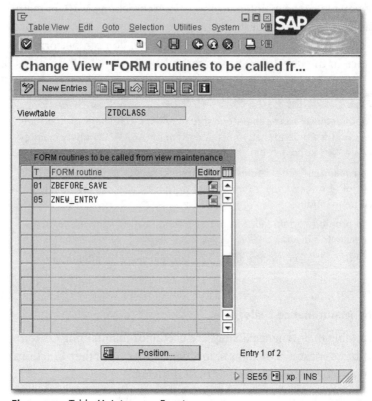

Figure 7.11 Table Maintenance Events

In this example, the ZBEFORE_SAVE form is called for event 01 before the newly added, changed or deleted entries are saved. ZNEW_ENTRY is called when a new entry is created and confirmed using Return.

It is useful to create the form routines in the same function group where you also generate the maintenance view. You are not required to add a prefix to the form routines; however, it is done here to prevent naming conflicts with routines delivered with the standard SAP system, and also to make it easier for users to find their own routines again in the overview.

Prefix

We will now present a generic check service you can use for any plausibility functions of events 01 and 05, but in which you can only make a minimum number of adjustments. The basic idea is to define an interface that only has to be implemented. In this case, it consists of three methods, as shown in Listing 7.1.

Check service

```
interface Z_IF_TABLE_MAINT_CHECK
  public .
  class-methods CHECK_SINGLE_ENTRY
    importing
      !IV_ENTRY type ANY
    Exceptions
      ERROR .
  methods ADD_ENTRY
    importing
      !IV_ENTRY type ANY .
  methods CHECK_ENTRIES
    exceptions
      ERROR .
endinterface.
```

Listing 7.1 Interface of a Generic Plausibility Check for Table Maintenance

The CHECK_SINGLE_ENTRY( ) method is static because it only checks a single record, whereas the two other methods work with an instance of the check object. This means that you can save all relevant records by calling the ADD_ENTRY( ) method, check them as a whole using CHECK_ENTRIES( ), and thereby also relate table entries in a check to each other.

If you want to use these functions in a table maintenance dialog, all you have to do is define two constants and one variable in the include where you develop the implemented table maintenance (see Listing 7.2).

```
*----------------------------------------------------------------*
***INCLUDE LZTTDCLASSF01 .
*----------------------------------------------------------------*
CONSTANTS:
  lc_tabname   TYPE tabname    VALUE 'ZTDCLASS',
  lc_classname TYPE seoclsname VALUE 'Z_CL_DATE_CHECK'.

DATA lr_maint_check TYPE REF TO z_cl_date_check.
```

Listing 7.2 Non-Generic Part of the Plausibility Service

The first constant, lc_tabname, is the name of the maintained table and the second, lc classname, is the name of the class that implements the Z_IF_TABLE_MAINT_CHECK interface mentioned. The variable contains a reference to this class, in this case, a date checker class called Z_CL_DATE_CHECK. In this example, you must check whether the start date is earlier than or the same as the end date for the ZTDCLASS table that manages time-dependent data for the class and also whether the amount of data for this table is complete. To do this, you only have to create form routines for events 01 and 05, where you call the date checker class using defined constants and variables.

Include programs

Both form routines for events 01 and 05 are completely generic and you can store and incorporate them into an *include program*. You create include programs like normal reports but with type "I".

> **Multiple Use of Includes**
>
> We would advise you not to use an include multiple times in different programs because this poses major risks in terms of using the package concept and the Enhancement Framework. There are also software reasons not to do this: Developers do not expect include programs to be reused; therefore, maintenance will be prone to errors. Include programs especially cannot be tested individually. Modularization obtained this way (using includes) is not good from a software perspective because includes, unlike classes, do not have explicit interfaces.

You can check a single entry using the source code shown in Listing 7.3.

```
*&---------------------------------------------------------------*
*&      Form  ZNEW_ENTRY
*&---------------------------------------------------------------*
*         Time 05
*---------------------------------------------------------------*
FORM znew_entry.
  FIELD-SYMBOLS <fs> TYPE ANY.
  ASSIGN (lc_tabname) TO <fs>.
  CALL METHOD (lc_classname)=>check_single_entry
    EXPORTING
      iv_entry = <fs>
    EXCEPTIONS
      error    = 1
      OTHERS   = 2.
  IF sy-subrc <> 0.
    MESSAGE ID sy-msgid TYPE sy-msgty NUMBER sy-msgno
              WITH sy-msgv1 sy-msgv2 sy-msgv3 sy-msgv4.
  ENDIF.
ENDFORM.                         "ZNEW_ENTRY
```

Listing 7.3 Check for a Single Entry Before Saving

The form routine first dynamically accesses a field that has exactly the same name as the underlying table or the maintenance view. The field is then transferred to the check routine. All changed entries are tested in the same way (see Listing 7.4).

Testing all changed entries

```
*&---------------------------------------------------------------*
*&      Form  ZBEFORE_SAVE
*&---------------------------------------------------------------*
*         Time 01
*---------------------------------------------------------------*
FORM zbefore_save.
  FIELD-SYMBOLS <fs> TYPE ANY.

  ASSIGN (lc_tabname) TO <fs>.
  CREATE OBJECT lr_maint_check.

  LOOP AT total.
    IF <action> = new_entry OR
```

```
              <action> = change OR
              <action> = original.
*       Check entry
        CALL METHOD (lc_classname)=>check_single_entry
           EXPORTING
              iv_entry = <vim_ctotal>
           EXCEPTIONS
              error    = 1
              OTHERS   = 2.
        IF sy-subrc <> 0.
          MESSAGE ID sy-msgid TYPE 'S' NUMBER sy-msgno
                      WITH sy-msgv1 sy-msgv2 sy-msgv3 sy-msgv4
                      DISPLAY LIKE sy-msgty.
        ENDIF.
        lr_maint_check->add_entry( <vim_ctotal> ).
      ENDIF.
    ENDLOOP.
* Check entries
  CALL METHOD lr_maint_check->check_entries
    EXCEPTIONS
      error  = 1
      OTHERS = 2.
  IF sy-subrc <> 0.
    MESSAGE ID sy-msgid TYPE 'S' NUMBER sy-msgno
              WITH sy-msgv1 sy-msgv2 sy-msgv3 sy-msgv4
              DISPLAY LIKE sy-msgty.
  ENDIF.
ENDFORM.                               "ZBEFORE_SAVE
```

Listing 7.4   Check for a Single Entry Before Saving

The <total> field symbol from the generated source code is accessed here. Assigning the <total> header line in the loop also implicitly changes the <vim_ctotal> field symbols for the current entry and the <action> field symbol that specifies the change status of a record. Consider only the original and changed records in the loop, not the records that were created and deleted. They are initially checked as single records and then transferred to the check class by the ADD_ENTRY( ) method. Subsequently, the records are checked as a whole. If an error occurs, use the MESSAGE command to issue a status message that looks like an error (DISPLAY LIKE addition). If you were to issue a real error message, or a warning, the entire dialog would be terminated, which does not make sense because users will want to be able to correct their entries.

It now remains for us to show you how to implement the date checker class, which represents any plausibility check the Z_IF_TABLE_MAINT interface implements.

Implementing the date checker class

It is easy to check a single entry using the CHECK_SINGLE_ENTRY( ) method. The generic iv_entry parameter is typed first, and then a check is performed to verify whether the end date is earlier than or the same as the start date (see Listing 7.5).

```
METHOD z_if_table_maint_check~check_single_entry.
  DATA lv_date TYPE DATS.

  lv_date = iv_entry.

  IF lv_date-begda IS INITIAL AND lv_date-endda IS INITIAL.
    MESSAGE e000 RAISING error.
  ELSEIF lv_date-begda > lv_date-endda and
         lv_date-endda is NOT INITIAL.
    MESSAGE e001 with lv_date-begda lv_date-endda
          RAISING error.
  endif.
endmethod.
```

Listing 7.5 Date Check for a Single Entry

The ADD_ENTRY( ) method adds a new record after the typing in a date type by an APPEND in an internal mt_dates table (see Listing 7.6).

```
METHOD z_if_table_maint_check~add_entry.
  DATA lv_date TYPE DATS.

  lv_date = iv_entry.
  IF lv_date-endda is INITIAL.
    lv_date-endda = '99991231'.
  ENDIF.
  APPEND lv_date TO mt_dates.
ENDMETHOD.
```

Listing 7.6 Saving an Entry Temporarily

Checking for completeness

Set the maximum value for an initial end date to make it easier to perform the following check for data completeness (see Listing 7.7):

```
METHOD z_if_table_maint_check~check_entries.
  DATA:
    lv_last       TYPE t_line,
    lv_current    TYPE t_line,
    lv_tomorrow TYPE DATS.

  SORT mt_dates BY class begda.
  READ TABLE mt_dates into lv_last INDEX 1.

  LOOP AT mt_dates INTO lv_current FROM 2.
    IF lv_current-object = lv_last-object.
      lv_tomorrow = lv_last-endda + 1.
      IF lv_current-begda <> lv_tomorrow.
        MESSAGE e002 RAISING error.
      ELSEIF lv_current-begda = lv_last-begda.
        MESSAGE e003 WITH lv_current-begda RAISING error.
      ENDIF.
    ENDIF.
    lv_last = lv_current.
  ENDLOOP.
ENDMETHOD.
```

Listing 7.7 Check for Completeness of Time-Dependent Data

Old source code

This example is instructional in several ways. The SAP system contains old source code that you should not reuse in an object-oriented context. This is because tables with header lines cannot be used in methods as this will cause activation errors. When you use other table maintenance events, you are actually forced to manipulate sy-subrc. You can assume the following based on these factors:

▶ Integrating your own application logic into a generated maintenance dialog is complicated. If the application logic is complex, you should use another GUI technology for robustness and maintenance reasons.

▶ Using event maintenance requires a lot of expertise and is prone to errors. It therefore makes sense to have an expert perform this work. If necessary, implement a generic solution like the one described, of which users will only have to apply a small, non-generic part, and otherwise only have to implement a plausibility class.

Calling Table Maintenance from ABAP Programs

You have two options you can use if you want to call table maintenance dialogs from applications. You can create a transaction, as shown in Figure 7.12, or you can use one of the function modules from the SVIM function group, as follows:

Two options

▶ VIEW_MAINTENANCE_CALL

▶ VIEW_MAINTENANCE

▶ VIEW_MAINTENANCE_LOW_LEVEL

▶ VIEW_MAINTENANCE_SINGLE_ENTRY (for displaying a single table entry)

These function modules are described in the SAP Library under BC - Extended Applications Function Library • Extended Table Mainte-nance. Detailed documentation is also available as function module documentation in the system. You can call a table maintenance dialog in change mode as follows:

Calling table maintenance dialogs

```
CALL FUNCTION 'VIEW_MAINTENANCE_CALL'
  EXPORTING
    action    = 'U'
    view_name = 'ZTDCLASS'
  EXCEPTIONS
    OTHERS    = 15.
```

The most important functions are specifying selection options using the TABLES parameter DBA_SELLIST and deactivating single functions using entries in the TABLES parameter EXCL_CUA_FUNCT. If you enter the DELE value there, for example, you will not be able to delete any more entries. In the entries for DBA_SELLIST, you can specify the records to be dis-played by indicating the field in the VIEWFELD component, an operator such as EQ for "equal" and NE for "not equal" in the OP component, and the value in the VALUE field.

You can also call the view cluster from a transaction. Figure 7.12 shows how you must define this transaction. Create a transaction code for Transaction SM30, skip the initial screen by selecting the correspond-

Calling view clusters using a transaction

ing checkbox, set the name of the maintenance view in the VIEWNAME screen field, and specify X in the UPDATE screen field to enable you to change data.

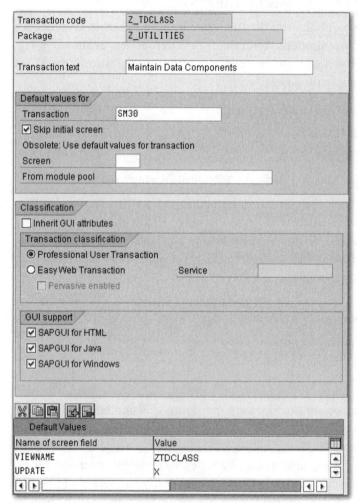

Figure 7.12 Calling a Maintenance View Using a Transaction

7.2.2 View Clusters

View clusters are a dialog technique related to table maintenance dialogs. Figure 7.13 shows an example of this dialog type.

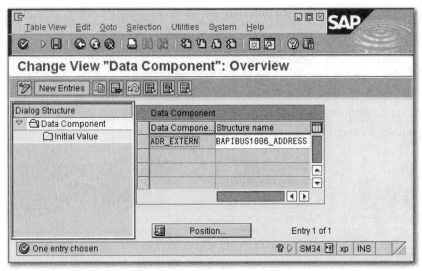

Figure 7.13 Initial Screen of a View Cluster

You can maintain a range of tables in one joint dialog. Tables or views to be maintained are displayed in a tree-like structure on the left. By double-clicking on them, you can navigate to the corresponding data records, which then appear on the right of the screen. This results in the following advantages:

- The information is displayed in a clearer and more user friendly way **Advantages** when you want to display or maintain a number of tables together. For example, this enables you to edit the entire Customizing of an application, which is particularly useful if there are logical relationships between the entries of different tables.

- You can edit tables together with tables that depend on them: You can navigate directly from a table entry to dependent entries and also use a record to delete or (in the case of Customizing) transport all dependent records.

Next, you will create a view cluster and enhance this example the way you did when maintaining table maintenance dialog events.

Here, we have chosen a view cluster with one table and a dependent **Example** table as the example (see Figure 7.13). This example shows a scenario that is controlled by Customizing (as frequently occurs when you map data structures).

Assigning dependent entries

In this example, you manage a number of data components that are defined by a name (for example, ADR_EXTERN). You can assign dependent entries to a single data component in the view cluster by selecting the data component (ADR_EXTERN here) and then selecting INITIAL VALUE, as shown in Figure 7.14.

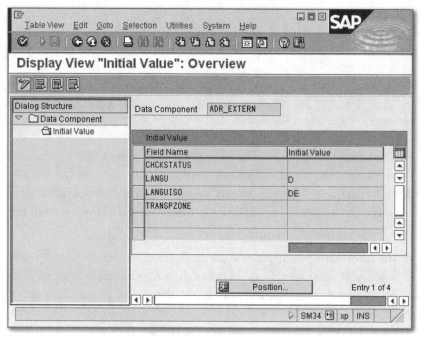

Figure 7.14 Navigating to a Subset

Constants as initial values

You can use this approach in the sample application to define which components (for example, TRANSPZONE or LANGU) of the ADR_EXTERN structure are supposed to have constants as initial values. In a mapping scenario, you can define fixed values flexibly and transparently in this way when converting values of one structure into another. For this purpose, you create two Customizing tables and two maintenance views, as shown in Figure 7.15 and Figure 7.16.

It is important here that you define the "S" (for subset) maintenance attribute for the MPART field, as displayed in Figure 7.16. When you call this type of view in Transaction SM30, a modal dialog appears, requesting a value for this field.

Maintenance attribute S

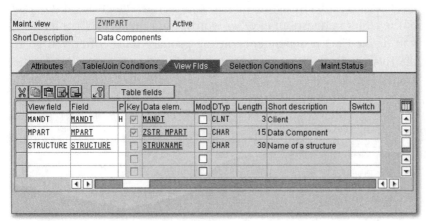

Figure 7.15 Maintenance View for Main Table

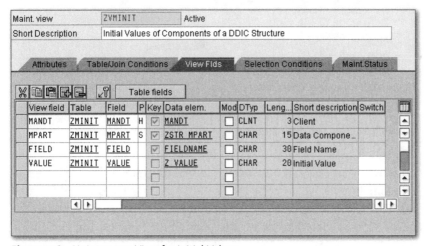

Figure 7.16 Maintenance View for Initial Values

You use the Subset attribute to relate both tables in a view cluster to each other and enable navigation such as the one shown in Figure 7.14. You first define a view cluster via Transaction SE54 and use the EDIT VIEW

253

CLUSTER button. You can then create and test the view cluster. First, define an object structure as shown in Figure 7.17. Use the PREDECESSOR and DEPENDENCIES entries to determine the hierarchical dependencies.

Generating field dependencies

You must then generate the field dependencies. This is easiest if you have already correctly defined the foreign key dependencies at the level of the tables in question; in other words, from the MPART component, you defined a 1:n dependency in the primary table. After you go to the HEADER ENTRY, you can activate the view cluster and maintain it in Transaction SM34.

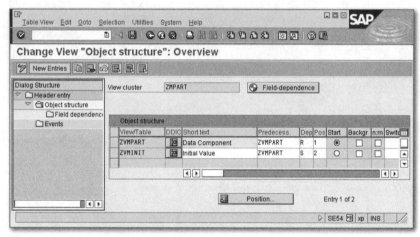

Figure 7.17 Creating a View Cluster

View cluster event maintenance

Enhancing view clusters

You can enhance view clusters with event maintenance in exactly the same way that you can enhance table maintenance dialogs using separate functions, as we described in Section 7.2.1, Generating and Enhancing Table Maintenance Dialogs. Technical background information for items such as view cluster events—for which you can integrate your own source code—is available in the SAP Library under CUSTOMIZING (BC-CUS) • BC – GENERATE TABLE MAINTENANCE DIALOG. You use event maintenance for the following purposes:

▶ For event 03, you can query whether there are specific authorizations for jumping to a detail dialog.

▶ You can use event 05 to manipulate data in tables that are not maintained by the view cluster. You can also perform checks across all tables when you save your data. You do this by saving the references to management and data tables for each subobject before you call the view maintenance module for a subdialog in a service class. This means that you will also be able to determine and transfer entries from higher-level tables when you create a new entry.

If you want to define your own application logic in a view cluster, unlike with table maintenance dialogs, there is no generated function group available where you can create an include. This means that you must create your own include program.

Your own include program

Access to Table Entries of a View Cluster

In this section, you will learn how to access data from other tables that are maintained in a view cluster. In a programming example, you will maintain initial values for components of a structure, as shown in Figure 7.14. When you maintain an initial value for a component, a check in the generated table maintenance dialog should ensure that the component is also located in the ABAP Dictionary structure. This structure's name is contained in the higher-level table.

If you want to access the table data that is maintained in a view cluster, you must use view cluster functions that are defined in the LSVCMCOD include. First, set the <VCL_TOTAL> field symbol to the table data by calling vcl_set_table_access_for_obj. You can then copy the data into a separate internal table and return it, as happens in the function module shown in Listing 7.8.

View cluster functions

```
FUNCTION z_get_vcl_table.
*"----------------------------------------------------------
*"*"Local interface:
*"  IMPORTING
*"     REFERENCE(IV_TABLE) TYPE  TABNAME
*"  EXPORTING
*"     REFERENCE(ER_TABLE) TYPE REF TO  DATA
*"  EXCEPTIONS
*"       NOT_FOUND
*"----------------------------------------------------------
```

```
DATA:
  lv_vcl_object TYPE vim_name,
  lv_error      TYPE c,
  lr_table      TYPE REF TO data,
  lv_field      TYPE string.

FIELD-SYMBOLS:
  <line>        TYPE ANY,
  <table>       TYPE INDEX TABLE,
  <vcl_data>    TYPE INDEX TABLE.

INCLUDE LSVCMCOD.

lv_vcl_object = iv_table.

* Set variable <vcl_total> to specified table
  PERFORM vcl_set_table_access_for_obj IN PROGRAM saplsvcm
          USING lv_vcl_object
          CHANGING lv_error.
  IF lv_error = 'X'.
*    Table is not contained in viewcluster
     RAISE not_found.
  ELSE.
*    Create return table
     CREATE DATA lr_table TYPE TABLE OF (iv_table).
     ASSIGN lr_table->* TO <table>.
     lv_field = '(SAPLSVCM)<VCL_TOTAL>[]'.
     ASSIGN (lv_field) TO <vcl_data>.
     LOOP AT <vcl_data> ASSIGNING <line>.
       APPEND <line> TO <table>.
     ENDLOOP.
  ENDIF.
  er_table = lr_table.
ENDFUNCTION.
```

Listing 7.8 Creating a Copy of View Cluster Data

In general, you cannot assume that the variables defined in the LSVCM-COD include are defined in the same main program as that in the calling program. If you want to access variables in the view cluster, you must call the form routines in the SAPLSVCM program. You can use the following statements to access the <VCL_TOTAL> field symbol in the SAPLSVCM main program:

```
lv_field = '(SAPLSVCM)<VCL_TOTAL>[]'.
ASSIGN (lv_field) TO <vcl_data>.
```

The just described access to variables defined in a view cluster must be programmed as a function module. You cannot use the LSVCMCOD include in classes because it uses obsolete language constructs.

Obsolete language constructs

Calling View Clusters

You can create a transaction when you call a view cluster, as shown in Figure 7.18.

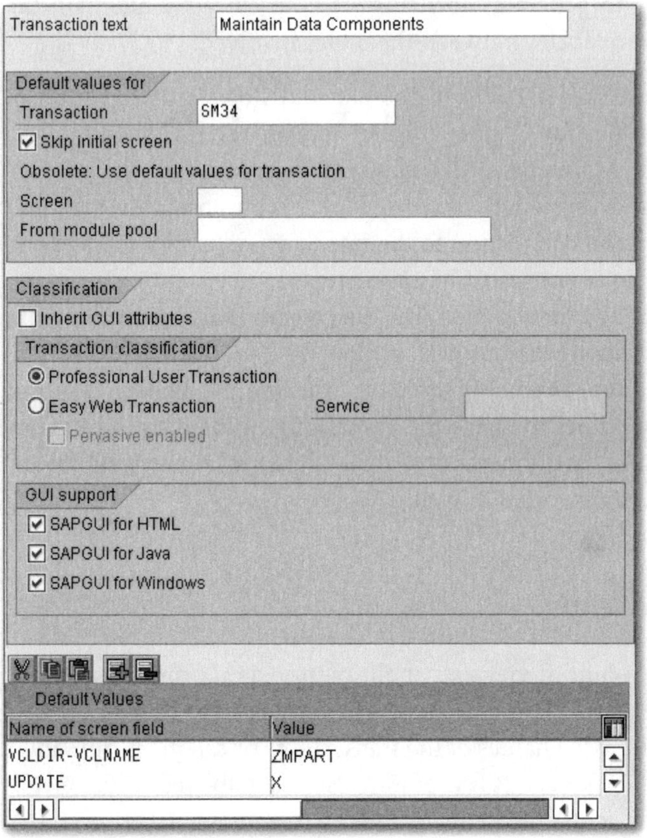

Figure 7.18 Calling a View Cluster

Alternatively, you can use the VIEWCLUSTER_MAINTENANCE_CALL function module. As is the case when you call table maintenance dialogs using the SVIM function group function modules, you can define a wide range of parameters, such as quantities of selected data, and processing parameters.

7.2.3 Tips for Handling Maintenance Views and View Clusters

If you are looking for functional enhancement examples of table maintenance dialogs and view clusters, you can use the RSVIMT_NON_UC_VIM_AREAS report to determine event maintenance dialogs of table maintenance dialogs or view clusters for which event maintenance enhancements were implemented.

The easiest way to generate view clusters is to correctly maintain the foreign key dependencies between the tables involved.

Connecting to the transport system

One of the main uses of table maintenance dialogs is the creation of maintenance dialogs for Customizing. In Section 7.2.1, Generating and Enhancing Table Maintenance Dialogs, you learned about the connection to the transport system to be created for this purpose. However, you can create your own connection to the transport system by transferring the object directory entries to be saved to the TR_OBJECTS_CHECK and TR_OBJECTS_INSERT function modules. This means that you can program your own Customizing dialogs with greater ease, which will enable you to export and import Customizing data from the file system. You can also use these modules to check the granularity of the data to be transported and ensure that, for example for a higher-level entry, all lower-level entries are transported as well.

7.3 Area Menus

From the user's point of view, an application system primarily consists of a number of transactions and reports that act as an entry point. Experienced users know the names of the transactions or call them from their Favorites menu. However, it is useful to also make the number of available transactions accessible in an area menu (see Figure 7.19).

Area menus are hierarchically structured so that you can arrange them according to topics or subapplications. In addition to the most important application transactions, you should use this approach to make the following functions available:

Hierarchical structure

► **Customizing**
Even if Customizing maintenance is generally deactivated in live systems, experienced users or application consultants can analyze the system settings in this way to explain system behavior.

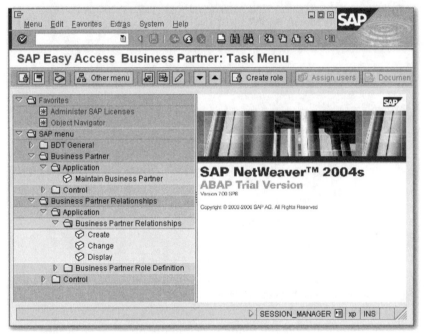

Figure 7.19 Example of an Area Menu

► **Evaluation and check reports**
Numerous reporting applications, such as search services for application objects or displaying incorrect application objects, do not arise from functional requirements, but instead emerge during development and developer testing. These are often of interest to experienced users and application consultants and can be made available in a separate node.

In Section 2.1.2, Functional Requirements, and Section 2.1.3, Non-Functional Requirements, we mentioned other examples such as user and administration cockpits you can make available to users in an area menu. You use Transaction SE43 to create and edit area menus, and you can see an example of an area menu of the SAP Business Partner application in Figure 7.20.

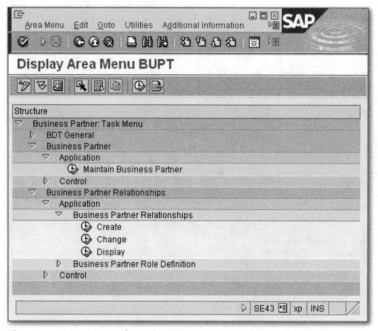

Figure 7.20 Area Menu from the SAP Business Partner Product

Components   An area menu can have the following components:

▶ Folders

▶ References to other submenus

▶ Reports, such as ABAP and SAP Query reports

▶ Transactions

For more information and tips and tricks, see the BASIS SERVICES • AREA MENU MAINTENANCE section in the SAP Library. Note that area menus are also useful when defining roles because you can integrate them into role-specific user menus.

7.4   Object-Oriented Screen Programming

The standard SAP system provides options to wrap elements of classic screen programming in an object-oriented way. Examples include the User Interface Framework (BC-SRV-UIF) for mobile applications and MEREQ as part of SAP ERP. We present the BUS Screen Framework here to illustrate how classic screen programming can be carried out in an object-oriented way and to introduce a framework from the SAP Business Partner area that you can use in your own applications.

BUS Screen Framework

[+]	**No External Release**

The BUS Screen Framework is used in many areas of the standard SAP system, but is not released externally. For some areas such as the Locator Framework, which you will learn about in Section 8.2, Business Partner Extension, it is often crucial to have knowledge of the framework.

Even if you do not want to use the BUS Screen Framework, this section will provide you with sufficient suggestions for advanced, and, in particular, object-oriented screen programming.

7.4.1   Pros and Cons of Subscreens

Why should you work with subscreens at all? Ultimately, as a developer, you could argue that you can achieve a great deal with normal screens, or even just with selection screens, that is, without ever working with the Screen Painter. Programming with subscreens is more complicated (and therefore more prone to errors), consequently, some people regard it as a special discipline of ABAP development. The most important arguments in favor of subscreens are flexibility, modularization, and extensibility, as follows:

Complicated and prone to errors

▶ **Flexibility**

You gain flexibility because a subscreen you create once can later be integrated everywhere. You can use it in full screens, on dialog boxes and tabstrips, in different dialogs of your own application, and as an element in frameworks of the standard system, such as in the SAP Business Workflow or Business Data Toolset (BDT). (This also lets you integrate subscreens into standard SAP system applications, such as the central business partner, or industry solutions created using the BDT, such as banks, insurance companies, and financial service providers.)

▶ **Modularization**
You can quickly and easily combine new screens and screen sequences from a modular building block system of subscreens. You can implement general screens for recurring tasks and separate these from special screens. This increases the reusability of screens. The combined screens can come from different programs and function groups that conceal their internal statuses from each other and communicate with one another through interfaces.

Screen BAdI ▶ **Extensibility**
Because you can also integrate subscreens dynamically, they are eminently suitable for extending applications without modifications. There is even a special BAdI type with the *Screen BAdI* available for this task.

7.4.2 Subscreens as a Modularization Unit

In modern, flexible, and therefore technically complex applications such as SAP Business Partner, numerous subscreens from different function groups are often displayed at the same time. Even with simple navigation (for example, you call Transaction BP, select a business partner, and display the address), several dozen subscreens can easily be run.

Main program   In this case, several subapplications are integrated in the background by a main program that does not statically identify the screens to be integrated, but instead accesses Customizing tables to determine the screens and function modules that should be displayed and called at runtime.

Examples of (possible or actually existing) subapplications are bank and finance data, customer data, employee data, and external providers. These subapplications are independent of each other, know nothing about one another, and can be individually activated or deactivated in a specified system.

In the program, each subapplication ensures that it can be accessed in a certain way (for example, using the interface parameters of function modules specified by the program), and therefore fulfills its part of an interface contract. Subscreens are the smallest modularization unit because you can decide for each individual subscreen whether and where it is integrated into the subapplication.

If the program is programmed in such a way that it can dynamically integrate each subapplication (and the subapplication can integrate each subscreen) that fulfills the same interface contract, the result is a flexible overall application that you can extend without modification. This is enormously important because it is the only way you can add new screens and functions and replace existing ones without modifying the program's (here, the standard SAP system's) development objects.

In every software development project, designers should ask themselves whether and to what extent they want their product to be extended by a third party (customers, users, and add-on developers). In the meantime, in the SAP environment a high degree of flexibility and extensibility has become the norm.

Extensibility by a third party

7.4.3   Encapsulating with Screens

Another aspect of classic screen programming is the issue of encapsulation. With classic screen programming this usually takes place at the program or function group level because you cannot declare any local or private data in Process Before Output (PBO) and Process After Input (PAI) modules. Even work areas and field symbols for loop passes and auxiliary variables that are declared in modules can be globally displayed and changed within the function group or executable program. (You can, of course, store parts of the functions in form routines, where you can also declare local variables.) Data that logically belongs to only one screen therefore does not have any inherent or obvious assignment to this. The different screens of a function group are therefore only encapsulated and differentiated from one another to a small extent.

7.4.4   Message Handling with Screens

A typical question with highly modularized screen applications, for which screens of external function groups (including dynamic ones) are also integrated, concerns the exchange of messages between a screen and the application framework.

The framework application normally has a lot of information to communicate to a subscreen:

▶ Which application object has just been selected? (The program may also deliver the detail data to be displayed.)

▶ Are you in edit or change mode? Do fields have to be ready for input?

▶ Which function code did the user trigger? Should I save data? Must I release data or locks?

Equally, the subscreen has some messages for the program:

▶ Were the inputs made by the user correct, or have errors occurred? If so, which errors? (You may have to summarize the errors of all subscreens in a log.)

▶ Is the data entered in the subscreen correct?

▶ Which function code (for example, using a button) was triggered in the subscreen that is handled by the program?

▶ Could a function code transferred by the program be handled successfully? Has the subscreen declared itself responsible?

If there are subscreens and programs in different function groups, as is typical for extensible applications, the result is generally more of a complicated number of function module calls between the two components. This is due to the fact that there is a significant lack of standardized, robust mechanisms for exchanging data between a subscreen and its environment at runtime.

7.4.5   BUS Screen Framework

The BUS Screen Framework provides an object-oriented framework for implementing screens as ABAP classes. In this case, you create the screen layout using the Screen Painter.

[»]

> **Screen Flow Logic**
>
> You program the *screen flow logic* of a screen in the Screen Painter. You use a special set of commands, which, within the blocks PROCESS BEFORE OUTPUT (before you output the screen) and PROCESS AFTER INPUT (handling user inputs), define the sequence in which modules that control the screen initialization and system response to user inputs are called.
>
> For example, a module can have the task of jointly checking the values entered in three related grouped screen fields A, B, and C.
>
> The definition in the screen flow logic is that the CHECK_A_B_C module is called for the three fields. This causes all three fields, A, B, and C, to be ready for input at the same time if an error occurs.

Unlike classic procedural screen programming, a standard call that is always the same and that delegates further control of the screen logic to the BUS Screen Framework is entered in the flow logic. You then encode the actual functions of the screen, such as filling the screen before output and responses to user inputs, within an ABAP class that is derived from the screen classes of the framework for normal screens and subscreens.

Always the same standard call

The framework provides basis classes for subscreen screens and main screens. When you create your own applications, you usually create a local subclass for each screen and implement the application-specific behavior of the screen into it, as shown in Figure 7.21.

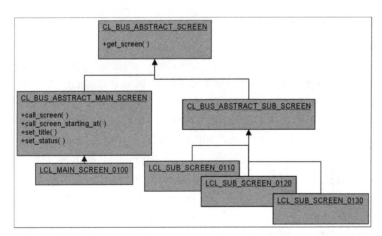

Figure 7.21 Static Class Diagram of BUS Screen Framework with Derived Application-Specific Classes

Inheritance, encapsulation, and polymorphy

This means that the characteristics of object-oriented programming (primarily, inheritance, encapsulation, and polymorphy) are also available for screens' flow logic. The framework also provides several functions, such as object-oriented representation of tabstrips and tabs, reading and setting the cursor position, setting the screen title and GUI status, suppressing functions of the GUI status, highlighting screen fields after incorrect entries, and managing messages.

7.4.6   Advantages of Object-Oriented Screens

Object-oriented programming with ABAP Objects has generally made it easier to create extensible, clearly modularized, encapsulated applications. The following list names the most important characteristics of object-oriented screens:

▸ **Extensibility**
In main programs you program against interfaces and extensions implement the program interfaces. This guarantees a seamless integration of application and extension.

▸ **Standardization**
For many of the issues mentioned, in an object-oriented screen framework you can create standardized solutions that can be used in completely different contexts. Once a developer is familiar with the framework, he can quickly access and extend source code and architecture of a wide variety of applications that use the framework.

▸ **Inheritance**
In an object-oriented framework you can implement the general application-independent properties and functions of screens in basis classes. For application-specific characteristics, you can create the necessary interfaces or specialized (basis) classes that guarantee uniform interfaces (for example, for exchanging check results) or consistent behavior.

▸ **Encapsulation**
Internal screen statuses are stored in the attributes of the screen objects. This means that, first, they are clearly assigned and, second, you can declare them as `private`. Therefore, they can only be displayed within the relevant screen class.

7.4.7 Uses for the BUS Screen Framework

An example illustrates how the BUS Screen Framework emphasizes the advantages mentioned and can help maintain clarity in a complex, highly parameterizable and extensible application.

The *Locator Framework* enables you to integrate search screens and search functions into application transactions. By customizing and programming against defined interfaces, you can also subsequently integrate modification-free searches into standard SAP system applications, for example, into the search functions for business partners in Transaction BP (business partner maintenance).

Locator Framework

Because the Locator is used in several standard SAP system applications and is graphically uniform in appearance, the user will recognize the Locator Framework when he encounters it in new applications. Transaction LOCA_CUST gives you an overview of the standard applications that use the Locator Framework.

7.4.8 Normal Screens and Modal Dialog Boxes

The framework provides the CL_BUS_ABSTRACT_MAIN_SCREEN basis class for main screens (identified as a *normal screen* or *modal dialog box* in the Screen Painter, in contrast to *subscreen*). You implement them in a local class derived from the basis class.

Within the executable program or function group that contains the screen, you must define and implement a local class for this, where the abstract methods of the CL_BUS_ABSTRACT_MAIN_SCREEN class are implemented as shown in Listing 7.9. You can also implement any additional screen attributes and functions.

The LCL_MAIN_SCREEN_0100 local screen class is defined for a main screen in the example shown in Listing 7.9. It does not include any application-specific features; it only contains the methods you absolutely must implement, because, for technical reasons, they are defined as abstract in the basis class.

Defining a local screen class

```
CLASS lcl_main_screen_0100 DEFINITION
  INHERITING FROM cl_bus_abstract_main_screen.
  PROTECTED SECTION.
```

```
     METHODS call_screen               REDEFINITION.
     METHODS call_screen_starting_at REDEFINITION.
ENDCLASS.

CLASS lcl_main_screen_0100 IMPLEMENTATION.
  METHOD call_screen.
    CALL SCREEN iv_dynpro_number.
  ENDMETHOD.
  METHOD call_screen_starting_at.
    CALL SCREEN iv_dynpro_number
      STARTING AT iv_xstart iv_ystart
      ENDING   AT iv_xend   iv_yend.
  ENDMETHOD.
ENDCLASS.
```

Listing 7.9 Simple Main Screen Class

[+]

Recurring Tasks

If your application covers several main screens, you can create an LCL_MAIN_SCREEN local basis class based on the example from Listing 7.9 and derive the different main screens from it.

You will require some source code components repeatedly when working with the BUS Screen Framework, for example:

▶ Defining and implementing the basis class for a main screen

▶ PBO modules DYNPRO_PBO, DYNPRO_PBO_BEGIN, DYNPRO_PBO_END

▶ PAI modules DYNPRO_PAI, DYNPRO_PAI_BEGIN, DYNPRO_PAI_END

▶ Interface of the BUS_SCREEN_CREATE form routine

Although using include programs is not ideal for multiple use purposes, their use is justified in this case.

Alternatively, you can create a function group as a template that contains the commonly recurring local implementations.

The reason for implementing the CALL_SCREEN( ) and CALL_SCREEN_STARTING_AT( ) methods locally is that the CALL SCREEN command must always be in the executable program or function group to which the called screen belongs. This command is therefore not allowed within global classes, and the class for a main screen must be abstract.

7.4.9   Defining Flow Logic

The flow logic you create in the Screen Painter is standardized and uni-form because preferably all special features of the relevant screen will be encapsulated within the screen class. The screen flow logic in the Screen Painter therefore only contains what is absolutely necessary to transfer control to the framework. If the screen does not contain any subscreen areas, the flow logic looks as follows:

Flow logic of a screen without a subscreen area

```
* Dynpro nnnn in program xyz
PROCESS BEFORE OUTPUT.
  MODULE dynpro_pbo.

PROCESS AFTER INPUT.
  MODULE dynpro_pai.
```

The modules called here are responsible for delegating processing to the framework, which in turn determines the responsible screen object (it may first create an instance for this purpose) and then calls its PBO and PAI methods. These are created in the executable program or in the function group that contains the screen. Listing 7.10 shows the standardized modules that are created in each program or function group that use the BUS Screen Framework.

Delegating the processing to the framework

```
* Delegate PBO processing to framework
MODULE dynpro_pbo OUTPUT.
  cl_bus_abstract_screen=>dynpro_pbo(
    iv_dynpro_number = sy-dynnr
    iv_program_name  = sy-repid ).
ENDMODULE.

* Delegate PAI processing to framework
MODULE dynpro_pai INPUT.
  cl_bus_abstract_screen=>dynpro_pai(
    iv_dynpro_number = sy-dynnr
    iv_program_name  = sy-repid ).
ENDMODULE.
```

Listing 7.10   DYNPRO_PBO and DYNPRO_PAI Modules

The DYNPRO_PBO( ) and DYNPRO_PAI( ) class methods use the received values for screen number and program name to request an instance of the relevant screen class and call the PBO_BEGIN( ) and PBO_END( ) methods or PAI_BEGIN( ) and PAI_END( ) methods on this.

Their use is equivalent to calling DYNPRO_PBO_BEGIN( ) and DYNPRO_PBO_END( ) (or the corresponding PAI methods). You use the BEGIN and END methods if you want to process a subscreen between BEGIN and END.

7.4.10 Creating Instances

Program name and screen number

To create an instance of a screen class, the framework always calls the BUS_SCREEN_CREATE form routine in the program or function group to which the screen belongs. The form routine has the parameters *program name* and *screen number* and returns a reference to a screen object that must be derived from CL_BUS_ABSTRACT_SCREEN.

In the form routine shown in Listing 7.11, as the developer you encode the assignment between a specific screen and the corresponding screen object. (You can cheat a little here and use the same screen class and even the same object instance for several screens.)

```
FORM bus_screen_create USING     VALUE(iv_program_name)
                                 VALUE(iv_dynpro_number)
                       CHANGING       cr_screen.
  CASE iv_dynpro_number.
  WHEN '0100'.
    CREATE OBJECT cr_screen TYPE lcl_main_screen_0100
      EXPORTING
        iv_program_name  = iv_program_name
        iv_dynpro_number = iv_dynpro_number.
  WHEN '0200'.
    CREATE OBJECT cr_screen TYPE lcl_screen_0200
      EXPORTING
        iv_program_name  = iv_program_name
        iv_dynpro_number = iv_dynpro_number.
  ENDCASE.
ENDFORM.
```

Listing 7.11 Creating Application-Specific Screen Object Instances

7.4.11 Calling Screens

You can jump to a screen by calling the SHOW( ) instance method or displaying SHOW_AS_POPUP( ) as a popup. To access the screen object whose CALL method you want to call use the GET_SCREEN( ) method of the CL_BUS_ABSTRACT_SCREEN framework basis class, which also performs the task of instance management.

Listing 7.12 shows how you obtain and call an instance of screen 0100 of the ZVEHICLE_DIALOG function group (SAPLZVEHICLE_DIALOG main program). Screen 0100 here must be a main screen. You can also call an instance from outside the function group in this way.

Screen 0100 must be a main screen

```
DATA lr_screen_0100 TYPE REF TO cl_bus_abstract_main_screen.
CALL METHOD cl_bus_abstract_screen=>get_screen
  EXPORTING
    iv_program_name  = 'SAPLZVEHICLE_DIALOG'
    iv_dynpro_number = '0100'
  IMPORTING
    ev_dynpro        = lr_screen_0100.
CALL METHOD lr_screen_0100->show.
```

Listing 7.12 Calling Screen 0100

7.4.12 Sequence of Processing Events

In the PBO block, starting with the main screen, first PBO_BEGIN( ), then any included subscreens, and finally PBO_END( ), are called in each case. PBO_BEGIN( ), included subscreens, and PBO_END( ) are called again in each subscreen.

After the PBO block, the PAI block is processed using the same procedure. At the end of the PAI block, the PROCESS_AFTER_INPUT event of the main screen is triggered, which, as an event parameter, has the function code created by the user and can be registered for any event handler. The system calls the event handlers in the order in which they are registered.

Figure 7.22 and Figure 7.23 illustrate the flow.

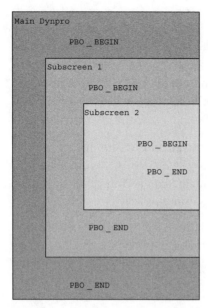

Figure 7.22 Nesting in the PROCESS BEFORE OUTPUT Processing Block

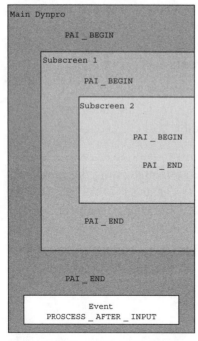

Figure 7.23 Flow of the PROCESS AFTER INPUT Processing Block

7.4.13 Defining Your Own Screen Logic

To implement the flow logic for the PROCESS BEFORE OUTPUT and PROCESS
AFTER INPUT events, you can redefine the PBO_BEGIN( ), PBO_END( ),
PAI_BEGIN( ) and PAI_END( ) methods. The first call within the method
should always apply as the corresponding method of the superclass as
follows, for example:

```
METHOD PBO_BEGIN.
  super->pbo_begin( ).
  … (my flow logic)
ENDMETHOD.
```

Upward delegation
in PBO_BEGIN( )
method

Important: Upward Delegation at the Right Time   **[!]**

It is essential that in each case you call the methods of the framework basis
classes at exactly the right time in their redefined methods because otherwise
inconsistencies may occur. The result would be unwanted application behavior, such as incorrect cursor positions.

7.4.14 Setting Titles and GUI Statuses

You set the title using the SET_TITLE( ) method and the call should occur
within the PBO_BEGIN( ) method.

You use the SET_STATUS( ) method to set the GUI status, with the
program and status ID of the GUI status to be displayed transferred as
parameters of the method.

```
METHOD PBO_BEGIN.
  ...
  set_title( 'My screen title!'(001) ).
  set_status( iv_status_program = sy-repid
              iv_status_key     = 'STATUS_0100' ).
  super->pbo_begin( ).
  ...
ENDMETHOD.
```

Example: Setting
titles and GUI
statuses

7.4.15 Handling User Inputs

In this section we compare the handling of user input when using classic screen programming or when using the object-oriented BUS Screen
Framework.

Function Codes in Classic Screen Programming

OK field In classic screen programming, an OK field is usually defined in the main screen. For this purpose, you use a global field (for example, GV_OKCODE) of the program that contains the main screen. The system automatically transports the SY-UCOMM function code triggered by the user to this GV_OKCODE field before the PAI block, where it is usually evaluated at the end of the PAI block of the main screen. An example is shown in Figure 7.24.

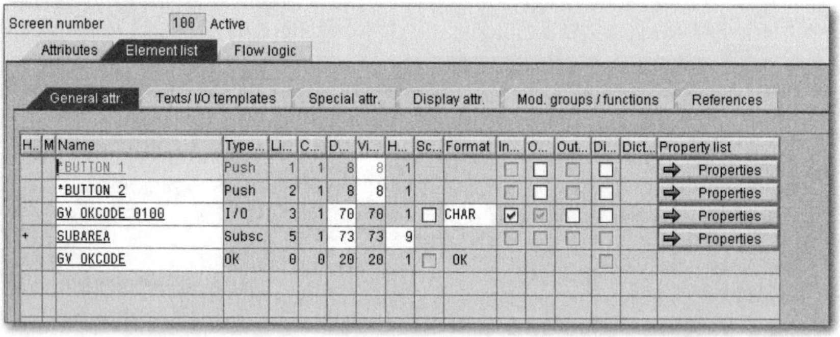

Screen number	100	Active											

Attributes	Element list	Flow logic

General attr.	Texts/ I/O templates	Special attr.	Display attr.	Mod. groups / functions	References

H..	M	Name	Type...	Li...	C...	D...	Vi...	H...	Sc...	Format	In...	O...	Out...	Di...	Dict..	Property list
		▸BUTTON 1	Push	1	1	8	8	1			☐	☐	☐	☐		⇒ Properties
		▸BUTTON 2	Push	2	1	8	8	1			☐	☐	☐	☐		⇒ Properties
		GV_OKCODE_0100	I/O	3	1	70	70	1	☐	CHAR	☑	☑	☐	☐		⇒ Properties
+		SUBAREA	Subsc	5	1	73	73	9			☐	☐	☐	☐		⇒ Properties
		GV_OKCODE	OK	0	0	20	20	1	☐	OK				☐		

Figure 7.24 Defining the OK Field in the Element List of the Main Screen

If subscreens from other programs and function groups are involved, they cannot access the GV_OKCODE function code directly because its visibility is limited to the function group of the main screen.

Evaluating function code Because subscreens have access to the SY-UCOMM system field, developers like to use it to evaluate the function code. Unfortunately, the behavior of SY-UCOMM and GV_OKCODE (or a differently named OK field of the main screen) differ from each other if the user triggers an empty function code (for example, by pressing the Enter key). The PAI block will run as normal. GV_OKCODE is initial here, while SY-UCOMM has the value of the last non-initial function code.

If the user triggers a function code (for example, by clicking on a button), and then presses the Enter key twice, the main screen receives the function code of the button in the first PAI run, and an initial function code in the next two PAI runs. However, an integrated subscreen that evaluates SY-UCOMM receives the function code of the button three times, as if the user had clicked on it three times consecutively. This is the case even if the function code originates from a button on the same subscreen. The main screen can prevent the unwanted effect of an old function code from being sent repeatedly by also initializing SY-UCOMM in the OK code handling at the very end of its PAI block. Unfortunately, however, this is often omitted.

Another option in addition to evaluating SY-UCOMM that developers like to choose is communication using function modules. The function group of the main screen can have a function module that the screens involved can use at the time of the PAI to query the function code triggered by the user. This procedure works but has some disadvantages, one of which is that it is not very sophisticated. Last but not least, there is a problem with the two procedures described so far if you, as the function code handler, want an independent piece of software rather than a screen.

Communicating using function modules

Function Code as OO Event

The BUS Screen Framework uses a different path. The framework triggers the PROCESS_AFTER_INPUT event at the end of the PAI processing of the main screen, after the PAI_BEGIN( ) and PAI_END( ) methods of the main screen and all subscreens have been processed. The event is triggered as an instance event of the main screen that is currently active and inherently has the function code as the event parameter.

Every piece of software that has been registered as a handler on this event is now called and receives a reference to the triggering main screen and the value of the function code. The event handlers can, but do not have to, be screens. In fact, it is often advisable to separate application logic and screens.

Separating application logic and screens

By publishing the function code as an OO event, you achieve a degree of de-coupling, which may be desirable in some scenarios, for example, in loosely coupled applications and frameworks. This may, however, also cause problems in scenarios with components that are logically more closely coupled if it is unclear whether a function code has found a suitable handler. Function codes can therefore either be handled several times or not at all, without this being recognized by a central instance, which may produce an error message.

**Application class
as an event
handler**

One possible design that addresses these issues and has proven itself is creating an application class that is registered centrally as an event handler. This application class has a dispatcher method that initially tries to handle the function code itself. It also calls other potential handlers, such as the Control Framework, to handle function codes from custom controls such as the ALV grid adequately, and integrates more technically distinct handlers.

Each potential handler must confirm, in a result parameter, whether the function code has found its relevant handler; in this case, the central dispatcher ends the processing and, if appropriate, issues a success message. The dispatcher will issue an error message if it reaches the end of its processing without the function code having been executed.

Fortunately, it does not matter whether event handlers belong to the same executable program or function group as the main screen. They also do not have to be screens; any local or global classes can instead have a method that is registered as the handler on the PROCESS_AFTER_INPUT event. Listing 7.13 contains an example for implementing an application class for handling function codes.

```
CLASS lcl_application DEFINITION.
  TYPE-POOLS abap.
  PUBLIC SECTION.
    METHODS handle_process_after_input
      FOR EVENT process_after_input
        OF cl_bus_abstract_main_screen
      IMPORTING sender
                iv_function_code.
    METHODS dispatcher
      IMPORTING iv_function_code TYPE bus_screen-function_code.
ENDCLASS.          "lcl_application DEFINITION
CLASS lcl_application IMPLEMENTATION.
  METHOD handle_process_after_input.
    CALL METHOD me->dispatcher
      EXPORTING
        iv_function_code = iv_function_code.
  ENDMETHOD.          "handle_process_after_input
  METHOD dispatcher.
    DATA lv_dispatched TYPE abap_bool.
* Handle function code
```

```
...
IF lv_dispatched = abap_false.
  MESSAGE 'Could not handle function
          code'(001) TYPE 'S'.
ENDIF.
ENDMETHOD.                     "dispatcher
ENDCLASS.      "lcl_application IMPLEMENTATION
```

Listing 7.13 Defining and Implementing the Event Handler

The following sample source code shows how an instance of the application class is created and the handler method is registered:

Registering event handlers

```
DATA lr_application TYPE REF TO lcl_application.
CREATE OBJECT lr_application.
SET HANDLER lr_application->handle_process_after_input
  FOR cl_bus_abstract_main_screen=>gv_current_main_screen.
```

You use a similar syntax to cancel the registration:

Canceling a registration

```
SET HANDLER lr_application->handle_process_after_input
  FOR cl_bus_abstract_main_screen=>gv_current_main_screen
  ACTIVATION abap_false.
```

[!]

Be Careful of Forgotten Event Handlers!

If objects the developer has forgotten and that do not have a defined internal status have inadvertently remained registered on an event, confusing errors that are also difficult to analyze in debugging can result. This is because these object instances often look very similar to expected handlers and therefore can be confused with one another, and errors often occur only when you call a function repeatedly.

Always ensure to dereference object instances you no longer require and, if necessary, remove the registration on the event using the SET HANDLER ... ACTIVATION SPACE command.

7.4.16 Collecting and Issuing Error Messages

In classic screen programming, you can assign checks (for example, input checks on allowed values) to individual screen fields. If an error occurs, not only is a message issued, but the cursor is subsequently placed on the corresponding field, which is highlighted in color.

This is also possible in a similar fashion with the BUS_SCREEN framework. The CL_BUS_MESSAGE class encapsulates a message to be directed to the user. Each message has a reference to a screen, one or more screen fields, and another field where the cursor should be positioned. (The maximum length of the full field name must not exceed 30 characters; otherwise, it cannot be highlighted by the framework.)

During the PAI processing, any number of objects of the CL_BUS_MESSAGE class can be created and appended to the internal GT_MESSAGES[] table of the relevant screen. During the PBO processing, each screen propagates its messages on the main screen and highlights the selected screen fields in each case.

[+] **Highlighting IDs**

If you also want the label next to your screen fields to be highlighted, assign them the same element name preceded by "*". For example, if the label of the ZVEHICLE-VEHICLE_ID screen field has the name *ZVEHICLE-VEHICLE_ID, it will also automatically be highlighted by the framework.

Listing 7.14 shows how a message object is created with a T100 message when an error occurs. If the IV_CURSOR_SCREEN constructor parameter is provided with a reference to the current screen object, the message object is automatically appended to the message table.

```
METHOD pai_end.
  DATA:
    ls_but000 TYPE          but000,
    lr_msg    TYPE REF TO cl_bus_message,
    lv_dummy  TYPE          string.
  SELECT SINGLE * FROM  but000 INTO ls_but000
    WHERE partner = mv_partner.
  IF sy-subrc NE 0. " No entry found? Error!
* Generate T100 message and fill with the
* message variables SY-MSGTY, MSGID, MSGNO, MSGV1.
* The constructor of the message object copies
* these values if we don't forward any others.
* Advantage: The where-used list for the message
* works
    MESSAGE e001(zvehicle) WITH mv_partner INTO lv_dummy.
* Generate CL_BUS_MESSAGE-Objekt.
    CREATE OBJECT lr_msg TYPE cl_bus_message
```

```
      EXPORTING
        iv_cursor_screen     = me
        iv_highlighted_field = 'LCL_SCR_100=>MV_PARTNER'.
    ENDIF.
    super->pai_end( ).   " upward delegation
  ENDMETHOD.               "pai_end
```

Listing 7.14 Creating a Message Using the CL_BUS_MESSAGE Class

Although the framework already has functions to collect messages and to evaluate them in terms of screen fields and cursor positions to be highlighted, it is the developer who must program the issuing of messages and initializing of the message table before the next PBO/PAI cycle.

This means that the developer can specify the time when messages are issued. For example, issuing messages at the end of the PBO block is a good time (that is, in the PBO_END( ) of the main screen after upward delegation). This way the screen is already fully set up, all messages have been collected on the main screen, and all fields are highlighted in accordance with the message table.

Time when messages are issued

Listing 7.15 shows how you determine the message with the greatest severity level along with the short text of the message. This is accomplished by using a static method of the CL_BUS_MESSAGE class from the message table. The message is then issued as an "S" (success) message in the status bar of the application, without affecting the application flow.

```
METHOD pbo_end. " in the main screen class
  DATA:
    lv_text TYPE c LENGTH 255.
* Firs upward delegation
  super->pbo_end( ).
* GT_MESSAGES[] is set.
* We determine the most severe message.
  CALL METHOD cl_bus_message=>get_most_severe_message
    EXPORTING
      it_messages = gt_messages
    IMPORTING
      ev_message  = gv_message.
  IF gv_message IS BOUND.
* Determine short text for message
    CALL METHOD gv_message->get_short_text
      IMPORTING
        ev_text = lv_text.
```

279

```
* Issue as message of type "S"
    MESSAGE lv_text TYPE 'S'.
  ENDIF.
* Initialize messages after issue
  CLEAR gt_messages[].
ENDMETHOD.                      "pbo_end
```

Listing 7.15 Simple Issuing of a Message

[+]

Issuing Messages According to Message Type

If you want to issue the message according to the message type (for example, in red and with an error icon for an error message), you can use the syntax that follows to issue the message. This will enable you to prevent error messages (types A, E, or X) from causing terminations or other unwanted side effects.

```
MESSAGE lv_text TYPE 'S'
  DISPLAY LIKE gv_message->gs_message-msgty.
```

7.4.17   Embedding the Business Application Log

Sometimes, it is not enough to just issue a message; you may instead want the entire message table to be displayed in the form of a log. You can do this using tools from the *Business Application Log*, which we discuss in detail in Section 9.1, Implementing the Application Log.

Docking container   Listing 7.16 shows how you can display an application log in a docking container at the bottom of a screen. You then extend the main screen class with certain instance attributes that refer to a log, container, and control, and also add a method where they are displayed.

```
CLASS lcl_scr_100 DEFINITION
  INHERITING FROM cl_bus_abstract_main_screen.
  ...
  PRIVATE SECTION.
    DATA:
      mr_container  TYPE REF TO cl_gui_docking_container,
      mv_loghandle  TYPE        balloghndl,
      mv_balcnthndl TYPE        balcnthndl.
    METHODS display_messages_as_log.
```

```
ENDCLASS.                    "lcl_scr_100 DEFINITION
```

Listing 7.16 Defining the Main Screen Class

You implement the new method as follows: First, you create the required *Custom Container*, *Log* and *Log Control* objects. You initialize the log control using a display profile, for which you activate the SUPPRESS TOOLBAR option.

Implementing the new method

You then extract the messages that are in the internal GT_MESSAGES[] table, transfer them to the BAL log, and select the option whether to display the log (depending on whether there are any messages).

In the calls shown in Listing 7.17, the objects are not created again, but rather the log content is deleted and a new one is created from the message table.

```
METHOD display_messages_as_log.
* In the first pass, all objects are generated:
* log, docking container and log container.
* In each pass, the log is cleared and the
* current messages are attached. If there are
* no messages, the docking container will be
* hidden.
* When you exit the program, container, control
* and log are released.
  DATA:
    lt_loghandle TYPE bal_t_logh,
    ls_log       TYPE bal_s_log,
    ls_prof      TYPE bal_s_prof,
    ls_msg       TYPE bal_s_msg,
    lr_message   TYPE bu_message.

* First pass? Then, MV_LOGHANDLE is initial
* and we must generate all objects.
  IF mv_loghandle IS INITIAL.
* Generate docking container
    CREATE OBJECT mr_container
      EXPORTING
        side  = mr_container->dock_at_bottom
        ratio = 10.
* Generate log
    CALL FUNCTION 'BAL_LOG_CREATE'
```

```
         EXPORTING
           i_s_log      = ls_log
         IMPORTING
           e_log_handle = mv_loghandle.
       APPEND mv_loghandle TO lt_loghandle.
* Display profile for log
     CALL FUNCTION 'BAL_DSP_PROFILE_NO_TREE_GET'
         IMPORTING
           e_s_display_profile = ls_prof.
       ls_prof-no_toolbar = 'X'.
* Generate log control and link to container
     CALL FUNCTION 'BAL_CNTL_CREATE'
         EXPORTING
           i_container           = mr_container
           i_s_display_profile = ls_prof
           i_t_log_handle       = lt_loghandle
         IMPORTING
           e_control_handle      = mv_balcnthndl.
     ENDIF.
* Clear log
   CALL FUNCTION 'BAL_LOG_MSG_DELETE_ALL'
       EXPORTING
         i_log_handle = mv_loghandle.
* Loop at all messages and attach to log
   LOOP AT gt_messages INTO lr_message.
* Convert message in BAL structure
     CLEAR ls_msg.
     ls_msg-msgty = lr_message->gs_message-msgty.
     ls_msg-msgid = lr_message->gs_message-msgid.
     ls_msg-msgno = lr_message->gs_message-msgno.
     ls_msg-msgv1 = lr_message->gs_message-msgv1.
     ls_msg-msgv2 = lr_message->gs_message-msgv2.
     ls_msg-msgv3 = lr_message->gs_message-msgv3.
     ls_msg-msgv4 = lr_message->gs_message-msgv4.
* Attach message to log
     CALL FUNCTION 'BAL_LOG_MSG_ADD'
         EXPORTING
           i_log_handle = mv_loghandle
           i_s_msg      = ls_msg.
   ENDLOOP.
* No messages? Then hide container
   IF sy-subrc NE 0.
     mr_container->set_visible( space ).
```

```
    ELSE.
      mr_container->set_visible( 'X' ).
    ENDIF.
*   Refresh control to display log data
    CALL FUNCTION 'BAL_CNTL_REFRESH'
      EXPORTING
        i_control_handle = mv_balcnthndl.
*   Flush to send control status to GUI
    cl_gui_cfw=>flush( ).
ENDMETHOD.                      "display_messages_as_log
```

Listing 7.17 Issuing all Screen Messages as a Log Control

7.4.18 Table Controls and ALV-Grids

When you display data objects in screens in table form, as a developer you can choose between table controls and ALV grids. The ALV grid is the more modern and more user-friendly technology. With a few lines of source code you can create—as if by magic—tables in the dialog that leave nothing to be desired: selection, filter, sort and totals functions are implemented, as is the ABAP Dictionary connection with the full range of capabilities of search helps, value lists, and ⌐F1⌐ documentation.

ALV grid: Modern and user-friendly

At runtime, you can change the structure and appearance of the grid control and, to a large extent, determine its responses to user interaction. In contrast, table controls act like outdated technology. In particular, they require enormous effort on the programmer's part to achieve approximately the same high level of user-friendliness achieved with the ALV grid.

> **Compatibility with the SAP GUI for HTML**   **[+]**
>
> If you want your dialogs to be compatible with the SAP GUI for HTML, we recommend that you check the current SAP Notes related to this question in SAPNet before you decide whether to use table controls or the ALV grid.

7.4.19 Screens with Subscreen Areas

You cannot call subscreens directly. Instead, you must always incorporate them into another screen (either a normal screen or another subscreen). The higher-level screen must have a subscreen area where the subscreen is integrated, as shown in Figure 7.25. In screens with subscreen areas, the most important factor is that the framework methods are processed at the right time.

The processing is divided into three phases:

1. BEGIN: Before the subscreen(s)

2. Subscreen(s)

3. END: After the subscreen(s)

When you integrate subscreens into a subscreen area, there are two variants: *static* and *dynamic*. Integrating a subscreen statically means that the program name and screen number to be integrated are known at design time and can be specified in the source code accordingly.

In the example shown in Listing 7.18, we assume that a normal screen with the number 0100 has a subscreen area called SUBSCREEN_AREA_0100. The subscreen with number 0130 is statically integrated into this subscreen area. Listing 7.18 shows the flow logic of the higher-level 0100 screen in the Screen Painter:

```
PROCESS BEFORE OUTPUT.
  MODULE pbo_begin.
  CALL SUBSCREEN subscreen_area_0100
    INCLUDING 'SAPLZVEHICLE_DIALOG'
            '0130'.
  MODULE pbo_end.

PROCESS AFTER INPUT.
  MODULE pai_begin.
  CALL SUBSCREEN subscreen_area_0100.
  MODULE pai_end.
```

Listing 7.18 Flow Logic with Statically Integrated Subscreen

Dynamically integrating a subscreen means that the program and screen number are not known at the time of programming. For example, it may be necessary to dynamically integrate a screen whose program name and screen number are not known at design time, but are read from a Customizing table at runtime. In this case, the program containing the higher-level screen must possess global variables for the program name and screen number of the screen to be integrated. You can define this as a global data object in a structure, as follows:

```
DATA:
  BEGIN OF gs_subscreen_0100,
    repid TYPE syrepid,
    dynnr TYPE sydynnr,
  END OF gs_subscreen_0100.
```

The following sample source code for the flow logic of framework screen 0100 shows how this global data is used in the flow logic:

```
* Dynpro 0100 in Program SAPLZVEHICLE_DIALOG
process before output.
  MODULE pbo_begin.
  CALL SUBSCREEN subscreen_area_0100
    INCLUDING gs_subscreen_0100-repid
              gs_subscreen_0100-dynnr.
  MODULE pbo_end.

process after input.
  MODULE pai_begin.
  CALL SUBSCREEN subscreen_area_0100.
  MODULE pai_end.
```

Class and Instance Attributes   [+]

Instead of using global variables, as in the previous code example, you can also use class and instance attributes.

A frequently occurring error we want to warn you about happens when the CALL SUBSCREEN … INCLUDING command is reached in the flow logic of the framework screen, but the variables for program and screen have not yet been set. If the variables are first set in the PBO_END( ) method of the current screen by mistake and they are still initial, a runtime error that cannot be caught will occur when the flow logic reaches the CALL SUBSCREEN statement.

Frequent error

7.4.20 Defining Subscreens

Defining screen classes for subscreens is easier than for main screens. You must derive the screen class of subscreens from the abstract CL_BUS_ ABSTRACT_SUB_SCREEN basis class. Since this does not have any abstract methods, the derived screen class may also be a global class. (In this case, however, you must solve the issue of access to screen fields from outside the program or function group.)

Simplest definition of a subscreen class

You create instances exactly like normal screens within the BUS_SCREEN_ CREATE form routine of the program or the screen's function group. In the simplest definition, you can even forego a class implementation, because no methods are redefined or added:

```
CLASS lcl_sub_screen DEFINITION INHERITING FROM
  cl_bus_abstract_sub_screen.
ENDCLASS.  "lcl_sub_screen DEFINITION
```

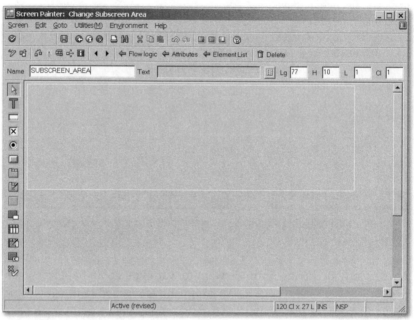

Figure 7.25 Subscreen Area in Screen Painter

7.4.21 Data Transfer Between Screen Fields and Screen Class

Simple and robust

The most simple and robust option is to use global data of the main program on the screen. This option is frequently chosen, but the disadvantage is that the assignment of the global data object to screen and screen class is not clear or unambiguous.

A second option available that will make the assignment to the screen field more explicit involves defining an attribute in the screen class as a data reference to the program's global data object. When you create the screen object, or in the first PBO_BEGIN( ) run, GET REFERENCE OF … INTO … can then establish the connection between the global variable and attribute. Only the data reference will be accessed within the class.

The third alternative entails not using global data objects for screen fields and working with instance or class attributes. If you want to use an instance attribute, you must define a TYPE REF TO (screen class) global variable in the program that will point to the screen object at runtime. In the Screen Painter, you can then define screen fields that are linked to attributes of the screen class (for example, GR_SCR_0100->MV_FIRST_NAME).

If you want to use class attributes, you do not need a global data object and you can directly use the static attributes of the screen class on the screen (for example, LCL_SCR_0100=>MV_FIRST_NAME).

There are two major advantages to the second and third options: First, the idea of encapsulation is expressed and, second, modularization units outside of the current program can also use this programming model to obtain read and write access to the screen contents (provided you allow this, know a screen instance, and the screen structure type is known).

However, there is a prerequisite to ensure that the link between the screen field and attribute works at runtime. That is, you must instantiate the data object at runtime before the PBO block of the screen is reached. You do this by accessing any component of the class by, for example, creating an instance, calling a method, or accessing an attribute. Despite this restriction, we prefer the latter option and will use it in the following examples.

Prerequisite

7.4.22 Tabstrips

The BUS_SCREEN framework provides support for tabstrips in the form of the CL_BUS_TABSTRIP and CL_BUS_TAB classes. One object of the CL_BUS_TABSTRIP class represents a single tabstrip. Like a subscreen, it can be integrated into any screen.

Tabs The objects of the `CL_BUS_TAB` class represent the tabs, that is, the individual tab titles. Each tab title refers to a subscreen that is displayed when the relevant tab title is active.

In the example, you can see how a tabstrip with three tab titles is integrated into a screen, in this case, main screen 0100. Depending on which tab title is active, subscreens 0110, 0120 or 0130 should be displayed in the tabstrip.

Declaring tabstrip control You must first declare the tabstrip control globally in the main program. This is also where you assign its name. In our `TABSTRIP_0100` example this is:

```
CONTROLS tabstrip_0100 TYPE TABSTRIP.
```

This is the only declaration you must perform globally in the program. You can perform all other declarations in the screen class in accordance with the idea of encapsulation.

Declaring a tabstrip object You will need a reference to the tabstrip object that still has to be created.

```
CLASS lcl_main DEFINITION INHERITING FROM
  cl_bus_abstract_main_screen.
  PUBLIC SECTION.
    DATA       mr_tabstrip TYPE REF TO cl_bus_tabstrip.
    ...
```

Structure for tabstrip fields Furthermore, you require a data object for the tabstrip fields. It must be typed on the BUS_SCREEN_TABSTRIP data class, and contains the headings of the tab titles and the current subscreen for each.

You create this data object as a public class attribute of the screen class:

```
CLASS-DATA ms_tabstrip TYPE bus_screen_tabstrip.
```

Defining a function code prefix Tabstrips work internally with function codes, where each tab title behaves like a pushbutton element whose function code is triggered when you click on the tab title. The function codes in our tabstrip example consist of a prefix (which you can choose as you wish) and the suffix _TAB_nn, where *nn* represents the number of tab titles between 01 and 20.

In this example, select the FKT prefix to produce the function codes FKT_TAB_01, FKT_TAB_02, and so on, up to FKT_TAB_20.

> **Name Length Restriction** [!]
>
> The full name of the BUS_SCREEN_TABSTRIP data object for the tabstrip fields (in this example, LCL_MAIN=>MS_TABSTRIP) must not be longer than 25 characters. The length of the function code prefix must not exceed 15 characters.

The content of the tabstrip is displayed in a subscreen area. Depending on which tab title is active, the subscreen assigned to it is integrated into the subscreen area. In this example, call it SUBAREA_0100.

Defining a subscreen area

Before you call the Screen Painter, in Table 7.1 you will find a summary of the names and IDs we previously assigned.

Name of control	TABSTRIP_0100
Structure for tabstrip fields	LCL_MAIN=>MS_TABSTRIP
Prefix for function codes	FKT
Name of subscreen area	SUBAREA_0100

Table 7.1 Freely Defined Tabstrip Name Components

In the Screen Painter, you must now create the tabstrip control, with up to 20 tab titles. (You only need to create the actual number of tab titles you will use. In our example, we have restricted the number to three.)

Creating tabstrips in the Screen Painter

Call the Screen Painter and add a tabstrip control with the properties shown in Table 7.2.

Screen element	Tabstrip
Name	TABSTRIP_0100
Tab title	3

Table 7.2 Tabstrip Control Properties

Create a subscreen area inside the tabstrip and call it SUBAREA_0100.

Creating tab titles Now, edit the first tab title and assign it the properties shown in Table 7.3.

Screen element	Button
Name	LCL_MAIN=>MS_TABSTRIP-TAB_01
Visible length	20
Function code	FKT_TAB_01
Reference field	SUBAREA_0100
Output field	Yes

Table 7.3 Properties of the First Tab Title

Create the other tab titles in the same way. The name of the second tab title is LCL_MAIN=>MS_TABSTRIP-TAB_02 and the function code is FKT_TAB_02.

Flow logic Next, maintain the flow logic of the screen to ensure that the subscreen area can be taken into account (see Listing 7.19).

```
PROCESS BEFORE OUTPUT.
  MODULE dynpro_pbo_begin.
  CALL SUBSCREEN subarea_0100
    INCLUDING lcl_main=>ms_tabstrip-area-program_name
              lcl_main=>ms_tabstrip-area-dynpro_number.
  MODULE dynpro_pbo_end.

PROCESS AFTER INPUT.
  MODULE dynpro_pai_begin.
  CALL SUBSCREEN subarea_0100.
  MODULE dynpro_pai_end.
```

Listing 7.19 Flow Logic of a Screen with Subscreen Area

You have now completed your screen, and will turn your attention again to the main screen's LCL_MAIN screen class where you will program the creation of the tabstrip and tab title objects. You do this in the PBO_BEGIN( ) method, which you redefine for this purpose as shown in Listing 7.20.

```
METHOD pbo_begin.
  IF mr_tabstrip IS NOT BOUND.
```

```
    CALL METHOD add_tabstrip
      EXPORTING
        iv_field_name_prefix    = 'LCL_MAIN=>MS_TABSTRIP'
        iv_function_code_prefix = 'FKT'
      IMPORTING
        ev_tabstrip             = mr_tabstrip
      CHANGING
        cs_tabstrip_control     = tabstrip_0100
        cs_tabstrip_fields      = lcl_main=>ms_tabstrip.
    ...
  ENDIF.
  super->pbo_begin( ).
ENDMETHOD.
```

Listing 7.20 Implementing the PBO_BEGIN( ) Method

Transfer the name of the structure for screen fields as the IV_FIELDNAME_ PREFIX parameter, the structure itself as CS_TABSTRIP_FIELDS, the function code prefix as IV_FUNCTION_CODE_PREFIX, and the tabstrip control as CS_TABSTRIP_CONTROL.

Note that the upward delegation using SUPER->PBO_BEGIN( ) occurs only at the end of the method. This is important because unwanted behavior, including runtime errors, may otherwise occur. After you have created the tabstrip, create three tab titles that you must link to subscreens 0110, 0120 and 0130 (see Listing 7.21).

Upward delegation

```
    DATA:
      lr_tab  TYPE REF TO cl_bus_tabstrip_tab,
      ls_area TYPE          bus_screen_area.

    CLEAR: lr_tab, ls_area.
    ls_area-program_name  = sy-repid.
    ls_area-dynpro_number = '0110'.
    CALL METHOD mr_tabstrip->add_tab
      IMPORTING
        ev_tab = lr_tab.
    lr_tab->set_area( ls_area ).
    lr_tab->set_caption( 'First Tabstrip' ).

    CLEAR: lr_tab, ls_area.
    ls_area-program_name  = sy-repid.
    ls_area-dynpro_number = '0120'.
```

```
CALL METHOD mr_tabstrip->add_tab
  IMPORTING
    ev_tab = lr_tab.
lr_tab->set_area( ls_area ).
lr_tab->set_caption( 'Second Tabstrip' ).

CLEAR: lr_tab, ls_area.
ls_area-program_name  = sy-repid.
ls_area-dynpro_number = '0130'.
CALL METHOD mr_tabstrip->add_tab
  IMPORTING
    ev_tab = lr_tab.
lr_tab->set_area( ls_area ).
lr_tab->set_caption( 'Third Tabstrip' ).
```

Listing 7.21 Adding Three Tab Titles to a Tabstrip

Screens 0110 to 0130 embedded in this way can be any subscreens that either are not in the same main program or must not use the BUS Screen Framework. The layout of the completed tabstrip with the embedded subscreen 0110 is displayed in Figure 7.26.

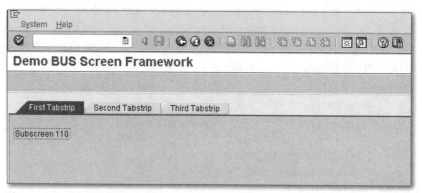

Figure 7.26 Tab Title with Subscreen 0110

Transferring function code Before the tabstrip can work correctly and respond when you click on the tab title, you must transfer to it the function code triggered by the user at the time of the PAI.

In this program, you have already created an event handler for the main screen's PROCESS_AFTER_INPUT event. You extend this method with a call for the tabstrip object, to which you pass the function code (see Listing 7.22).

```
METHOD handle_pai.
  DATA lv_dispatched TYPE abap_bool.
  CALL METHOD mr_main_screen->mr_tabstrip->dispatch
    EXPORTING
      iv_function_code = iv_function_code
    IMPORTING
      ev_dispatched    = lv_dispatched.
  IF lv_dispatched = abap_true.
    EXIT.
  ENDIF.
* Further handling of the function code
  ...
ENDMETHOD.
```

Listing 7.22 Handling Function Code

This is all you need to implement a fully functional tabstrip. Next, we describe a few other functions that make working with tab titles easier and more flexible.

The CL_BUS_TABSTRIP and CL_BUS_TABSTRIP_TAB classes enable you to change the layout and appearance of the tabstrip control at runtime.

The CL_BUS_TABSTRIP tabstrip class provides the following methods: **CL_BUS_TABSTRIP**

- The ADD_TAB( ) method lets you add new tab titles.
- The REMOVE_ALL_TABS( ) method lets you remove existing tab titles.
- The GV_ACTIVE_TAB attribute contains a reference to the tab title that is currently active.
- The GET_TAB_BY_KEY( ) method provides a reference to the tab title identified by an application-defined key.
- The SET_ACTIVE_TAB( ) and SET_ACTIVE_TAB_BY_KEY( ) methods let you change the active tab title.
- The NEW_TAB_SELECTED event is triggered if you have selected a new tab title. As an event parameter, it contains a reference to the new tab title.

The CL_BUS_TABSTRIP_TAB tab title class enables you to access individual   **CL_BUS_**
tab titles: **TABSTRIP_TAB**

▶ The SET_CAPTION( ) method lets you set the caption.

▶ The SET_VISIBLE( ) method lets you change the display options of a tab title.

▶ The SET_AREA( ) and SET_SUBSCREEN( ) methods let you assign a screen to the tab title. You can transfer this either using the name (program and screen number) or as a reference to a screen object.

▶ The SET_KEY( ) method lets you set the application-defined key of the tab title.

▶ The SET_ICON( ) method lets you set the icon and quick info text.

7.4.23 For Advanced Users: Selection Screens and Screen Painter

Selection criterion

The *selection criterion*, which consists of two input fields and one button for multiple selections, is the ideal design element for entering complex selections. You will recognize it from the selection screens of classic ABAP reports, where it is created using the SELECT-OPTIONS language element. Unfortunately, it is not available in the Screen Painter. However, you can use it by creating a selection screen with a selection criterion and integrating the selection screen into the application as a subscreen.

[+] | **Events on Selection Screens**

During selection screen processing, the system triggers the following events in a specific sequence and for certain user interactions:

▶ AT SELECTION-SCREEN OUTPUT

▶ AT SELECTION-SCREEN ON {para|selcrit}

▶ AT SELECTION-SCREEN ON END OF selcrit

▶ AT SELECTION-SCREEN ON BLOCK block

▶ AT SELECTION-SCREEN ON RADIOBUTTON GROUP radi

▶ AT SELECTION-SCREEN { }

▶ AT SELECTION-SCREEN ON {HELP-REQUEST|VALUE-REQUEST} FOR {para|selcrit-low|selcrit-high}

▶ AT SELECTION-SCREEN ON EXIT-COMMAND

The system also handles all OK codes for execution, cancelation, printing, and variant management purposes and, if necessary, triggers the START-OF-SELECTION processing block.

Rather than dealing with selection screen options, this section instead covers the interaction options of selection screens and normal screens created using the Screen Painter. We will briefly describe three scenarios and then make some comments about using the BUS Screen Framework for selection screens.

Selection Screen as Main Screen

This is the simplest option and is generally well-known. You can define selection screens in executable programs and function groups. You do not specifically need to define the selection screen with the `SELECTION-SCREEN BEGIN OF SCREEN nnnn` statement in an executable report because all `PARAMETERS`, `SELECT-OPTIONS`, and `SELECTION-SCREEN` statements that are not explicitly assigned to another screen automatically belong to standard selection screen (1000 in this case). In a function group, these statements must be within the selection screen definition because there is no standard selection screen in this case:

Selection screen 0100 with business partner selection criterion

```
DATA:
  gs_but000 TYPE but000.

SELECTION-SCREEN BEGIN OF SCREEN 100.
SELECT-OPTIONS:
  so_partn FOR gs_but000-partner.
SELECTION-SCREEN END OF SCREEN 100.
```

Figure 7.27 Selection Screen 0100

You can now call screen 100 using `CALL SELECTION-SCREEN 100`. Because it is a selection screen, it differs from a normal screen in several ways:

- The program cannot set the GUI status because the system automatically sets a specific GUI status for selection screens.

Differences to a normal screen

▶ Instead of the screen flow logic programmed for normal screens in the Screen Painter, the *selection screen processing* is run, whereby the system calls specific event blocks such as AT SELECTION-SCREEN OUT-PUT in the program.

▶ The screen is linked to variant management, which means that the user can create, change, and transport variants, as well as use all functions known from the classic selection screens of executable programs.

▶ If the user exited the selection screen by selecting EXECUTE, the value in the SY-SUBRC field will subsequently be 0. If the user exited the selection screen by selecting CANCEL or EXIT, the value in this SY-SUBRC field will be 4.

[!]   **Calling Selection Screens**

It is important that you only call selection screens using CALL SELECTION-SCREEN, not CALL SCREEN, because otherwise the selection screen processing will not be performed correctly and in a worst-case scenario, terminations will occur.

Selection Screen as Main Screen Integrating Subscreen

The selection screen variant that involves a selection screen as a main screen integrating a subscreen is rarely used because awareness about it is low. For years, before delving into the depths of selection screen processing, even the authors of this book used normal screens instead of selection screens if there was a requirement to integrate (without tab titles) one or more subscreens that only became known at runtime.

Integrating subscreens
The process to integrate a subscreen on a selection screen is simple. However, the selection screen in this case must not be a subscreen itself. To integrate a subscreen on a selection screen you have to alter the example a little, as shown in Listing 7.23:

1. First, define a subscreen area called SUBSCREEN_AREA on screen 100.

2. Integrate subscreen 200 into the SUBSCREEN_AREA subscreen area at runtime.

3. You create subscreen 200 as a normal screen in the Screen Painter, as shown in Figure 7.28. It must have a checkbox that is linked to the G_CHECK global variable.

```
REPORT  z_call_selection_screen.

* Global variables
DATA:
  gs_but000 TYPE but000,     " for selection criterion
  gv_check  TYPE c LENGTH 1. " Checkbox

* Main screen: selection screen 0100
SELECTION-SCREEN BEGIN OF SCREEN 100.
SELECT-OPTIONS:
  so_partn FOR gs_but000-partner. " business partner
SELECTION-SCREEN BEGIN OF TABBED BLOCK subscreen_area FOR 10 LINES.
SELECTION-SCREEN END OF BLOCK subscreen_area.
SELECTION-SCREEN END OF SCREEN 100.

AT SELECTION-SCREEN OUTPUT.
* Assign subscreen 0200 at runtime
  subscreen_area-prog  = sy-repid.
  subscreen_area-dynnr = '0200'.

START-OF-SELECTION.
* Call main screen
  CALL SELECTION-SCREEN 100.
* Issue SY-SUBRC
  WRITE: / sy-subrc.
```

Listing 7.23 Selection Screen with Subscreen Area

The SELECTION-SCREEN BEGIN OF TABBED BLOCK area language command, which is normally used to define tabstrips on selection screens, was used to provide a subscreen area on a selection screen. By specifying FOR 10 LINES, you define that the subscreen area has a total of ten lines. (The width is automatically set in the system to 116 characters.)

A global data object with the same name as the relevant subscreen area and the PROG, DYNNR and ACTIVETAB components is automatically created for each subscreen area.

Global data object

ACTIVETAB is not relevant for this example and is used with tabstrips to identify the active tab titles. The PROG and DYNNR components contain the program name and screen number of the subscreen to be integrated and must be set before the selection screen is sent, in other words, at the time of PROCESS BEFORE OUTPUT at the latest. In selection screen processing, this corresponds to the AT SELECTION-SCREEN OUTPUT event. After you exit the selection screen, issue SY-SUBRC on the basic list.

[»]   **Variants and Subscreens**

If you experiment a little with this example, you will discover that you can create and manage variants, but the elements of the integrated subscreen will be ignored if it is not a selection screen. Variant management covers integrated subscreens, but only selection screens, not normal screens.

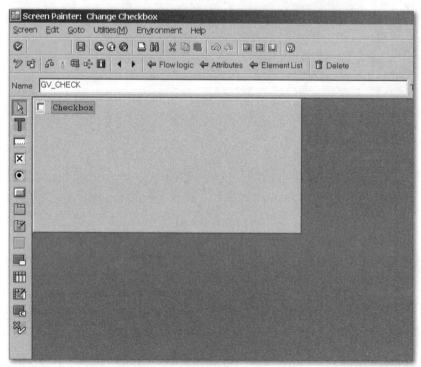

Figure 7.28 Subscreen 0200 in the Screen Painter

Normal Screen as Main Screen Integrating Selection Screen

The third scenario shows how a normal main screen created in the Screen Painter can integrate a selection screen that is defined as a subscreen.

This time you vary the example as follows in Listing 7.24:

Process

1. In the program, define a global structure called GS_SCREEN_0100, which is typed on BUS_SCREEN-AREA and contains the components PROGRAM_NAME and DYNPRO_NUMBER. You use this structure to define the subscreen to be integrated at runtime.

2. In the Screen Painter, create a main screen 100 that gets a subscreen area called SUBSCREEN_AREA.

3. In the flow logic of screen 100, specify that the screen named in the GS_SCREEN_0100 structure is to be integrated into the SUBSCREEN_AREA subscreen area at runtime.

4. Define a selection screen 200 with the *Business partner* selection criterion. The AS SUBSCREEN addition defines the selection screen as a subscreen rather than as a main screen.

5. Before you call main screen 0100, specify the program name and screen number of selection screen 200 in the GS_SCREEN_0100 structure.

```
REPORT  z_call_selection_screen_3.

DATA:
* Structure for screen known at runtime
  gs_screen_0100 TYPE bus_screen-area,
* Structure for selection option
  gs_but000      TYPE but000.

* Selection screen 0200 as subscreen
SELECTION-SCREEN BEGIN OF SCREEN 200 AS SUBSCREEN.
SELECT-OPTIONS:
  so_partn FOR gs_but000-partner.
SELECTION-SCREEN END OF SCREEN 200.

START-OF-SELECTION.
* Specify screen number and program name for structure
  gs_screen_0100-program_name = sy-repid.
  gs_screen_0100-dynpro_number = '0200'.
* Call main screen
```

```
CALL SCREEN 100.
WRITE: / sy-subrc.
```

Listing 7.24 Integrating the Selection Screen as a Subscreen in the Main Screen

```
PROCESS BEFORE OUTPUT.
  CALL SUBSCREEN subscreen_area
    INCLUDING gs_screen_0100-program_name
              gs_screen_0100-dynpro_number.

PROCESS AFTER INPUT.
  CALL SUBSCREEN subscreen_area.
```

Listing 7.25 Screen Flow Logic of Main Screen 100

No predefined GUI status

Because the main screen is a normal screen, not a selection screen, unlike with the first and second examples, there is no predefined GUI status and no link to variant management in this example. The selection screen processing with its AT SELECTION-SCREEN {Event} event blocks is only run for subscreen 200, not for main screen 100, for which corresponding modules would have to be defined in the flow logic.

7.4.24 Selection Screens in Conjunction with the BUS Screen Framework

When you use the BUS Screen Framework in conjunction with selection screens, the different behavior of normal screens and selection screens can cause problems if you do not proceed very carefully. When you use the standard screen classes, you may, for example, execute the SET PF-STATUS command at a time when this is not allowed, which will result in a termination. In addition, the basis class of the framework does not provide for any static methods for events on selection screens.

We therefore recommend that in most cases, you only use the BUS Screen Framework for normal screens, not for selection screens.

Because there is no reason not to, we recommend that normal screens integrate selection screens and vice versa. This way, you can develop normal screens using the BUS Screen Framework, and selection screens following the classic programming model, that is, you program event blocks.

If, for reasons of uniformity, you need to create screen classes for selection screens, we recommend that you only do this for selection screens that are subscreens. (This can be necessary, for example, when integrating selection screens into an application that requires using the BUS Screen Framework.)

Uniformity

To encapsulate the flow logic completely within your screen class, and to do this in as similar a way as possible to the structure of the framework, you can proceed as we explain next.

Suggestion: Extend the framework for selection screens

First, extend the basis class of the framework by deriving a new subclass. Create new static methods similar to the existing DYNPRO_PBO( ) and DYNPRO_PAI( ) methods in a new subclass of the CL_BUS_ABSTRACT_SCREEN Framework basis class. A suitable static method is set up for every selection screen processing event. This method has the IV_PROGRAM_NAME and IV_DYNPRO_NUMBER parameters and may also have a parameter for the name of the relevant element (see Table 7.4). The result is displayed in Listing 7.26.

Method	Additional Parameter
EVENT_ON_ELEMENT( )	IV_ELEMENT
EVENT_ON_END_OF_ELEMENT( )	IV_ELEMENT
EVENT_ON_BLOCK( )	IV_BLOCK
EVENT_ON_RADIOBUTTON_GROUP( )	IV_GROUP
EVENT_ON_HELP_REQUEST( )	IV_ELEMENT
EVENT_ON_VALUE_REQUEST( )	IV_ELEMENT
EVENT_ON_EXIT_COMMAND( )	

Table 7.4 Methods for Selection Screen Events

```
CLASS zcl_bus_abstract_screen DEFINITION
  PUBLIC
  INHERITING FROM cl_bus_abstract_screen
  ABSTRACT
  CREATE PUBLIC .

*"* public components of class ZCL_BUS_ABSTRACT_SCREEN
*"* do not include other source files here!!!
```

```
PUBLIC SECTION.

  CLASS-METHODS event_on_element
    IMPORTING
      !iv_element TYPE bus_screen-field_name
      !iv_program_name TYPE bus_screen-program_name
      !iv_dynpro_number TYPE bus_screen-dynpro_number .
  CLASS-METHODS event_on_end_of_element
    IMPORTING
      !iv_element TYPE fieldname
      !iv_program_name TYPE bus_screen-program_name
      !iv_dynpro_number TYPE bus_screen-dynpro_number .
  CLASS-METHODS event_on_block
    IMPORTING
      !iv_block TYPE c
      !iv_program_name TYPE bus_screen-program_name
      !iv_dynpro_number TYPE bus_screen-dynpro_number .
  CLASS-METHODS event_on_radiobutton_group
    IMPORTING
      !iv_group TYPE c
      !iv_program_name TYPE bus_screen-program_name
      !iv_dynpro_number TYPE bus_screen-dynpro_number .
  CLASS-METHODS event_on_help_request
    IMPORTING
      !iv_element TYPE bus_screen-field_name
      !iv_program_name TYPE bus_screen-program_name
      !iv_dynpro_number TYPE bus_screen-dynpro_number .
  CLASS-METHODS event_on_value_request
    IMPORTING
      !iv_element TYPE bus_screen-field_name
      !iv_program_name TYPE bus_screen-program_name
      !iv_dynpro_number TYPE bus_screen-dynpro_number .
  CLASS-METHODS event_on_exit_command
    IMPORTING
      !iv_program_name TYPE bus_screen-program_name
      !iv_dynpro_number TYPE bus_screen-dynpro_number .
```

Listing 7.26 Defining the Extended ZCL_BUS_ABSTRACT_SCREEN Basis Class

Implementing methods

The implementations of the seven new static methods follow the example of the DYNPRO_PBO( ) and DYNPRO_PAI( ) framework methods. The screen object is requested first, and then the corresponding method for the event is executed (see Listing 7.27).

```
METHOD event_on_element.
  DATA lv_screen TYPE REF TO zcl_bus_abstract_sel_screen.
  CALL METHOD get_screen
    EXPORTING
      iv_program_name  = iv_program_name
      iv_dynpro_number = iv_dynpro_number
    IMPORTING
      ev_screen        = lv_screen
    EXCEPTIONS
      OTHERS           = 1.
  IF sy-subrc IS INITIAL.
    RETURN.
  ENDIF.
  CALL METHOD lv_screen->on_element
    EXPORTING
      iv_element = iv_element.
ENDMETHOD.
```

Listing 7.27 Implementation for the AT SELECTION-SCREEN ON Event

Next, implement the other six methods using the same pattern shown for the first method.

Then create a ZCL_BUS_ABSTRACT_SEL_SCREEN class as the subclass of the CL_BUS_ABSTRACT_SUB_SCREEN framework class. This means that you create a specialization of the screen class for subscreens that is responsible for subscreens of the selection screen type. You define the interface as shown in Listing 7.28.

Specializing the screen class

```
CLASS zcl_bus_abstract_sel_screen DEFINITION
  PUBLIC
  INHERITING FROM cl_bus_abstract_sub_screen
  CREATE PUBLIC .

*"* public components of class ZCL_BUS_ABSTRACT_SEL_SCREEN
*"* do not include other source files here!!!
PUBLIC SECTION.

  METHODS on_element
    IMPORTING
      !iv_element TYPE bus_screen-field_name .
  METHODS on_end_of_element
    IMPORTING
```

```
            !iv_element TYPE bus_screen-field_name .
       METHODS on_block
          IMPORTING
            !iv_block TYPE c .
       METHODS on_radiobutton_group
          IMPORTING
            !iv_group TYPE c .
       METHODS on_help_request
          IMPORTING
            !iv_element TYPE bus_screen-field_name .
       METHODS on_value_request
          IMPORTING
            !iv_element TYPE bus_screen-field_name .
       METHODS on_exit_command .
```

Listing 7.28 Defining the Screen Class for Subscreens of the Selection Screen Type

The implementations of the new methods in the ZCL_BUS_ABSTRACT_SEL_
SCREEN class should be empty. You should not force the user to redefine
all methods; therefore, do not create them as abstract methods.

For the integration into the program, create a local screen class where you
can redefine individual methods of the ZCL_BUS_ABSTRACT_SEL_SCREEN
class (see Listing 7.29). In this example, call the class LCL_SCR_0200 and
redefine the ON_VALUE_REQUEST( ) method.

```
CLASS lcl_scr_0200 DEFINITION
  INHERITING FROM zcl_bus_abstract_sel_screen.
  PUBLICSECTION.
    METHODS on_value_request REDEFINITION.
ENDCLASS.                 "lcl_scr_0200 DEFINITION

CLASS lcl_scr_0200 IMPLEMENTATION.
  METHOD on_value_request.
    MESSAGE iv_element TYPE 'I'.
  ENDMETHOD.                  "on_element
ENDCLASS.                  "lcl_scr_0200 IMPLEMENTATION
```

Listing 7.29 Screen Class for Selection Screen 200

As always, create a form routine that will create the object instance for
the screen class (see Listing 7.30).

```
FORM bus_screen_create USING     iv_program_name
                                 iv_dynpro_number
                     CHANGING cr_screen.
  CASE iv_dynpro_number.
    WHEN ,0200'.
      CREATE OBJECT cr_screen TYPE lcl_scr_0200
        EXPORTING
          iv_program_name  = iv_program_name
          iv_dynpro_number = iv_dynpro_number.
  ENDCASE.
ENDFORM.                          "bus_screen_create
```

Listing 7.30 Creating an Instance of the LCL_SCR_0200 Screen Class

You now have to ensure that the framework will actually be called in the program. To do this, you program event blocks for all selection screen events that are handled by the screen class (see Listing 7.31).

Programming event blocks

```
* Event PBO
AT SELECTION-SCREEN OUTPUT.
  cl_bus_abstract_screen=>dynpro_pbo(
    iv_dynpro_number = sy-dynnr
    iv_program_name  = sy-repid ).


* Event PAI
AT SELECTION-SCREEN.
  cl_bus_abstract_screen=>dynpro_pai(
    iv_dynpro_number = sy-dynnr
    iv_program_name  = sy-repid ).


AT SELECTION-SCREEN ON VALUE-REQUEST FOR so_partn-low.
  CALL METHOD zcl_bus_abstract_screen=>event_on_value_request
    EXPORTING
      iv_program_name  = sy-repid
      iv_dynpro_number = sy-dynnr
      iv_element       = 'SO_PARTN-LOW'.
```

Listing 7.31 Calling the Extended Basis Class in Event Blocks

[!]

> **Event Blocks and Standard Functions**
>
> Caution: When you program an event block such as AT SELECTION-SCREEN ON VALUE-REQUEST FOR …, the selection screen processing calls this event block *instead of* the otherwise standard functions that are provided automatically. The standard functions such as calling search help or F1 documentation are suppressed.
>
> Preferably program the AT SELECTION-SCREEN … event blocks only if you really want to replace the standard functions with your own functions. If you are satisfied with the standard functions for a screen element, simply omit that particular event block.

7.4.25 Outlook

The example we have been working with shows that you can extend the framework with special functions for selection screens, and indicates what this extension could look like.

Risks Depending on the demands the development of your applications places on a framework for screen development, the BUS Screen Framework may suit your needs exactly, or it may be too basic or too powerful (and complicated). There certainly are risks involved in using an unreleased framework and you should take these on only if you thoroughly understand the framework and can replace it with your own solution at any time, if required.

Irrespective of any specific framework, the examples show that ABAP Objects is a modern programming language you can use to support the object-oriented programming paradigm in all areas of SAP application development.

7.5 Web Dynpro

Web Dynpro is the most recent and most advanced GUI technology in AS ABAP. It contains solutions for the classic techniques of ALV grids, ALV trees, creating business graphics, comprehensive solutions for integration into the Enterprise Portal, and Adobe integration for creating Adobe Interactive Forms. Web Dynpro applications are also web-enabled: The SAP GUI is no longer available as a client; you use a web browser instead.

Experience shows that you can create applications more quickly and maintain them more easily using Web Dynpro than using classic screen technology. The reason for this is an advanced development environment where you can develop graphical applications extensively and generate a large part of the application source code automatically using the *Web Dynpro Code Wizard*.

Web Dynpro Code Wizard

Due to lack of space, we will only provide a brief introduction into Web Dynpro technology and focus instead on software factors of Web Dynpro development. We will cover the basic principles of dynamic programming and show you that as far as modification-free extensibility is concerned, Web Dynpro is just as good as predecessor technologies, such as the Business Data Toolset.

7.5.1 Basic Principles

The prerequisites for using Web Dynpro and the settings required in AS ABAP are described in the WEB DYNPRO ABAP CONFIGURATION and WEB DYNPRO ABAP ADMINISTRATION sections under WEB DYNPRO FOR ABAP in the SAP Library. The main thing you must do is activate ICF NODES in Transaction SICF, as explained in SAP Note 517484. Once you have fulfilled the prerequisites, you can begin programming.

The smallest programming unit of a Web Dynpro application is the *component*. To be able to call a component and edit it in a web browser, you must define an *application*.

Component

We recommend that when you begin a Web Dynpro project, you refer to specialist literature on the subject, such as *Web Dynpro for ABAP* by Ulli Hoffmann (SAP PRESS 2006). The books *Next Generation ABAP Development* by Thomas Jung and Richard Heilmann (SAP PRESS 2007) and *ABAP Objects* by Horst Keller and Sascha Krüger (SAP PRESS 2007) provide very good introductions into this technology. Even if you find Web Dynpro technology quick and easy to learn, you should follow some basic rules to achieve comprehensible and maintainable applications.

Separating Application Logic and Visual Components

In Section 7.4, Object-Oriented Screen Programming, we introduced you to an example of object-oriented screen programming. You encapsulated subscreens for objects, in whose attributes you save application data. You can define the same type of interfaces for these objects and thereby integrate methods for PAI and PBO handling and interfaces for plausibility checks, and for saving data.

Although this enables you to modularize applications, you cannot separate visual components of a dialog and of the application logic, or achieve a uniform concept of communication of individual objects of the overall application.

MVC design pattern

The Web Dynpro framework provides a separate uniform design methodology for this, similar to the Model-View-Controller (MVC) design pattern. Application data is stored in a *model* and displayed in another component, the *view*. The *controller* receives user interactions, delegates these to the model, and updates the view. The objective of this separation is to create maintainable applications, where you can change the layout and application logic with ease.

Basic rules

To achieve this, you must observe several rules:

▶ Store application data in the context of the component controller and map this data to the context of the corresponding views: The view is a pure data consumer.

▶ Delegate data manipulations and general user interactions from the view to the component controller context, but do not manipulate any application data in the view.

▶ The same principle also applies for controlling the application; this should never occur using view components.

Web Dynpro Programming Model

Use the Web Dynpro programming model to create maintainable applications. The result of adhering to the Web Dynpro programming model is that at the same time, programming guidelines can be established for developers. This means that you can achieve homogeneous Web Dynpro components that you create in accordance with the same procedure and that are therefore easier to understand and maintain.

Componentizing Applications

You should not implement larger applications in a component; instead, use a sensible breakdown:

Useful breakdown

▸ **Search services**
As with the Locator Framework in classic ABAP Dynpro applications, in Web Dynpro applications you need components with search functions for central applications objects.

▸ **Editing the application object**
You need display and processing dialogs for central application objects.

▸ **Detail views**
In addition to dialogs for application objects, you need detail dialogs for dependent objects.

▸ **Components that are not displayed**
You can also create the previously described displayed components on components that are not displayed and are used only to store data.

Creating Web Dynpro applications differs from classic screen programming in many ways. No dialog standards such as the ones introduced in Section 7.1, Ergonomic Examples and Dialog Standards, have yet become widely accepted. This does not cause problems for small programming projects, but it does pose the following challenges for big Web Dynpro programming projects that consist of a large number of components:

Challenges for big projects

▸ **Consistency**
You must ensure that the look and feel of all components is identical for the user. In addition, there are also requirements for portal integration. Technically speaking, registering or triggering portal events is very easy, but we recommend that you use a consistent design methodology for this.

▸ **Reusability**
The Web Dynpro framework enables you to componentize applications. From a technical perspective, you do this by creating usage definitions. You define component interfaces in the components used, which enables you to create method and event interfaces. You should

also use the same design methodology for this to ensure that you can integrate the components.

[+]
> **Chief Designer Role**
>
> In big Web Dynpro projects, it makes sense to assign a chief designer role. Together with sold-to parties, the chief designer defines the overall application, breaks down the components, and specifies regulations and guidelines for developers.

7.5.2 Creating a Sample Application

We will now create an example of a Web Dynpro application for the Vehicle Management sample application. Although this application only consists of one search dialog (see Figure 7.29), you will implement it with several components. A component displays detail vehicle data on the EQUIPMENT tab title. In Section 7.5.3, Modification-Free Extensions Using Dynamic Programming, you will see how you can display additional components. This is controlled dynamically using Customizing. Clicking on the SEARCH VEHICLE button should update all vehicle data displayed on the screen.

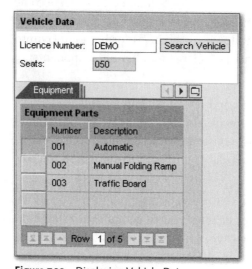

Figure 7.29 Displaying Vehicle Data

In the ABAP Workbench, create a Web Dynpro component called Z_
VEHICLE_DISPLAY with a W_MAIN window, as shown in Figure 7.30.

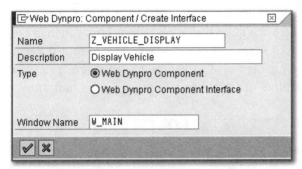

Figure 7.30 Creating a Web Dynpro Component

If you look at the component in the ABAP Workbench (more specifically, in the Web Dynpro Explorer) – Figure 7.31 shows the parts of the completed component – you see that the following objects were created:

Structure of a Web Dynpro component

▶ *Component Controller*: Used to implement the data retention and central services of the component.

▶ *Window*: Contains a number of *views* that form the components actually displayed.

▶ *Component Interface*: Creates a component interface for other components and for the application. Each window has an *Interface View* of the same name.

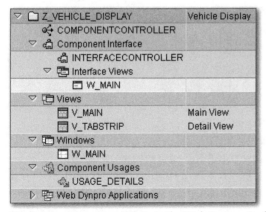

Figure 7.31 Component Parts in the Web Dynpro Explorer

Defining nodes

You will proceed as follows for the Web Dynpro application: In the context of the component controller, define a node with several attributes that correspond to the data elements in the display. For this purpose, go to change mode and use the CREATE NODE context menu to create the VEHICLE node in the CONTEXT. For the ZVEHICLE structure, you then use the CREATE USING WIZARD ATTRIBUTES FROM COMPONENTS context menu to create the components displayed in Figure 7.32. Because you only want to display the number of seats, also set the READ-ONLY indicator.

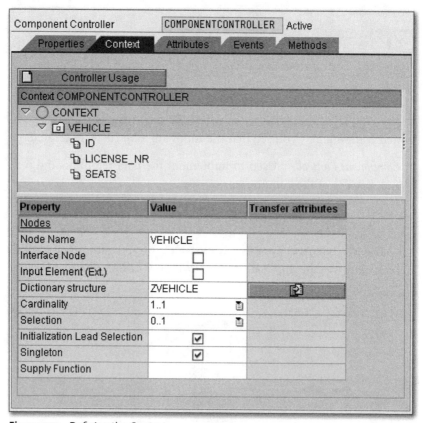

Figure 7.32 Defining the Context

You then define a V_MAIN view using the context menu for the Z_VEHICLE_DISPLAY component (see Figure 7.31). In this view, you will also find a CONTEXT tab title, to which you can drag and map the VEHICLE node from CONTEXT COMPONENTCONTROLLER to CONTEXT V_MAIN using drag and drop. This enables you to link the data structures of the view to the context. You then define the graphical design on the LAYOUT tab title, as shown in Figure 7.33. You can also use a graphical editor here.

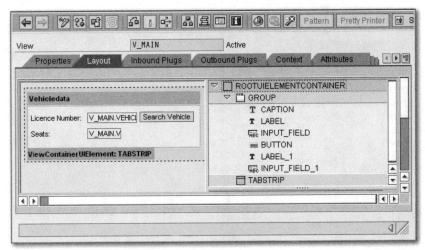

Figure 7.33 Layout of the Vehicle Data Display

In this section, you must edit the properties of the elements displayed in Figure 7.33. You can edit these properties on the lower right of the screen. We recommend that you define the LABEL and LABEL_1 text fields using the LABELFOR entry as the text field for INPUT_FIELD and INPUT_FIELD_1. You also connect these two fields to the V_MAIN.VEHICLE. LICENSE_NR and V_MAIN.VEHICLE.SEATS context elements using the VALUE property field, so that the values from the context are displayed on the view. Define a RELOAD event for the BUTTON element, which will be triggered when you click on it, as shown in Figure 7.34.

Editing properties of elements

You must first define the RELOAD event using the ACTIONS tab title and implement the ONACTIONRELOAD method under the METHODS tab title (see Figure 7.35).

When you click on the W_MAIN window in the Web Dynpro Explorer, you can embed the V_MAIN view on the Window tab title using the W_MAIN context menu.

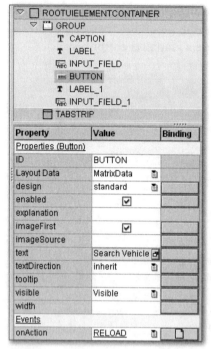

Figure 7.34 Triggering an Event Using a Button

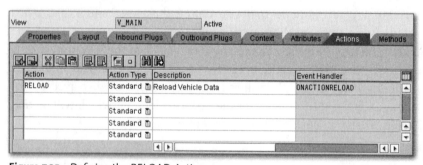

Figure 7.35 Defining the RELOAD Action

Implementing data retrieval

You could previously create the component completely using the Web Dynpro Explorer, with support from the graphical editor. Now you only have to implement data retrieval using the ONACTIONRELOAD() method, as shown in Listing 7.32.

```
DATA:
  lt_components     TYPE            wd_component_usage_group,
  lv_component      TYPE REF TO if_wd_component_usage,
  lr_controller     TYPE REF TO ziwci_z_vehicle_dynamic_ci.

DATA:
  node_vehicle      TYPE REF TO if_wd_context_node,
  elem_vehicle      TYPE REF TO if_wd_context_element,
  stru_vehicle      TYPE            if_v_main=>element_vehicle,
  item_license_nr LIKE             stru_vehicle-license_nr.

* navigate from <CONTEXT> to <VEHICLE> via lead selection
  node_vehicle = wd_context->get_child_node( name =
    if_v_main=>wdctx_vehicle ).

* get element via lead selection
  elem_vehicle = node_vehicle->get_element( ).

* get single attribute
  elem_vehicle->get_attribute(
    EXPORTING
      name =  `LICENSE_NR`
    IMPORTING
      value = item_license_nr ).

  wd_comp_controller->reload_context( item_license_nr  ).
```

Listing 7.32 Implementing the Reload Operation in the View

You can almost completely generate the source code using the Web Dynpro Code Wizard (⎡Ctrl⎤ + ⎡F7⎤), by reading a context node and then calling the RELOAD_CONTEXT( ) method with the entry in the component controller. This is the first time you do encoding without any help from code generations tools. After you load the data to be displayed, you can also use the Web Dynpro Code Wizard to help you connect this data to the context using the SET_ATTRIBUTE( ) method (see Listing 7.33).

Web Dynpro Code Wizard

```
DATA:
  lr_vehicle     TYPE REF TO z_if_vehicle,
  ls_attributes TYPE            zstr_vehicle_data.

DATA:
```

```
node_vehicle      TYPE REF TO if_wd_context_node,
elem_vehicle      TYPE REF TO if_wd_context_element,
stru_vehicle      TYPE
               if_componentcontroller=>element_vehicle,
item_license_nr  LIKE stru_vehicle-license_nr.
* navigate from <CONTEXT> to <VEHICLE> via lead selection
node_vehicle = wd_context->get_child_node( name =
   if_componentcontroller=>wdctx_vehicle ).

* get element via lead selection
elem_vehicle = node_vehicle->get_element(   ).
TRY.
    lr_vehicle =
      zcl_vehicle=>z_if_vehicle~load_by_license_nr(
          iv_nr = iv_license_nr ).
    ls_attributes = lr_vehicle->get_attributes( )
  CATCH zcx_object_not_found.
    clear ls_attributes.
ENDTRY.
* set single attribute
  elem_vehicle->set_attribute(
      name  = `LICENSE_NR`
      value = iv_license_nr ).

* set single attribute
  elem_vehicle->set_attribute(
      name =  `SEATS`
      value = ls_attributes-seats ).

* set single attribute
  elem_vehicle->set_attribute(
      name =  `ID`
      value = ls_attributes-id ).
```

Listing 7.33 Setting the Context Attributes for the Application Object Using the RELOAD_CONTEXT( ) Method

By defining a Web Dynpro application using the Web Dynpro Explorer, you have almost completed the display dialog. All that remains is implementing the detail displays of the Equipment tab title (see Figure 7.29). An equipment parts component and an auxiliary class are defined for this, where customers can add other components dynamically that are displayed as additional tabs on the tab title.

7.5.3 Modification-Free Extensions Using Dynamic Programming

You can also use the Web Dynpro framework dynamically, which means that you can dynamically change, delete, or add almost all development objects, such as context objects or views. Applications that result from using this option are more complex and are also not as easy to understand as normal Web Dynpro applications. Nevertheless, you will extend the application dynamically to enable you to display other detail data on tab titles (see Figure 7.29).

Increased complexity

First create a Customizing table called ZWDCUSAGE, where you will save the components to be embedded, as is shown in an entry in Figure 7.36. In the Z_VEHICLE_DISPLAY component, you will embed a Z_EQUIPMENT_ DISPLAY component on the first position on the tab title. The label of the corresponding component on the tab title will be EQUIPMENT.

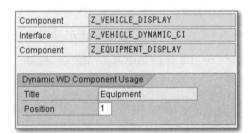

Figure 7.36 Components To Be Embedded

By adding other table entries, you extend the tab title with entries in which additional views are embedded. All of these views need to implement the Z_VEHICLE_DYNAMIC_CI interface (see 7.37). This means that customers can integrate their own dialogs and extend the data model of the central application object without modifications. In the additional, dynamically integrated components in the customer namespace, you manage customer data that has a logical dependency on the central application object.

Extending tab titles

Figure 7.37 Defining a Component Interface

Help Functions for Dynamic Embedding

Constructor You can save the data for the embedding in a component context. At this point, however, you need to implement a reusable solution to extend your own components dynamically. To do this, create a Z_CL_WB_TAB_ TOOLSET class that will load the ZWDCUSAGE table entries in the constructor and perform the embedding. Primarily, two attributes are filled in the constructor:

- Component usages are saved in the mt_usages attribute. The first use access is transferred to the constructor in the ir_wd_intf parameter, whereas you create the others from the first use by calling the CRE-ATE_COMP_USAGE_OF_SAME_TYPE( ) method. For the sake of simplicity, they are assigned the name of the component to be embedded, whose name is stored in Customizing.

- The use access names are stored in the mt_usage_names attribute.

Listing 7.34 shows the source code of the constructor of the Z_CL_WB_ TAB_TOOLSET auxiliary class:

```
METHOD constructor.
  DATA:
    ls_configuration TYPE       ZWDCUSAGE,
    lv_usage_name    TYPE       string,
    lr_usage         TYPE REF TO if_wd_component_usage.

  SELECT * FROM zwdcusage
    INTO CORRESPONDING FIELDS OF TABLE mt_component_usage
    WHERE component = iv_component_name AND
          wdcusage = iv_interface_name  AND
          pos > 0
    ORDER BY pos.
  IF sy-subrc = 0.
    APPEND ir_wd_intf TO mt_usages.
    APPEND iv_usage_name to mt_usage_names.
```

```
    LOOP at mt_component_usage FROM 2 INTO ls_configuration.
      lv_usage_name = ls_configuration-implementation.
      lr_usage = ir_wd_intf->create_comp_usage_of_same_type(
        lv_usage_name ).
      APPEND lr_usage TO mt_usages.
      APPEND lv_usage_name to mt_usage_names.
    ENDLOOP.
  ENDIF.
ENDMETHOD.
```

Listing 7.34 Constructor of Z_CL_WB_TAB_TOOLSET Auxiliary Class

The preparations you have made make it easy for you to now implement another method, PREPARE_NAVIGATION( ), of the Z_CL_WB_TAB_TOOLSET auxiliary class (see Listing 7.35).

```
METHOD prepare_navigation.
  DATA:
    lv_component_name TYPE string,
    lv_usage_name     TYPE string,
    lv_position       TYPE string,
    ls_configuration  TYPE zwdcusage,
    lv_count          TYPE i.
  FIELD-SYMBOLS <usage> TYPE REF TO if_wd_component_usage.
  LOOP AT mt_component_usage INTO ls_configuration.
    lv_count = sy-tabix.
    lv_component_name = ls_configuration-implementation.
    READ TABLE mt_usage_names into lv_usage_name INDEX
         lv_count.
    CONCATENATE iv_target_embedding_position lv_usage_name
                INTO lv_position SEPARATED BY `/`.
    TRY.
        ir_view_controller->prepare_dynamic_navigation(
            source_window_name       = iv_source_window_name
            source_vusage_name       = iv_source_vusage_name
            source_plug_name         = iv_source_plug_name
            target_component_name    = lv_component_name
            target_component_usage   = lv_usage_name
            target_view_name         = iv_target_view_name
            target_plug_name         = iv_target_plug_name
            target_embedding_position = lv_position ).
      CATCH cx_wd_runtime_repository.
        RAISE EXCEPTION TYPE cx_wdr_rt_exception.
```

```
      ENDTRY.
      READ TABLE mt_usages ASSIGNING <usage> INDEX lv_count.
      IF <usage>->has_active_component( ) IS NOT INITIAL.
        <usage>->delete_component( ).
      ENDIF.
      <usage>->create_component( lv_component_name ).
    ENDLOOP.
ENDMETHOD.
```

Listing 7.35 Dynamic Embedding

PREPARE_
NAVIGATION()
method

The PREPARE_NAVIGATION( ) method of the Z_CL_WB_TAB_TOOLSET auxiliary class reads, in a loop, the component usages to be implemented
and embeds the iv_target_view_name interface view of the lv_compo-
nent_name component for them. This component must implement the
component interface that corresponds to the lv_usage_name component
usage. From the source of the embedding, you must specify the name
of the iv_source_window_name window and the iv_source_vusage_name
view usage of the view to be embedded. In this example, it will be
the V_TABSTRIP_USAGE_3 view usage of the V_TABSTRIP node shown in
Figure 7.38. You also need to transfer the name of the outbound plug
and inbound plug of the iv_target_view_name interface view to ensure
that a navigation link is created between them. The lv_component_name
target component originates from Customizing and was determined in
the constructor. You determine the lv_position embedding position by
attaching the component to be embedded to the name of a container
(iv_target_embedding_position transfer parameter) using the "/" sepa-
rator. This is how you obtain a unique name.

Dynamic Extension

You can now extend the Z_VEHICLE_DISPLAY component using the Z_CL_
WB_TAB_TOOLSET auxiliary class. Proceed as follows:

Component
interface as
standard interface
of components to
be embedded

1. Specify that all components to be embedded dynamically must define
   a Z_VEHICLE_DYNAMIC_CI component interface (see Figure 7.37). In
   this component interface, create a SET_CONTEXT( ) method that you
   call for all dynamically used components at the end of the RELOAD_
   CONTEXT( ) method of the component controller:

```
DATA:
  lt_components TYPE         wd_component_usage_group,
  lv_component  TYPE REF TO if_wd_component_usage,
  lr_controller TYPE REF TO ziwci_z_vehicle_dynamic_ci.
lt_components = wd_this->get_used_components( ).

LOOP AT lt_components INTO lv_component.
  lr_controller ?= lv_component->get_interface_controller(
    ).
  lr_controller->set_context( ls_attributes-id ).
ENDLOOP.
```

2. To enable you to embed components that implement the Z_VEHICLE_   **Creating a usage**
   DYNAMIC_CI component interface, you must define a USAGE_DETAILS
   usage for the Z_VEHICLE_DYNAMIC_CI component interface. You need
   this component usage because you require a static component usage
   first before you can create other component usages dynamically from
   it using the CREATE_COMP_USAGE_OF_SAME_TYPE( ) method. In the
   component controller of the component, create a wd_this->mc_usage_
   manager attribute of the Z_CL_WD_TAB_TOOLSET class. The constructor
   is called in the wddoinit( ) method of the component controller. This
   method is called directly when the controller is initialized:

```
METHOD wddoinit .
DATA: lr_usage TYPE REF TO if_wd_component_usage.

  lr_usage = wd_this->wd_cpuse_usage_details( ).
  wd_this->mc_usage_manager = z_cl_wd_tab_toolset=>create(
      iv_component_name = 'Z_VEHICLE_DISPLAY'
      iv_interface_name = 'Z_VEHICLE_DYNAMIC_CI'
      iv_usage_name     = 'USAGE_DETAILS'
      ir_wd_interface   = lr_usage ).
ENDMETHOD.
```

3. Define views and their embedding as shown in Figure 7.38. The   **View embedding**
   application only runs in the W_MAIN window where you embed the
   V_MAIN view: The V_MAIN view (see Figure 7.33) contains a ViewCon-
   tainerUIElement TABSTRIP, where you embed the V_TABSTRIP view
   by dragging the V_TABSTRIP element from the left in Figure 7.39 to
   the TABSTRIP view container. V_TABSTRIP consists of a TABSTRIP tab-

strip element. This view has a FROM_MAIN inbound plug, for which you create a navigation link to the TO_TABSTRIP outbound plug using the drag and drop function, as shown in Figure 7.40.

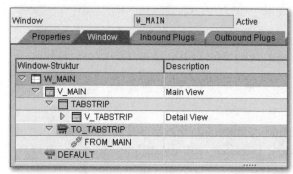

Figure 7.38 View Embeddings

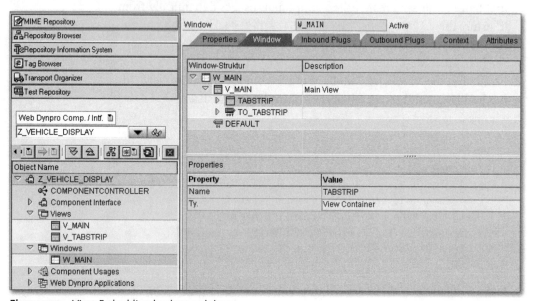

Figure 7.39 View Embedding by drag and drop

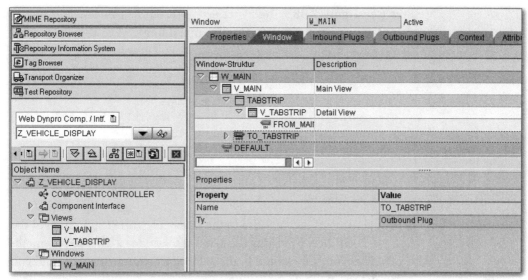

Figure 7.40 Creating a Navigation Link

4. When you initialize the V_MAIN view, you must call the runtime API of the View Controller by activating the PREPARE_DYNAMIC_NAVIGATION( ) method in the WDDOINIT( ) method; you do this through the delegation to the View Controller using the CREATE_TABSTRIPS( ) method. You then trigger the TO_TABSTRIP outbound plug, which causes the program to navigate to all dynamically created subsequent views:

Calling runtime APIs of the View Controller

```
DATA:
  l_view_controller_api TYPE REF TO
  if_wd_view_controller.

l_view_controller_api = wd_this->wd_get_api( ).
wd_comp_controller->create_tabstrips(
   ir_view_controller  = l_view_controller_api ).
wd_this->Fire_To_Tabstrip_Plg( ).
```

5. The called CREATE_TABSTRIPS( ) method is implemented in the component controller and delegates the call to the PREPARE_NAVIGATION( ) method of the Z_CL_WB_TAB_TOOLSET object. We have described the implementation of this earlier in the chapter. In addition to the View Controller window, the view and plug are specified from the source and target. The iv_source_vusage_name parameter corresponds to the view usage of the V_TABSTRIP view in the TABSTRIP view contain-

er (see Figure 7.38). The `iv_target_embedding_position` parameter contains the path position for the embedding:

```
wd_this->mc_usage_manager->prepare_navigation(
    ir_view_controller          = ir_view_controller
    iv_source_window_name       = `W_MAIN`
*   usage of V_TABSTRIP in Window W_MAIN
    iv_source_vusage_name       = `V_TABSTRIP_USAGE_3`
    iv_source_plug_name         = `TO_TABSTRIP`
    iv_target_plug_name         = `DEFAULT`
    iv_target_view_name         = `W_MAIN`
    iv_target_embedding_position =
        `V_MAIN/TABSTRIP.V_TABSTRIP` ).
```

Naming Tabstrips 6. Set the name of the tab titles in the `WDDOMODIFYVIEW( )` method of the V_TABSTRIP view by calling the `NEW_TAB( )` and `NEW_CAPTION( )` methods. The names are stored in the ZWDUSAGE Customizing table and you can determine them by calling a `GET_TABSTRIP_NAMES( )` component controller method that delegates them to the Z_CL_WB_TAB_TOOLSET class (see Listing 7.36).

```
METHOD wddomodifyview .
    DATA: l_cmp_usages        TYPE wdapi_component_usages,
          l_tabstrip          TYPE REF TO cl_wd_tabstrip,
          l_tab               TYPE REF TO cl_wd_tab,
          l_content           TYPE REF TO cl_wd_uielement,
          l_caption           TYPE REF TO cl_wd_caption,
          l_id                TYPE string,
          l_container_name    TYPE string.

    IF first_time = abap_true.
      l_tabstrip ?= view->get_element( 'TABSTRIP' ).
      l_tabstrip->remove_all_tabs( ).
      DATA:
        lt_info    TYPE ztab_usage_info,
        ls_info    TYPE zstr_usage_info,
        lv_text    TYPE string,
        lv_counter TYPE i.
      lt_info = wd_comp_controller->get_tabstrip_names( ).
      LOOP AT lt_info INTO ls_info.
        lv_counter = sy-tabix.
        CONCATENATE 'TAB_' ls_info-pos INTO l_id.
        l_tab = cl_wd_tab=>new_tab(
```

```
                id   = l_id
                view = view ).
      CONCATENATE 'CAP_' ls_info-pos INTO l_id.
      lv_text = ls_info-name.
      l_caption = cl_wd_caption=>new_caption(
                  id   = l_id
                  view = view
                  text = lv_text ).
      l_tab->set_header( l_caption ).
      l_container_name =
        wd_comp_controller->get_usage_name( lv_counter ).
      l_content =
cl_wd_view_container_uielement=>new_view_container_uielement(
                     id   = l_container_name
                     view = view ).
      l_tab->set_content( l_content ).
      l_tabstrip->add_tab( l_tab ).
    ENDLOOP.
  ENDIF.
ENDMETHOD.
```

Listing 7.36 Creating and Naming Tab Titles

Creating a Component To Be Embedded

To complete the example displayed earlier in Figure 7.29, you still have to present a Z_EQUIPMENT_DISPLAY component for displaying the equipment data. This is a generally useful procedure. If you allow customers to extend an application with other components, you should create a sample component that can be used as a model for the extensions.

Sample components

Create a component that implements the Z_VEHICLE_DYNAMIC_CI component interface. Because you want to display a number of equipment parts for a vehicle ID, create all of this data in the context using "cardinality 0 ... n". You create the equipment data by right-clicking and selecting CREATE USING WIZARD ATTRIBUTES FROM COMPONENTS OF STRUCTURE from the context menu. Then set up a view, use drag and drop to drag the EQUIPMENT node to the view context, and map it to the view context (see Figure 7.41).

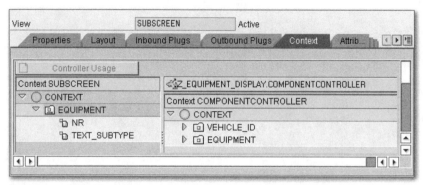

Figure 7.41 View Context

Table view element for data in tables

To display data contained in tables, use the *table view element* of the Web Dynpro framework. You will be able to display data in a table view element by setting DATA SOURCE to SUBSCREEN.EQUIPMENT in PROPERTIES (see Figure 7.42). This view element is a *composite view element* because you can assign other low-level view elements, such as TableColumn views, to it.

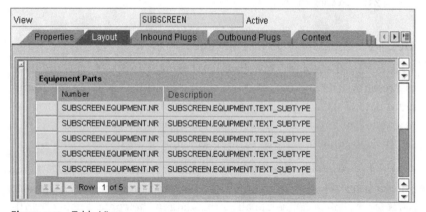

Figure 7.42 Table View

Supply functions

When you then implement the SET_CONTEXT( ) method of the Z_VEHI-CLE_DYNAMIC_CI component interface by saving the transferred vehicle ID in an attribute and then invalidating the context using wd_context->invalidate( ), you can load the data for the context using a supply function. *Supply functions* are data sources for context nodes. They populate the nodes if these are initial or have been invalidated, as is the case here.

7.6 Best Practices

In this chapter, you have learned important techniques for implementing graphical user interfaces. In Chapter 8, SAP Business Partner, we describe another technology with the Business Data Toolset. If you want to use one of these techniques in a development project, you must ask yourself two questions: Which technology is the right one, and how do I apply it correctly?

7.6.1 Choosing the Right GUI Technology

The most important factor is that you know the criteria for choosing the right technology for creating graphical user interfaces. Table maintenance dialogs and view clusters are only suitable for maintaining very basic master and transaction data or Customizing tables. If, due to specialized requirements, you are forced to manipulate existing screens and program comprehensive event maintenance, it is senseless to use table maintenance dialogs; you should preferably use classic screen programming. If you design more complex dialogs, you should use object-oriented encapsulations, as we recommended in Section 7.4.25, Outlook.

Knowing criteria

Web Dynpro is the first choice for programming web applications. Experience shows that you cannot avoid programming with Business Server Pages (BSP) in some situations. This applies in particular when you create graphically challenging applications that are subject to very demanding design requirements. In this case, we recommend that you refer to specialist books like *Web Programming in ABAP with the SAP Web Application Server in ABAP by* Frédéric Heinemann and Christian Rau or *Advanced BSP Programming* by Brian McKellar and Thomas Jung (both titles by SAP PRESS). You face two major challenges when developing BSP applications: How do you achieve a consistent layout, and how do you deal with browser incompatibilities? We recommend the following:

Business Server Pages

▶ Always use the W3C HTML Validator (*http://validator.w3.org/*). Only create correct HTML.

- Use Cascading Stylesheets (CSS) to set element properties. Use the W3C CSS Validator (*http://jigsaw.w3.org/css-validator/*) in this case. Also take CCS incompatibilities into account (*http://www.css4you.de/browsercomp.html*).

- Use the DOCTYPE switch, and set this correctly. You will find a good summary of this topic under *http://www.oreillynet.com/pub/a/javascript/synd/2001/08/28/doctype.html* and *http://www.ericmeyeroncss.com/bonus/render-mode.html*.

7.6.2 Software Factors

Separating display logic from application logic

Regardless of the technology you use to create graphical user interfaces, you should always remember not to combine display logic with application logic. If you ignore this rule, you will create applications that will exceed any budget in terms of the costs that will be required to maintain and further develop them. Furthermore, these types of applications are not sustainable because you will not be able to perform the following changes with reasonable effort:

- **Changing the GUI technology**
  The problems of combining a graphical interface too closely connected with an application technology become obvious immediately when you have to web-enable the application dialogs, for example. In this case, you will need a completely new development, including comprehensive tests.

- **Changing the channel**
  You may have a situation where you not only want to enter data using an input dialog, but where you also want to use a new channel, such as BAPI interfaces or web services. You may have the same specialized requirement in terms of accuracy for this channel as you do in the dialog application, and stronger or weaker checks are possible.

One of the strengths of the Web Dynpro framework is that you can separate display logic from data retrieval, and also from checks. You should follow this rule when developing maintainable applications, irrespective of which GUI technology you choose.

7.6.3   Key Transactions

In this chapter, we used the transactions shown in Table 7.5 to create user dialogs.

Transaction Code	Description
BIBS	Ergonomic examples
SE43	Area menu maintenance
SE54	Access to tables and view maintenance
SE55	Table maintenance generator
SM30	Table maintenance
SM34	View cluster maintenance

Table 7.5   Key Transaction Codes

"Frameworks store experience; problems are solved once and the business rules and designs are used consistently. This allows an organization to build from a base that has been proven to work in the past." (Juha Hautamäki)

8 SAP Business Partner

Business partner data must be stored in virtually every application in the SAP environment. Even though the business partner is hardly ever the central application object, he is almost as important for business processes as the application object itself.

The business partners relevant for the application can be private or business customers, employees, service providers, vendors, sales, logistics and other partners, creditors, debtors, competitors, parent companies, or subsidiaries. It is most likely that they are linked with their application objects and that they play a central role in their business processes.

As part of the SAP_ABA software component, SAP delivers a sophisticated business partner application you can use for your ABAP applications. Based on a simple example, this chapter describes how you can extend SAP Business Partner with customized attributes, and search for business partners based on these attributes, using the SAP Locator. For this purpose, we first provide you with an overview of SAP Business Partner, to which you will add new data fields and a business role. You will then create and test a Locator search that lets you search for business partners based on the new data fields.

Sophisticated business partner application

8.1 Background Information

Before detailing the extension of the SAP Business Partner application, we will first provide you with background and historical information about SAP Business Partner, and the fundamental concepts implemented in this application.

8.1.1 The Creation of SAP Business Partner

Cross-application component

SAP Business Partner evolved from the consolidation of multiple application-specific business partner administrations available at the time. Its concept includes a cross-application component in which a business partner can be found in multiple roles. Each of these roles specifies multiple maintainable attributes. (Attributes can also occur in multiple roles.)

> **Business Partner Role**
>
> A *business partner role* describes the function of a business partner with regard to your enterprise. Examples for business partner roles are employee, private customer, or external service provider.
>
> The configuration of a role involves the attributes that are relevant for the function. Each business partner can assume multiple roles. For the maintenance of a business partner with a specific role, you are only shown the attributes related to that role.

Attributes

The concept of SAP Business Partner focuses on three main aspects.

- **Divisibility**
  Because the applications that use the business partner administration include several hundreds of attributes, you should be able to divide the maintenance into multiple parts in which only the fields relevant for a certain specialist context are visible. This resulted in the development of the business partner role concept.

- **Configurability**
  The customer operating the software should be able to select only the fields relevant for him from the available fields and hide the others. To avoid that the user has to click through a vast number of almost empty screens, the remaining fields were supposed to be distributed flexibly to entry screens to achieve a lean and ergonomic screen sequence.

- **Extensibility**
  Central business partner attributes, such as name, address, and bank details, are part of the core application. Moreover, you can

extend business partners by additional attributes and roles without modifications.

This method is used in new applications of the SAP standard and in customer developments, as well as in implementation projects of customers who want to add individual fields or tables without any modifications.

During the creation of SAP Business Partner (which originally used to be called Central Business Partner or CBP), the business partner relationships were also developed. It was established that in these two parts of the project, similar technical problems had to be solved. As a result, these were abstracted from the concrete entities, business partner and business partner relationship, to create the *Business Data Toolset* framework (BDT), which facilitates the development of large SAP applications and simultaneously supports configurability, divisibility, and extensibility. Since then, along with SAP Business Partner, the BDT has been used primarily in SAP industry solutions.

Business Data Toolset

> ### Business partner relationships
>
> *Business partner relationships* is an application you can use to manage the relationships between business partners, based on the relationship category and additional attributes. This enables you, for example, to map corporate structures, complex business relationships, or the relationships between customers and service representatives or subsidiaries.

8.1.2 Conceptual Overview

The BDT development focuses on the *application object* (Examples: business partner, business partner relationship). For each application object, multiple applications can exist, whereas exactly one application that owns the application object leads.

Application object

An application can have any number of *tables*, but the application that owns the tables is known and fixed for each table. In its event function modules, the application ensures that the data of its tables is transferred, checked, completed, and saved correctly.

Applications don't have to contain all data in their own tables, but can share the tables of other applications via table appends. The *participating*

Participating application

application exclusively owns certain attached fields of the external table. Therefore, the participating application doesn't own the entire table, but only the attached fields. The application that owns the tables provides event function modules (which can be used by the participating application to query the content read by the database), and collects the changes submitted by the participating applications using other function modules, before it saves its tables to the database.

All objects created within BDT Customizing belong to BDT applications. An application can be activated or deactivated as a whole.

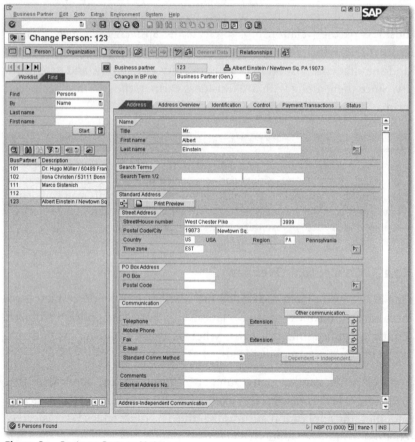

Figure 8.1 Business Partner Maintenance

8.1.3 First Impression

To get a first impression of SAP business partner administration, call Transaction BP (see Figure 8.1). The locator on the left side of the screen enables you to search for business partners; the actual application runs on the right side of the screen. You are either shown the business partner you last processed, or you can use an input field to select a business partner using the search help.

If an error occurs during creation of a business partner, you should check whether the basic Customizing is missing. To do so, call the Implementation Guide using Transaction *SPRO*. Under CROSS-APPLICATION COMPONENTS • SAP BUSINESS PARTNER • BUSINESS PARTNER • BASIC SETTINGS • NUMBER RANGES AND GROUPINGS you can find the activities Define Number Ranges (see Figure 8.2) and Define Groupings And Assign Number Ranges (see Figure 8.3).

Basic Customizing

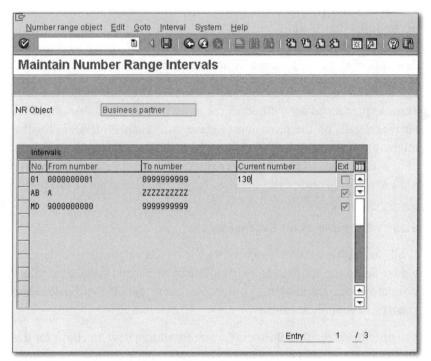

Figure 8.2 Number Range Intervals for the Business Partner

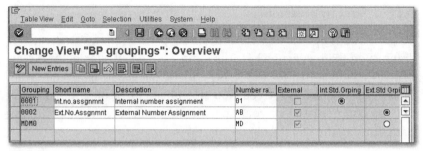

Figure 8.3 Business Partner Groupings and Intervals

You need to check the settings and ensure that the partner types 0001 and 0002 exist and that these are assigned with number range intervals, including the appropriate assignment type (internal or external).

8.2 Business Partner Extension

In the following sections, you will perform a modification-free extension in SAP Business Partner. You are also provided with a step-by-step description of how you can add new functions using Customizing and programming.

These explanations are limited to the extension of the dialog interface. Further details on the provision of mass data capable interfaces for the migration of (legacy) data, development of BAPI interfaces, connection of new data fields to the archive, creation of change documents, etc. are not provided, because this would go far beyond the scope of this book.

8.2.1 Example of an Extension

While in implementation projects of existing SAP applications only individual fields are attached to existing business partner roles (and many standard fields are hidden), you require more detailed extensions for creating new applications.

Creating a Vehicle Manufacturer business partner role

You need to extend SAP Business Partner by adding new functions for the application. You will create a new Vehicle Manufacturer business partner role that can be maintained by business partners of type Organization.

The role is supposed to include a new tab, on which you can maintain the attribute (see Figure 8.4). The conditions can have the values *Vehicle Conditions*, *Replacement Part*, or *Scale of Discount*.

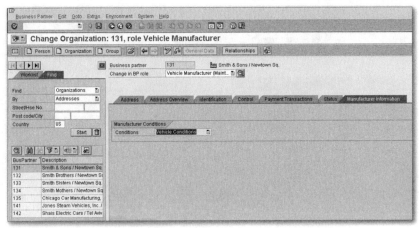

Figure 8.4 SAP Business Partner Extension

In BDT language: In addition to the BUPA application object of the BUP application (which owns the application object), you also create a new ZVHM application (which is the application that owns the table ZVHMCON-DITIONS). In the first step, you need to create a transparent table, ZVHM-CONDITIONS, in which information is saved (see Figure 8.5).

BDT language

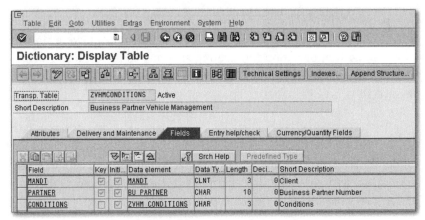

Figure 8.5 ZVHMCONDITIONS Table

The CONDITIONS field contains a domain in which the possible values for the manufacturer conditions are defined (see Figure 8.5).

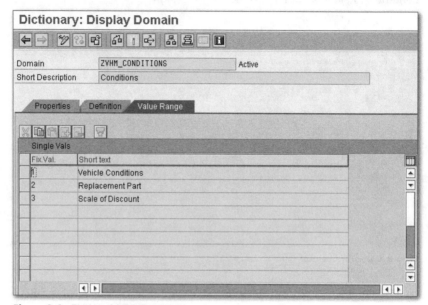

Figure 8.6 ZVHM_CONDITIONS Domain

Creating a Function Group

Then you create the ZVHM_BUPA function group, which needs to contain the coding and screens for this extension. First, you create an empty screen 0100 of the *Subscreen* type and activate it.

You perform the next steps in the configuration environment for the Business Data Toolset (BDT). Start the BUPT area menu. You were already provided with information for creating area menus in Section 7.3, Area Menus. You can find the menu points required for this purpose under BUSINESS PARTNER • CONTROL.

8.2.2 Maintaining the Application

Under the APPLICATIONS menu item (Transaction *BUS1*), add a new ZVHM application and enter the description "Vehicle Management". Activate the ACTIVE checkbox (see Figure 8.7).

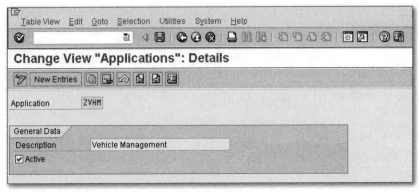

Figure 8.7 Application Vehicle Management

8.2.3 Maintaining the Data Set

Under DATA SETS (Transaction BUS23), add a new entry with the ZVHM key and the name "Vehicle Management" (Figure 8.8).

Figure 8.8 Data Set Vehicle Management

8.2.4 Maintaining Tables

Under TABLES (Transaction BUSG), add an entry for the ZVHMCONDITIONS table (see Figure 8.9).

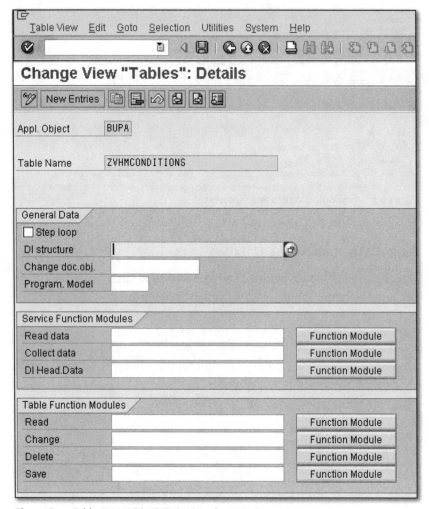

Figure 8.9 Table ZVHMCONDITIONS in the BDT Customizing

8.2.5 Maintaining Field Groups

Field group   A *field group* is a group of fields whose ready-for-input status is determined collectively. For example, for each field group you can specify within the field modifications whether fields are ready for input, have required entry fields, or should be hidden.

Under FIELD GROUPS (Transaction BUS2), create a new field group 600 with the description "Vehicle Management: Manufacturer Conditions". Enter the structure and field name for the input field in the screen under FIELD GROUPS • FIELDS.

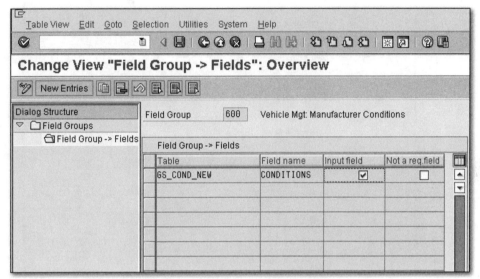

Figure 8.10 Field Group and Fields for the Manufacturer Conditions

8.2.6 Views (Transaction BUS3)

Field groups are combined into a *view*. All attributes of a view are always displayed and checked collectively. From a technical perspective, a view is identical to a subscreen.

View is identical to subscreen

Create a ZVHM view, and assign the view to the ZVHM application and the ZVHM data set. At runtime, the BDT considers all views currently to be displayed by dynamically displaying the appropriate subscreens.

Enter the SAPLZVHM_BUPA program name and screen number 0100, to make the maintenance screen known to the BDT. Activate the ENTRY VIEW, DIALOG VIEW, and DATA SCREEN options for this view and assign the differentiation type 0, as you can see in Figure 8.11.

Creating a view

UNDER VIEW • FIELD GROUPS, assign field group 0600 to the view (see Figure 8.12).

Assigning the view to a field group

341

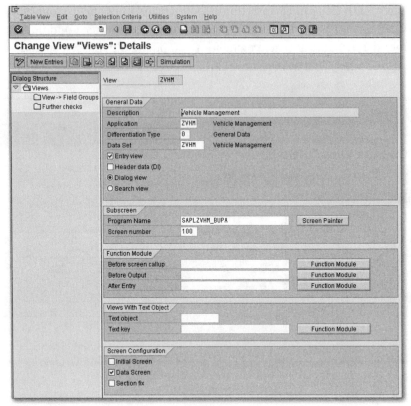

Figure 8.11 BDT View of Vehicle Management

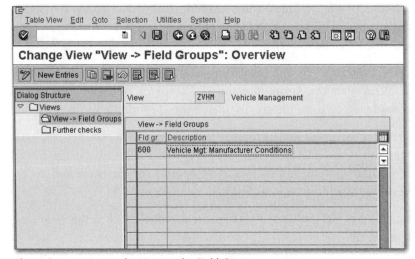

Figure 8.12 Assigning the View to the Field Group

8.2.7   Sections (Transaction BUS4)

One or more views are combined into a *section*. The BDT automatically   Creating a section
sets a frame around each section, and displays the title of the section
in the upper left corner of the frame. (Exception: The first section of a
screen is used for header data and is framed.)

Create a ZVHM section called "Manufacturer Conditions". One section
can consist of one or more views. The section creates a frame around the
contained views in the display; the name entered here is displayed as the
text of the frame in the dialog. Create the assignment to the ZVHM view,
and enter the item number 1000010, as shown in Figure 8.13.

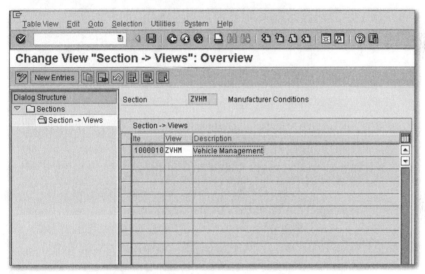

Figure 8.13 Assigning the Section to the View

8.2.8   Screens (Transaction BUS5)

Create a screen ZVHM with the name "Manufacturer Information" (see   Creating a screen
Figure 8.14). This will later be displayed as a tab. Maintain the DATA
SCREEN screen type, the BDT screen origin, and the NORMAL screen type.
Then, assign the EMPTY (Item 1000010) und ZVHM (Item 1000011) sec-
tions to the screen (see Figure 8.15).

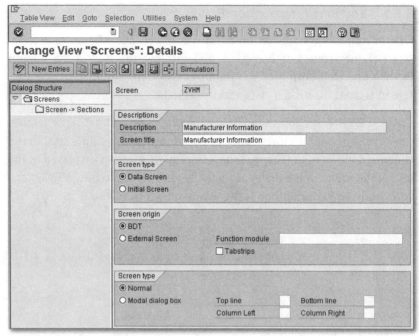

Figure 8.14 BDT Screen Manufacturer Information

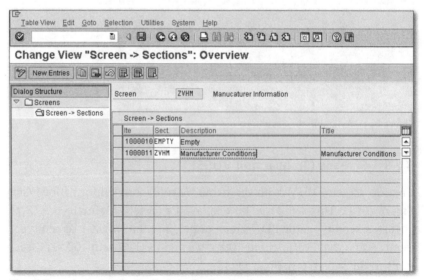

Figure 8.15 Assigning the Sections to the Screen

8.2.9 Screen Sequences (Transaction BUS6)

Create a new ZVHM screen sequence, and assign it to the ZVHM screen of item 1000010.

8.2.10 BP Views (Transaction BUSD)

Create a ZVHM BP view ZVHM with the name "Vehicle Management". Accept the data sets that are assigned to the view 000000 (general business partner), and add the ZVHM data set (see Figure 8.16).

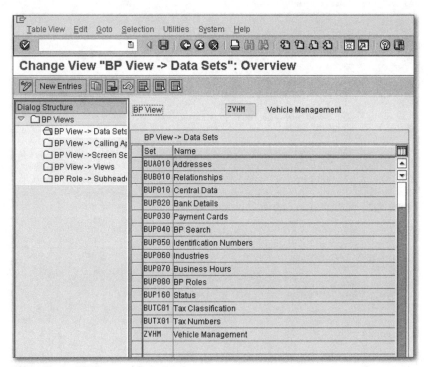

Figure 8.16 BP View and Data Sets

8.2.11 Creating Role Categories and Roles

Display the Implementation Guide using Transaction SPRO. Under CROSS-APPLICATIONS COMPONENTS • SAP BUSINESS PARTNER • BUSINESS PARTNER • BASIC SETTINGS • BUSINESS PARTNER ROLES you can find the DEFINE BP ROLES activity (see Figure 8.17).

Implementation Guide

First, create the ZVHM role category with the name "Vehicle Manufacturer." Assign the differentiation type 0 and the possible business partner
category, Organization (see Figure 8.18).

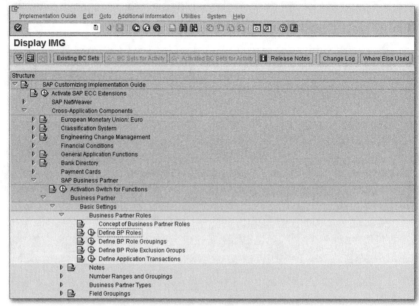

Figure 8.17 SAP Business Partner Implementation Guide

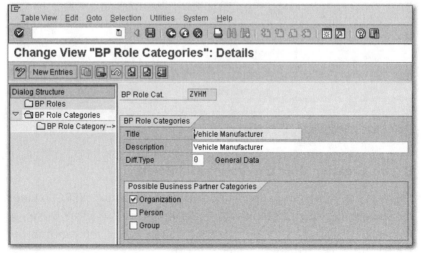

Figure 8.18 Vehicle Manufacturer Role Category

Now create the new ZVHM role with the name "Vehicle Manufacturer". The name maintained here will be displayed as the role name in the dialog. Assign the ZVHM BP role category to the role, and select the STANDARD ASSIGNMENT BETWEEN BP ROLE • BP ROLE CATEGORY check box. Enter ZVHM as the assigned view (see Figure 8.19).

Creating a role

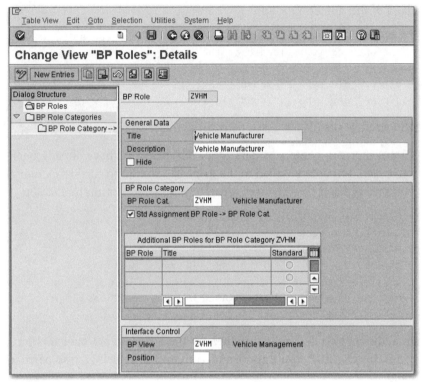

Figure 8.19 Vehicle Manufacturer Role

Before you complete Customizing, consider turning your attention to the ZVHM_BUPA function group to program the screen and program logic.

8.2.12 ZVHM_BUPA Function Group

The function group is used to encapsulate the "Vehicle Management" application. It contains function modules that are called at specific events by the BDT, all vehicle management screens, and global data to map the respective status of the application.

Current memory

This includes *current memory* and *global memory* in particular. Current memory always refers to the currently processed business partner and comprises the old status, the status read from the database when starting the maintenance, and the current status (which has possibly been changed by dialog entries). This means that you declare two field strings with the structure of the ZVHMCONDITIONS table in the TOP include (global data) of the function group:

```
* Current memory: Old and new condition of the current
* instance as it is loaded at the ISDAT event.
data:
  gs_cond_old type zvhmconditions,
  gs_cond_new type zvhmconditions.
```

You also use the GS_COND_NEW field string in the screen.

Global memory

Global memory comprises data of all instances that have already been processed, but not yet saved to the database. Similar to current memory, you save old and new statuses separately, however, in internal tables:

```
* Global memory: Old and new statuses of all
* instances processed.
DATA:
  gt_cond_new TYPE STANDARD TABLE OF zvhmconditions
    WITH KEY partner,
  gt_cond_old TYPE STANDARD TABLE OF zvhmconditions
    WITH KEY partner.
```

In addition, you declare a structure for the BUT000 table, which is provided by the BUP application and contains central business partner data:

```
* Current. business partner - the BUPA application which
* owns the application object provides these at the
* ISDAT event.
DATA:
  gs_but000  TYPE but000.
```

8.2.13   Screen 0100

Simple layout

Screen 0100 has a very simple layout. You use the GS_COND_NEW-CONDITIONS field and display it as a listbox with visible length 20. In addition, you use a text field named *GS_COND_NEW-CONDITIONS, display it as designation to the left, and assign the text "Conditions".

The flow logic is very simple as well. It comprises one PBO module and one PAI module:

Flow logic

```
PROCESS BEFORE OUTPUT.
  MODULE pbo.

PROCESS AFTER INPUT.
  MODULE pai.
```

In the modules, control is transferred to the BDT, which assumes responsibility for all subsequent processes. The BDT evaluates the SY-REPID and SY-DYNNR system fields to determine the currently displayed screen. In BDT Customizing, it finds the assigned field groups and implements the configured field modifications, calls check and other function modules saved in Customizing, and ensures that the screen is smoothly integrated into the flow of the BDT application. Create the PBO and PAI module within the function group as shown in Listing 8.1.

Control transferred
to the BDT

```
MODULE pbo OUTPUT.
  CALL FUNCTION 'BUS_PBO'.
ENDMODULE.                 " pbo  OUTPUT

MODULE pai INPUT.
  CALL FUNCTION 'BUS_PAI'.
ENDMODULE.                 " pai  INPUT
```

Listing 8.1 Coding of the PBO and the PAI Module to a BDT View

8.2.14 Events

The BDT data maintenance process follows a uniform structure that is valid across applications. The BDT defines events, which are performed in a specific sequence and with a specific activity.

Uniform structure

The applications involved can (or must) implement these events by providing the appropriate function modules, which perform the defined activity and make it known in BDT Customizing.

In this example, you only implement the most essential events for initializing an application and for loading, checking, and saving application data. Additionally, there are numerous optional events for different subjects, for example archiving, authorizations, change documents, dialog menu, deletion, and direct input. It would go far beyond the scope of this book to describe and implement all of these.

Event maintenance
You can access the event maintenance and obtain an overview of the events defined by the BDT using Transaction BUS7 (see Figure 8.20).

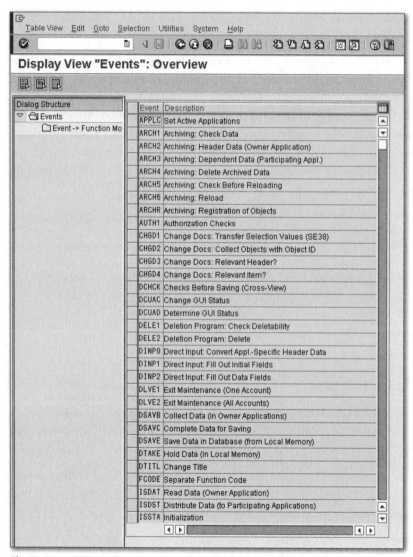

Figure 8.20 BDT Events

Each event can be assigned with multiple function modules, which are called in a sequence defined by the item number. Each function module is assigned to an application and is called when the application is active.

You can use the CALL field to control whether the function module is always called, even if the selected role contains no screen of your application. In this case, you enter an asterisk (*) in the field. In this example, the function module is only supposed to be implemented if one of your screens is involved in the dialog. Therefore, you enter the value "X" in the CALL field (see Figure 8.21).

Call field

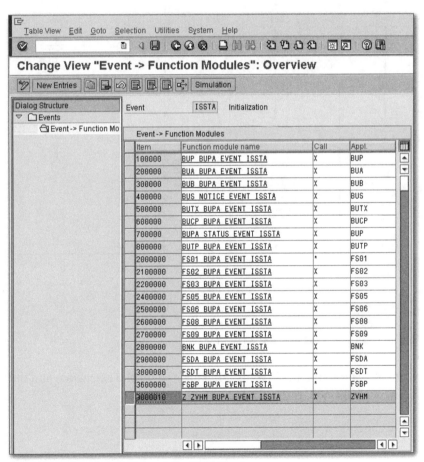

Figure 8.21 Function Modules at the ISSTA Event

Figure 8.22 shows the processing scheme, including all events involved in the BDT data maintenance.

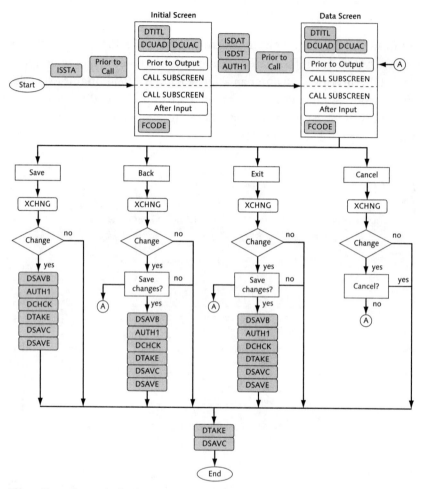

Figure 8.22 Events in the Business Data Toolset

Table 8.1 shows the BDT events implemented for the extension, and the activity performed, respectively.

Event	Activity
ISSTA	*Initialize the application*
	You initialize the application and request the start parameter from the BDT. By calling the BUS_PARAMETERS_ISSTA_GET function module, you determine the status of the BDT instance. In this example, this is the E_XUPDTASK parameter, which defines whether saving to the database is performed synchronously or asynchronously (IN UPDATE TASK).
ISDAT	*Read data*
	Read the data for the current instance from the database. For this purpose, request the ID of the application object (in other words, the current business partner number) from the BUP application which owns the application object using the BUP_BUPA_BUT000_GET function module, and then read the manufacturer information for this business partner from the database table.
DCHCK	*Check data*
	Here, you program consistency checks that are implemented before saving. Error messages created here are displayed as popups and prevent that the data is saved.
	You transfer the messages to the BDT by calling the BUS_MESSAGE_STORE function module of the BDT Message Handler.
XCHNG	*Check whether data has been changed*
	For this event, the current status of the displayed instance in the dialog is compared with the last status available in the database. You use the E_XCHNG parameter to indicate whether data has been changed.
	Accordingly, the BDT displays a popup when you exit the maintenance to inform you about possible loss of data and to allow saving of data.
DTAKE	*Transfer data to the global memory*
	In addition to the current memory, which includes the old and new status of the current instance, each application also manages a global memory that contains the old and the new status of all maintained instances that have not yet been saved.

Table 8.1 BDT Events

Event	Activity
	Usually, the BDT is in *save mode*, in which only one instance is processed and then saved or discarded. The management of multiple unsaved instances in the global memory is relevant in the *transfer mode,* in which you maintain (or create) multiple instances and then save them collectively.
	For performance reasons, this can be desirable for initial data transfer including many instances. It is also required for technical reasons, if two business partners and their relationship are recorded in an SAP LUW, and the data is to be saved collectively or not at all.
DSAVC	*Complete data*
	This event is implemented to complete data before saving. In particular, temporary IDs assigned during object creation are now replaced by final IDs. (Temporary IDs are often used to prevent gaps in the assignment of consecutive IDs from number ranges that are caused by terminated new creations.)
DSAVE	*Save data*
	This event is used to save data. All datasets from the global memory whose old and new statuses deviate are saved.
	Here, the E_XUPDTASK parameter is considered, which was requested during the ISSTA event by the BDT frame. It determines whether saving is performed asynchronously via the update, or synchronously. In both cases, the same update module is called. To save via the update, you call the function module with the IN UPDATE TASK addition.
DLVE1	*Initialize current memory*
	This event is used to initialize the current memory. The data of the current instance (old and new status) must be initialized completely.
DLVE2	*Initialize the global memory*
	This event is used to initialize the global memory. You must initialize the old and new status of the global memory.

Table 8.1 BDT Events (Cont.)

In the following sections, you create function modules for the events shown in Table 8.1 in your example application. The task of each function module can also be found in Table 8.1. In addition, the listings that follow include inline documentation to explain further details.

Creating function modules

ISSTA Event – Initialize the application

```
FUNCTION Z_ZVHM_BUPA_EVENT_ISSTA .
*"----------------------------------------------------------------
*"*"Local interface:
*"----------------------------------------------------------------
* Initialize the application and request the start
* parameter from the BDT. Must data be saved in the
* update (IN UPDATE TASK) at the DSAVE event or
* synchronously?

  CALL FUNCTION 'BUS_PARAMETERS_ISSTA_GET'
    IMPORTING
      e_xupdtask = gv_xupdtask.

ENDFUNCTION.
```

Listing 8.2 ISSTA Event Function Module

Of course, you must declare the GV_XUPDTASK global variable that you set here, and the ABAP type pool used in the TOP include of the function group:

```
TYPE-POOLS:
  abap.

* Is data to be saved in the update(IN UPDATE TASK)
* at the DSAVE event or synchronously?
* Is requested by the BDT frame at ISSTA event.
DATA:
  gv_xupdtask TYPE abap_bool.
```

ISDAT Event – Load Data

```
FUNCTION Z_ZVHM_BUPA_EVENT_ISDAT .
*"----------------------------------------------------------------
*"*"Local interface:
*"----------------------------------------------------------------
* Load current instance:
* 1. First get the BUT000 main table from the BUP
*    application which owns the applicaton object to
*    determine the currently displayed business partner.
* 2. Then delete the current memory. The new and
*    old status is read from the database.
*    If no record exists on the database yet, the old status
*    is saved initially in the current memory and the new
*    status is saved with client and business partner.
*    Therefore, the comparison of old and new at the XCHNG
*    event shows that changes were made.
  DATA:
    ls_vhm     TYPE zvhmconditions.

  CALL FUNCTION 'BUP_BUPA_BUT000_GET'
    IMPORTING
      e_but000 = gs_but000.

  SELECT SINGLE * FROM  zvhmconditions
                  INTO  ls_vhm
                  WHERE partner = gs_but000-partner.
  IF sy-subrc EQ 0.
    gs_cond_new = ls_vhm.
    gs_cond_old = ls_vhm.
  ELSE.
    gs_cond_new-mandt   = sy-mandt.
    gs_cond_new-partner = gs_but000-partner.
  ENDIF.

ENDFUNCTION.
```

Listing 8.3 ISDAT Event Function Module

DCHCK Event – Check Data

Here, the error message 001 of the ZVHM message class is generated to demonstrate how an error message is output after a check:

```
FUNCTION Z_ZVHM_BUPA_EVENT_DCHCK .
*"----------------------------------------------------------
*"*"Local interface:
*"----------------------------------------------------------

  IF gs_cond_new-conditions EQ '4'.
    CALL FUNCTION 'BUS_MESSAGE_STORE'
      EXPORTING
        arbgb     = 'ZVHM'
        msgty     = 'E'
        txtnr     = '001'
        tbfld_strg = 'GS_COND_NEW-CONDITIONS'
        msgv1     = gs_cond_new-conditions.
  ENDIF.

ENDFUNCTION.
```

Listing 8.4 DCHCK Event Function Module

XCHNG Event – Check Whether Data Has Been Changed

```
FUNCTION Z_ZVHM_BUPA_EVENT_XCHNG .
*"----------------------------------------------------------
*"*"Local interface:
*"  EXPORTING
*"     VALUE(E_XCHNG) LIKE  BUS000FLDS-XCHNG
*"----------------------------------------------------------
* Check whether changes have been made. Compare the
* old and the new status of the current memory.

  IF gs_cond_new NE gs_cond_old.
    e_xchng = abap_true.
  ENDIF.

ENDFUNCTION.
```

Listing 8.5 XCHNG Event Function Module

DTAKE Event – Transfer Data to the Global Memory

```
FUNCTION Z_ZVHM_BUPA_EVENT_DTAKE .
*"----------------------------------------------------------------
*"*"Local interface:
*"----------------------------------------------------------------
* Transfer current memory to the global memory.
*
* 1. Transfer the new status from the current memory via
*    INSERT or MODIFY to the global memory for new records
*    depending on whether a record is already marked
*    with the same key.
* 2. If no record is marked with the same key in the global
*    memory for old records, it is transferred from the
*    current memory.

  READ TABLE gt_cond_new TRANSPORTING NO FIELDS
                  WITH KEY partner = gs_cond_new-partner.
  IF sy-subrc EQ 0.
    MODIFY TABLE gt_cond_new FROM gs_cond_new.
  ELSE.
    INSERT gs_cond_new INTO TABLE gt_cond_new.
  ENDIF.

  READ TABLE gt_cond_old TRANSPORTING NO FIELDS
                  WITH KEY partner = gs_cond_old-partner.
  IF sy-subrc NE 0.
    INSERT gs_cond_old INTO TABLE gt_cond_old.
  ENDIF.

ENDFUNCTION.
```

Listing 8.6 DTAKE Event Function Module

DSAVC Event – Complete Data

```
FUNCTION Z_ZVHM_BUPA_EVENT_DSAVC .
*"----------------------------------------------------------------
*"*"Local interface:
*"----------------------------------------------------------------
* For new creations, work with a temporary business
* partner number up to the DSAVC event. At the DSAV event,
* request the final number from the BUPA application
* which owns the application object and replace the
```

```
* temporary number by the final number in the current and
* global memory.

    DATA:
      ls_but000   TYPE but000,
      lv_temp_nr  TYPE bu_partner,
      lv_final_nr TYPE bu_partner.

    FIELD-SYMBOLS:
      <ls_cond>   TYPE zvhmconditions.

* Determine old - or temporary - business partner number
    lv_temp_nr = gs_cond_new-partner.

* Determine final business partner number
    CALL FUNCTION 'BUP_BUPA_BUT000_GET'
      IMPORTING
        e_but000 = ls_but000.
    lv_final_nr = ls_but000-partner.

* Change global memory from old to new number
    LOOP AT gt_cond_old ASSIGNING <ls_cond>
      WHERE partner = lv_temp_nr.
      <ls_cond>-partner = lv_final_nr.
    ENDLOOP.
    LOOP AT gt_cond_new ASSIGNING <ls_cond>
      WHERE partner = lv_temp_nr.
      <ls_cond>-partner = lv_final_nr.
    ENDLOOP.

* Change current memory
    IF gs_cond_new-partner = lv_temp_nr.
      gs_cond_new-partner  = lv_final_nr.
    ENDIF.
    IF gs_cond_old-partner = lv_temp_nr.
      gs_cond_old-partner  = lv_final_nr.
    ENDIF.

ENDFUNCTION.
```

Listing 8.7 DSAVC Event Function Module

DSAVE Event – Save Data

In this module, you use a global type and a constant, which you first must declare in the TOP include of the function group:

```
* Type for DB operation
TYPES:
  g_typ_operation(1) TYPE c.

* Insert and change constants for DB operation
CONSTANTS:
  BEGIN OF gc_operation,
    insert TYPE g_typ_operation VALUE 'I',
    update TYPE g_typ_operation VALUE 'U',
  END OF gc_operation.
```

The event function module calls the update module, which implements the actual database change:

```
FUNCTION Z_ZVHM_BUPA_EVENT_DSAVE .
*"----------------------------------------------------------
*"*"Local interface:
*"----------------------------------------------------------
* Save all instances in the global memory which are new
* or have been changed. Check for all new statuses
* whether a corresponding old status exists.
*
* If an old status exists, implement an update.
* If no old status exists, implement an insert.
*
* At the ISSTA event it was requested from the BDT frame
* whether the data is to be saved in the update or
* synchronously.
* Evaluate the GV_XUPDTASK result to  call the
* Update module IN UPDATE TASK or synchronously.

  DATA:
    lv_operation    TYPE g_typ_operation,    " DB-Operation
    ls_cond_new     TYPE zvhmconditions,     " new status
    ls_cond_old     TYPE zvhmconditions.     " old Status

  LOOP AT gt_cond_new INTO ls_cond_new.
```

```
* Does an old status exist?
   READ TABLE gt_cond_old INTO ls_cond_old
                  WITH KEY partner = ls_cond_new-partner.
   IF sy-subrc NE 0.
     lv_operation = gc_operation-insert.
   ELSE.
     lv_operation = gc_operation-update.
   ENDIF.

   IF gv_xupdtask EQ abap_true.              " Update?
     CALL FUNCTION 'Z_ZVHM_BUPA_UPDATE' IN UPDATE TASK
       EXPORTING
         is_conditions_new = ls_cond_new
         is_conditions_old = ls_cond_old
         iv_operation      = lv_operation.
   ELSE.
     CALL FUNCTION 'Z_ZVHM_BUPA_UPDATE'
       EXPORTING
         is_conditions_new = ls_cond_new
         is_conditions_old = ls_cond_old
         iv_operation      = lv_operation.
   ENDIF.
 ENDLOOP.
ENDFUNCTION.
```

Listing 8.8 DSAVE Event Function Module

Update Module

The update function module is not an event module, but is called by the DSAVE event function module. Provided that the update is used and called with the IN UPDATE TASK addition, the call is only registered at the DSAVE event; the registered function module is performed when the BDT frame has triggered a COMMIT WORK.

If the update is not active and if the DSAVE module calls the update task without the IN UPDATE TASK addition, the update module is implemented immediately like a regular function module, without any changes to the database.

Ensure that the update module's processing type setting is set to START IMMED. (start immediately; see Figure 8.23).

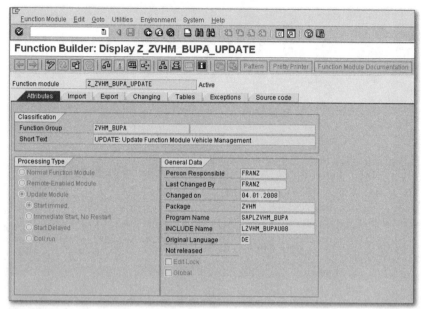

Figure 8.23 Properties of the Update Module

```
FUNCTION Z_ZVHM_BUPA_UPDATE .
*"----------------------------------------------------------------
*"*"Update function module:
*"
*"*"Local interface:
*"  IMPORTING
*"     VALUE(IS_CONDITIONS_NEW) TYPE  ZVHMCONDITIONS
*"     VALUE(IS_CONDITIONS_OLD) TYPE  ZVHMCONDITIONS OPTIONAL
*"     VALUE(IV_OPERATION) TYPE  CHAR1
*"----------------------------------------------------------------

  CASE iv_operation.
    WHEN gc_operation-insert.
      INSERT zvhmconditions FROM is_conditions_new.
    WHEN gc_operation-update.
      UPDATE zvhmconditions FROM is_conditions_new.
  ENDCASE.

ENDFUNCTION.
```

Listing 8.9 Update Module

DLVE1 Event – Initialize the Current Memory

```
FUNCTION Z_ZVHM_BUPA_EVENT_DLVE1 .
*"----------------------------------------------------------
*"*"Local interface:
*"----------------------------------------------------------
* Initialize current memory

  CLEAR:
    gs_cond_new,
    gs_cond_old.

ENDFUNCTION.
```

Listing 8.10   DLVE1 Event Function Module

DLVE2 Event – Initialize the Global Memory

```
FUNCTION Z_ZVHM_BUPA_EVENT_DLVE2 .
*"----------------------------------------------------------
*"*"Local interface:
*"----------------------------------------------------------
* Initialize global memory

  CLEAR:
    gt_cond_new,
    gt_cond_old.

ENDFUNCTION.
```

Listing 8.11   DLVE2 Event Function Module

8.2.15   BDT Naming Conventions

The following naming conventions apply:

- You may only create new *application objects* after consulting SAP.   **Application objects**
- *Applications* from customers start with Y or Z, followed by an alphabetic string.

▸ *Views, sections, screens, screen sequences, screen sequence categories, menu entries, field grouping criteria, object parts,* and *object parts groupings* all start with the abbreviation of the application, which is followed by a numeric string (example: ZVHM01).

Field groups ▸ The range between 600 and 749 is reserved for customer *field groups*.

▸ *Event function modules* start with Y or Z, followed by the abbreviation of the application and of the application object, the word EVENT and the key of the event, each separated by an underscore (example: Z_ZVHM_BUPA_EVENT_ISSTA). Prefix namespaces are also permitted.

Item numbers ▸ *Item numbers* are allocated during the assignment between any objects to ensure that the sixth digit is not equal to 0 and the seventh digit is equal to 0 for the customer (example: 1234510, 1234520, 0000030).

▸ If the customer has a two-level development system (headquarters and subsidiaries), the seventh digit is not equal to 0 for item numbers at the second level.

▸ Because most objects names are very short (only four to six characters), prefix namespaces are not supported for BDT-specific object types; for general Workbench and Dictionary object types, such as programs, function modules, and tables, they are also valid in the BDT.

8.2.16 Testing the Extension

The extension is now complete and ready for testing. Call Transaction BP and create a business partner of type *Organization* (BUSINESS PARTNER • CREATE • ORGANIZATION).

Maintain the TITLE and NAME, and select the VEHICLE MANUFACTURER role. A popup window is displayed, querying whether you want to save the business partner first in the BP role "Business Partner (General)". Click on SAVE to confirm (see Figure 8.24).

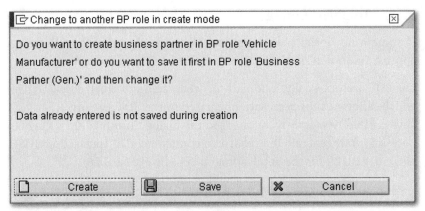

Figure 8.24 Confirmation Prompt for Role Change

You are now shown the MANUFACTURER INFORMATION tab for the maintenance of the VEHICLE MANUFACTURER role. Select this tab and maintain the manufacturer conditions (see Figure 8.25).

Maintaining manufacturer conditions

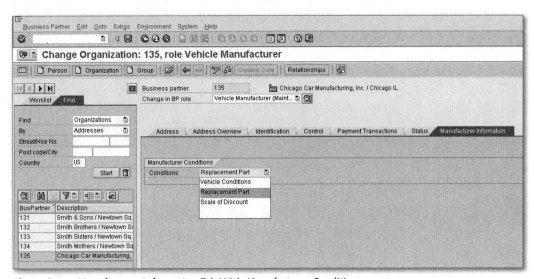

Figure 8.25 Manufacturer Information Tab With Manufacturer Conditions

You can then save the business partner and exit the transaction. During the next call, you can check whether the data was saved correctly and read in the database.

8.2.17 Troubleshooting

If something doesn't work as expected, you can use the following approaches to determine the error:

Generating subscreen containers
The BDT uses internally, automatically generated subscreen containers in which different subscreens are integrated in the BDT screens. After you have created new screens or changed the dialog Customizing, it may be necessary to regenerate the subscreen containers. Call Transaction BUSP and enter BUPA for the application object (see Figure 8.26).

> **Screen Container**
>
> A screen container is a dynpro – usually a main screen – with one or more subscreen areas. Its main purpose is to function as a frame for the contained subscreens.

Checking the Customizing using the BDT Analyzer
You can find Customizing errors, such as forgotten or erroneous assignments, using the *BDT Analyzer*. Use Transaction SE38 to start the BDT_ ANALYZER program, and select the BUPA application object (business partner) and your application (see Figure 8.27).

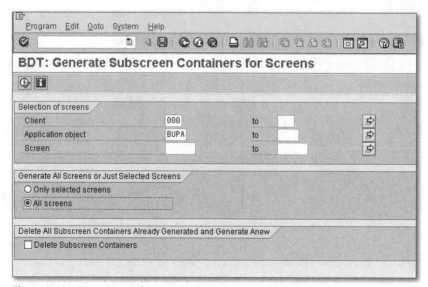

Figure 8.26 Generating Subscreen Containers

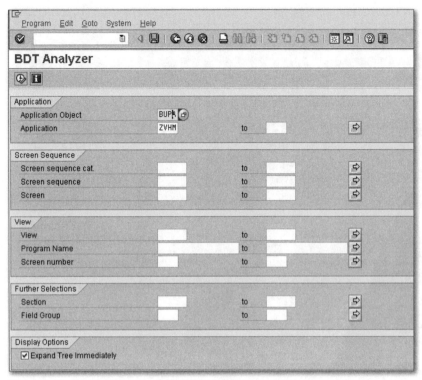

Figure 8.27 Selection Screen of the BDT Analyzer

Click on a tree node to go to the respective Customizing maintenance transaction (see Figure 8.28).

Starting the BDT Analyzer	**[+]**
You can start the BDT Analyzer from any BDT application by entering the BDT_ANALYZER character string into the command field of the SAP GUI.	

To ensure that the Customizing and program logic of the event function modules are free of errors, you can set breakpoints in the function modules. To debug the update module, you can first set a breakpoint in the DSAVE module and activate update debugging in the debugger settings (see Figure 8.29).

Event debugging

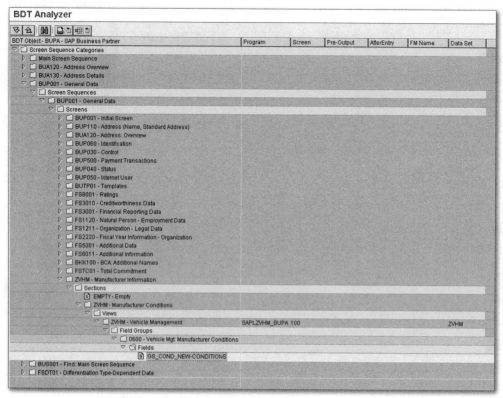

Figure 8.28 Tree Display of the BDT Analyzer

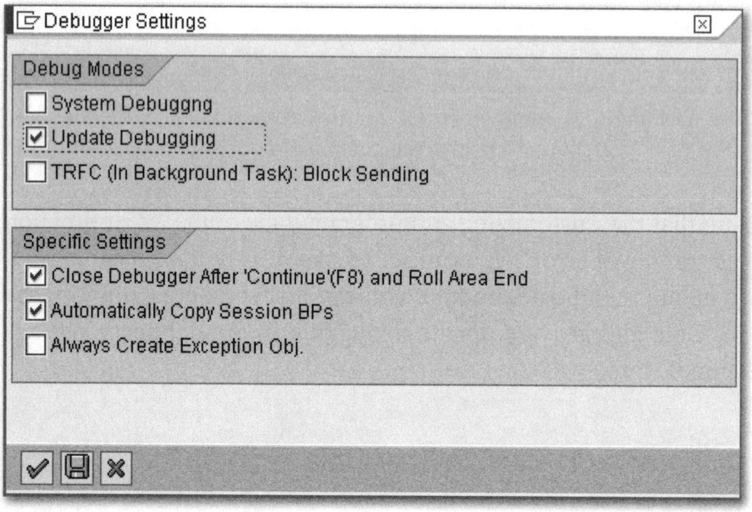

Figure 8.29 Debugger Settings

8.2.18 Summary

This section provided an overview of the SAP business partner administration and the Business Data Toolset, on which it is based. It introduced
SAP Business Partner extension concept, which you used by developing
a new BDT application and integrating it in the business partner maintenance. You developed a new transparent table, a screen, and multiple
event function modules, assigned them to a new business partner role,
and tested the extension. Finally, you were provided with information
on the BDT naming conventions and troubleshooting options. For more
information, refer to the section *Business Data Toolset* in the SAP Library.

8.3   SAP Locator Extension

The following sections provide descriptions about the SAP Locator,
which is located on the left side of the screen, and which enables you to
select and search for application objects. The existing business partner
searches will be supplemented by additional ones, which enable searching for business partners based on the additional data fields created in
Section 8.1, Background Information.

8.3.1   Introduction to the SAP Locator

The *SAP Locator* is a tool that supports the user in the selection of business objects to be processed. It is integrated in the application dialogs
and, using a multilevel selection, enables the user to specify the search
to be implemented.

Specifying the search

In the first list field, the user can select the object type for which to
search (example: organizations). In the second list field, the user can
select the criterion based on which the search is performed (example:
address). Depending on the selections specified, the appropriate search
fields are displayed.

If the user executes a search, and there are hits, they are displayed in the
lower part of the Locator in a table control. If the user double-clicks on
the found object, he can select it for processing. Additionally, the user is
provided with functions for adding objects to the user-specific worklist

Enlarging, reducing, hiding the Locator

(My Objects) and the option to integrate further application-specific functions. The user can enlarge, reduce or completely hide the Locator as required, to have more space available for displaying the application dialog.

Since its introduction, the Locator has been used in SAP Business Partner, in *Customer Relationship Management* (CRM), in industry solutions, and in partner developments. Thanks to its high degree of user-friendliness and user recognition, it is recommended to use the Locator for developing your own applications.

Extensions without modification

You can extend Locator dialogs without any modifications. In other words, new searches can be integrated in existing searches without changing the dialogs themselves. Therefore, it is possible to also extend the Locator dialog in the business partner maintenance with a search without any modification of the business partner application.

8.3.2 Aim of the Extension

After you have extended the business partner with another attribute, you should now develop the extension by supplementing the Locator with another search.

The new search is supposed to permit the search for organizations to be based on the manufacturer conditions in the business partner maintenance transaction. Moreover, the first two name fields of the business partners are supposed to be available as search criteria. Figure 8.30 shows what the search screen should look like when it is integrated in the business partner application.

8.3.3 Transaction LOCA_CUST

Transaction LOCA_CUST provides an overview of the searches available for the business partner. The existing searches are part of a three-level hierarchy.

Search Applications

The topmost level is SEARCH APPLICATIONS. A Locator dialog can only be started with a search application – for the business partner application, this search application is called BUPA_LOCATOR (see Figure 8.31).

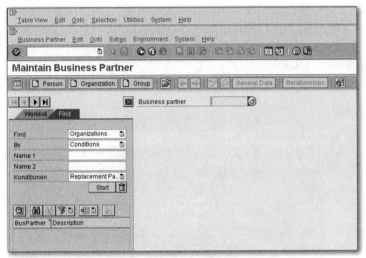

Figure 8.30 Search Organizations By Conditions

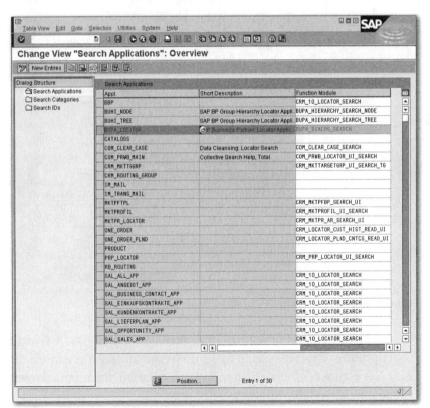

Figure 8.31 Search Applications in Locator Customizing

Search Categories
The second level of the hierarchy is SEARCH CATEGORIES. These are the objects for which you can search. The selection list of the Locator provides search options for BUSINESS PARTNER, PERSONS, ORGANIZATION, or GROUPS (see Figure 8.32).

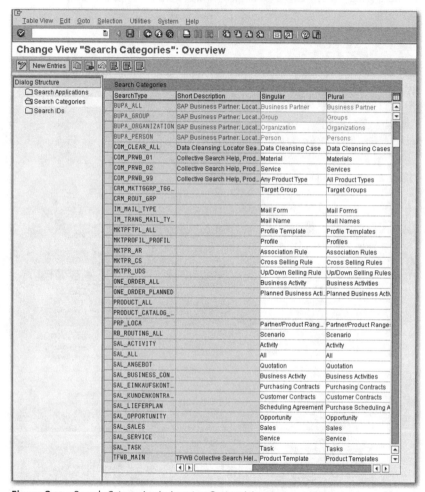

Figure 8.32 Search Categories in Locator Customizing

Search IDs
The third and last level of the hierarchy includes SEARCH IDS. A Search ID characterizes a specific search by a search criterion, such as address or name (see Figure 8.33). Based on this search criterion, the user is shown the input fields suitable for the selected search ID.

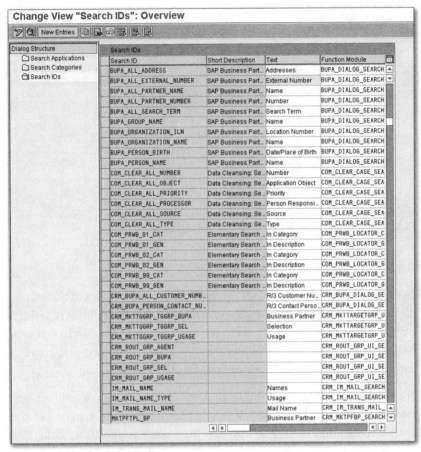

Figure 8.33 Overview of Search IDs

The name for the search ID of the function module that will implement the search later on is stored in Customizing. To display and determine the search criteria in the dialog, you enter a screen number and the corresponding program name (see Figure 8.34).

Because the user can change the size of the Locator area in the dialog, you can also define a second screen, whose input fields may be wider, in addition to the default screen.

Size of the Locator area

373

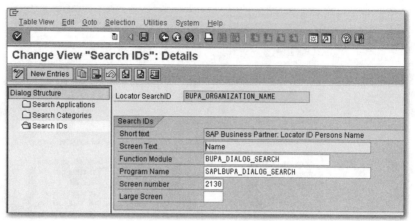

Figure 8.34 Details of a Search ID of the SAP Standard

8.3.4 Definition of the Hierarchy

In Customizing Transaction LOCA_CUST, you saw the nodes of the hierarchy, but not the links between them. The structure of the links is defined in the ABAP Dictionary as collective search helps. A collective search help can include other (collective) search helps. This way, you create a hierarchy to evaluate the Locator framework.

Collective search help | A collective search help of the same name exists for each search application and each search category. The search categories are assigned to the search application in such a way that the search application's collective search help includes the search categories' collective search helps. The search IDs are represented by elementary search helps and assigned to the search categories using search help inclusions.

If you select the BUPA_LOCATOR search help using Transaction SE11, you can see that this includes the search helps BUPA_ALL, BUPA_PERSON, BUPA_ORGANIZATION, and BUPA_GROUP. This corresponds to a search application and defines your search categories.

BUPA_PERSON, in turn, is a collective search help that includes the search helps BUPA_ALL_PARTNER_NUMBER, BUPA_ALL_SEARCH_TERM, BUPA_ALL_EXTERNAL_NUMBER, BUPA_PERSON_NAME, BUPA_PERSON_BIRTH, and BUPA_ALL_ADDRESS. In this case, the relationships between the BUPA_PERSON search category and its search IDs are mapped.

This way, search applications, search categories, and search IDs, which are stored in Customizing, are linked to a hierarchy that you can extend easily using append search helps.

Hierarchy of the searches

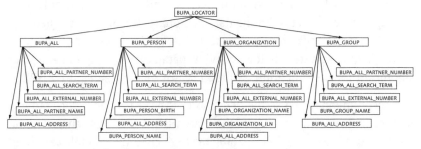

Figure 8.35 Hierarchy of Business Partner Searches

8.3.5 Creating an Append Search Help

You can integrate the new search in the tree as a search ID below the FIND ORGANIZATIONS search category. To do so, you call the BUPA_ORGA-NIZATION collective search help in display mode in Transaction SE11, and select the menu path GO TO • APPEND SEARCH HELP to create an *append search help*. This is a modification-free extension of the existing standard search help. Enter the name ZVHM_BUPA_ORGANISATION_APPEND for the append search help (see Figure 8.36).

Modification-free extension

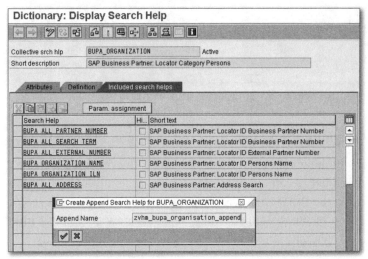

Figure 8.36 Creating the Append Search Help for BUPA_ORGANISATION

8.3.6 Creating the Elementary Search Help

You now create an *elementary search help* whose name must be identical to the search ID. Enter the name ZVHM_BUPA_ORGANISATION_COND. Like all other search helps described in this section, this search help is only used to map the tree structure in the data dictionary. It is never assigned to a data element as a search help, because its definitions – selection method, search help parameter, dialog behavior, parameter assignment – are not significant for the functioning of the Locator dialog (see Figure 8.37).

Recommendations It is recommended to use the definition of the search help declaratively to describe the functionality of the search ID. You can use the selection method and the search help parameter to declare which tables are used in the search and which result category is delivered.

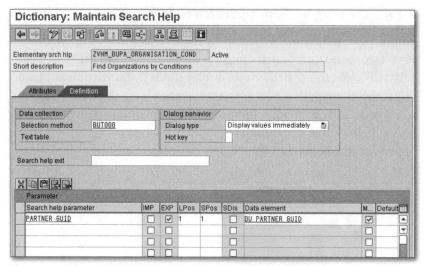

Figure 8.37 Search Help ZVHM_BUPA_ORGANISATION_COND

8.3.7 Assigning the Search Help to the Append Search Help

You assign the new elementary search help to the previously created append search help as an included search help, as you can see in Figure 8.38. Click on the PARAMETER ASSIGNMENT button to display and accept the suggestion of the system. The new search is now completely integrated in the hierarchy, and you can start to define its functionality.

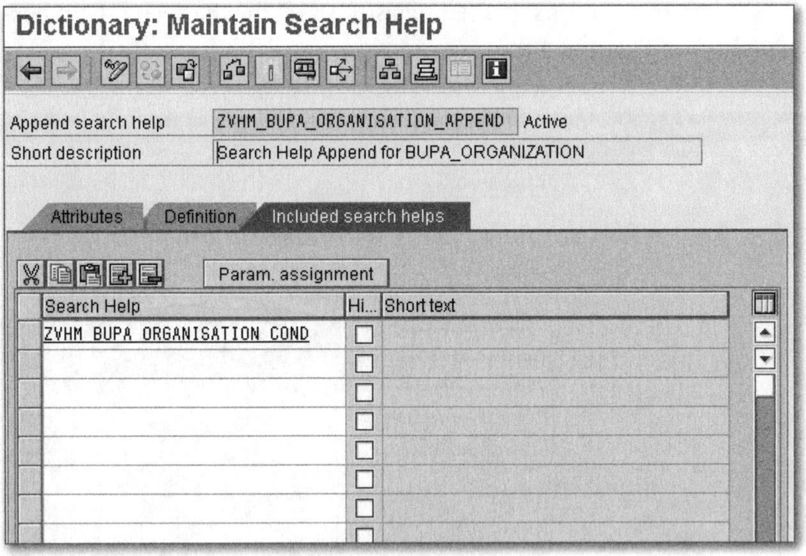

Figure 8.38 Accepting a New Search Help in Append

8.3.8 Creating a Function Group

To implement new search IDs for the "Vehicle Management" application, you create a new function group with the name ZVHM_LOCA_PROVIDE. It will comprise the entire search functionality and the search screens for vehicle management. First, you must define the GS_SEARCH_FIELDS structure used in the screen in the TOP include of the function group. For this purpose, proceed as follows:

Defining the search structure

```
TYPES:
  BEGIN OF g_typ_search_fields,
    name_org1  TYPE but000-name_org1,
    name_org2  TYPE but000-name_org2,
    cond       TYPE zvhm_conditions,
  END OF g_typ_search_fields.

DATA:
  gs_search_fields TYPE g_typ_search_fields.
```

8.3.9 Creating a Search Screen

Then, you create a search screen 2000 for your own search ID. Display the CONDITIONS field as a listbox (see Figure 8.39). Just like for the screen fields, enter an additional preceding asterisk (*) for the search field designations (see Figure 8.40).

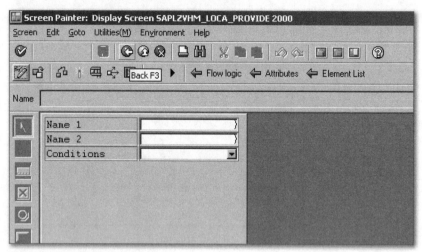

Figure 8.39   Search Screen 2000

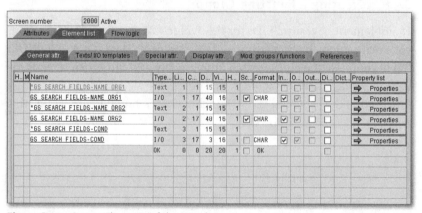

Figure 8.40   Screen Elements of the Search Screen

Screen flow logic   The screen flow logic is simple:

```
PROCESS BEFORE OUTPUT.
  module dynpro_pbo.

PROCESS AFTER INPUT.
  module dynpro_pai.
```

The underlying PBO and PAI modules use the BUS Screen Framework:

```
MODULE dynpro_pbo OUTPUT.
  cl_bus_abstract_screen=>dynpro_pbo(
    iv_program_name  = sy-repid
    iv_dynpro_number = sy-dynnr ).
ENDMODULE.              " dynpro_pbo  OUTPUT

MODULE dynpro_pai INPUT.
  cl_bus_abstract_screen=>dynpro_pai(
    iv_program_name  = sy-repid
    iv_dynpro_number = sy-dynnr ).
ENDMODULE.              " dynpro_pai  INPUT
```

Because you also want to enter a large screen in Customizing, copy screen 2000 and all its flow logic to screen 2100 and change the visible length of the first two search fields to 40 characters (see Figure 8.41).

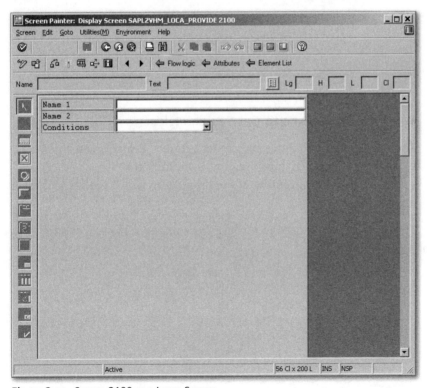

Figure 8.41 Screen 2100 as a Large Screen

8.3.10 Form Routine to Initialize the Search

For each change to a new search ID (and when starting the Locator dialog), the Locator frame calls the `bus_locator_set_search_id` form routine to initialize the search in the program associated with the search screen.

Initializing the search

The form routine is optional and doesn't have to be implemented. In this example, you will create an empty implementation, because you might use this routine to implement other searches in future:

```
*&--------------------------------------------------*
*&      Form  bus_locator_set_search_id
*&--------------------------------------------------*
FORM bus_locator_set_search_id
     USING iv_search_application
        TYPE bus_locator-search_application
           iv_search_type
        TYPE bus_locator-search_type
           iv_search_id
        TYPE bus_locator-search_id.
* Do nothing
ENDFORM.                    "bus_locator_set_search_id
```

8.3.11 Form Routine to Get Search Fields

The Locator frame queries the content from the search screen entered by the user. For this purpose, the user calls the `bus_locator_get_search_fields` form routine of the program to which the search screen belongs.

Getting search fields

The form routine is used to retrieve the content of the search structure:

```
*&--------------------------------------------------*
*&      Form  bus_locator_get_search_fields
*&--------------------------------------------------*
FORM bus_locator_get_search_fields
     USING    iv_search_application
        TYPE bus_locator-search_application
     CHANGING ev_search_fields
        TYPE bus_locator-search_fields.
  ev_search_fields = gs_search_fields.
ENDFORM.           "bus_locator_get_search_fields
```

8.3.12 Form Routine to Set Search Fields

To increase user-friendliness, the Locator frame saves the search history for every user and provides the content of the last search the next time a Locator dialog is called. This means that the Locator frame must be able to predefine the fields of the search screen. The function group provides the `bus_locator_set_search_fields` form routine (see Listing 8.12) for this purpose.

Search history

```
*&----------------------------------------------*
*&      Form  bus_locator_set_search_fields
*&----------------------------------------------*
FORM bus_locator_set_search_fields
     USING iv_search_application
        TYPE bus_locator-search_application
           iv_search_fields
        TYPE bus_locator-search_fields.
  DATA:
    lr_error TYPE REF TO cx_sy_conversion_error.
  TRY.
       gs_search_fields = iv_search_fields.
    CATCH cx_sy_conversion_error INTO lr_error.
      MESSAGE lr_error TYPE 'S'.
  ENDTRY.
ENDFORM. "bus_locator_set_search_fields
```

Listing 8.12 Setting Search Fields

Runtime Error **[!]**

After changes to the search structure, the search history of individual users can still contain content that was saved for the old structure. If this content is assigned in the `bus_locator_set_search_fields` form routine of the current search structure, runtime errors may occur, for example, if character-type values are to be included in a numeric field.

You should ensure stable programming and make sure to catch exceptions from assignments that are not permitted.

8.3.13 Form Routine To Create the Screen Object

As you already noticed in the code of the PBO and PAI modules, the Locator frame uses the BUS Screen Framework. The BUS Screen Frame-

Large screen

work queries the function groups—using the `bus_screen_create` form routine—to obtain the screen instance of the default screen and, if available, the large screen.

Here, you can create an object of the `CL_BUS_LOCATOR_SEARCH_SCREEN` class—or a class derived from it—and transfer it to the frame (see Listing 8.13). You do not necessarily require this form routine for the Locator dialog to function, but if you omit it, the Locator frame cannot switch to a possibly existing large screen when you increase the Locator area.

```
*&---------------------------------------------------*
*&      Form  bus_screen_create
*&---------------------------------------------------*
*       Generate screen object
*---------------------------------------------------*
*       -->IV_PROGRAM_NAME    Program name
*       -->IV_DYNPRO_NUMBER  Dynpro number
*       -->EV_SCREEN          Dynpro object
*---------------------------------------------------*
FORM bus_screen_create USING    iv_program_name
                          TYPE bus_screen-program_name
                                iv_dynpro_number
                          TYPE bus_screen-dynpro_number
                        CHANGING ev_screen
                                TYPE any.
  CREATE OBJECT ev_screen
    TYPE        cl_bus_locator_search_screen
    EXPORTING   iv_program_name  = iv_program_name
                iv_dynpro_number = iv_dynpro_number.
ENDFORM.                        "bus_screen_create
```

Listing 8.13 Generating the Screen Object

8.3.14 Creating a Function Module

After the user has entered the search criteria and started the search, the Locator frame calls the search function module saved in Customizing and transfers all information relevant for the search to the IV_SEARCH importing parameter with the REF TO CL_BUS_LOCATOR_SEARCH category.

This is a search object whose attributes can be found in the SEARCH APPLICATION, SEARCH CATEGORY, and SEARCH ID of the function module.

Moreover, the filled search structure and the maximum number of hits are transferred. The Locator frame expects the search function module to attach the hit list to the GT_SEARCH_RESULTS tabular attribute of the search object.

Before you program a function module, you must make a design decision. Because you will presumably implement additional business partner searches in the future, and because the code should still have a clear structure, you use the structure of the BUPA_DIALOG_SEARCH standard search module and swap the actual search strategy to a local helper class, LCL_SEARCHER. The function module has the CASE structure. This structure is used to decide which search method of the helper class will implement the search, based on the search application, search category, and search ID (see Listing 8.14).

Design decision

```
FUNCTION Z_VHM_LOCA_SEARCH.
*"----------------------------------------------------------
*"*"Local interface:
*"  IMPORTING
*"     VALUE(IV_SEARCH) TYPE REF TO CL_BUS_LOCATOR_SEARCH
*"  EXCEPTIONS
*"     SEARCH_VALUES_MISSING
*"----------------------------------------------------------
  DATA:
    ls_src_fields    TYPE g_typ_search_fields,
    lt_partner_guids TYPE bus_partner-guid_table.

  ls_src_fields = iv_search->gv_search_fields.

  CASE iv_search->gv_search_id.

    WHEN lcl_searcher=>mc_src_by_cond.
      lcl_searcher=>search_by_conditions(
        EXPORTING
          is_search_fields = ls_src_fields
          iv_maximum_rows  = iv_search->gv_maximum_rows
        IMPORTING
          et_partner_guids = lt_partner_guids ).
      lcl_searcher=>append_guids_to_result(
        EXPORTING
          it_partner_guids = lt_partner_guids
        CHANGING
```

```
                        ct_search_result = iv_search->gt_search_result ).
          WHEN OTHERS.
            CLEAR sy-subrc.
        ENDCASE.

        CASE sy-subrc.
          WHEN 1.
            RAISE search_values_missing.
        ENDCASE.
      ENDFUNCTION.
```

Listing 8.14 Search Function Module

8.3.15 Creating a Local Search Class

You first create the definition of the local search class, LCL_SEARCHER, in the TOP include of the function group (see Listing 8.15).

```
*-------------------------------------------------------------*
*          CLASS lcl_searcher DEFINITION
*-------------------------------------------------------------*
*          Helper class for the Locator search
*-------------------------------------------------------------*
CLASS lcl_searcher DEFINITION.
  PUBLIC SECTION.
    CONSTANTS:
      mc_src_by_cond
        TYPE bus_locator-search_id
          VALUE 'ZVHM_BUPA_ORGANISATION_COND'.
    CLASS-METHODS search_by_conditions
      IMPORTING
        value(is_search_fields)
          TYPE g_typ_search_fields
        value(iv_maximum_rows)
          TYPE i
      EXPORTING
        value(et_partner_guids)
          TYPE bus_partner-guid_table.
    CLASS-METHODS append_guids_to_result
      IMPORTING
        value(it_partner_guids)
          TYPE bus_partner-guid_table
      CHANGING
```

```
            ct_search_result
          TYPE bus_locator-search_result.
  PRIVATE SECTION.
    CONSTANTS:
      mc_partner_guid
        TYPE fieldname VALUE 'PARTNER_GUID'.
ENDCLASS.                     "lcl_searcher DEFINITION
```

Listing 8.15 Definition of a Local Search Class

Currently, the LCL_SEARCHER class only owns the SEARCH_BY_CONDI-TIONS( ) search method; if you want to perform additional searches in the future, they are implemented as additional search methods. It is important that the parameters defined in the method signature are transferred per value and not per reference, so that you can change the values within the method without any impact on the calling program.

The APPEND_GUIDS_TO_RESULT( ) method is used to convert the found business partner GUIDs into the format of the result structure. Because this task will also occur in future searches, you need to separate it from the actual search strategy.

APPEND_GUIDS_
TO_RESULT( )
method

The implementation of the search strategy is described in Listing 8.16. Asterisks (*) and empty fields are transformed into the percentage symbol suitable for the database searches. Subsequently, you implement a search in the tables, BUT000 and ZVHMCONDITIONS, using an INNER JOIN.

```
*--------------------------------------------------------------*
*       CLASS lcl_searcher IMPLEMENTATION
*--------------------------------------------------------------*
*       Helper class for the Locator search
*--------------------------------------------------------------*
CLASS lcl_searcher IMPLEMENTATION.
  METHOD search_by_conditions.
    REPLACE ALL OCCURRENCES OF '*'
      IN is_search_fields WITH '%'.
    IF is_search_fields-name_org1 IS INITIAL.
      is_search_fields-name_org1 = '%'.
    ENDIF.
    IF is_search_fields-name_org2 IS INITIAL.
      is_search_fields-name_org2 = '%'.
    ENDIF.
```

```
    IF is_search_fields-cond IS INITIAL.
      is_search_fields-cond = '%'.
    ENDIF.
    SELECT  partner_guid
      FROM  but000 AS b
      INNER JOIN zvhmconditions AS c
      ON    c~partner    EQ   b~partner
      UP TO iv_maximum_rows ROWS
      INTO  TABLE et_partner_guids
      WHERE b~type       EQ   '2'
      AND   b~name_org1  LIKE is_search_fields-name_org1
      AND   b~name_org2  LIKE is_search_fields-name_org2
      AND   c~conditions LIKE is_search_fields-cond.
  ENDMETHOD.                       "search_by_conditions

METHOD append_guids_to_result.
  DATA:
    ls_result_line TYPE ddshretval.
  LOOP AT it_partner_guids INTO ls_result_line-fieldval.
    ls_result_line-fieldname = mc_partner_guid.
    ls_result_line-recordpos = sy-tabix.
    APPEND ls_result_line TO ct_search_result.
  ENDLOOP.
  ENDMETHOD.                       "append_guids_to_result
ENDCLASS.                          "lcl_searcher IMPLEMENTATION
```

Listing 8.16 Implementing the Search Class

8.3.16 Providing the Search ID in the Locator Customizing

To enable the Locator frame to call the search using the search screen and the search module, you must provide it in the Locator Customizing. For this purpose, you create a new search ID, ZVHM_BUPA_ORGANI-SATION_COND, under Search IDs using Transaction LOCA_CUST. Here, you maintain the SCREEN TEXT, CONDITIONS, the PROGRAM NAME (SAPLZ-VHM_LOCA_PROVIDE), the default SCREEN NUMBER 2000, and the SCREEN NUMBER 2100 of the LARGE SCREEN (see Figure 8.42).

Function module Z_VHM_LOCA_SEARCH

Moreover, you enter the Z_VHM_LOCA_SEARCH function module, which implements the search (see Figure 8.42). This is required only if the function module deviates from the default function module maintained in the search application.

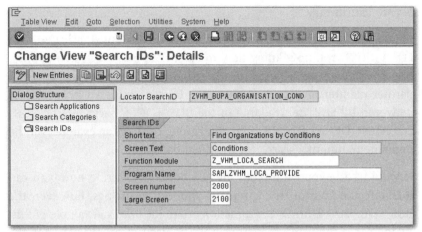

Figure 8.42 Details about the Search ID in the Locator Customizing

8.3.17 Testing the Search

You can now call the new search for the first time. Call Transaction BP to reach the business partner maintenance. If you selected the SEARCH ORGANIZATIONS search category, the selection list of the Locator now provides the BY CONDITIONS search ID.

After you entered the search criteria, you can execute the search by clicking on Start; the hitlist is then displayed in the lower part of the Locator.

Hit list

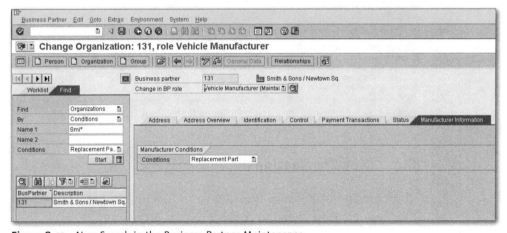

Figure 8.43 New Search in the Business Partner Maintenance

8.3.18 Summary

Sample
implementations

This section described the SAP Locator and its Customizing Transaction LOCA_CUST. You now know how to extend an existing search application by a new search, program the search, and test it in the business partner maintenance environment. The Locator framework and demos delivered by SAP are available in the BUS_TOOLS package. The BUS_LOCATOR_DEMO_PROVIDE function group contains an example for the implementation of a search for the flight database.

Integrating the
Locator in
customized
application dialogs

It would go beyond the scope of this book to describe how you can integrate the Locator in customized application dialogs; however, the BUS_LOCATOR_DEMO_USE function group includes an example of this. At the same time, this function group is used as an example for the use of the BUS Screen Framework, because both the Locator and the demo application displayed on the right side of the screen are implemented using this framework. You can also call this demo via Transaction LOCA.

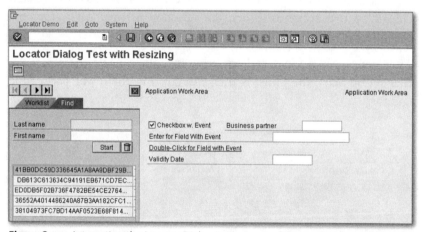

Figure 8.44 Integrating the Locator Dialog in Customized Transactions

8.4 Key Transactions

The transactions shown in Table 8.2 were used in this chapter to extend SAP Business Partner and to create a Locator dialog.

Transaction Code	Function
BUPT	Area Menu Business Partner, BDT Configuration
BP	Maintain Business Partner
BUSG	BDT: Tables
BUS1	BDT: Applications
BUS2	BDT: Field Groups
BUS3	BDT: Views
BUS7	BDT: Events
BUS23	BDT: Data Sets
BUSP	Generate Screen Containers
SPRO	SAP Implementation Guide
LOCA_CUST	Locator Customizing
LOCA	Locator Demo
SE11	Data Dictionary

Table 8.2 Key Transactions

"Technology is the effort to reduce effort." (José Ortega y Gasset)

9   Application Programming Techniques

This chapter will familiarize you with two important aspects of application programming: the implementation of application logs, and parallelization. Whereas parallelization techniques are mainly used in application systems handling mass data, logging is a central topic in virtually every development project. After processing large amounts of data in a mass report, a log is required that indicates the actions implemented and, in particular, the errors that occurred.

Also, more complex actions are triggered in the dialog from time to time, whose progress and success or failure are not sufficiently described with a simple message in the status bar. In such cases, you expect to see a popup or control, with a log of the triggered action included.

Sometimes it can be useful to equip a business object with a *persistent log* that documents all technical actions that have been implemented during its life cycle by dialog users, background jobs, and other channels. This documentation enables you to trace the current state of the object.

Persistent log

Administrators with specialized knowledge must be able to get an overview of the overall status of the application at any time. Are all traffic lights set to red because the more critical periodic reports have produced a vast amount of errors? Or is it *business as usual* instead, perhaps with some minor errors here and there that are displayed in a practical list and that need to be clarified?

Section 9.1, Implementing the Application Log, first describes the business application log. This section introduces the concept and provides programming examples on how you can easily implement a high-performance logging and interactive log display using standard tools. Section

9.2, Parallel Processing of Applications, deals with the techniques of parallelization and, based on programming examples, introduces *asynchronous RFC for parallel processing*.

9.1 Implementing the Application Log

Convenient

The business application log enables you to log application messages. In addition, convenient research and display options exist, as shown in Figure 9.1.

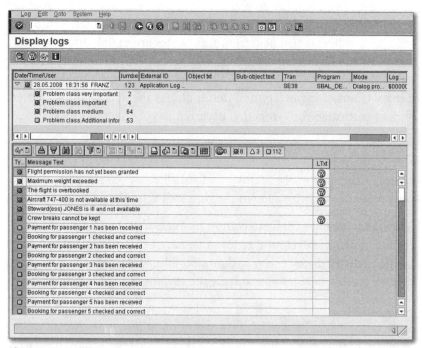

Figure 9.1 Log Research

Release Status of the Business Application Log (BAL)

The BAL is released only internally for use within SAP AG; you are provided with neither customer support nor interface stability guarantees. Nevertheless, because it is applied at numerous points in the standard SAP system, it is advisable to use it.

9.1.1 Log Recipients

When planning logging, you should consider the log recipients. It would be useless to send a log filled with technical messages about tablespaces and profile parameters to business users or persons responsible, and it would be superfluous to send a log that includes thousands of individual log messages – or even worse, thousands of logs – to a technical administrator who just wants to get an overview of an application's overall status.

Dividing these aspects to an extreme extent can result in the consistent separation of technical and business logging, always using two different logs. In practice, however, it is problematic to implement this approach pragmatically because it is difficult to clearly separate business and technical messages. Further, technical messages frequently cannot be interpreted without the business context (or vice versa).

Separating business and technical messages

9.1.2 Log Research as a Business Process

The safest way to obtain highly detailed logging is to analyze and model the log research like a business process. Developers can use the frequently asked questions we present in this section as a guide.

It is usually too early for customers to provide detailed and appropriate specifications for logging during the initial project design and development phases. If the project procedure permits it, you can postpone this subject until the first processes have been implemented in the system and the customer has a realistic impression of the software. At that point, logging requirements will be obvious to the customer. The questions that follow should help to clearly define and implement requirements, instead of confusing and overburdening the customer.

Sometimes, analyzing customer requirements can lead to exotic results. Nonetheless, we tried to provide answers, which were successfully used in other development projects:

Requirements

▶ **Who wants to read the logs?**
Usually, the customer has application administrators or specialized administrators who provide a combination of specialized and technical skills and who serve as a link between persons responsible and system administrators working across applications.

Specialized administrator

For example, these application administrators or key users are often assigned the task of maintaining the Customizing tables, opening SAP-Net messages, and performing similar interface functions between technology and specialization. When you create your logging concept, you can assume that the application administrator will regularly check the results of the periodically scheduled jobs using logs.

▶ **Which search paths or search criteria are used to determine the relevant logs?**
For log research in the business application log, the standard SAP system provides Transaction SLG1. Here, you can use different search criteria to restrict your selection. For example, you are provided with the fields LOG OBJECT, LOG SUB-OBJECT, USER (CREATED BY), DATE AND TIME, PROGRAM, and TRANSACTION CODE SUBOBJECT.

Typically, the administrator will use the time criteria to select the current logs, and the LOG OBJECT and LOG SUB-OBJECT fields to select logs of a specific process (in other words, one or more related background jobs).

Transaction SLG0
The possible values for LOG OBJECT and LOG SUB-OBJECT are maintained in Transaction SLG0. It is recommended that you already provide these fields in the logging concept as primary selection conditions for the application administrator. This means that a log object is maintained for an application and individual log sub-objects for different specialized processes (background jobs).

If the application creates all logs according to this requirement, the application administrator can readily review all current logs for the entire application. Furthermore, he can systematically search for the logs of individual processes, for example for the logs of an important periodic settlement run.

▶ **Which information needs to be provided to users immediately, and which detailed information will be provided as required?**
You have different options to make additional information and interactive functions available in the application log. These options can be linked with individual log messages or the log header. When you define message texts for the log, you can take into consideration that

the message doesn't have to contain all details of the logged situation. Instead, you can display these details in another application dialog.

▶ **Is a standalone log display sufficient or should the log display be integrated into an application transaction?**
You can integrate the log display into an application dialog as a separate screen in the application's dialog sequence or as a modal or amodal popup window. Moreover, you can integrate the log into a subscreen area of the current dialog, or dock it to the current screen in a docking container at the top, bottom, left, or right.

Modal or amodal popup

▶ **Does the user have to navigate to other application transactions to perform his task?**
Comprehensive options exist in the application log to integrate navigation options and function calls that you can use to make the application transactions available for log message completion.

▶ **When is the log research completed?**
Logs can be marked as completed. Does this make sense for the current application case? Is there a defined end of the log research, for example after all errors have been checked? Is this supposed to have a technical effect, for example subsequent selecting, deleting or archiving of the log?

▶ **For how long must the log data be available?**
Upon creation, you can determine a validity date for the logs. This prevents that they are deleted prematurely. Are there any retention periods for logs for revision purposes? Does a requirement exist to retain logs for a specific period of time, for example to check the results of settlement runs within three months?

Validity date

▶ **Do logs have to be archived afterwards?**
If many logs are created in a system, you will sooner or later need to reduce the load on the BAL's tables by deleting some of the logs. You can save the logs prior to deletion—to an optical archive, for example—to provide them for archive research.

9.1.3 Business Application Log (BAL)

The Business Application Log is a flexible logging framework in the standard SAP system that you can use for various purposes. This framework provides you with functions for creating, changing, displaying, and managing logs. It also enables you to integrate separate flow logic in the log display using callbacks, and to store additional information. BAL knows logs that are in main memory, logs that are also in the database, and finally, logs contained in the archive.

9.1.4 BAL Data Model

Log handle

An application log consists of a header and a list of messages. It has a unique ID – referred to as the *log handle* – that you can use to store the log in the database. Each log is assigned to a *log object* and a *log sub-object* during creation. These categorizations help you find and manage logs, because, for example, all logs of a specific work area or an application are assigned to a log object, and all logs of a specific process are assigned to a sub-object.

When logs are created, they have a predefined lifetime, which prevents administrators from accidentally deleting logs. They also contain information about their creation, such as user, time, report, and transaction code.

9.1.5 Application Programming Interface (API)

The BAL provides a multitude of options, but the obstacles you need to overcome for the initial steps are not particularly high. You only need to know a few central function modules and data types to create, display, and manage logs.

Interfaces for developers

The following function modules are the most critical interfaces for developers:

- **BAL_LOG_CREATE**
  Used to create a log in the main memory

- **BAL_LOG_MSG_ADD**
  Used to add a message to a log

- **BAL_DSP_LOG_DISPLAY**
  Used to display logs

▶ **BAL_DB_SAVE**
Used to save a log that exists in main memory to the database

▶ **BAL_DB_LOAD**
Used to load a log from the database into main memory

The most important data types are:

Data types

▶ **BALLOGHNDL**
Data element for character-type handle of the BAL log. It is consistently used to identify a single log.

▶ **BAL_S_MSG**
Structure for a single message in the log. This deep structure contains the MSGTY, MSGID, MSGNO, and MSGV1 to MSGV4 fields in particular, which are required for saving T100 messages.

▶ **BAL_S_MSG**
Structure for the log header. To save a log, you must at least fill the OBJECT and SUBOBJECT fields. (the possible values for OBJECT and SUBOBJECT can be maintained in Transaction SLG0.)

▶ **BAL_S_PROF**
Structure for the log display options. Among others, they are passed to the BAL_DSP_LOG_DISPLAY function module. This structure includes the MESS_FCAT tabular component, in which you can transfer the fields for log display.

9.1.6 Example: Creating and Displaying a Log

As a simple example you are shown a report that creates a log, adds a message, and subsequently calls the log display (see Listing 9.1).

```
*&---------------------------------------------------------*
*& Report  ZBAL_DEMO1
*&---------------------------------------------------------*
*& Demo program for creating a log
*&---------------------------------------------------------*

REPORT  zbal_demo1 MESSAGE-ID zvhm.
```

```
DATA:
  balloghndl  TYPE balloghndl,  " Handle for the log
  t_balhndl   TYPE bal_t_logh,  " Table of handles
  ballog      TYPE bal_s_log,   " Header of the log
  balmsg      TYPE bal_s_msg.   " Structure for a message

START-OF-SELECTION.
* Create a log
  CALL FUNCTION 'BAL_LOG_CREATE' " Create log
    EXPORTING
      i_s_log      = ballog       " Header structure
    IMPORTING
      e_log_handle = balloghndl. " Log handle

* Prepare message
  CLEAR balmsg.
  balmsg-msgty = 'S'.         " Error, info, success, etc.
  balmsg-msgid = 'ZVHM'.      " Message class vehiclemgt
  balmsg-msgno = '047'.       " Element & was added to vehicle &
  balmsg-msgv1 = '00123'.     " Message variable 1
  balmsg-msgv2 = '00456'.     " Message variable 2
  balmsg-msgv3 = space.       " Message variable 3
  balmsg-msgv4 = space.       " Message variable 4

* Add message to the log
  CALL FUNCTION 'BAL_LOG_MSG_ADD'" Add message
    EXPORTING
      i_log_handle = balloghndl  " Log handle
      i_s_msg      = balmsg.     " Content of message

* Output log
  INSERT balloghndl INTO TABLE t_balhndl.
  CALL FUNCTION 'BAL_DSP_LOG_DISPLAY'
    EXPORTING
      i_t_log_handle = t_balhndl.
```

Listing 9.1 Creating and Displaying a Log

This results in the log display in Figure 9.2.

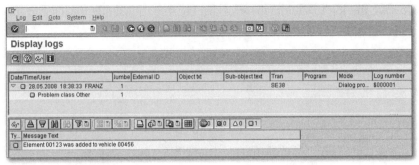

Figure 9.2 Log Display

This example includes a minor flaw: The use of Message 047 of the ZVHM   **Flaw**
message class is not recorded by the where-used list for messages, as
happens when using the MESSAGE statement. This is accomplished by
using the call in Listing 9.2.

```
DATA: dummy TYPE string.

MESSAGE ID   'ZVHM' TYPE 'S' NUMBER '047'
        WITH '00123' '00456'
        INTO dummy.

CLEAR balmsg.
balmsg-msgty = sy-msgty.      " Message type
balmsg-msgid = sy-msgid.      " Message class
balmsg-msgno = sy-msgno.      " Message number
balmsg-msgv1 = sy-msgv1.      " Message variable 1
balmsg-msgv2 = sy-msgv2.      " Message variable 2
balmsg-msgv3 = sy-msgv3.      " Message variable 3
balmsg-msgv4 = sy-msgv4.      " Message variable 4
```

Listing 9.2 Filling the Message Structure Using the Where-Used List

You can also use the short form, MESSAGE S047(ZHVM) ....

9.1.7   Example: Saving the Log

When saving logs, you must specify a log object and log sub-object. The
possible values for these fields need to be maintained in advance using
Transaction SLG0. In this example, you create the ZVHM log object and
the ZREP sub-object.

Saving the log in the database

To save the log to the database to display it for subsequent calls and for other users, the additional code shown in Listing 9.3 is required.

```
START-OF-SELECTION.
* Vor BAL_LOG_CREATE: Prepare header
  ballog-object    = 'ZVHM'.  " NEW: Object from TA SLG0
  ballog-subobject = 'ZREP'.  " NEw: Sub-object from TA SLG0
  ...
* At the end: Save log
  CALL FUNCTION 'BAL_DB_SAVE'       " NEW: Save log(s)
    EXPORTING                       " NEW
      i_t_log_handle = t_balhndl.   " NEW: Handle(s)
```

Listing 9.3 Saving a Log to the Database

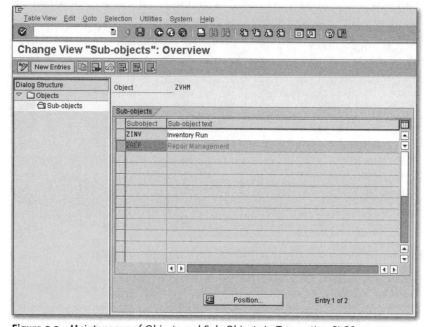

Figure 9.3 Maintenance of Objects and Sub-Objects in Transaction SLG0

Transaction SLG1

Logs that were saved to the database can be displayed using Transaction SLG1. Figure 9.4 shows the selection mask for logs, in which you can enter numerous criteria. After a search has been run, the system navigates to the already known log display.

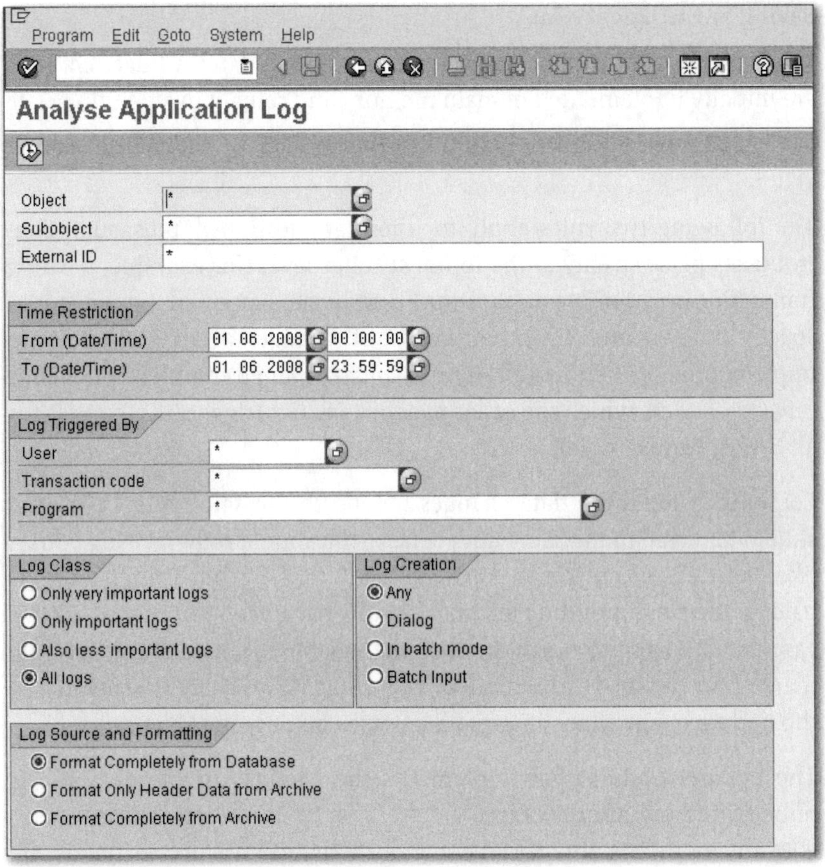

Figure 9.4 Selecting Application Logs

9.1.8 Transaction Concept

You should also include transaction security in logging. If the application uses this technique only after the update, database changes are implemented after a COMMIT WORK. Do you want to write the log entries only after the COMMIT WORK in the same SAP LUW in the database, together with the application data?

Including security

When saving logs, the caller can select whether the database changes should be implemented immediately or in the update task. This is controlled with the I_IN_UPDATE_TASK parameter of the BAL_DB_SAVE function module, which may have the value SPACE (false) or X (true).

Saving in the Update Task

Many recent applications consistently use the update: All data changes are initially implemented in main memory and remain in a pending state until they are committed by the update modules in the database after COMMIT WORK.

Physical data changes are strictly transactional

The following two rules apply for these applications: Transaction control takes place strictly at the topmost caller level (for example, a dialog transaction or a remote application), and data changes are implemented strictly transactional (in other words, all changes of an SAP LUW are implemented or none at all). Here, each data change completely depends on COMMIT WORK which the caller may or may not trigger (this applies for all BAPIs, for example).

Log entries for these data changes belong to the same SAP LUW, and should be saved in the same update task. You should only save log entries like "Address of customer ABC changed" or "The bill was marked as paid" if the corresponding technical results have been committed. In this case the changes are not written to the database immediately, but only marked for saving. For each call of BAL_DB_SAVE, an entry is generated in the update queue that contains all changes belonging to the call.

ROLLBACK WORK

The update module that implements the changes in the database is only carried out after an explicit COMMIT WORK. In the case of no COMMIT WORK, the module is not carried out and the changes are not written to the database. An explicit or implicit ROLLBACK WORK removes entries from the update queue. (This is done after a termination, for example.)

Saving without the Update Task

There are also applications – generally older ones – in which database changes are implemented immediately and that don't depend on a COMMIT WORK by the caller. If the application does not use the update, it is not certain that an explicit COMMIT WORK is triggered after the transaction has been properly concluded. In this case, you must ensure that the log entries don't wait for the COMMIT WORK, but are permanently persisted beforehand.

If you select immediate saving without update task, the behavior of the database changes is the same as after other database changes carried out with the Open-SQL command set: The changes are immediately visible across the modes. They are revoked only if there is an explicit ROLLBACK WORK, or a situation that results in an implicit rollback (a program termination, for example), before the next COMMIT WORK statement. However, a COMMIT WORK is no longer required to persist changes.

Immediate saving without the update task

Special Case: Logging in Own SAP LUW

The application might trigger an implicit ROLLBACK WORK intentionally or after a technical error occurred. As a general rule, logs that logically belong to the database changes should only be stored together with them; that is, in the same SAP LUW. If one is discarded, the other is also invalid.

In exceptional cases, it may be desirable for a log message to survive the termination of a transaction and not be rolled back. This may be required if you want to log technical errors – the occurrence and cause of the rollback – or if the rollback is the result of a specialist error (for resetting pending update entries, for example) that should be documented in the application log.

Exception

Selecting the Right Mode for Saving

Selecting the save mode for a given log depends on the transaction concept of the logged transaction: Usually, you should implement logging in the same SAP LUW and use the same transaction concept.

9.1.9 Enriching Logs

In addition to mere message contents you can enrich logs by adding information to identify the specialist, technical, or time-based context, or to enable navigation to help texts, documents, or application functions.

Environment Information

Often the business context in which a message or log was created is not obvious from the log messages. A message the user can easily understand

Often the context is not clear

in the object dialog or the document he just edited might be completely incoherent and cryptic when it appears in a log.

Therefore, when you create a log, you can supply a context for each message and log header. This context is any character-type ABAP Dictionary structure. You enter its name in the CONTEXT-TABNAME field and the structure content in the CONTEXT-VALUE field.

Listing 9.4 shows how you can fill a business context structure and enrich the message before it is written to the log.

```
DATA:
* Context structure for messages
  balcontext TYPE zvhm_balcontext.

* Prepare context
  CLEAR balcontext.
  balcontext-vehicle      = '00456'.
  balcontext-element      = '00123'.
  balcontext-customer     = '0000001001'.
  balcontext-repairorder = 'N00124'.
* Filling DDIC structure name
  balmsg-context-tabname = 'ZVHM_BALCONTEXT'.
  balmsg-context-value    = balcontext.          " Content
```

Listing 9.4 Filling Own Context Structure

Purpose of environment information

The environment information thus supplied can be used for multiple purposes:

- ▶ It can be displayed as message details, as shown in the popup window visible in Figure 9.5.

- ▶ All fields in the context structure can be used as columns in the message area of the log output. For this purpose, you must publish them in the display profile by entering them in the BAL_S_PROF structure's MESS_FCAT table.

- ▶ Additionally, you can use the context structure's fields as nodes and column headers in the log navigation tree setup. Here, you need to enter them in the BAL_S_PROF structure's tables LEV1_FCAT to LEV9_FCAT (for the corresponding level one to nine of the navigation tree).

► The context structure's fields can be used as sort criteria in the message area and for setting up the navigation tree. To do that, you must enter them in the table, MESS_SORT or LEV1_SORT to LEV9_SORT, of the BAL_S_PROF structure.

Listing 9.5 shows how you can integrate the Vehicle and Order columns of the ZVHM_BALCONTEXT context structure into the log display. First, you need to read the default profile template for displaying single logs, using the BAL_DSP_PROFILE_SINGLE_LOG_GET function module.

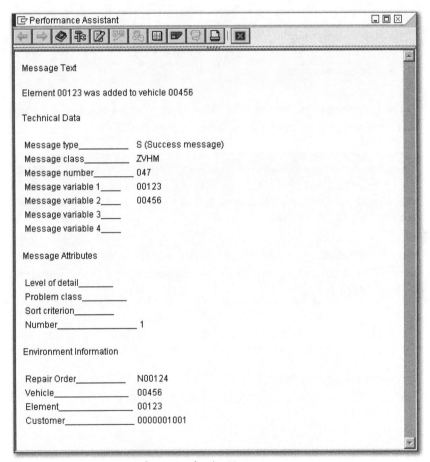

Figure 9.5 Environment Information for the Message

> **Default Profile Template for Logs**
>
> The following function modules provide you with the default profile templates for the log display:
>
> ▶ BAL_DSP_PROFILE_SINGLE_LOG_GET
> (Default profile template)
>
> ▶ BAL_DSP_PROFILE_DETLEVEL_GET
> (Hierarchy according to DETLEVEL)
>
> ▶ BAL_DSP_PROFILE_NO_TREE_GET
> (Without tree, fullscreen)
>
> ▶ BAL_DSP_PROFILE_POPUP_GET
> (Without tree, popup)
>
> ▶ BAL_DSP_PROFILE_STANDARD_GET
> (Standard, many logs)

In the following step, you add the ORDER and VEHICLE fields of the context structure to the field catalog in the display profile.

[+]

> **Additional Fields and Sortings**
>
> The field catalog BAL_S_PROF-MESS_FCAT enables you to add fields to the log display. Similarly, you can use table BAL_S_PROF-MESS_SORT to define sort criteria for the log output.

Calling the log display

You use the display profile to which you added fields to call the log display (see Listing 9.5). The result should correspond to the log view shown in Figure 9.6.

```
DATA:
    ls_prof TYPE bal_s_prof,   " BAL display profile
    ls_fcat TYPE bal_s_fcat.   " one row of the field catalog

* Read standard profile
  CALL FUNCTION 'BAL_DSP_PROFILE_SINGLE_LOG_GET'
    IMPORTING
      e_s_display_profile = ls_prof.

* Extend field catalog of the standard profile
  ls_fcat-ref_table = 'ZVHM_BALCONTEXT'.
  ls_fcat-ref_field = 'REPAIRORDER'.
  APPEND ls_fcat TO ls_prof-mess_fcat.
```

```
    ls_fcat-ref_table = 'ZVHM_BALCONTEXT'.
    ls_fcat-ref_field = 'VEHICLE'.
    APPEND ls_fcat TO ls_prof-mess_fcat.
    ...
* Output log
    CALL FUNCTION 'BAL_DSP_LOG_DISPLAY'
      EXPORTING
        i_s_display_profile = ls_prof          " Display profile
        i_t_log_handle      = t_balhndl.
```

Listing 9.5 Displaying Additional Columns in the BAL Context

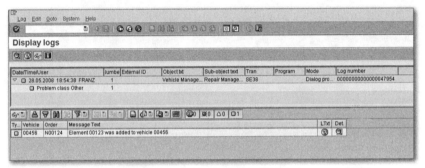

Figure 9.6 Vehicle and Order Columns from the Context

Detailed Information for the Message as Dialog Text

You can also enrich the log message with data and functions by append-   **Appending dialog**
ing a dialog text that can be displayed as detailed message information.   **text**
This is an SAPscript text maintained in Transaction SE61 (Document
maintenance) of the *Text in dialog* document class, to which you can add
any number of placeholders for variables. Save the variable values as
additional data for the log message. When you display the text, they are
added to the text.

Not only can you maintain placeholders and formatted text in SAPscript   **SAPscript texts**
texts, but you can also include references to other texts, text blocks and
executable links to ABAP programs and transactions. Therefore, they are
a powerful tool to integrate application functionality into the log display
in a user-friendly way. Figure 9.7 shows the initial document maintenance screen, Figure 9.8 shows the maintenance of dialog texts in the
graphical editor, and Figure 9.9 shows the text-based editor.

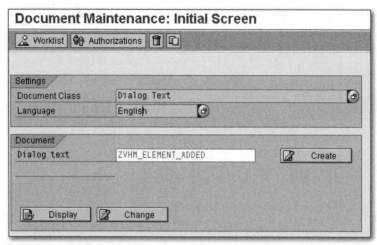

Figure 9.7 Initial Screen of the Document Maintenance (Transaction SE61)

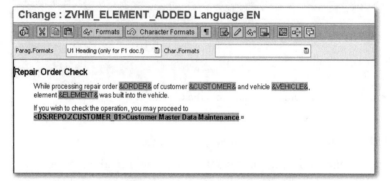

Figure 9.8 Dialog Text Maintenance in the Graphical Editor

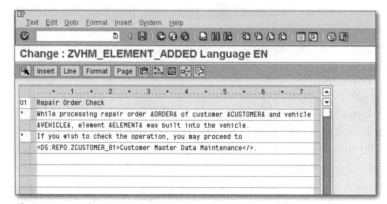

Figure 9.9 Dialog Text Maintenance in the Text-Based Editor

Listing 9.6 shows you how to add a dialog text to a message and how you supply the parameters.

Adding a dialog text

```
* Prepare display of dialog text
  data: ls_par type bal_s_par.            " Parameter


* Fill SE61 dialog text
  balmsg-params-altext = 'ZVHM_ELEMENT_ADDED'.

  ls_par-parname        = 'VEHICLE'.    " Name in dialog text
  ls_par-parvalue       = '00456'.      " Value
* Add message
  APPEND ls_par TO balmsg-params-t_par.

  ls_par-parname        = 'ORDER'.
  ls_par-parvalue       = 'N00124'.
  APPEND ls_par TO balmsg-params-t_par.

  ls_par-parname        = 'CUSTOMER'.
  ls_par-parvalue       = '0000001001'.
  APPEND ls_par TO balmsg-params-t_par.

  ls_par-parname        = 'ELEMENT'.
  ls_par-parvalue       = '0123'.
  APPEND ls_par TO balmsg-params-t_par.
```

Listing 9.6 Adding Dialog Text and Parameters to a Message

As an immediate result an additional icon displays, showing detailed information for the message (see Figure 9.10).

Additional icon

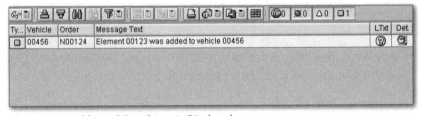

Figure 9.10 Additional Detail Icon is Displayed

Clicking on the detail icon opens the dialog text with the added parameters from the log message. You can also navigate to an ABAP report, as shown in Figure 9.11.

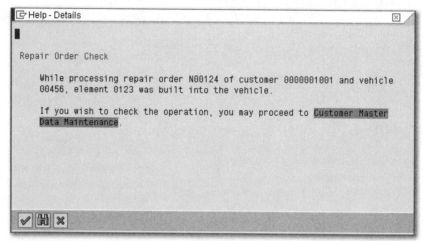

```
Help - Details                                                    ☒

Repair Order Check

    While processing repair order N00124 of customer 0000001001 and vehicle
    00456, element 0123 was built into the vehicle.

    If you wish to check the operation, you may proceed to Customer Master
    Data Maintenance.



✓ 🔛 ✖
```

Figure 9.11 Interactive Dialog Text

Detailed Information for the Message as Callback Routine

Callback routine   As an alternative to the dialog text you can also specify a callback routine in the message, which is executed when you click on the Detailed Information icon. You can implement this either as a function module or a subroutine. In both cases, you transfer the parameter using the parameter table, which you have already used for the variables in the dialog texts shown in Listing 9.6.

The BAL_S_MSG-PARAMS-CALLBACK structure contains the fields USEREXITP, USEREXITF, and USEREXITT:

▶ USEREXITT specifies the callback routine type and is allocated F for a function module and SPACE for a subroutine.

▶ USEREXITF contains the name of the function module or the subroutine.

▶ USEREXITP includes – in the case of a subroutine – the name of the main program that contains it.

The function module or subroutine must have a TABLES transfer parameter, I_T_PARAMS, with the SPAR structure. You use this parameter to add the name-value pairs to the subroutine, which have been transferred to the BAL_S_MSG-PARAMS-T_PAR table during the message creation.

Listing 9.7 shows you how to specify a callback routine for a message that results in the display of a decision popup. If you use a callback routine, you must not transfer a dialog text at the same time. Therefore, the BAL_S_MSG-PARAMS-ALTEXT field must remain blank.

Decision popup

```
* Fill SE61 dialog text
* balmsg-params-altext = 'ZVHM_ELEMENT_ADDED'.
* Callback routine
  balmsg-params-callback-userexitf = 'CALLBACK_FORM'.
  balmsg-params-callback-userexitp = sy-repid.
  balmsg-params-callback-userexitt = space.
  ...
```

Listing 9.7 Specifying a Callback routine

The callback routine is implemented as shown in Listing 9.8.

```
*&---------------------------------------------------*
*&      Form  callback_form
*&---------------------------------------------------*
FORM callback_form TABLES i_t_params STRUCTURE spar.
  DATA: lv_text TYPE string.
  CONCATENATE 'Do you wish to proceed with Customer'
              'or Vehicle Maintenance?'
              INTO lv_text SEPARATED BY space.
  CALL FUNCTION 'POPUP_TO_CONFIRM'
    EXPORTING
      titlebar      = 'Jump to detail maintenance'
      text_question = lv_text
      text_button_1 = 'Customer'
      icon_button_1 = 'ICON_CUSTOMER'
      text_button_2 = 'Vehicle'
      icon_button_2 = 'ICON_CAR'.
  ...
ENDFORM.                    "callback_form
```

Listing 9.8 Example of a Callback Routine

Click on the detail icon in the message to see the decision popup shown in Figure 9.12.

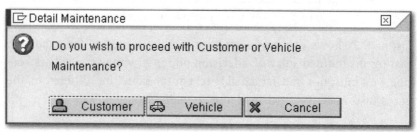

Figure 9.12 Decision Popup of the Log Callback

Detailed Information on the Log Header

The options for enriching individual messages using the structures BAL_S_MSG-CONTEXT and BAL_S_MSG-PARAMS are also provided with regard to the log header. Therefore, you can use the same techniques to add environment information, dialog texts, or function calls to the detail icon.

Filling structures For this purpose, use the same techniques to fill the structures BAL_S_LOG-CONTEXT and BAL_S_LOG-PARAMS. You can call the stored environment and detailed information by clicking on the magnifying-glass and the glasses icon in the menu bar of the log display (see Figure 9.13).

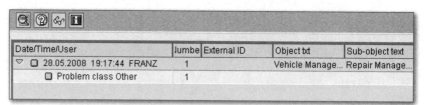

Figure 9.13 Icons for Environment and Details in the Log Display

9.1.10 Saving Complex Data

Saving tabular additional data If your application requires you to save additional data for the log header or the messages, it is possible that the methods discussed so far – BAL_S_CONT for environment information and BAL_S_PARM for parameters – are not sufficient. For example, it may be necessary to save additional data in tabular form. In this case you can save the additional data in the *data cluster* BAL_INDX. Here, LOGNUMBER is used as a key and is returned to the BAL_DB_SAVE module after saving.

To save the sample log, insert two rows—which you use to indicate the log object and log sub-object—after calling BAL_LOG_CREATE:

```
ballog-object    = 'ZVHM'.
ballog-subobject = 'REP'.
```

Immediately before the log output, enter the code shown in Listing 9.9 using the BAL_DSP_LOG_DISPLAY module.

```
* Log number as row and table type
  DATA:
    ls_lognumber  TYPE bal_s_lgnm,
    lt_lognumber  TYPE bal_t_lgnm.
* Save log to keep log numbers
  CALL FUNCTION 'BAL_DB_SAVE'
    EXPORTING
      i_t_log_handle   = t_balhndl
    IMPORTING
      e_new_lognumbers = lt_lognumber.

* Determine log number for current log handle
  READ TABLE lt_lognumber
    INTO ls_lognumber
    WITH KEY log_handle = balloghndl.
  IF sy-subrc EQ 0.
* Save additional data as CONTEXT in BAL_INDX
    EXPORT context = balcontext
         TO DATABASE bal_indx(al)
         ID ls_lognumber-lognumber.
  ENDIF.
```

Listing 9.9 Saving Additional Data in Table BAL_INDX

> ### Data Cluster
>
> The SAP Library describes a data cluster as a grouping of data objects for the purpose of storing them in a storage medium that can only be processed using ABAP statements.
>
> Various storage media exist for data clusters — shared memory, and shared buffers, for example.
>
> The *INDX-type tables* are relevant for this purpose. You can access them using the command EXPORT...TO DATABASE dbtab(ar)...ID id, or the corresponding import command, as well as the class CL_ABAP_EXPIMP_DB. Here, multiple data objects (including complex data objects) can be stored and read under one shared key.
>
> For more information on this subject refer to the ABAP keyword documentation at ABAP • REFERENCE • SAVING DATA EXTERNALLY • DATA CLUSTERS.

Reading additional data

You have read access to additional data stored in the BAL_INDX table, which you can display in the detail callback. The code example in Listing 9.10 shows you how to read additional data.

```
*&---------------------------------------------------*
*&      Form  callback_form
*&---------------------------------------------------*
FORM callback_form TABLES i_t_params STRUCTURE spar.
  DATA:
    ls_balcontext TYPE zvhm_balcontext,
    ls_param      TYPE spar,    " Workarea Parameter
    lv_lognumber  TYPE balognr. " Lognummer
  READ TABLE i_t_params
    INTO ls_param
    WITH KEY param = '%LOGNUMBER'.
  IF sy-subrc EQ 0.
    lv_lognumber = ls_param-value.
    IMPORT context = ls_balcontext
      FROM DATABASE bal_indx(al)
      ID ls_lognumber-lognumber.
  ENDIF.
  ... " Output data in LS_BALCONTEXT
ENDFORM.
```

Listing 9.10 Read Access to Additional Data in BAL_INDX

Archiving additional data

The additional data stored in Table BAL_INDX is automatically connected to archiving, and is therefore archived together with the log header and message data, using the default procedure. When you delete logs – using Transaction SLG2, or the BAL_DB_DELETE function module – all additional data is also automatically deleted.

Pros and Cons of BAL_INDX
Pros:
▶ Connection to archiving
▶ Connection to the delete function
▶ High-performance storage and reading of multiple (possibly complex) data objects with database access
Cons:
▶ No high-performance search across logs
▶ Storage format not transparent
▶ Error-prone if the structure of additional data is changed
▶ INDX-type tables not obsolete, but also not well-known among developers
▶ Update module must be developed individually

9.1.11 Using Additional Callbacks in the Display

You can use certain callback routines in the log display to develop application-specific functions. You define these in the BAL_S_PROF display profile's structure, and transfer them when calling BAL_DSP_LOG_DISPLAY. They include the callbacks listed in Table 9.1.

Developing application-specific functions

Callback	Function
CLBK_READ	*Read external data for the display*
	The routine is called for all fields that have the IS_EXTERN attribute with value 'X' in the field catalogs, LEV1_FCAT to LEV9_FCAT, or in MESS_FCAT.
CLBK_UCOM	*Execute own user commands*
	In this routine, you can edit your own function codes the user triggered in the log display.
	For example, you can edit the %EXT_PUSH1 to %EXIT_PUSH4 function codes of the user-defined buttons.

Table 9.1 Callbacks in Log Display

Callback	Function
CLBK_UCBF	*Before executing user commands* This routine is called for user-defined function codes and certain default BAL function codes before user commands are executed.
CLBK_UCAF	*After executing user commands* see CLBK_UCBF
CLBK_PBO	*Before Output* This callback is called before the log output, at the point of `PROCESS BEFORE OUTPUT`. Here you can set your own GUI status to override the default menu.
CLBK_TOOLB	*Modifying the toolbar* This callback enables you to modify the log toolbar (only in the ALV display). You can integrate your own functions, and even menus with subitems, in the toolbar.

Table 9.1 Callbacks in Log Display (Cont.)

Details   Refer to the online documentation on the `BAL_DSP_LOG_DISPLAY` function module to get detailed information on these callbacks, and, in particular, on their parameterization.

9.1.12   User-Defined Buttons

You can use up to four user-defined buttons in the log display. For this purpose, use the components `BAL_S_PROF-EXT_PUSH1` to `EXT_PUSH4`. You can determine the position of the buttons, specify whether the buttons are active, and define texts, tooltip, and icons. When the user clicks on one of the buttons, a function code, `%EXT_PUSH1` to `%EXT_PUSH4`, is triggered, which you can define in the callback routine `CLBK_UCOM`.

[+]   **Changeable Log**

Defining your own function codes enables you to go beyond the mere log display. In many applications, logs are created at regular intervals, which are ideally checked and handled. You can, for example, use user-defined function codes to change the log and store it again when the user has marked critical messages as checked. This way, log displays can serve as the backbone of application-specific error management.

9.1.13 Deleting and Archiving Logs

To delete logs, call Transaction SLG2. This application log is connected to archiving. For this purpose, you are provided with the archiving object BC_SBAL and the programs `SBAL_ARCHIVE` and `SBAL_ARCHIVE_DELETE`, which are integrated in the *Archive Development Kit*. You can use Transaction SLG1 (Log display) to process logs from the archive.

Transaction SLG2

9.1.14 Summary

This section described the SAP application log. In addition, this section detailed conceptual considerations on the use of this tool and the interplay of application transaction concepts and logging. Moreover, you were provided with information about the programming interface, the parameterization of the output, various options for storing and displaying additional information, as well as the application log's callback interfaces.

9.1.15 Additional Information

▶ In addition to the core functionality, the SZAL package also contains several sample programs (`SBAL_DEMO_*`).

SZAL package

▶ You can find additional information on the application log in the SAP Library under BC – EXTENDED APPLICATIONS FUNCTION LIBRARY • APPLICATION LOG.

▶ Under APPLICATION LOG (BC-SRV-BAL), the SAP Library also contains the following documents: APPLICATION LOG • USER GUIDELINES • GUIDELINES FOR DEVELOPERS.

▶ The most comprehensive documentation on the application log can be obtained by calling the `BAL_LOG_CREATE` function module in the online documentation. Here, you can find many sources and examples, such as *Application Log: Technical Documentation*.

9.2   Parallel Processing of Applications

This section describes the basic approaches, prerequisites, techniques, and tools for parallel processing of an application. It deals extensively

Asynchronous RFC

with the parallelization technique recommended by SAP using asynchronous RFC, but also details alternative techniques such as scheduling of background jobs and the use of additional frameworks for parallel processing.

9.2.1 Use case

Parallelizability is the most critical prerequisite for the use of software in a mass data scenario. It is the primary criterion for specific software being used at large customers, and determines the limits to the growth of data to be processed.

Quantity structures often inaccurate

Experience shows that the quantity structures determined at the beginning of a development project are only rough estimates. When developers design an application, they usually don't know the exact size of the data the application needs to process in jobs that are scheduled daily or nightly.

Parallelization

But how can you ensure smooth operation? The answer is the parallelizability of the application. Parallelizing an application means that actions can be implemented concurrently (in parallel) instead of consecutively. This process allows you to use the available hardware resources and avoid idle time. Conversely, it means that you can reduce the runtime for mass reports by providing additional hardware resources.

Today, many data centers are equipped with servers that can be dynamically assigned with resources, such as additional CPUs and main memories, depending on the current requirements. Considering parallelizability of an application during the design phase allows for dynamic growth of the application in line with the available hardware.

Ideally Scaling Applications

Linear scaling

In the ideal case, an application features *linear* scaling. An application has linear scaling when the amount of data to be processed (the problem factor) and the resource requirement (time, processors, main memory) grow at the same rate.

The goal of parallelization is to make the resource types time, processors, and main memory convertible (with one another) to optimize specific parameters. This usually means that you optimize a mass report runtime to require, for example, only half the time for double the number of work processes. You can also reduce the runtime by upgrading the hardware.

Types of Scaling Behavior

In practice, the ideal of linear scaling and convertibility of resource types is usually like any other ideal – you can't always achieve it. The time, processors, and main memory resource types can't be exchanged completely; in other words, doubling the processor performance doesn't automatically mean reducing the required processing time by half. The reasons for this are based on the specific application:

Unachievable ideal

▶ **Constant efforts that do not depend on the problem factor**
For example, the time required to set up a connection in the network or other initializations can be consistent for a resource type.

▶ **Problems with inherent nonlinearity**
Imagine, for example, search and optimization problems that are similar to the problems of a field sales representative who has to visit different locations and needs to find the shortest routes. (In the environment of the existing vehicle application, this problem type could occur in the programming of an automated resource planning optimization.) In this case, the resource requirement, such as time or main memory, increases exponentially in relation to the amount of input data.

▶ **Applications with limited convertible resource types**
For example, the time available might be constant. In this case, the scaling would entail that a larger amount of data is processed within the same amount of time, but using more available work processes.

Parallelizability and Performance Optimization

It is essential that you don't think of parallelizability as a type of performance optimization that absolves the application developer from the necessity of identifying critical performance bottlenecks and resolving them through optimization. This is not the case.

Thorough performance analysis

Thorough performance analysis and performance optimization are still the first measures you should take to achieve a lean and fast application. In addition, you should also ensure linear scaling behavior (for example, for main memory consumption).

However, the optimization of source code, data model, and system parameterization does more harm than good if you go beyond a specific point. Therefore, if developers pull out all the stops to reduce runtimes, it is possible that the application deviates too much from the standards, is less flexible, and becomes less transparent. This reduces the maintainability of the entire application. The goal of parallelizing an application is to enable operators to achieve runtime reductions by providing additional resources.

9.2.2 Prerequisites

Packaging, processing, controlling

The parallelizability of an application initially depends on the structure of the problems to be solved. In other words, it depends on the specialization. You must be able to divide the amount of data to be processed into packages without any logical dependencies. The results of processing a package must not have any impact on the processing of other packages. The sequence in which packages are processed should not play a role either. The issue can be divided into three parts: packaging, processing, and control (see Figure 9.14).

Packaging

Packaging includes the creation of a worklist; that is, you select the data to be processed and create the packages. You are provided with different packaging strategies, depending on whether the number of packages or the package size is predefined:

Packaging strategy

▶ **Manual packaging**

The simplest strategy is setting a fixed number of packages along with the selection conditions for the individual packages. This is feasible for a relatively static dataset, such as monthly settlement runs in HR management. You can typically use this strategy if the main business object has master data-like characteristics.

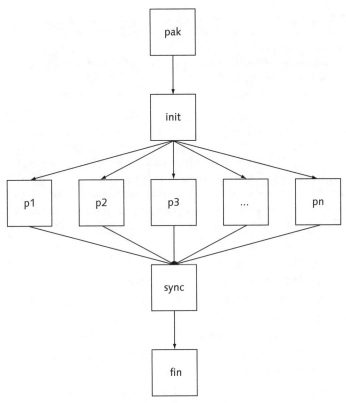

Figure 9.14 Schematic Diagram of a Parallelized Process

▶ **Predefined package size**

The second strategy is suitable for mass reports on a business object with document-like characteristics and many changes to the dataset. Here, you predefine the package size (e.g., as a parameter on the selection screen) and distribute the selected data to packages of the same size accordingly until the entire object quantity has been assigned.

▶ **Predefined number of packages**

The third strategy is to predefine the number of packages, and to uniformly distribute the object quantity to be processed to the defined packages.

[+]

> **Deluxe Packaging**
>
> In the most sophisticated variant we have encountered of this strategy, each object of the potentially relevant object quantity had a random GUID that was guaranteed to be unique and that was distributed almost evenly across the number range. Even for any subsets, the GUIDs were distributed almost evenly.
>
> Because you can cut the number range across which the GUIDs are distributed into areas of the same size without knowing the data to be processed, and use their upper and lower limits as selection conditions for the package definition, you can create the selection conditions for a specific amount of packages with an almost identical number of objects. Not only is this solution very elegant, it also prevents any overlapping of individual packages and saves expensive database accesses.

To determine the objects to be processed in a package, you can either define selection conditions for the package or save an explicit list of the objects to be processed. Selecting the right packaging strategy depends strongly on the specialization to be mapped. The specialist concurrencies (i.e., which specialist activities are independent of each other logically so they can be processed in any sequence, or even concurrently) determine which dependencies can be detected and resolved in advance between the business objects to be processed, and which activities are suitable for parallelization.

Processing of Packages

Good modularization pays off

The core functionality of package processing should be carried out as a simple call of an application function. Now it pays off if you modularized the application well and implemented the specialist functions in such a way that they can be used in different scenarios with only a few preconditions.

It is important for package processing that the package doesn't depend on changeable content or statuses of other packages, and doesn't impact them either. Such dependencies can occur if multiple packages access the same business objects, for example because documents that relate to the same business partners are distributed to multiple packages.

Such dependencies can also be indirect, for example, if the business objects of two packages refer to different business partners while a relationship existing between the two business partners is analyzed or changed during the package processing.

In these cases, you can set locks to prevent inconsistencies. Lock conflicts can also be dangerous if the lock requirements of two or more processes end up blocking each other. If the processes involved release a lock only if another lock is set, this can result in an alternating blockage (*deadlock*), causing a system standstill. (At the database system level, deadlock situations can occur due to competing accesses to the same data.)

To avoid deadlocks, you don't wait after a lock request has failed, but instead continue with the next object, leaving the object that is locked by another process in the worklist. Locks that are no longer required should be released soon.

Creating Packaging Criteria

If the relationship between a document and a business partner is not established until processing, because a business partner has been identified or created during the evaluation of name and address data contained in the document, you should think about the correct layout of the activity to be parallelized. You could carry out the business partner assignment without parallelization in an upstream step, and use the resulting business partner number as a grouping criterion for package creation.

Controlling and Monitoring the Overall Process

The subproblem of controlling and monitoring is highly significant for your parallelization concept because the consistency and operating security of your application depends on the answers to the following questions:

▶ How do you obtain an overview of the overall status of a parallelized program run? Is there a cockpit user interface?

▶ Can you establish which parts are still active, which parts have completed properly, and which have been canceled?

▶ What happens to the remaining objects that are contained in a package and have not been processed? Can these objects be resubmitted?

▶ Where and how are specialist and technical error and success messages from processing logged?

▶ Can you terminate a run manually?

▶ Can you continue or restart terminated parts, or the entire run? How do you ensure consistency of processing? (For example, objects that have been added in the meantime should not be considered in processing if a run is continued.)

▶ Can you retrace retroactively which user started which run? When was the run started and with which parameterization? Is reporting available?

▶ What happens if an unexpected technical error occurs, for example, if the system shuts down during processing? Is it possible to restore a consistent status?

Criteria for troubleshooting

For all of these questions and options, you should keep several things in mind, as you will see in a moment. For error handling of a parallelized run you can apply the same standards as for a traditional, non-parallelized report that was scheduled and implemented as a background job:

▶ During and after processing you are shown the overall status, indicating whether the run has been terminated.

▶ After the run, you receive a list or log.

▶ When an error occurs, you can decide whether the report is started again with the same or changed selection criteria.

▶ You can retroactively retrace scheduling details and parameterizations.

In the simplest case, individual packages or a run don't have to be reusable with exactly the same object quantity.

9.2.3 Asynchronous Remote Function Call (aRFC)

Special variant for parallel processing

For the implementation of parallel processing, SAP provides a special variant of *asynchronous RFC* (aRFC). It is called *asynchronous RFC for parallel processing*, and specifies an RFC server group instead of an RFC destination as the execution destination. It was developed to ensure parallelization of processes with an optimal combination of control, security, and load distribution, at a reasonable overhead. This section describes a parallelized program flow.

Initializing Parallel Processing

Initially, you can call the optional SPBT_INITIALIZE function module to check whether a correct RFC server group was specified. This module also provides information about the number of available work processes. You can use this information to adapt the package size.

Correct RFC server group

Calling the Function Module

For parallelization using the asynchronous RFC, the activity to be executed is implemented in a remote-capable function module, which is called repeatedly by a main program, in a loop. One package corresponds to one function module call.

When calling the function module, an *RFC server group*, not the RFC destination, is specified as the destination. The system automatically assumes load distribution and selects the correct server for processing the request.

RFC Server Group

You can define *RFC server groups* in Transaction RZ12. An RFC server group is a group of instances and is used for load distribution. For each server group specific threshold values are maintained, which determine the degree to which members of the group can provide resources for asynchronous RFCs.

If a program triggers an asynchronous RFC function module call against a server group (DESTINATION IN GROUP), the system automatically checks the utilization and determines the instance for processing the request. In addition to the server groups explicitly defined in Transaction RZ12, there is also the implicitly defined DEFAULT server group, which includes all instances of the current SAP system.

When calling the function module, you transfer an alphanumeric ID with up to four digits that can be used for managing triggered calls and assigning returns. For example, you can start with task ID 0001 and continue to increment after each successful call.

ID

Because you are usually interested in the results of the asynchronous RFC call, you enter a callback routine that is executed after the call has been processed. This can be a subroutine or a method. If you select a method, just like when calling CALL METHOD, you can define as the return destination either the named method of the separate object instance implicitly, or a method of another explicitly specified object instance. Naturally, you can also call static methods.

Handling Exceptions

Evaluating the
return code

After triggering the function module call, you again assume process control. You then evaluate the return code and check whether the call was successful, based on the exceptions.

At this point, one of the following occurred:

- **The call was triggered successfully**
  If no exception occurs, the system selected a suitable server from the server group and successfully sent the request to that server. The addressed server will process the function module call and return the results by calling a callback routine or callback method. To control the triggered calls that must still be carried out, you should use counter variables for all calls that must be triggered and that have already been triggered successfully, as well as for all implemented returns. This way, you can see whether calls still need to be implemented or whether all returns have been received.

- **A communication error occurred**
  The exception COMMUNICATION_FAILURE indicates that the addressed server could not be accessed. There might be an error in the server group configuration, or the system is temporarily not available. For error handling, you must determine the called system with the SPBT_GET_PP_DESTINATION function module, and exclude it from further processing using the SPBT_DO_NOT_USE_SERVER function module.

- **A system error occurred**
  Exception SYSTEM_FAILURE indicates that an internal error or a program error occurred in the addressed system. Error handling is identical to that for communication errors.

▶ **Temporarily, no work processes are available**

Wait for a moment and try again

Exception RESOURCE_FAILURE indicates that the call was not successful because all work processes are temporarily occupied. In this case, you should wait for a moment and then carry out the call again. If you use statement, WAIT UNTIL … UP TO … SECONDS, you can wait until all successfully triggered calls have been processed, up to a specific period of time (in seconds).

Control Loop

Normally, RFC calls are carried out within a control loop that is run until all planned packages have been successfully triggered. For this purpose, you can use the counter variables for triggered calls or for calls to be triggered. If a resource bottleneck occurs, loop processing is briefly interrupted. It continues when new resources are available.

Callback Routine

A callback routine that is implemented for each successful function module call after processing the package requires a USING parameter of type CLIKE for the transfer to the task ID. Based on the ID assigned during the RFC call, you can assign returns to specific calls.

Assigning returns

Within the routine, you use the RECEIVE RESULTS FROM FUNCTION language element to receive the function module's return values. (The exceptions SYSTEM_FAILURE and COMMUNICATION_FAILURE can occur here as well.) You should also increase the counter variable within the callback routine for the implemented returns.

Runtime errors	[!]

When programming the callback routine, you must take certain limitations into consideration. List output is not possible, and the following statements result in runtime errors:

```
WAIT UNTIL, WAIT UP TO, CALL SCREEN, CALL DIALOG, CALL TRANSACTION,
SUBMIT, MESSAGE W... and MESSAGE... I..., COMMIT WORK, ROLLBACK
WORK, COMMUNICATION RECEIVE, STOP, REJECT and EXIT FROM STEP-LOOP.
```

> **Runtime errors**
>
> More precisely, these statements are prohibited in the *return thread*, rather than within the *callback routine*. Therefore, if you call additional methods, subroutines, or function modules within the callback routine, you must ensure that they don't include prohibited statements. Otherwise, a non-catchable runtime error occurs. This also applies to handlers of events triggered in a callback routine. They are executed in the same thread and terminate if one of the mentioned statements is reached.
>
> For security reasons, it is recommended to clearly separate the code that the returns of the asynchronous RFC calls can run from the rest of the code. You can swap it to a separate class, for example.

Callback Method

Methods instead of subroutines

The return method must have a parameter called P_TASK of type CLIKE to inform you about the task ID. Otherwise, the programming of the callback method is identical to the corresponding subroutine. It is recommended to use methods instead of subroutines, to benefit from the enhanced options of ABAB Objects.

Concurrent Processing and Process Communication

No concurrent actions

No concurrent actions exist within the control program. The callback method or callback routine for the return is never processed at the same time as the main control flow of the program. Instead, the returns wait until the main program has reached the WAIT statement. Then, the callback routines for all pending returns are processed, before the main program is continued.

Consequently, each return is processed in the main program separately, and global and local variables are not changed by other returns or the main control flow. After each WAIT, the main program must assume that the returns changed global variables. This way, they communicate with the main program and with each other.

Synchronization

The process will usually include a synchronization point after the loop in which all calls were implemented has been completed. This synchronization point should run when all returns have been received. The WAIT command has already been used to wait for the release of new resources while simultaneously enabling return processes to enter the process. You can also use it to wait for all returns to be received.

Therefore, the termination condition of the WAIT command is that the number of returns must be identical to the total number of jobs started. You can query the SY-SUBRC system field to obtain information about the termination condition (see Table 9.2).

Termination condition

Flow Strategies

The WAIT command is a powerful tool you can use to implement your own strategy for the flow control of your parallelized process. You can use it to determine which prerequisites must be met to start new calls, receive returns, and reach synchronization points.

WAIT command

SY-SUBRC	Explanation
0	The logical condition was met.
4	No open asynchronous function calls exist.
8	When specifying the addition UP TO, the maximum time was exceeded.

Table 9.2 SY-SUBRC After WAIT Command

Your strategy could be, for example, to send all packages individually as fast as possible, and to receive all returns as fast as possible, to release new work processes. Alternatively, you could use a block procedure in which you trigger as many packages as possible before you receive returns and trigger packages again.

The following example uses a mixed scenario. While work processes are available, as many packages as possible are triggered without receiving returns. Whenever there is a resource bottleneck, however, you receive as many returns as possible before new packages are triggered.

Mixed form

Example

The program example shown in Listing 9.11 demonstrates the use of an asynchronous RFC. You can enter a business partner number in the selection mask.

Starting with the number entered in the mask, the program increments ten business partner numbers, and for each number calls an RFC function module of the SAP standard. The SAP standard returns some data relating to this business partner, as well as a message table if there is an error.

Logging in internal table

The triggered calls are logged in an internal table. Based on this table, the returns determine the appropriate datasets and supplement the call results.

After all returns have been received, the results are provided in a list.

```
*------------------------------------------------------------*
*& Report   ZARFC
*------------------------------------------------------------*

REPORT zarfc LINE-SIZE 256.

* First business partner number
* Based on this number it is incremented
* ten times and the data relating to the person
* is read via aRFC.
PARAMETERS:
  p_partn TYPE but000-partner.

*------------------------------------------------------------*
*         CLASS lcl_parallel DEFINITION
*------------------------------------------------------------*
CLASS lcl_parallel DEFINITION.

  PUBLIC SECTION.
* Execute parallelized application
    METHODS start.
* Callback methode
    METHODS on_return
      IMPORTING value(p_task) TYPE clike.
* Event after a task has been finished
```

```
      EVENTS   finished
        EXPORTING value(taskid) TYPE clike.


  PRIVATE SECTION.
* Type: Structure for tasks
    TYPES:
      BEGIN OF m_typ_s_task,
* Header data: task ID and server
        taskid    TYPE c LENGTH 4,
        rfcdest   TYPE rfcdes-rfcdest,
* Input data of task
        BEGIN OF input,
          partner   TYPE bu_partner,
        END OF input,
* Results of calls
        BEGIN OF results,
          cd       TYPE bapibus1006_central,
          cdpers   TYPE bapibus1006_central_person,
          return   TYPE bapiret2_t,
          message TYPE c LENGTH 80,
        END OF results,
      END OF m_typ_s_task,
* Type: Table of tasks with key TASKID
      m_typ_t_task TYPE HASHED TABLE
        OF m_typ_s_task WITH UNIQUE KEY taskid.
* Number of packages
    CONSTANTS:
      mc_ttl_jobs TYPE i VALUE 10.
    DATA:
* Triggered Packages
      mv_snt_jobs TYPE i,
* Received returns
      mv_rcv_jobs TYPE i,
* Tasks
      mt_tasks    TYPE m_typ_t_task.
* Output results
    METHODS output_results.
ENDCLASS.                  "lcl_parallel DEFINITION


DATA:
* Application object
  lr_application TYPE REF TO lcl_parallel.
```

```
START-OF-SELECTION.
* Create application object
  CREATE OBJECT lr_application.
* Start application
  lr_application->start( ).


*-------------------------------------------------------*
*         CLASS lcl_parallel IMPLEMENTATION
*-------------------------------------------------------*
*         Implementation of application class
*-------------------------------------------------------*
CLASS lcl_parallel IMPLEMENTATION.



*-------------------------------------------------------*
*         Main method of parallelized application
*-------------------------------------------------------*
  METHOD start.
    DATA:
      lv_partner TYPE n LENGTH 10, " Business partner
      ls_task    TYPE m_typ_s_task," WA for Task
      lv_taskid  TYPE n LENGTH 4,  " Task ID
      lv_rfcmsg  TYPE c LENGTH 80, " Error message
      lv_rfcdest TYPE rfcdes-rfcdest. " Server

* Initializations before first package
* Accept first partner number
    lv_partner = p_partn.
* Set first task ID
    lv_taskid = '0001'.

* Loop until all packages have been triggered
    WHILE mv_snt_jobs < mc_ttl_jobs.
      CLEAR lv_rfcmsg.
* The acutal function call as aRFC
* - Task ID LV_TASKID
* - RFC server group DEFAULT
* - Callback method ON_RETURN
      CALL FUNCTION 'BAPI_BUPA_CENTRAL_GETDETAIL'
        STARTING NEW TASK lv_taskid
        DESTINATION IN GROUP DEFAULT
        CALLING me->on_return ON END OF TASK
        EXPORTING
```

```
            businesspartner        = lv_partner
        EXCEPTIONS
            communication_failure = 1  MESSAGE lv_rfcmsg
            system_failure        = 2  MESSAGE lv_rfcmsg
            resource_failure      = 3.
      CASE sy-subrc.
        WHEN 0.
* Call was successfully triggered
* Remember the server
            CALL FUNCTION 'SPBT_GET_PP_DESTINATION'
                IMPORTING
                    rfcdest = lv_rfcdest.
* Update table of triggered jobs
            CLEAR ls_task.
            ls_task-taskid        = lv_taskid.
            ls_task-rfcdest       = lv_rfcdest.
            ls_task-input-partner = lv_partner.
            INSERT ls_task INTO TABLE mt_tasks.
* Update counter: sent jobs, next task ID
            ADD 1 TO mv_snt_jobs.
            ADD 1 TO lv_taskid.
            ADD 1 TO lv_partner.

        WHEN 1 OR 2.
* 1: Destination server not reached or communication
*    terminated
* 2: Program or system error
* We determine the last server called and
* exclude it from further processing.
            CALL FUNCTION 'SPBT_GET_PP_DESTINATION'
                IMPORTING
                    rfcdest = lv_rfcdest.
            CALL FUNCTION 'SPBT_DO_NOT_USE_SERVER'
                EXPORTING
                    server_name               = lv_rfcdest
                EXCEPTIONS
                    invalid_server_name       = 1
                    no_more_resources_left    = 2
                    pbt_env_not_initialized_yet = 3
                    OTHERS                    = 4.
        WHEN 3.
* Temporarily no resources - wait for one second
* and try again
```

433

```
              WAIT UNTIL mv_rcv_jobs = mv_snt_jobs UP TO 1 SECONDS.
      ENDCASE.
    ENDWHILE.
* Wait until all returns have been received.
    WAIT UNTIL mv_rcv_jobs = mv_snt_jobs.
* Output of results
    CALL METHOD output_results( ).
  ENDMETHOD.                      "start


*-------------------------------------------------------*
*        Callback method for aRFC calls
*-------------------------------------------------------*
  METHOD on_return.
    DATA:
      ls_task    TYPE m_typ_s_task. " WA für Tasks
* Remember task ID
    ls_task-taskid = p_task.
* Increment received returns
    ADD 1 TO mv_rcv_jobs.


* Receive results of RFC call
    RECEIVE RESULTS FROM FUNCTION 'BAPI_BUPA_CENTRAL_GETDETAIL'
      IMPORTING
        centraldata          = ls_task-results-cd
        centraldataperson    = ls_task-results-cdpers
      TABLES
        return               = ls_task-results-return
      EXCEPTIONS
        system_failure       = 1 message ls_task-results-
message
        communication_failure = 2 message ls_task-results-
message.
* Update task table
    MODIFY TABLE mt_tasks FROM ls_task TRANSPORTING results.
* Trigger event
    RAISE EVENT finished EXPORTING taskid = p_task.
  ENDMETHOD.                      "on_return


*-------------------------------------------------------*
*        Output results
*-------------------------------------------------------*
  METHOD output_results.
    DATA:
```

```
        ls_task    TYPE m_typ_s_task,
        ls_bapiret TYPE bapiret2.
      FORMAT COLOR COL_NORMAL.
* Loop for packages
      LOOP AT mt_tasks INTO ls_task.
* Header data for package: ID, server, partner number
        WRITE: / ls_task-taskid,
                 ls_task-rfcdest,
                 ls_task-input-partner.
* Type-independent header data
        IF ls_task-results-cd IS INITIAL.
          FORMAT COLOR COL_NEGATIVE.
        ELSE.
          FORMAT COLOR COL_POSITIVE.
        ENDIF.
        WRITE:   ls_task-results-cd-partnertype.
* Data about person
        IF ls_task-results-cdpers IS INITIAL.
          FORMAT COLOR COL_NEGATIVE.
        ELSE.
          FORMAT COLOR COL_POSITIVE.
        ENDIF.
        WRITE:   ls_task-results-cdpers-firstname,
                 ls_task-results-cdpers-lastname,
                 ls_task-results-cdpers-birthdate.
        FORMAT COLOR COL_NORMAL.
* RFC error message, if required
        WRITE: /5 ls_task-results-message.
* Bapiret-Table
        LOOP AT ls_task-results-return INTO ls_bapiret.
          WRITE: /49 ls_bapiret-message+0(200).
        ENDLOOP.
      ENDLOOP.
    ENDMETHOD.                        "output_results
ENDCLASS.                       "lcl_parallel IMPLEMENTATION
```

Listing 9.11 Parallel Processing Using Asynchronous RFC

Security Mechanisms

The process features a high level of security, thanks to the close coupling   **High security**
of the parallelized processes and the main program. You can detect sys-

tem and resource error occurrences both when triggering the asynchronous RFC and when receiving the results of the called function module errors.

Moreover, the process is safeguarded against consumption of all resources in a system by one parallel job, which could result in system failure. This safeguard only applies for the use of asynchronous RFC via server groups, but not for direct use of RFC destinations.

Configuring the System

A background job using parallelization via asynchronous RFC occupies the *background work process* on the server on which it is started. In addition, each asynchronous RFC call occupies a dialog work process on the server on which it is executed.

Sufficient dialog processes

You should ensure that sufficient free dialog processes are available on the servers of the RFC server group that you use for parallelized applications. You can avoid having your parallelized jobs compete for dialog work processes with dialog users. To do so, in the RFC server group configuration, indicate servers that are different from those used by dialog users.

Background and Dialog Work Processes

Several different types of work processes exist in the SAP system. The configuration of each instance determines how many work processes are available for the individual types. For the various operation modes (e.g., daytime or nighttime operation) different profiles may apply, so that, for example, more background work processes than dialog work processes are run during the nighttime operation.

Dialog and background work processes differ in two respects. Dialog work processes have a runtime limitation that triggers a runtime error if more than 300 seconds pass before a database commit (you can adapt this value in the system profile parameter rdisp/max_wprun_time). This limitation doesn't exist for background work processes. The second difference is how memory is assigned to processes. For background work processes, this is adapted to work particularly well for processing large amounts of data that require large amounts of main memory.

9.2.4 Parallelization with Background Jobs

The simplest option for parallelization is to schedule multiple background jobs, each of which processes a specific portion of the data. If you fill the selection variants of the background jobs in such a way that the object quantities neither have overlappings nor gaps, you can parallelize processing with little programming effort. This procedure may be all that is necessary to ensure smooth operation (particularly, if the available time windows are too short for the background jobs to be processed).

Scheduling multiple background jobs

We will only briefly describe this procedure because it is very simple and doesn't require detailed explanation. Because of its limitations, it is also not suitable in a real mass data scenario.

Interfaces for Job Scheduling

In addition to manual scheduling, two procedures with corresponding programming interfaces exist for scheduling background jobs.

The *easy method* consists of two functions modules with lean parameterization. You use the BP_JOBVARIANT_SCHEDULE function module to schedule a job that entails only one job step and an ABAP report. Most of the options, such as printing parameters and list format, are predefined and can't be changed. A dialog is displayed in which the user selects an existing variant for the execution and enters the start time or periodicity of the execution.

Easy method

The second function module, BP_JOBVARIANT_OVERVIEW, displays a simple job overview and enables the evaluation of logs and spool lists, as well as navigation to a detail screen for changing the start time of a scheduled job.

The *full-control method* provides full job scheduling control via a broad programming interface. Jobs are defined in several steps:

Full-control method

1. The JOB_OPEN function module is used to create a new background job. The module returns an ID that is used in the function module calls that follow to uniquely identify the job.

2. The GET_PRINT_PARAMETERS function module is used to determine print parameters for steps that create list outputs. Depending on the

parameterization of the call, the function module displays a dialog for entering the print parameters or provides a consistent set of print parameters without a dialog.

3. The `JOB_SUBMIT` function module is used to add job steps to a job. These can be executable ABAP programs, but also external calls, such as operating system commands. As an alternative to the `JOB_SUBMIT` function module, you can also use the `SUBMIT` ABAP command with the `VIA JOBNAME … NUMBER …` addition. Although you can allocate selection parameters only by indicating a variant using the `JOB_SUBMIT` function module, the `SUBMIT` ABAP command enables you to directly allocate selection parameters and selection options with the `WITH` addition. If the ABAP program creates a list, you should supply the parameters for the print output to both alternatives.

4. If the user is supposed to determine the start time interactively, you can display a corresponding standard dialog using the `BP_START_DATE_EDITOR` function module.

5. The `JOB_CLOSE` function module completes the job definition. Here, you transfer the start time and periodicity of the execution.

You can use the `BP_CALCULATE_NEXT_JOB_STARTS` function module to determine the next execution times for a periodic job.

Limitations

Lack of load distribution
The weak points of this method are the lack of both load distribution and process communication. There is no load distribution by the RFC server groups. The method provides no counterpart to the sophisticated configuration of the RFC server groups in which you can set threshold values for the maximum load of individual servers. Therefore, it is the application that must determine suitable servers for scheduling background jobs.

Monitoring locally or remotely triggered background jobs is complex and tedious. To monitor the overall process, you must monitor the jobs active on the remote servers and respond appropriately if one of the servers terminates or completes successfully. Finally, you must implement the return or retrieval of processing results from the remote server using additional interfaces.

Overall, this method leaves a lot to be desired when compared to asynchronous RFC. To compensate for the shortfalls through additional programming would be much more tedious than using asynchronous RFCs with server groups, which were designed specifically for parallelization. Therefore, it is recommended to use parallelization with job scheduling and without aRFC for only the simplest of scenarios.

9.2.5 Parallelization with the Parallel Processing Tool BANK_PP_JOBCTRL

The BANK_PP_JOBCTRL package contains a standard framework for parallelizing batch processes with mass data. The framework is part of the SAP_ABA software component, and is therefore included in every AS ABAP installation.

Scope of Functions

Internally, this framework uses asynchronous RFC with server groups. However, it also provides comprehensive additional functions. It was developed specifically for use in scenarios with extremely large amounts of data, and can efficiently distribute extensive loads to numerous servers. Its particular strength lies in the packaging of large amounts of data and the support of consistently reusable processes. By defining package templates, you can reuse built packages in multiple runs.

Comprehensive additional functions

The framework comprises separate database tables and administration functions for packages, package templates, and initiated runs, as well as their history (which you can supplement via application-specific tables).

Using cockpits and API function modules, you can consistently reuse defined runs, even after errors occur. You can return objects to processing that have not been processed successfully, using the resubmission function. Here, the framework ensures that the object quantity and the technical and specialist parameters don't diverge when the run is executed again.

Implementation

Application-specific functions in the framework are implemented using multiple Customizing and generation transactions, as well as programming of generated callback function modules. Transactions BANK_CUS_PP and BANK_CUS_PPC are used to maintain the settings of the application types delivered by SAP or developed by customers. Here, you check and correct the settings of an application type, and maintain the list of methods implemented in your application.

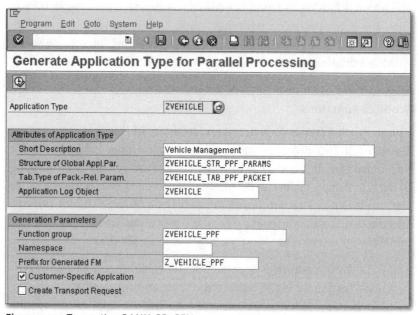

Figure 9.15 Transaction BANK_PP_GEN

To define a new application type, call Transaction BANK_PP_GEN (see Figure 9.15). Enter the key of the new application type, and the attributes of the application type and generation parameters shown in Table 9.3.

Attribute	Explanation
Short description	**Short description of the application type**
Structure of the global application parameter	These are application-specific parameters that are transferred at the start of a mass run and read at each restart of the run in the database. This parameter is considered when generating function module interfaces.
Table type of package-related parameters	Enter a table type for the application-specific data for packages. You must use a standard table type that includes the BANK_STR_PP_PACKAGEKEY structure. This parameter is considered when generating function module interfaces.
Application log object	Enter the application log object you can maintain using the transaction.
Function group	Enter an existing function group.
Namespace	If you develop a customer namespace (prefix namespace), you can enter it here to initiate the generation of objects in the namespaces by the code generator.
Prefix for generated function modules	This character string becomes the method key prefix of the generated function modules.
Customer-specific application	Controls whether the application is maintained as a standard SAP application using Transaction BANK_CUS_PP, or as a customer-specific application using Transaction BANK_CUS_PPC.
Create transport request	Controls whether a transport request is created. If you don't select this field, you must ensure that all required objects and table entries are collected in transport requests.

Table 9.3 Attributes of the Application Types

When you initiate the generation, the code generator generates several empty function modules according to your specifications. It also creates table entries that you can check and maintain in Transactions BANK_CUS_PP or BANK_CUS_PPC (see Figures 9.16 and 9.17).

Generating empty function modules

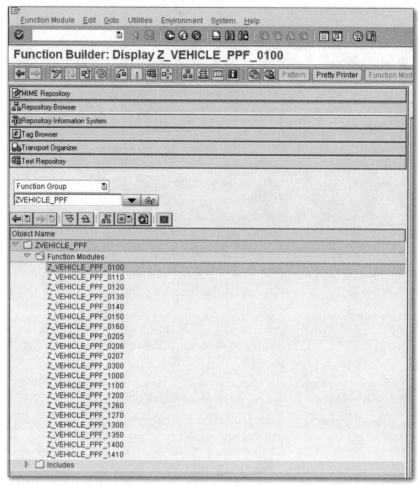

Figure 9.16 Generated Function Modules

Start Report and Report for Reuse

Copying and customizing

For an executable application, you require reports to start a new run or reuse a terminated run. For this purpose, you must copy the start reports and the reuse reports from the demo application, and customize them appropriately.

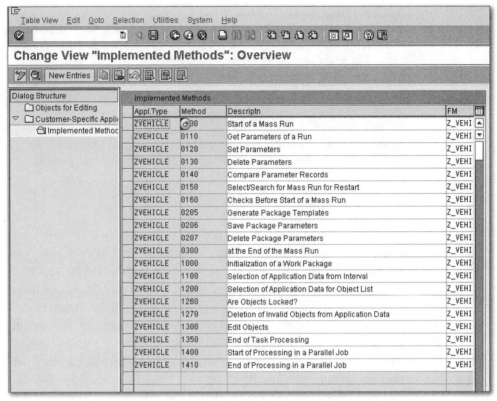

Figure 9.17 Generated Customizing

Test and Demo Application

An executable test application called PPF_TEST is available in the FS_
PPF_TEST package. It includes executable programs for generating application data, a separate data model, Customizing entries in the control
tables of the framework, callback function modules, as well as programs
for package creation and for starting the parallelized application. The
BANK_PP_JOBCTRL package also contains an executable demo application called DEMO. You can use both applications as templates for programming your own parallelized applications. In particular, you can use
the coding of the function modules as templates.

[+]

Configuration of the Mini SAP System

In some mini SAP systems, the test application is not executable because the configuration of the instances contains errors. In this case, you must call Transaction RZ04 and select the DUMMY operation mode.

Now, check whether the HOST NAME column or only the predefined WDFD00143292 entry is recorded in your local SAP installation. If you can't find an entry with your host name, you must create a new entry and replace the WDFD00143292 host name with the host name of your SAP system in the fields HOST NAME, APPLICATION SERVER, START PROFILE, and INSTANCE PROFILE.

9.2.6 Summary

This section started with the motivation and application cases for parallelization. Then, the prerequisites for the parallelization of processes were discussed. The section also described the basic strategies and solution approaches available in this context. Subsequently, you learned more about parallelization using asynchronous remote function call (aRFC), which was detailed based on a program example. The section concluded with information on the configuration of your system with regard to parallelization. You were also given explanations on the parallelization options without aRFC, only with background jobs, the programming interfaces, and the limitations of the process. Section 9.2.5, Parallelization with the Parallel Processing Tool BANK_PP_JOBCTRL, briefly described the parallel processing framework of SAP to give you an idea of the framework functions and the most critical setting and generation transactions. Moreover, you learned where to access demo and test applications to obtain more details on the implementation. You are now able to evaluate the use of parallelization techniques in your own development projects, select a suitable tool, and implement parallelization in your application.

9.2.7 Additional Information

Parallel Processing with aRFC

▶ For further information about asynchronous RFC, access the section BASIS PROGRAMMING INTERFACES (BC-DWB) • IMPLEMENTING PARALLEL PROCESSING in the SAP Library.

▸ COMPONENTS OF SAP COMMUNICATION TECHNOLOGY • CLASSICAL SAP TECHNOLOGIES (ABAP) • RFC • RFC PROGRAMMING IN ABAP • CALLING RFC FUNCTION MODULES IN ABAP • CALL FUNCTION • RFC (RFC VARIANTS) • USING ASYNCHRONOUS REMOTE FUNCTION CALLS • PARALLEL PROCESSING WITH ASYNCHRONOUS RFC can also be found in the SAP Library.

▸ You can find a detailed description, including examples, of the statement `CALL FUNCTION STARTING NEW TASK` in the ABAP documentation.

▸ You can find tips for selecting the correct RFC technique and for strategies to handle resource bottlenecks in SAP Note 597583 (Performance improvement using RFC parallel processing).

Background Jobs

▸ For further information about scheduling background jobs, access the section BASIS PROGRAMMING INTERFACES (BC-DWB) • SCHEDULING AND MANAGING JOBS: EASY METHOD or SCHEDULING AND MANAGING JOBS: FULL-CONTROL METHOD in the SAP Library.

Parallel Processing Framework

▸ For further information about the parallel processing tool, access the section PARALLEL PROCESSING OF MASS DATA (CA-GTF-TS-PPM) in the SAP Library.

▸ You can find the Customizing nodes for the parallel processing framework in the implementation guide (IMG) under CROSS-APPLICATION COMPONENTS • GENERAL APPLICATION FUNCTIONS • PARALLEL PROCESSING AND JOB CONTROL • PARALLEL PROCESSING.

9.3 Key Transactions

The transactions shown in Table 9.4 were used to create application logs.

Transaction	Description
SLG0	Application Log: Object Maintenance
SLG1	Analyse Application Log
SLG2	Delete Expired Logs
SLGN	Number range maintenance
SE61	Document maintenance

Table 9.4 Key Transaction Codes for Logging

The transactions shown in Table 9.5 were used for parallelization using jobs, asynchronous RFCs, and the parallelization framework.

Transaction Code	Description
SM37	Overview of Job Selection
RZ04	Maintain SAP Instances
RZ12	Maintain RFC Server Group Assignment
SARFC	Server Resources for Asynchr. RFC
BANK_CUS_PP	Settings for Parallel Processing
BANK_CUS_PPC	Customer-Specific Settings for Parallel Processing
BANK_PP_CHECK	Check Customizing for Parallel Processing
BANK_PP_GEN	Generate application type
BANK_PP_MONITOR	Monitor Parallel Processing Framework
BANK_PP_OVRVW	Overview of current mass runs
BANK_PP_SETTINGS	Current Parallel Processing Settings

Table 9.5 Key Transaction Codes for Parallel Processing

"We have to learn a lot to be able to ask about the things we do not know." (Jean-Jacques Rousseau)

10   Information Acquisition

Application developers who are fully qualified but have very little hands-on experience with SAP systems are confronted with the problem of how to become familiar with the SAP development environment and the standard SAP system.

Even proficient developers do not know everything there is to know about all APIs and AS ABAP technologies. Unlike beginners, however, they can identify sufficient information sources and technologies to enable them to quickly research the information they require.

This chapter introduces technologies and information sources that should be part of every developer's repertoire.

10.1   SAP Service Marketplace

The *SAP Service Marketplace* is a collection of individual SAP portals. These portals, which are briefly described in this section, contain valuable resources for developers.

Collection of individual portals

10.1.1   SAP Help Portal

The *SAP Help Portal* (*http://help.sap.com/*) contains, among other things, the *SAP Library* (see Figure 10.1). The SAP Library is the single most important source of documentation for the standard SAP system. Throughout this book, we have made numerous references to these resources because they provide detailed information about topics that we cannot discuss in detail in this book because of space limitations.

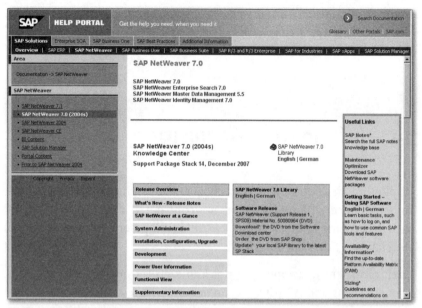

Figure 10.1 SAP Help Portal: Searching the SAP Library

10.1.2 SAP Support Portal

The *SAP Support Portal* is a central SAP service portal. It provides access to license and developer keys, as well as published SAP release notes (*http://service.sap.com/releasenotes*) that must be consulted for each release change.

SAP Notes   Here, you can also access the SAP Notes search in the Online Self Service (OSS). Furthermore, you can record problem messages for SAP and search for solution notes, as shown in Figure 10.2.

10.1.3 SAP Developer Network

The *SAP Developer Network* (*http://www.sdn.sap.com*) *(SDN)* is an online community of internal and external SAP developers. When combined with the *Business Process Expert Community* (BPX), it forms the *SAP Community Network*.

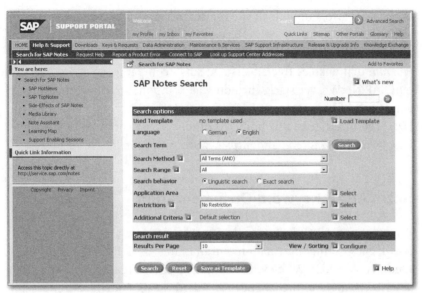

Figure 10.2 Searching for SAP Notes

Together, SDN and BPX have more than one million members, making them the largest and most important SAP communities. Here you will find, among other things, *forums* where you can ask and answer questions, as well as whitepapers and e-learning material. The range of topics is as vast as the world of SAP itself: from ABAP and Java development to integration technologies, business intelligence, or the service-oriented architecture.

Forums

The community is very creative and hands-on: *challenges* are set and good solutions rewarded. New technologies are tested immediately and *web logs* show, for example, how Internet technologies can be used to connect Google or route planners to the SAP system. The SDN also has podcasts and SDN TV. Furthermore, events are organized on a regular basis. SAP employees discuss the background of current technological developments in blogs. Such discussions provide the opportunity for constructive criticism. There are also *wikis* where SDN members can record and update their knowledge on a regular basis.

Blogs

An annual highlight is the *SAP Community Day*, where both internal and external SAP developers come together to get to know each other, participate in different expert groups, program systems together, and look for new and innovative solutions.

SAP Community Day

449

SDN Subscription
Program The SDN is also a download site for demo versions of SAP software (for example, the complete SAP NetWeaver Application Server) for training and evaluation purposes. We recently launched an *SDN Subscription Program* that enables freelancers and small companies to access the current SAP NetWeaver stack, including all components. This program also grants subscribers access to SAP Service Marketplace. In addition to the SDN, the Internet is also home to other related communities, such as *http://www.sapfans.com*, and *http://www.erpgenie.com*.

10.2   ABAP Keyword Documentation

To access the ABAP keyword documentation, press ⌷F1⌷ on your keyboard, click on the Information button in the ABAP Editor, or call Transaction ABAPHELP. We would also advise you to read the sections that describe changes to the language standard for the individual releases.

ABAP
programming
examples
ABAP programming examples are available in a) Transaction ABAPDOCU (which will be integrated into the ABAP keyword documentation as of the next release), and b) the *Reuse Library* (see Figure 10.3), which you can access by calling Transaction SE83. A detailed description is available in the SAP Library under *BC-DWB-UTL*.

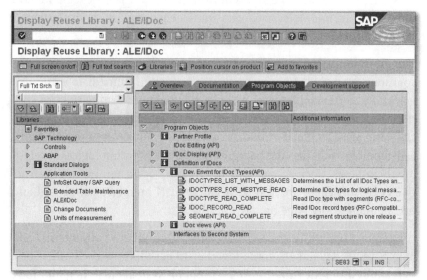

Figure 10.3   Reuse Library

10.3 SAP Design Guild

Another SAP portal, the *SAP Design Guild* (*http://www.sapdesignguild.org*), is a valuable resource for topics such as dialog design and user ergonomics. Here, you will find style guides, knowledge documents on all SAP GUI technologies, best practices, as well as discussions about poor interfaces, references to books, and information about upcoming events.

10.4 Internal Workings of AS ABAP

In ABAP development, most of the technologies available are "open source technologies", that is, using *where-used lists* and the debugger enables you to research and analyze sample applications. This helps you to precisely understand the AS ABAP software components .

Where-used list

10.4.1 Debugging

Because the entire SAP standard consists of open source code, clever debugging enables you to also quickly understand complex parts, and obtain an overview: create a breakpoint in a central location, analyze the call stack and, if necessary, choose another breakpoint.

You can debug ABAP programs by entering /h or /hs in the transaction line (for system debugging). If a dialog box does not have an input line, you can use a little trick: Click on the CUSTOMIZING OF LOCAL LAYOUT (Alt + F12) • CREATE SHORTCUT (or directly GENERATES A SHORTCUT) button to create a desktop shortcut you can use to activate the debugger. Then set the type to System command and enter the command /h as shown in Figure 10.4. If you now use drag and drop to drag the desktop shortcut to the dialog, this has the same effect as entering /h in the transaction line.

Debugging dialog boxes

Release 7.0 has a considerably improved debugger. Additional information is available in the SAP Library under ABAP – ANALYSIS TOOLS • DEBUGGER. Release 7.1 also has additional features, some of which are outlined below and can be used for program analysis:

Features in Release 7.1

▶ **Layer Debugging**
You can define selection criteria and therefore determine which modularization units (for example packages, classes, and function groups) you want to debug, and which you want to skip. In this way, you can define a software layer that you can analyze to determine which intermediate layers you want to skip.

▶ **New analysis tools**
New analysis dialogs have been created to enable you to analyze classical screens and Web Dynpro components.

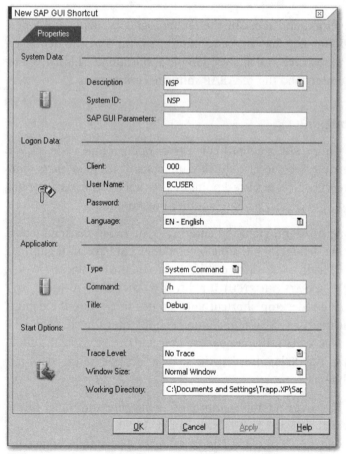

Figure 10.4 Creating a Desktop Shortcut for the Debugger

▶ **Script engine**
A script interface has been added to the ABAP Debugger that lets you automate debugger actions. This helps you, for example, to define breakpoints with complex situations, or generate automatic analyses and dumps of variable content in frameworks.

10.4.2 Information Sources in the SAP System

Even if you do not wish to explore this area in depth, you should be familiar with the following tricks that are a part of every SAP consultant's repertoire who wants to quickly become familiar with a new topic:

Tricks

▶ Use package interfaces (see Section 5.4.1, Package Interfaces and Checks) to check APIs.

▶ Use the Data Modeler (see Section 3.2.1, Structured Entity Relationship Model) to check SAP data models.

▶ Use the Easy Access Menu (Transaction S000) or table TSTCT to search for important transactions.

Easy Access Menu

▶ Use the *Implementation Guide* (IMG), which you access by calling Transaction SPRO and selecting SAP REFERENCE IMG, to gain insight into the system Customizing. Here, you will find a set of transactions that provides a point of entry to the underlying system control functions.

▶ Use the ABAP Workbench to search for programs with the name *DEMO*. This lets you find sample applications, which SAP frequently implements for the SAP standard framework.

▶ Use table DOKHL (see Figure 10.5) to search for development elements, which are all documented in the SAP system. You should search this table because you cannot search all data elements, function modules, classes, their associated methods, and so on.

▶ Use the F1 help for a data element and click on the Technical Info button to display a view that contains the current screen data (program name, screen number, field, and data element).

Screen data

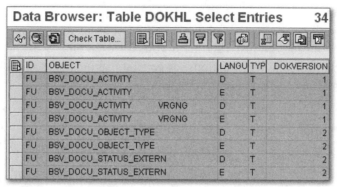

Figure 10.5 Searching for SAP Documentation

You can also use Transaction BAPI to search for BAPIs. BAPIs provide a standardized interface for the application objects in the standard SAP system. For example, in Figure 10.6 you see a function module interface for adding a business partner's address.

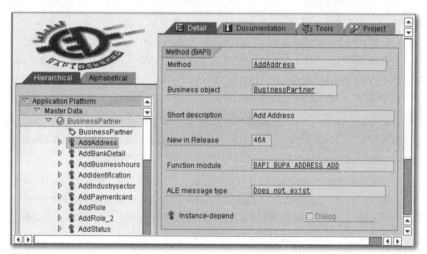

Figure 10.6 BAPI Interface for an SAP Business Partner

10.4.3 Runtime Analysis

Transaction SE30

If you wish to determine how a program, transaction, or function module works, you can use Transaction SE30 to perform a runtime analysis that includes a list of all functions called (see Figure 10.7).

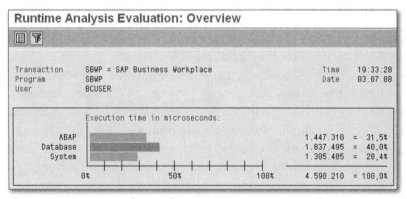

Figure 10.7 Transaction SE30

After you call Transaction SE30 (see Figure 10.7), enter the object to be tested (for example, Transaction SBWP), define a variant, and click on Execute to start the recording. If you click on Tips & Tricks, you will find sample code, including runtime analyses.

After you execute the test, you will see the program or transaction to be checked. To view the runtime analysis as shown in Figure 10.8, execute the function and click on Back ([F3]).

Runtime Analysis Evaluation: Overview

Transaction	SBWP = SAP Business Workplace	Time	19:33:28
Program	SBWP	Date	03.07.08
User	BCUSER		

Execution time in microseconds:

ABAP	1.447.310	= 31,5%
Database	1.837.495	= 40,0%
System	1.305.405	= 28,4%
	4.590.210	= 100,0%

0%   50%   100%

Figure 10.8 Runtime Analysis Evaluation

Detail view   You can then jump to the detail view, as illustrated in Figure 10.9. Here, you can see which programs, form routines, and function modules were called in Transaction SWBP.

Runtime Analysis Evaluation: Hit List

No.	Gross	=	Net	Gross (%)	Net (%)	Call
1	8.550.044		0	100,0	0,0	Runtime analysis
1	8.550.015		20.074	100,0	0,2	Call Transaction SBWP
1	8.383.241		79	98,0	0,0	Program SAPMSS00
1	8.287.191		102	96,9	0,0	Dynpro Entry
1	8.269.116		101	96,7	0,0	PBO Dynpro SAPMSS00
1	8.247.863		12.354	96,5	0,1	Module(PBO) TEST_PBO
1	5.677.879		3.753	66,4	0,0	Perform JUMP_TO_OFFICE
1	5.451.220		121.747	63,8	1,4	Call Func. SINWP_WORKPLACE_CREATE
1	4.158.779		44.073	48,6	0,5	Perform TREE_CONTROL_CREATE
1	3.537.214		28	41,4	0,0	Perform BUILT_TREE_TAB
1	3.205.273		928	37,5	0,0	Perform GET_INBOX_COUNTERS
2	3.204.031		80	37,5	0,0	Perform UPDATE_COUNTERS
1	2.930.336		226.230	34,3	2,6	Call Func. SIN_SET_COUNTER_WF
1	1.884.913		271.698	22,0	3,2	Call Func. SO_OFFICE_INIT
1	1.550.392		460	18,1	0,0	Call Func. SWL_WL_CONTEXT_GET
1	1.377.421		716	16,1	0,0	Call Func. RH_SUBSTITUTIONS_GET
2	1.305.879		222	15,3	0,0	Call Func. SET_BUILD
2	1.245.089		4.601	14,6	0,1	Perform OBJECTS_COLLECT
4	701.897		130	8,2	0,0	Perform BUILD_LEVEL
4	701.762		72.985	8,2	0,9	Perform READ_DB

Figure 10.9 Programs Called

The calls are displayed according to their call hierarchy, which is achieved by sorting the calls according to their gross runtime. However, for detailed performance analysis, it makes sense to sort the calls according to their percentage net runtime.

Best practices   Some best practices are in place for performance analyses. You should always endeavor to take the load from the database. You can evaluate the runtime analysis to see whether you have succeeded in your efforts. Experience has shown that several runtime analyses are necessary because they can vary greatly. First, optimize the sections of code that have a high net runtime. Frequently, the results are surprising because the perceived required runtime was incorrect: some accesses occur faster than expected, and sometimes a module is called more frequently than expected. Therefore, it is worth optimizing the code even further. This transaction was also revised, enhanced, and made more user-friendly in Release 7.1.

10.4.4 Database Trace

In Section 10.4.3, Runtime Analysis, we demonstrated how to check the ABAP call hierarchies. You will now learn how you can trace database accesses to locks (see Section 3.2.2, Data Modeling at ABAP Dictionary Level) and RFC calls.

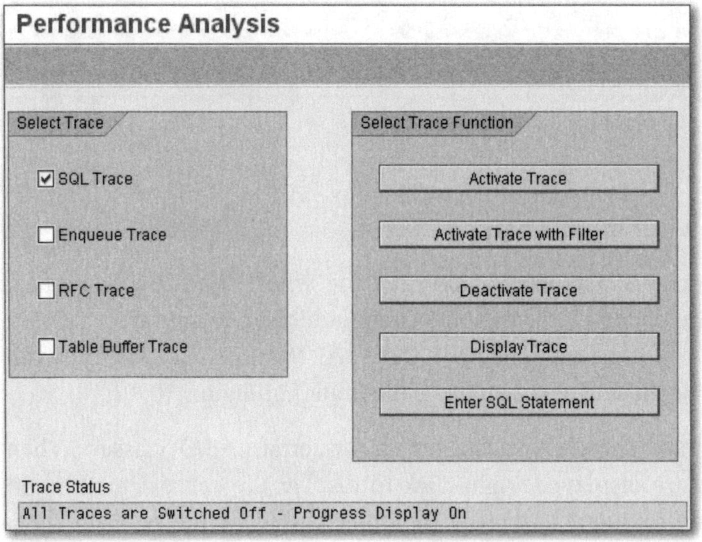

Figure 10.10 SQL Trace

In Transaction SE30 (see Figure 10.10), you click on Activate trace to activate the trace. In another session, you execute the action to be traced and, for example, call a transaction. Once the action has been traced, click on Deactivate trace and then click on Display trace. The system displays the results, as illustrated in Figure 10.11.

Process

Here, you see the native SQL implementations of the ABAP Open SQL statements and you can identify the database tables that were accessed. You can now double-click to navigate to the section of code where the corresponding ABAP SQL statement is coded. This trace function is extremely well-suited to finding and analyzing poorly performing database accesses.

Poor-performing database accesses

457

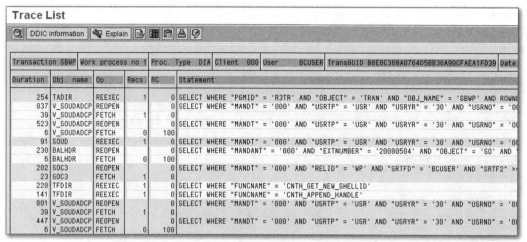

Figure 10.11 Result of the SQL Trace

10.4.5 Environment Analysis

Environment analysis exists alongside the where-used list. You call it from the Repository Information System, which you can start by clickin on the button of the same name in the ABAP Workbench. Here, you can perform a detailed object search, as illustrated in Figure 10.12.

Searching for ABAP classes
In the example shown, you can search for certain ABAP classes. When the results are displayed, right-click to display the context menu, and click on Environment to display the objects used by the relevant class. This helps you to quickly find the update modules for an application object, the connection from the business application log, as well as other objects in the standard SAP system.

Additional information about environment analysis is available in the SAP Library under the ABAP Workbench, as follows: INFORMATION ON DEVELOPMENT OBJECTS • THE REPOSITORY INFORMATION SYSTEM • ENVIRONMENT ANALYSIS.

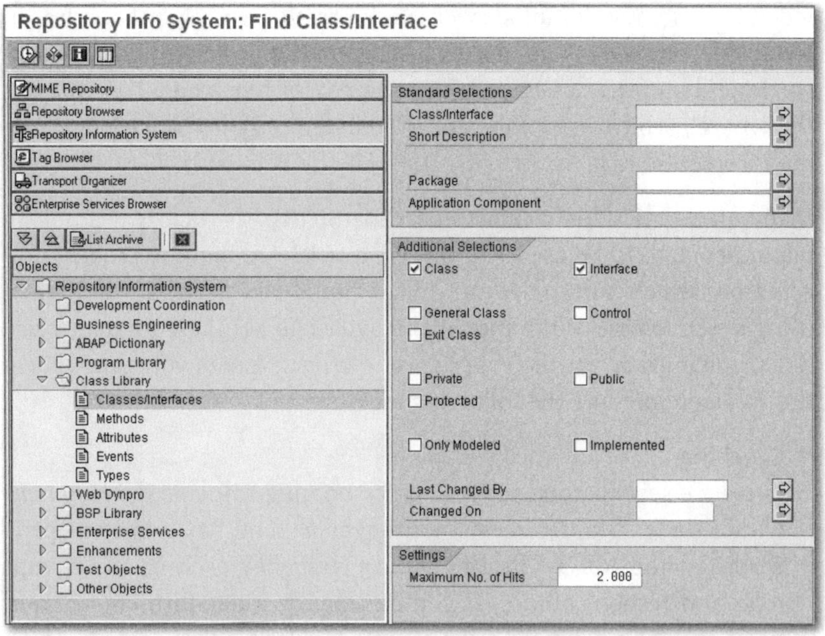

Figure 10.12 Searching the Repository Information System

10.5 Knowledge Management

This chapter has already introduced you to some key information acquisition methods. A big challenge facing any company or any software
development department is the need to produce synergy effects:

Synergy effects

▶ How can you ensure that knowledge is not only retained in the minds
of highly specialized experts (known as *knowledge monopolies*), but
also available to other employees in the company?

▶ Most employees want to further develop their skills. How can you
accommodate this need? How can you help employees identify more
with their work and, by doing so, increase job satisfaction? How can
you provide further training that challenges the experts among your
employees?

Because software development is knowledge work, knowledge is a key
requirement for successful software development projects. Nevertheless,
experience has shown that all of the technologies and resources pro-

Software
development is
knowledge work

459

vided in this book do not answer every pressing question that arises in a software project. If you always have to find a new solution for every single problem that arises, you run the risk of repeatedly "reinventing the wheel", which costs time and resources, and does not always produce a solution that works.

Many questions are of a fundamental nature: Is a particular technology mature enough to be used without great risk? Are there reference projects from which you can learn? What should you keep in mind when using a technology? What should you avoid? To ask these difficult questions, you must access the experience of others. A company can achieve this by implementing the following measures:

▶ **Coaching**
There are several good reasons for comparing software development with a trade. "Apprentices", "journeymen", and "master craftsmen" work together on a software project, but they each have different roles and responsibilities. If you develop this idea further, "apprentices" and "journeymen" must receive regular feedback from a "master craftsman", so that they can further develop their skills.

Knowledge exchange

▶ **Developer meetings**
Developer meetings provide an opportunity to exchange knowledge, get to know each other, and find the right experts to answer your questions.

▶ **Employee newsletter**
Many companies use company newsletters to keep employees informed. In special technical issues, employees can write articles about projects, products, technologies used, as well as their own experiences. Newsletters identify the areas of expertise within a company, as well as the experts themselves.

Training alternatives

In addition to fostering knowledge exchange, individual developers must be able to acquire the knowledge they require to perform their tasks, while remaining informed about any new developments. Most companies train their employees. However, there are also some training alternatives that foster individual initiatives. A company can allow its developers to devote a few days each year to their own personal programming projects. Of course, a few ground rules must be set: Is an employee allowed to use this time for a private open source project? Or must the programming project specifically refer to a company activity? If so, can a prototype for a new product or tool be used to simplify work processes? Such projects are successful because they motivate developers, give them the opportunity to determine their own further training, as well as test modern and possibly risky technologies.

Knowledge Documents	[+]
Encourage your employees to document any knowledge they acquire. For recurring workflows, they should document the process with numerous screenshots, so that colleagues can also perform these activities.	

Most of a company's knowledge is lost in a barrage of e-mails. Therefore, this medium is completely unsuitable for knowledge transfer. If the recipient group is small, the information is lost; if it is too large, departments drown in e-mails. It makes more sense to gather all relevant e-mails and place them in public folders. However, it is often difficult to search through and update these folders.

Blogs, wikis & co.

A better solution is *social software* such as blogs and wikis: employees can describe their special areas of expertise, their projects, or the technologies they deploy, and include links to the knowledge documents they have created. A wiki is a collaboration of work from many different authors and comprises easy-to-use search functions.

Take a look at the SAP Developer Network where you will be inspired by the many options you can introduce at your company. It is often good to first introduce and test the aforementioned cooperative types of knowledge transfer in an IT development department.

10.6 Key Transactions

Table 10.1 lists all of the transactions introduced in this chapter for information research and acquisition.

Transaction code	Description
ABAPDOCU	ABAP Documentation and Examples
ABAPHELP	ABAP Keyword Documentation
S000	SAP Easy Access Menu
SE30	Runtime Analysis
SE83	Reuse Library
SPRO	Implementation Guideline
ST05	Performance Analysis

Table 10.1 Key Transaction Codes

Appendices

"By ignoring the threat of negative outcomes — in the name of positive thinking or a can-do attitude — software managers drive their organizations into the ground." (From the cover of Waltzing With Bears, by Tom DeMarco)

A   Managing Development Projects

How do you successfully carry out a software development project? Unfortunately, there is no universal answer to this question, and recommendations made by those who favor agile methods — such as Scrum or Extreme Programming — will probably differ completely from recommendations made by supporters of "heavyweight" process models. However, there is agreement with regard to one aspect: Every IT project has risks. If you want to successfully complete software development projects, you must tackle these risks. This chapter primarily discusses technical risks and the strategies you can use to deal with them. The chapter also covers a number of errors that are frequently made in ABAP development projects.

Every IT project has risks

A.1   Roles in Development Projects

Is there any difference between ABAP development projects and other software development projects? How much do these differences affect the actual work in the course of ABAP development projects?

A.1.1   The Role of the Chief Software Designer

Project leads who don't want to or cannot assign the role of chief software designer to someone on their team make a big mistake as they will run the following risks:

▶ They will not have a complete overview of the application system to be developed. In addition, the risk exists that team members will not adhere consistently to basic decisions regarding the design of the system, or that a defined software structure is not implemented (see Chapter 5, Section 5.3, How To Structure a Software System).

A well-informed contact person

▶ There would not be a competent person for developers to contact to make decisions as to which of several alternative implementation options developers should use. If some of the developers on the team do not have much experience, they could make fundamental mistakes, for example, with regard to implementing the LUW concept.

What skills are necessary to design application systems? The following aspects are critical:

▶ A developer must have a vision of the final product.

▶ He needs to have detailed knowledge of the options provided by the SAP NetWeaver platform.

▶ Sound knowledge of ABAP programming is required.

The chief software designer should also be able to identify other team members' programming weaknesses and coach them accordingly.

A.1.2 Frameworks and Tools

Many projects require the creation of basic functions that must be made available as frameworks to all developers. Sometimes these basic functions can be complex frameworks; at other times they can be cross-sectional functions used to log system errors, or for tracing purposes. Creating these frameworks is the responsibility of the best developers on the team because if mistakes or poor design decisions are made at that stage, the consequences may seriously affect the entire development project. In the best case scenario, the framework's interfaces contain errors that make their usage inconvenient and result in increased development work. In the worst case scenario, a framework contains severe design errors that may affect the quality of the entire application.

Using tools

Tools that are created during the development phase also need to be taken into consideration. In this context, you should follow a simple rule of thumb: Tools should also be used by the people who develop them. This ensures that they are designed in such a way that they reduce the workload of the people who use them. If the creators of tools do not use them themselves, you should at least make sure that those who do can send their feedback to the responsible developers.

A.2 Quality Management

Quality management is one of the most difficult tasks in a software development project because using the term *software quality* only makes sense in conjunction with the term *risk*. Although quality criteria are defined by functional (technical accuracy, usability, etc.) and non-functional requirements (robustness, availability, flexibility, maintainability, performance, etc.), these requirements alone do not provide any indication as to how they should be weighed and measured.

We think that these aspects should be derived from *risk management*. There's no doubt that failing to meet functional and non-functional requirements involves risks; however, the level of severity of a risk depends on its degree of probability and the resulting damage. Let us take a look at an example: The flexibility of standard software such as SAP ERP is an absolute prerequisite for its success on a global scale. To require the same level of flexibility from a migration report that is used only once is unreasonable because the report's lack of adaptability and maintainability won't cause any damage.

A.2.1 Risk Management

Experience has shown that in many development projects, a high degree of uncertainty exists with regard to risk management. Sometimes this even results in the misunderstanding that conservative strategies are a useful means to avoid risks. Consequently, the risk management activities in many companies consist of using only "proven" technologies. However, this approach is all too often a one-sided method, as is made clear by the following questions:

Great uncertainty

▶ Why should serious risks be only of a technical nature? Don't unclear and changing content requirements, scheduling, or staff turnover represent a much greater risk?

▶ Can you be sure that a "proven" technology has not become obsolete, and that SAP hasn't discontinued its development in the meantime? Isn't it possible that some of these methods are outdated in a more contemporary environment, such as service-oriented applications?

Risks of ABAP programming

In our opinion, each software project requires risk management that enables you to identify risks, determine their probability indicators, and devise counter strategies. Everyone who wants to seriously look into this subject should read the book *Waltzing with Bears* by Tom de Marco. In the following sections, we'll move away from the general description of risk and focus on the specific risks involved in ABAP development.

The connection between bug fixing and continued development represents a major risk in project phases that follow the going live of an application or parts of an application. How can both aspects be ensured in a highly integrated SAP system?

Release changes

Release changes of SAP Basis components always involve risks. APIs can change: Some functions can become obsolete and can be replaced by new ones. If the development work was done too "close" to the standard, or if non-released APIs were used, severe errors may occur (which should be eliminated by running tests).

Risks of using new technologies

New technologies provide not only new opportunities; they also involve a lot of risks. Did SAP really implement the functionality to the extent they promised? How stable is the technology? Is a sufficient amount of documentation available? You should use a direct, no-nonsense approach to tackling these risks:

▶ **Prototyping**
The best way to evaluate new technologies is to employ an experimental prototype that allows you to test technical properties—such as robustness and performance—and store the results. Technical spike solutions enable you to evaluate the overall solution by implementing complete sub-processes. Sandbox systems often represent an appropriate development environment in these cases. Documenting your results is the basis of your know-how documents, and it enables you to repeat the tests and update the results when a new release is introduced.

▶ **Robustness**

Search the SAP Notes for information on the corresponding software component. How many current error messages are there? A decreasing number indicates the stabilization of the technology.

▶ **Community feedback**

How is a technology discussed in public forums, such as the SAP Developer Network (*http://www.sdn.sap.com*)?

A.2.2 Development Guidelines

You cannot achieve software quality by simply complying with regulations or mechanically processing checklists. It is therefore completely wrong to assume that development guidelines alone can be helpful. Nevertheless, they are necessary:

▶ Development guidelines can help prohibit dangerous statements. For example, if you are still using internal tables with headers because it was common to do so years ago, not only do you generate slow and complex code with many side-effects, you also cannot transfer the code into modern modularization units.

Prohibiting dangerous statements

▶ Guidelines may contain recommendations for proven programming methods. In this way, the knowledge of experienced developers is passed on to others.

▶ You can use consistent naming conventions for development objects, which will simplify applications. This is because you can easily tell at a glance which topical context a development object has, or if a transparent table contains application data or Customizing.

Consistent naming convention

Development guidelines may fail to have the desired effect. In this case, they can decelerate the development progress and turn into a significant cost factor. Meaningless guidelines may also lead to unnecessary conflicts between developers and the guideline creators.

Development guidelines may fail for various reasons:

Why guidelines fail

▶ **Development guidelines become obsolete**

For example, proven recommendations from the era of release 4.6C development, may be completely obsolete because ABAP has been optimized by further developing the kernel and language.

▶ **Overregulation**
Performance optimizations are a good example of the risks of over-regulation. For example, development guidelines exist that recommend to use field symbols as work areas in LOOP statements because this saves you a few milliseconds. Other guidelines require that data is transferred only as reference. If this becomes a guideline, you run the substantial risk of unintentionally changing the data.

▶ **Inflexible naming conventions**
Guidelines fail most frequently because of naming conventions for development objects are too detailed. If developers have to already follow specific rules that require strict compliance when naming local variables, then code wizards, persistent classes, generated table maintenance dialogs, or Enterprise Services programming cannot be used, for example, for Web Dynpro development.

[!] | **Guidelines have to be recommendations**

Establishing development guidelines for ABAP programming processes is quite difficult because developers sometimes have to use obsolete technologies. However, experience has shown that, in any programming language, there will always be situations where exceptions to the rules are required, even if sophisticated guidelines exist. It is therefore a quality characteristic of guidelines that specific statements are not prohibited but explanations are given or referenced why a statement has risks and how developers can find a better way to program a function. Consequently, development guidelines should be written by experts that are continuously informed of further ABAP developments and new APIs.

A.2.3 Code Inspections and Enhancement of the Code Inspector

Reviews and audits

Reviews and audits are analytical quality assurance measures. You can use them to ensure the code quality in an ABAP development project. The Code Inspector (Transaction SCI) is a tool to perform various checks for the source code of repository objects. This includes, for example, performance checks, syntax checks, or checks for compliance with naming conventions.

It is advisable to perform some of these checks during the development process already, to achieve consistent code quality and detect errors as early as possible. SAP offers a wide range of predefined checks.

Automatic Code Inspections   **[+]**

Code inspections are an indispensable means to achieve high software quality. However, their use often leads to interpersonal problems: Is the criticism constructive? Is it understood as constructive criticism by the person who is being criticized? Does he take it as a chance to learn from an experienced developer? Or is an inspection only the mechanical processing of a checklist? In the last case, automatic checks may make sense: If you detect that developers always make the same mistakes, you can have programs search for these errors automatically, which simplifies and rationalizes discussions about errors.

This section describes how you can write your own checks for the Code Inspector. For detailed information, refer to ABAP - ANALYSIS TOOLS • CODE INSPECTOR in the SAP Library.

Figure A.1 shows the initial screen of the Code Inspector. When you create a check, you must select a check variant, that is, you have to create the check variant first. This also applies to the quantity of the objects that are supposed to be tested. When you perform a code inspection, use a check variant for an object quantity, and test the result afterwards. It makes sense to run the checks in parallel, which is supported by the tool in a convenient way.

Check variant

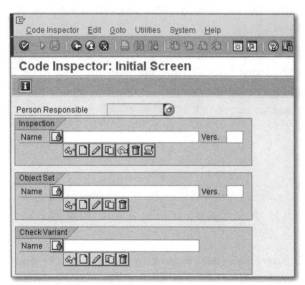

Figure A.1 Code Inspector

Separate checks During your ABAP development project, you may decide to add customized checks to the Code Inspector's default checks.[1] Such a situation may occur in the later phases of a development project as a result of the following:

- Developers forgot to run an exception handling correctly, which is indicated by empty TRY CATCH blocks.

- For various code positions, developers entered a "TODO" or "TO DO" comment but forgot to actually run these activities.

- If exceptions are caught by CATCH … INTO and new exceptions are created in this block, are those linked by using the PREVIOUS parameter? If this is not the case, the information on the original errors as well as on the original error source is lost, which makes troubleshooting more difficult.

"TODO" comments The second example in this list is described in more detail here. The "TODO" comments mentioned should be handled in a proactive way; even if forgotten "TODO" comments are a significant source of errors, there is no reason why you shouldn't use this procedure. Developers are often interrupted by calls, meetings, colleagues, and so on. Sometimes, they cannot use development objects that are provided by another team because the necessary robustness is missing. In this case, a "TODO" comment in the source code is quite useful. However, you then have to find the respective source code lines.

The goal of this section is to write a customized test for the Code Inspector that searches for the word "TODO" in comments and generates a warning for each found location. Moreover, it should be possible to add further variants of the search term (such as "TO DO") when the test runs, as shown in Figure A.2.

Separate Category

Defining the category Each check is assigned to a category, with which it is displayed in the Code Inspector. Therefore, the category has to be defined first. To do so,

---

1 In this context, it is strongly recommended not to create your own tools because the quantity of the objects that need to be tested increases from release to release and you have to maintain the tools on a regular basis.

copy the CL_CI_CATEGORY_TEMPLATE class from the S_CODE_INSPECTOR package to ZCL_CI_CATEGORY_MYTESTS.

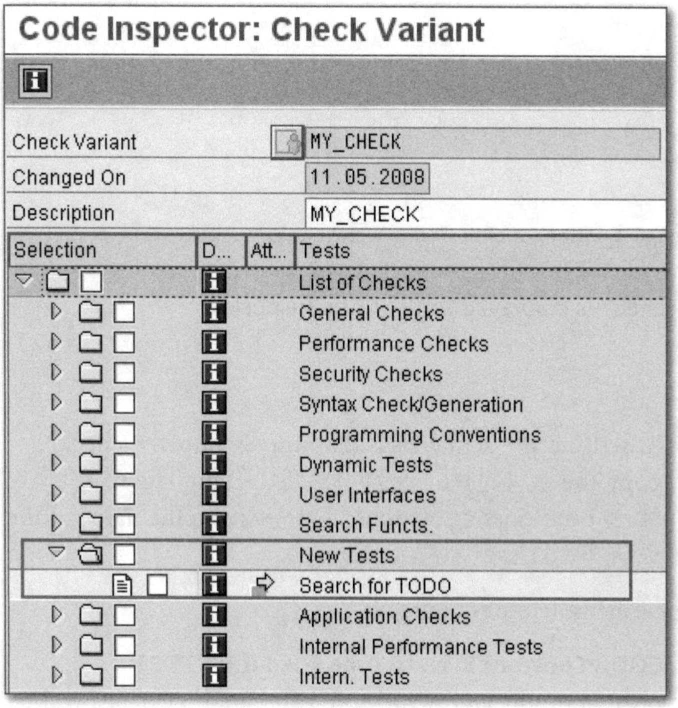

Figure A.2 Extending the Check Variant

In the constructor of the class (see Listing A.1), you now have to modify three attributes:

- **Description**
  A short description of the category, displayed in the Code Inspector.

- **Category**
  The name of the top-level category, in most cases: CL_CI_CATEGORY_TOP (highest category to which all checks are added). Of course, you can also add a new category under the existing one, for example CL_CI_CATEGORY_SECURITY, to extend the list of the security checks by your new check. In most cases, for the sake of clarity, you should add your new category under the top-level category and extend it, if required, by subcategories.

▶ **Position**

The position where the category appears in the list (when selected in the check variant).

```
METHOD CONSTRUCTOR .
  super->constructor( ).
  Description = 'New Tests'(000).
  Category    = 'CL_CI_CATEGORY_TOP'(001).
  Position    = '099'.
ENDMETHOD.
```

Listing A.1 Sample Constructor of the "New Tests" Category

This way the check is displayed in the Code Inspector.

Check Class

The next task is writing the actual class that implements the check. For this purpose, copy the CL_CI_TEST_SCAN_TEMPLATE template to ZCL_CI_ TEST_SCAN_TODO. Set the existing attribute C_MY_NAME to the name of the ZCL_CI_TEST_SCAN_TODO class.

Defining attributes You define the other attributes yourself:

▶ **C_ERROR_CODE Constant Private Type SCI_ERRC 'TD01'**
This is the error code through which the generated messages will be output.

▶ **SEARCH_STRINGS Instance Attribute Protected Type SCI_SRCHSTR**
In this attribute, you store the "TODO" search variants. This includes those defined by you and those users can add during the test. This enables you to have the system search for "TO DO" or other variants as well. The following text discusses this method in detail. The Code Inspector also lets you define various search parameters for a check. Figure A.3 illustrates how you can parameterize the Search Functions default check by clicking on the selected arrow to, for example, search the ABAP code for user-defined criteria.

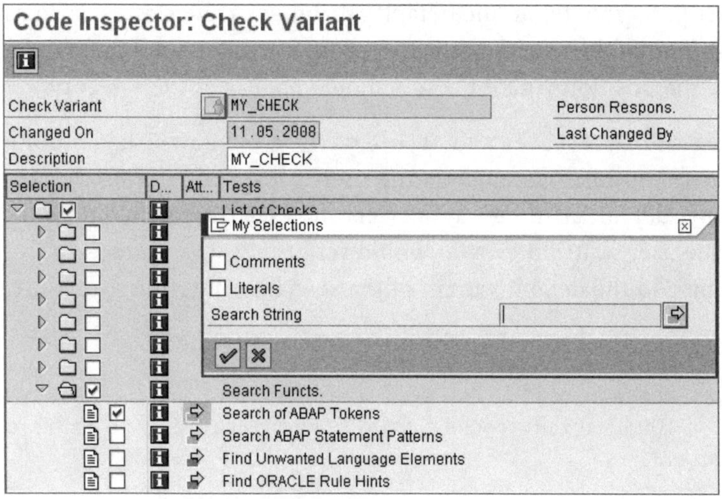

Figure A.3 Entering Search Criteria

In this example, you should be able to define variants with your own search strings for which the system should search in addition to "TODO." The handling of these search strings is critical for almost all methods that are redefined as follows.

First, adapt the constructor (see Listing A.2):

```
METHOD constructor.
  DATA:
    l_var_sstring TYPE LINE OF sci_srchstr.

  super->constructor( ).

  Description      = 'Search for TODO '(001).
  Category         = 'ZCL_CI_CATEGORY_MYTESTS'.
  version          = '000'.
  position         = '001'.               "optional
  has_attributes = c_true.                "optional
  attributes_ok  = c_true.                "optional

  "Add default variants
  l_var_sstring = 'TODO'.
  APPEND l_var_sstring TO search_strings.
ENDMETHOD.
```

Listing A.2 Constructor of the Check Class

In the first part, you define the default attributes of the classes, such as the description of the test, the categorization, a version number (mandatory), and the position where the test should appear in the category.

The values, has_attributes and attributes_ok, are new. They indicate that there are optional parameters the user can specify during the test and that the default attributes are correct. In a test that wouldn't work without the user's attributes, you would set attributes_ok to c_false. Finally, you add the default variant of the search term to the search list.

Method for the output of the check

Next, you generate the method for the output of the check:

```
METHOD get_message_text .
 p_text = 'TODO variant found in following location: &1'(101).
ENDMETHOD.
```

To enable the transfer of additional search parameters, you must redefine several methods as follows:

```
METHOD get_attributes.
  "Exporting optional search strings
  EXPORT search_strings = search_strings
        TO DATA BUFFER p_attributes.
ENDMETHOD.
```

In this way, you export parameters (only the table of the TODO variants) so that they can be changed in a search mask:

```
METHOD put_attributes.
  IMPORT
        search_strings = search_strings
        FROM DATA BUFFER p_attributes.
ENDMETHOD.
```

As a result, you import the parameters that have been modified by the users, as well as the method that enables the users to enter the parameters (see Listing A.3).

```
METHOD if_ci_test~query_attributes.
CLASS:
      cl_ci_query_attributes DEFINITION LOAD.
```

```
DATA:
  l_attributes     TYPE sci_atttab,
  l_attribute      LIKE LINE OF l_attributes,
  l_search_strings LIKE search_strings,
  l_search_string  LIKE LINE OF search_strings,
  l_strlen         TYPE i,
  l_message(72)    TYPE c.

DEFINE fill_att.
  get reference of &1 into l_attribute-ref.
  l_attribute-text = &2.
  l_attribute-kind = &3.
  append l_attribute to l_attributes.
END-OF-DEFINITION.

  l_search_strings = search_strings.
  l_strlen = 0.
  fill_att l_search_strings 'search string(s)'(204) ' '.

*-- At least 3 characters
  WHILE l_strlen < 3.
    l_strlen = 999999.
    IF cl_ci_query_attributes=>generic(
            p_name       = c_my_name
            p_title      = 'Additional TODO variants'(005)
            p_attributes = l_attributes
            p_message    = l_message
            p_display    = p_display ) = 'X'.
*-- = 'X' --> 'Exit' Button pressed on PopUp
      RETURN.
    ENDIF.
    IF l_search_strings IS INITIAL.
      l_message = 'Specify at least 1 variant'(902).
      l_strlen = 0.
    ELSE.
      LOOP AT l_search_strings INTO l_search_string.
        TRANSLATE l_search_string USING '* + '.
        CONDENSE l_search_string.
        IF STRLEN( l_search_string ) < l_strlen.
          l_strlen = STRLEN( l_search_string ).
        ENDIF.
      ENDLOOP.
```

```
        IF l_strlen < 3.
          l_message = 'Enter at least 3 letters'(901).
        ELSE.
          CLEAR l_message.
        ENDIF.
      ENDIF.
    ENDWHILE.

    search_strings = l_search_strings.
    attributes_ok  = c_true.
ENDMETHOD.
```

Listing A.3 Method for the Generation of a Selection Popup for Search Variants

The code is based on the SAP template of the `CL_CI_TEST_ROOT` class and has been adapted only slightly.

run( ) method

Now, you only have to write the method that executes the actual check, the run( ) method (*see Listing A.4*).

```
METHOD run .
  DATA:
    l_var_include        TYPE sobj_name,
    l_var_line           TYPE token_row,
    l_var_column         TYPE token_col,
    l_var_tokennr        LIKE statement_wa-from,
    l_var_errcnt         TYPE sci_errcnt,
    l_var_position       TYPE i,
    l_var_param_1        TYPE string,
    l_var_searchstring   TYPE string.

* Generate ScanObject
  IF ref_scan IS INITIAL.
    CHECK get( ) = 'X'.
  ENDIF.

  CHECK ref_scan->subrc = 0.

  l_var_errcnt = 0.
  " Loop at the statements
  LOOP AT ref_scan->statements INTO statement_wa
    where type = 'P'.
```

```
        CHECK statement_wa-from <= statement_wa-to.

        l_var_position = sy-tabix.
        "Loop at the individual commands of statement
        LOOP AT ref_scan->tokens INTO token_wa
              FROM statement_wa-from TO statement_wa-to.

          l_var_tokennr = sy-tabix.
          IF token_wa-str CS c_my_name.
            RETURN. "Don't check SCI check class
          ENDIF.
*         Search for search string variants
          LOOP AT search_strings INTO l_var_searchstring.
            IF ( token_wa-str CS l_var_searchstring ).

              l_var_include = get_include( ).
              l_var_line    = get_line_abs( l_var_tokennr ).
              l_var_column  = get_column_abs( l_var_tokennr ).
              l_var_errcnt  = l_var_errcnt + 1.
              l_var_param_1 = l_var_line.

*             Generate message as warning
              inform( p_sub_obj_type = c_type_include
                      p_sub_obj_name = l_var_include
                      p_position     = l_var_position
                      p_line         = l_var_line
                      p_column       = l_var_column
                      p_errcnt       = l_var_errcnt
                      p_kind         = c_warning
                      p_test         = c_my_name
                      p_code         = c_error_code
                      p_param_1      = l_var_param_1 ).
            EXIT.
          ENDIF.
        ENDLOOP."search_strings
      ENDLOOP."tokens
    ENDLOOP."statements
ENDMETHOD.
```

Listing A.4 Check Routine

Here are some explanations of the check routine's functionality: **Explanations**

▶ By means of `get()`, an object of the `CL_CI_TEST_SCAN` class is created that provides output similar to that of a parser. This output can then be searched easily.

▶ The `statements` table contains all statements of an include. Statement chains and macros are broken down into individual complete statements. Additional information include: the tokens contained, the statement type, and so on. (Here, a `LOOP` loop contains only statements of the type "P" because these statements include all comments as tokens of the type "C" and the search strings should only be found in comments.)

Tokens ▶ The `tokens` table contains all tokens of the current include. Tokens are the individual "words" of statements. Moreover, the type provides additional information on the word type (comment = "C", etc.), and the `str` attribute contains the word itself.

▶ `inform( )` is used to create the message that will be displayed in the Code Inspector. Among other things, the position of the found location and the message type (warning, error, information) is transferred. Here, it would also be possible to transfer a pseudo comment via the optional `p_suppress` parameter. This comment could be used to mask the found location (similar to "`#EC NOTEXT`).

▶ We only used the `CHECK` statement because we wanted to shorten the listing. In general, this statement is problematic for a variety of reasons, for example, because it can easily lead to errors.

[+]   **Pseudo Comments to Suppress SCI Messages**

The Code Inspector sometimes gives redundant warnings and error messages. The ABAP commands, `TOLOWER` or `TOUPPER`, do not necessarily lead to errors in a multilingual system. In this case, you can suppress an error message by using the "`#EC CALLED` pseudo comment. Such a comment also indicates at a code position that no error occurred and that the developer has checked the situation.

A.2.4   Creating a Documentation

You still have to create documentation for the category and check class that can be called in the Code Inspector. For this purpose, use Transaction SE61, as shown in Figure A.4.

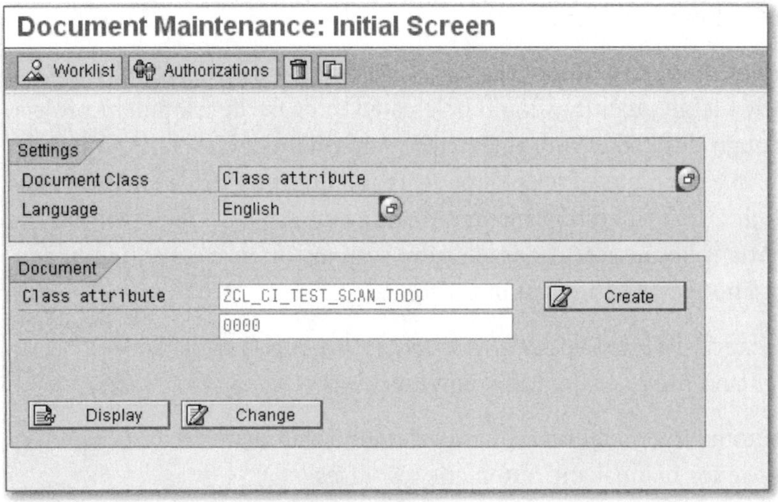

Figure A.4 Maintenance of the Documentation

A.2.5 Enabling a Check

To be able to use a check, you must activate it in the Code Inspector:
GOTO • MANAGEMENT OF TESTS (see Figure A.5).

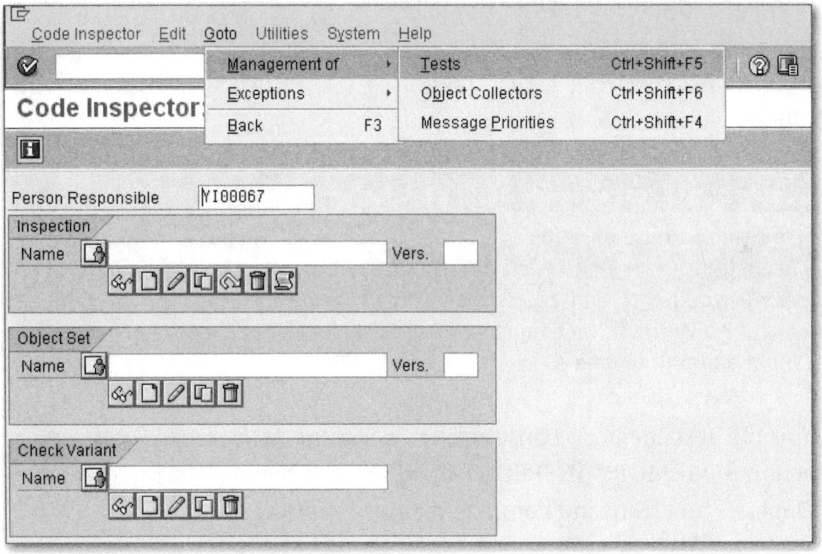

Figure A.5 Enabling the Check

A.2.6 Software Test

Chapter 4, Classes, Interfaces, and Exceptions, mentioned unit tests of which a large quantity should be created in every development project. Although this can ensure the accuracy of individual modules, it doesn't solve the problem of automatic tests for the interaction of individual modules, that is, testing integration-relevant aspects. These aspects are important because ABAP application systems often have a high parameterization level as a result of Customizing.

eCATT

The *extended Computer Aided Test Tool* (eCATT) is part of the test workbench and provides the following functions:

- Automatic generation of master data and transaction data as a prerequisite for manual and automatic test cases.

- Performing system tests: You record test case data and have the system compare screen mask data with stored values.

- Performing integration tests: In some cases, you only want to ensure that a specific process runs, certain objects are created, or subsequent processes have been started, without having to check the technical accuracy of changes made to data. You can also use eCATT to call ABAP methods, which run these checks.

For more information, refer to the section TEST WORKBENCH OR ECATT: EXTENDED COMPUTER AIDED TEST TOOL (BC-TWB-TST-ECA) in the SAP Library.

Using eCATT test data for ABAP Unit tests

You can also use an eCATT test data container to keep information that is needed in ABAP Unit tests. You can create test data containers within the ABAP workbench and access their content using the class CL_APL_ECATT_ TDC_API. With this technique you can easily handle test cases with complex input and output data

---

Memory Inspector

You can test memory consumption using the *Memory Inspector* (Transaction S_MEMORY_INSPECTOR), which is integrated in the debugger. Deploy it to create and compare memory extracts.

For programs that are mass data capable and scalable, you absolutely have to check memory consumption. If it increases more than in a linear fashion, the processing of mass data may cause problems. These problems are not easy to detect: A termination due to lack of memory can occur not only when incorrect large data objects are accessed, but also when small, but frequently used data objects are accessed. Such difficulties have always existed, particularly with regard to internal tables, but have been reduced by using objects and data references. The Memory Inspector makes memory consumption more transparent. When analyzing memory extracts, you must differentiate between bound and referenced memory. Bound memory is the memory consumption of the object itself; this is the minimum amount of memory that becomes free when an object is released. *Referenced memory* is the consumption of the object itself, and all referenced objects.

Tackle Memory Waste as Early as Possible!   **[+]**

You can tackle memory waste as early as during the development phase:

► Using CLEAR, release data and object references that are no longer needed. This prevents too many references to an object from existing, and simplifies memory management. It also helps to make programs easier to understand, because the life cycle of an object is also simplified.

► If large internal tables are no longer used, you should release the memory using FREE instead of only deleting the content with CLEAR.

► Schedule mass tests. Even though a program with small data volumes provides high performance doesn't mean that it can also process large data volumes.

For more information, refer to ABAP - ANALYSIS TOOLS • MEMORY INSPECTOR in the SAP Library.

A.2.7 Documentation

There is no question that to be maintained and further developed, software has to be documented. However, many questions arise how this can be done. The main problem with documentation is that it can be maintained in two locations: in the SAP system and in external documents. You must decide which object is documented in which location:

What is documented where?

► In the SAP system, you can provide short and long descriptions for all modularization units (reports, function modules, classes, methods, etc.) and also for the entire Data Dictionary. This information can be read together with metainformation, and you can generate parts of DP concepts. If all texts are available in a word processing system, you can easily perform spell checks, and the corrected texts can be transferred (manually, if required) to the SAP system.

Data Modeler
▸ You can use the Data Modeler to describe data models in the SAP system and connect them with the ABAP Dictionary.

▸ Information on software structuring, basic design decisions, dynamic program behavior, and knowledge that has been acquired during development cannot easily be stored in the SAP system — it belongs to external concepts instead.

[!] **Duplicate Documentation as a Quality Risk**

Documentation redundancy involves a great deal of effort creating and maintaining the documentation. Experience has shown that it cannot be guaranteed that information is globally updated in all locations. This questions the quality of the entire documentation.

Mandatory documentation components
A pragmatic strategy is recommended for the documentation. A DP concept or documentation must contain certain mandatory components. These include:

▸ **Supported business processes**
A few sentences should describe which business transactions and business application cases are supported by this application.

▸ **Embedding in the enterprise architecture**
This provides information about descriptions on the integration with other applications. This applies not only to external applications but also to SAP system components.

▸ **Technologies used**
You should list the technologies used: Do you use only the ABAP stack or also the Java stack? Which dialog technology (Web Dynpro, BSP, Business Data Toolset, etc.) do you use? If output is generated, is this done by spools of reports, SAP Smartforms, or Adobe Interactive Forms?

Implementation view
The implementation view is another mandatory component. It describes the structures of the application system, such as packages or classes, but also external components. For application systems that consist of more

than one package, an overview should provide information on the packages and background of the package concept. Chapter 5, Section 5.3, How To Structure a Software System, describes possible concepts for the structure of packages. You should also define the relationship between the described objects and thus, specify their interfaces. You can map classes in a UML class diagram.

The data model is the backbone of any business application. In most cases, it is sufficient to refer to a data model the Data Modeler uses. In some cases it may be necessary to refer to a data model in a technical concept and provide the connection between the two.

Data view

The runtime view contains dynamic aspects of a software system, which can be best described using UML activities or collaboration diagrams. In systems with many batches, these views describe the order, prerequisites, and post-conditions of reports, as well as concepts you use so that dynamic scheduling scales optimally. In other applications, they provide details of the interaction of classes.

Runtime view

At the latest, you will define general rules during development. This is true for naming conventions for development projects, and also for regulations for the LUW concept, for example. Is the traditional or the object-oriented transaction concept being used? Where does a transaction start and where does it end? The error concept is another critical aspect: How do you manage system errors? Where are they neutralized? Where and how are they logged? How is the authorization concept used? You can include this information in the document, or refer to external documents.

Development guidelines

An SAP system contains many development objects, and you can never document all objects or request that all are described in a DP concept. It also would make absolutely no sense to create a shared document template for DP concepts that includes all possible development objects. For this reason, you should use a "modular design principle:" Standardized and proven patterns are provided for central development elements, such as Web Dynpro components, BSP applications, or workflow patterns. These patterns are transferred to the DP concept that should be created and populated there.

Modular design principle

A.2.8 Key Transactions

The transactions shown in Table A.1 are helpful for software tests.

Transaction Code	Description
SCI	Code Inspector
SE61	Document maintenance
SLIN	Extended syntax check
S_MEMORY_INSPECTOR	Memory Inspector
SCOV	Coverage Analyzer

Table A.1 Key Transaction Codes

B Bibliography

ABAP

Keller, Horst; Krüger, Sascha: *ABAP Objects*. 2nd updated and extended edition. SAP PRESS 2007.

The updated and extended edition provides a complete description of the ABAP Objects language and the most important tools. It also discusses external interfaces, such as the Internet Connection Framework or Web Services. Because this book explains concepts up to Release 7.0, such as shared objects or common expressions, it is a must-have for every ABAP developer.

Rickayzen, Alan; Dart, Jocelyn, Brennecke, Carsten; Schneider, Markus: *Practical Workflow for SAP*. SAP PRESS 2002.

This definitive book on workflow programming provides all of the information needed for workflow projects. In addition to programming, it discusses the administration of the Webflow Engine, troubleshooting, agent determination, non-technical challenges of a workflow project, and e-process interfaces. It also describes the different system types (SAP CRM and EBP). Tips, tricks, and checklists round off the book.

Jung, Thomas; Heilman, Rich: *Next Generation ABAP Development*. SAP PRESS 2007.

This book contains what its title promises: It introduces APIs to Master Data Management, describes the use of Adobe Forms, and explains the development of BSP and Web Dynpro applications. Furthermore, it discusses web services provided via ABAP server proxies and ABAP Unit, and much more. If you want to develop innovative ABAP applications, you need to use this book.

Agile Methods

Agile methods have had considerable influence on software development. Hardly any projects still use the common "cascade model" because the rigid order of technical concept, DP concept, implementation, and test has proven to be inflexible and costly. For projects with dynamically changing requirements in particular (or those that use completely new technologies), agile methods are very useful. Agile methods focus on short development cycles. This way, parts of the system can be shown to future users quickly, and those users can provide feedback at an early stage. Automatic tests are often part of the development process and enable you to manage changes proactively. No matter which procedure you decide is best suited for your specific development project, you should always be aware of the pragmatic view of agile methods. This is because they focus on the software products that should be developed, their quality, as well as efficient and effective development methods.

Schwaber, Ken; Beedle, Mike: *Agile Software Development with Scrum.* Prentice Hall 2001.

Scrum provides a wide range of methods for agile project management. Sprints are characteristic for Scrum; this includes development cycles of 30 days, with defined goals the product owner specifies in collaboration with the development team. At the end of the sprint, the functions should be developed and tested by developers; the status is then presented to the product owner as a review. Because, during the sprint phases, the team should focus only on these goals, and the decisions how the goals should be achieved are made only within the team, this method concentrates on the team's internal organization, but also on the identification with the project. The development cycles should provide an early presentation of defined parts to the product owner, which makes the development progress more transparent, and also makes it possible to refine, change, or reprioritize requirements. The development team can learn from mistakes and successes, and the internal processes and technical procedures are optimized on an ongoing basis. As a project management method, Scrum is not bound to a specific software development procedure, and traditional controlling mechanisms are not overridden. However, Scrum shifts the responsibilities in such a way that both the product owner and the product developer can focus on their core competencies, while planning the product progress together and communicating with each other in defined cycles of the product to be developed.

Jeffries, Ronald E.; Anderson, Ann; Hendrickson, Chet: *Extreme Programming Installed*. Addison-Wesley 2000.

Many Extreme Programming technologies have changed the programming style; thus, ABAP Unit and Refactoring, for example, have become part of the ABAP Objects language. For this reason alone, you should take a closer look at this software development method to understand its background. This book is currently available on the Internet under *http://www.XProgramming.com/xp_installed.htm*.

SAP NetWeaver Application Server

Schneider, Thomas: SAP Performance Optimization Guide. SAP PRESS, 5th updated and revised edition 2008.

This definitive book is a must-have if you want to develop performance-intensive applications. It describes methods of analyis for hardware and databases, performance analyses, load distribution, table buffering, locks, and much more.

Risk Management

DeMarco, Tom; Lister, Timothy: Waltzing with Bears. Dorset House Publishing Company, Incorporated, 2003.

IT projects involve high risks. The authors of Waltzing with Bears are of the opinion that this needs to be this way because otherwise competitors will provide more innovative and optimized products. This definitive book about risk management describes how you can tackle these risks. Not only is Tom DeMarco a software pioneer and project management expert, he is also a structured thinker and precise writer, which makes reading this book even more enjoyable.

C   List of Quotations

Chapter 2

Quoted from: Loos, Adolf: »Architektur«. *Gesammelte Schriften 1900–1930*. Publisher: Adolf Opel. Wien 1982. (German only.)

Chapter 3

Quoted from: Rumbaugh, James; Blaha, Michael; Premerlani, William; Eddy, Frederick; Lorensen, William: *Object-Oriented Modeling and Design*. Prentice Hall International 1990.

Chapter 4

Quoted from: Coplien, James O: *Advanced C++ Programming Styles and Idioms*. Addison-Wesley 1992.

Chapter 5

Quoted from: Kremerskothen, Josef (editor): *Große Architekten Band 1. Menschen, die Baugeschichte machten*. Gruner + Jahr 1990. (German only.)

Chapter 7

Quoted from: *http://en.wikiquote.org/wiki/Philippe_Kahn*. Orally: On stage to Bill Gates at a PC Forum.

Chapter 8

Quoted from: Hautamäki, Juha: *A Survey of Frameworks*. Department of Computer Science, University of Tampere 1997.

Chapter 9

Quoted from: Ortega y Gasset, José: *Betrachtungen über die Technik*. Deutsche Verlags-Anstalt 1949. (German only.)

Chapter 10

Quoted from: Rousseau, Jean Jacques: Julie, or the New Heloise. 1805.

Appendix

Quoted from: DeMarco, Tom; Lister, Timothy: Waltzing with Bears. Dorset House Publishing Company, Incorporated, 2003.

D   The Authors

Thorsten Franz is a software architect at AOK Systems GmbH. For ten years, he has been working as a developer, coach, consultant, and trainer and has managed the rollout of ABAP development projects. He was also responsible for architecture and development management in a large strategic project in cooperation with SAP AG.

His work revolves around the development of SAP-based applications and frameworks, as well as application integration. He is particularly interested in the SAP NetWeaver platform and the options to make it available for new applications. His current focus is on enterprise architecture and includes topics such as SOA, Web Services, Composite Applications, NetWeaver for Java, and Web Dynpro.

In previous projects, Thorsten worked with many different components, frameworks, and technologies of the SAP world, such as HCM, BI, FS-PM, CRM, BP, Workflow, ALE, BDT, and BRF. He has given several presentations on these subjects at the SAP Developer's Summit 2002 in Las Vegas.

Tobias Trapp is a software developer at AOK Systems GmbH. His areas of expertise include ABAP development, XML and Web 2.0 technologies. He has more than ten years of experience in software development on various platforms, and using different programming languages for both custom and standard software.

His current work focuses on error management, printing and document processes, as well as programming in a large ABAP development project. In addition, he is interested in all aspects of SAP programming, agile development methods, knowledge management, and operations research. He also participates in the SAP Mentor program.

You can often find him on the SDN, as a speaker at the SAP Community Day, or in lectures on SAP programming for students. Furthermore, he is the author of the book *XML Data Exchange using ABAP* (SAP PRESS 2006).

Index

A developer's guide to new
technologies and techniques in
SAP NetWeaver 7.0 (2004s)

Discusses the new ABAP Editor,
ABAP Unit testing, regular
expressions, shared memory
objects, and more

485 pp., 2007, with CD, 69,95 Euro / US$ 69,95
ISBN 978-1-59229-139-7

Next Generation
ABAP Development

www.sap-press.com

Rich Heilman, Thomas Jung

Next Generation ABAP Development

This book takes advanced ABAP programmers
on a guided tour of all the new concepts,
technologies, techniques, and functions
introduced in the new ABAP release 7.0. The
unique approach of the book gives you a front
row seat to view the entire process of design,
development, and testing — right through the
eyes of a developer. You'll quickly learn about
all of the new ABAP programming options at
your disposal, while virtually experiencing a
detailed series of actual scenarios that could
easily be encountered in your own upcoming
projects.

Basic principles, architecture, and configuration

Development of dynamic, reusable UI components

Volumes of sample code and screen captures for help you maximize key tools

360 pp., 2006, 69,95 Euro / US$
ISBN 1-59229-078-7

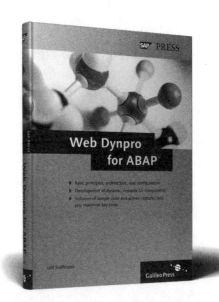

Web Dynpro for ABAP

www.sap-press.com

U. Hoffmann

Web Dynpro for ABAP

Serious developers must stay ahead of the curve by ensuring that they are up-to-date with all of the latest standards. This book illustrates the many benefits that can be realized with component-based UI development using Web Dynpro for ABAP. On the basis of specifically developed sample components, readers are introduced to the architecture of the runtime and development environment and receive highly-detailed descriptions of the different functions and tools that enable you to efficiently implement Web Dynpro technology on the basis of SAP NetWeaver 2004s. Numerous code listings, screen captures, and little-known tricks make this book your indispensable companion for the practical design of modern user interfaces.

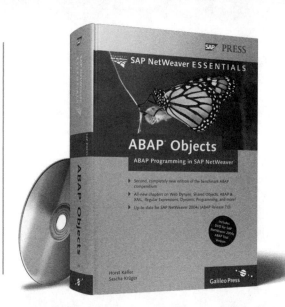

ABAP Objects

www.sap-press.com

H. Keller, S. Krüger

ABAP Objects

ABAP Programming in SAP NetWeaver

This completely new third edition of our best-selling ABAP book provides detailed coverage of ABAP programming with SAP NetWeaver. This outstanding compendium treats all concepts of modern ABAP up to release 7.0. New topics include ABAP and Unicode, Shared Objects, exception handling, Web Dynpro for ABAP, Object Services, and of course ABAP and XML. Bonus: All readers will receive the SAP NetWeaver 2004s ABAP Trial Version ("Mini-SAP") on DVD.

The ABAP
Quick Reference

www.sap-press.com

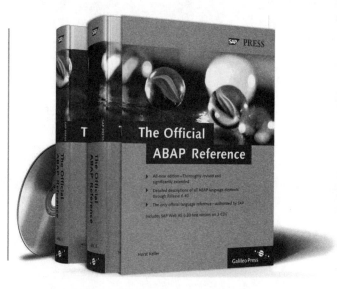